The "Other" New York
Jewish Intellectuals

REAPPRAISALS IN JEWISH SOCIAL
AND INTELLECTUAL HISTORY
General Editor: Robert M. Seltzer

*Martin Buber's Social and Religious Thought:
Alienation and the Quest for Meaning*
LAURENCE J. SILBERSTEIN

The American Judaism of Mordecai M. Kaplan
EDITED BY EMANUEL S. GOLDSMITH, MEL SCULT,
AND ROBERT M. SELTZER

On Socialists and "the Jewish Question" after Marx
JACK JACOBS

Easter in Kishinev: Anatomy of a Pogrom
EDWARD H. JUDGE

*Jewish Responses to Modernity:
New Voices from America and Eastern Europe*
ELI LEDERHENDLER

Rabbi Abraham Isaac Kook and Jewish Spirituality
EDITED BY LAWRENCE J. KAPLAN AND DAVID SHATZ

The "Other" New York Jewish Intellectuals
EDITED BY CAROLE S. KESSNER

EDITED BY CAROLE S. KESSNER

THE "OTHER" NEW YORK JEWISH INTELLECTUALS

NEW YORK UNIVERSITY PRESS
NEW YORK & LONDON

NEW YORK UNIVERSITY PRESS
New York and London

Library of Congress Cataloging-in-Publication Data
The "Other" New York Jewish intellectuals / edited by Carole S.
Kessner.
p.   cm. — (Reappraisals in Jewish social and intellectual
history)
Includes bibliographical references and index.
ISBN 0-8147-4659-4.—ISBN 0-8147-4660-8 (pbk.)
1. Jews—New York (N.Y.)—Biography. 2. Jews—New York (N.Y.)—
Intellectual life. 3. Intellectuals—New York (N.Y.)—Biography.
4. Zionists—New York (N.Y.)—Biography. 5. American literature—
Jewish authors—Biography. 6. Jewish scholars—New York (N.Y.)—
Biography. 7. New York (N.Y.)—Biography. I. Kessner, Carole S.,
1932–   . II. Series.
F128.9.J5087 1994
974.7'1004924'00922—dc20
[B]   94-17491
                                                              CIP

New York University Press books are printed on acid-free paper,
and their binding materials are chosen for strength and durability.

Manufactured in the United States of America
10   9   8   7   6   5   4   3   2   1

Dedication
Mi Dor L'dor
For Marion and Milton Schwartz
Joan, Barbara, and Judith

Contents

PART THREE
Spiritual Leaders

List of Illustrations

Acknowledgments

The idea for a volume devoted to the many committed Jewish intellectuals who were influential and played an important role in American Jewish life in the critical years of the 1930s, 1940s, and 1950s originated at a panel entitled "The Other New York Jewish Intellectuals: Hayim Greenberg, Maurice Samuel, and Marie Syrkin" that I organized for the Conference for the Association for Jewish Studies in 1989. Ben Halpern was present at that meeting, and it was at his suggestion that I began to think of a book on the subject. The AJS panel was followed by an expanded conference on the same subject sponsored by the Joseph and Ceil Mazer Institute for Research and Advanced Study in Judaica of the Graduate School of City University of New York and the Judaic Studies Department of the State University of New York at Stony Brook. For this latter conference I am grateful to Robert Seltzer for his proposal that we hold such a meeting and for his efforts to help organize it. Earlier versions of some of the essays in this volume were presented at the two conferences. I am also grateful to the American Jewish Archives at Hebrew Union College in Cincinnati for awarding me a Lowenstein-Weiner fellowship for research on Marie Syrkin. It was while I was working on her biography at the Archives that I came to realize that there were two clearly distinguishable groups of Jewish intellectuals active in America in the first half of this century, and that one of them had never been properly recognized. Finally, I am indebted to Thomas Kranidas who gave me, as always, his own unique combination of intellectual insight and emotional support.

CAROLE S. KESSNER

xi

Introduction

Carole S. Kessner

Everyone knows the New York Jewish Intellectuals; but this book is not about them. This is about another group of intellectual Jews who lived and worked mainly in New York, men and women who were in no way ambivalent about their Jewishness. Although there is much that the two groups have in common, it is the role that Jewishness played in their identities, their ideas, and their activities that set them upon divergent paths which were to meet up only after 1967.

Recently, considerable attention has been lavished on the adventures and achievements of the New York Jewish Intellectuals. In addition to the numerous full-length historical and literary studies, a special issue of *American Jewish History*[1] was devoted entirely to them. There have been countless articles and essays, and in the last fifteen years an outpouring of personal memoirs by such luminaries as William Phillips, Irving Howe, Sidney Hook, William Barrett, Lionel Abel, and Leslie Fiedler. If we add the names Philip Rahv, Daniel Bell, Lionel Trilling, Saul Bellow, Delmore Schwartz, Alfred Kazin, Clement Greenberg, Isaac Rosenfeld, Harold Rosenberg, and Meyer Schapiro, we have a fairly representative list of the Jewish members of the New York Intellectuals of the thirties, forties, and fifties.

The fact that this outpouring of scholarship has happened somewhat belatedly—after all, their major work was done over thirty years ago—brings to mind an insight that Irving Howe had about the flowering of Jewish writing in the mid-twentieth century. Comparing two literary regional subcultures, the Jewish and the Southern, Howe claimed that, "in both instances, a subculture finds its voice and its passion at exactly the moment that it approaches disintegration."[2] His report of the death of American Jewish writing was a bit premature, for we find that the genre continues with subjects other than immigrant life. Yet his statement is perhaps apposite to the recent profusion of memoirs and scholarly retrospectives by and about the New York Intellectuals, and particularly in the light of Eugene Goodheart's penetrating essay "Abandoned Legacy."[3] Goodheart points out that the legacy of the New York Intellectuals has been ignored by the contemporary literary academy and he argues that one reason for the abandoned legacy is the radical difference between the Marxism of the Old Left and contemporary academic Marxism, the public intellectualism of the former and the hermetic intellectualism of the latter. Hence the contemporary academic theorists, finding no useful model in the older Marxists, have left them for dead. This premature burial may also be the inevitable consequence of the older group's universalist aspirations at the expense of the particular.

Admittedly, this book too, arrives late. The "other" New York Jewish Intellectuals have never enjoyed proper celebrity. Few wrote memoirs; some individuals have been the subject of recent scholarship, but for the most part they have not been thought of as a group or community of intellectuals, despite the fact that their lives so frequently interacted and that they probably were more ideologically cohesive than the more prominent intellectual group. The justification for the studies in this book, however, is not eulogy but recuperation. Unlike those contemporary academics who can find little usable from the past, the contemporary scholars of Jewish life and letters who have written the essays in this volume have found much to admire and to emulate in these proudly affirmative Jews who in many cases were their teachers or their colleagues. The effort is a very Jewish one: commitment to the preservation of the worthy past and its incorporation into the present for the sake of the future.

Let me turn back now for a brief description of the New York Jewish Intellectuals so that we shall be able to measure the subjects of this book against them. Admittedly, the emblematic figure of this group, Irving Howe, never really coined the term *New York Jewish Intellectual*, though the coinage gained currency after his well-known essay "New York Intellectuals" appeared in *Commentary* in October 1968.[4] Remarking that although American intellectuals, including the Transcendentalists, have done their work mostly in isolation, one apparent exception is the group of writers (of which he himself was a member) who mostly had been resident in New York in the 1930s and 1940s and who rose to prominence in mainstream American intellectual life in the 1950s. The group primarily cohered around *Partisan Review*, which held the view that it was not only possible, but also natural, to unite aesthetic avant-gardism with political radicalism. Thus, in a bold act of literary miscegenation, Marxism and T. S. Eliotism found themselves under the same covers. Writing in 1968, Howe goes on to explain that the New York Intellectuals

> appear to have a common history, prolonged now for more than thirty years; a common political outlook, even if marked by ceaseless internecine quarrels; a common style of thought and perhaps composition; a common focus of intellectual interests; and once you get past politeness—which becomes, these days, easier and easier—a common ethnic origin. They are, or until recently have been, anti-Communist; they are, or until some time ago were, radicals; they have a fondness for ideological speculation; they write literary criticism with a strong social emphasis; they revel in polemic; they strive self-consciously to be "brilliant"; and by birth or osmosis, they are Jews.[5]

In addition to this last defining clause, that "by birth or osmosis they are Jews," Howe informs us that this was the "first group of Jewish writers to come out of the immigrant milieu who did not define themselves through a relationship nostalgic or hostile to memories of Jewishness."[6] These last two statements call for some examination. If they did not define themselves through nostalgia or hostility, then how did they define themselves Jewishly—simply through the accident of birth? The answer is a bit more complicated: they defined themselves Jewishly through their alienation from their Jewishness. This is an important point that I shall return to later. Furthermore, once Howe asserted of the New York Intellectuals that "by birth or osmosis, they are Jews," it was inevitable that the word "Jewish" would be inserted into his more inclusive term; thus, New York *Jewish* Intellectuals, not always used by non-Jews without a hint of pejorative. From the reference to "osmosis" we can conclude that the New York Intellectuals included non-Jews who absorbed certain Jewish characteristics. The statement, however, does not suggest the opposite, which is also true. By the same "osmosis," the Jewish members of the group absorbed certain qualities of such non-Jews in the group as F. W. Dupee, Dwight MacDonald, Edmund Wilson, William Barrett, and Mary McCarthy. Indeed, it was a symbiotic affair in which the Yale-educated critics, who had not quite broken free from a sense of American inferiority, loved the up-from-the-ghetto, City College-educated men (at the outset there weren't any women in this group) for their universalism, their cosmopolitanism, their Europeanness, their exoticism, and, not the least, their brains. The City College types loved their non-Jewish counterparts for their particularism, their authentic Americanness, and for the ticket they provided for entry into the mainstream. It was an intermarriage made in atheist's heaven.

Now, a few words about each of the terms of the descriptive label *New York Jewish Intellectuals*. First, the geographic locale. New York in this context functions more as metaphor than fact. Whereas it is true that all those in the group were not native New Yorkers and that some, like Saul Bellow, were identified with other cities, they became New Yorkers through their association with *Partisan Review*, and, as Eugene Goodheart has put it, "they belonged to a fraternity of intellect and sensibility."[7] This fraternity had its headquarters in New York.

What is meant by "intellectual" is more difficult to pin down. Russell Jacoby points out in *The Last Intellectuals* that "until recently arguments about 'intellectuals' took their cue from the Dreyfus Affair of the 1890's. The artists, writers, and teachers, including Emile Zola, who challenged the state's prosecution of Dreyfus, became known as the 'intellectuals.' " For the anti-Dreyfusards they were a new and objectionable group. But as Jacoby further explains, the Russian term *intelligentsia*, which dates to the 1860s, "gradually passed into English or at least rubbed off on 'intellectuals,' darkening its oppositional hues." The role of *intelligentsia*, says Jacoby, was to pave the way for the Russian Revolution and it was almost exclusively defined by "its alienation from and hostility towards the state."[8] This definition is particularly interesting in light of Irving Howe's claim that the "New York Intellectuals are perhaps the only group America has ever had that could be described as an intelligentsia." Howe quotes the historian of Russian culture, Martin Malia, who describes the intelligentsia as "more than intellectuals in the ordinary sense. Whether merely 'critical thinking' or actively oppositional, their name indicates that [in Russia] they thought of themselves as the embodied 'intelligence' . . . or 'consciousness' of the nation. They clearly felt an exceptional sense of apartness from the society in which they lived."[9]

It is this "sense of apartness" that is theme to the variations of almost every attempt to describe and define the Jewish intellectual, beginning with Thorstein Veblen's emphasis on marginality in his 1919 essay "The Intellectual Pre-eminence of Jews in Modern Europe." Veblen's theme can be heard in variations written by Daniel Bell, Lewis Coser, Isaac Deutscher, John Murray Cuddihy, Paul Mendes Flohr, Amos Funkenstein, and Sander Gilman. If we apply their insights to the case of the New York Jewish Intellectuals, it appears that they are intellectuals *par excellence*; doubly marginal, they are voluntarily estranged from the culture they were born into, involuntarily alienated from the society into which they wish to assimilate. In all cases the leitmotif is alienation.

We return now to the word "Jewish" as it appears in connection with the New York Intellectuals. By the 1950s, this group was at the peak of its power, and its members had begun to hold down academic postions in a variety of American universities; as Howe explains, "Some writers began to discover that publishing a story in the *New Yorker* or *Esquire* was not a sure ticket to Satan; others to see that the academy, while perhaps less exciting than the Village, wasn't invariably a graveyard for the intellect . . ."[10] Mark Schechner has wittily added that this journey from the thirties to the fifties traveled the route from the Depression to depression— from radical politics to psychological neurosis.[11] This was inevitable because, as Howe himself has observed in two-thirds of a truth, "the New York writers came at the end of the modernist experience, just as they came at what may yet have to be judged the end of the radical experience, and they certainly came at the end of the Jewish experience." As he rightly points out, the great battle for modernism raged in the 1920s and by the 1930s, when the New York Intellectuals sent in their troops, the battle was already over except for "skirmishes and mopping-up operations."[12] By the time *Partisan Review* was founded in 1936, Picasso, Stravinsky, and Joyce had already been proclaimed victors in the battle of the arts. Moreover, a good number of literary modernists, such as the notable anti-Semites Pound and Eliot, frequently aligned themselves with the political right and took ethical positions antithetical to those of the New York Intellectuals. With the hindsight of half a century, Howe was to write in 1991, "Eliot . . . was our 'culture hero.' " We failed to find—this is a judgement of retrospect—a coherent and dignified public response to the troubling passages about Jews that lie scattered in Eliot's work, passages far less virulent than those of Pound but quite bad enough."[13]

That they came at the end of the radical experience of the first part of this century is also true. The battle for orthodox Marxism was over as well. The only significant radical movement in America had been the Communist party, but by the late thirties even the YCL was losing its grip. The politically radical fiction of the thirties was the so-called proletarian novel, written by men and women overtly identified with the Communist party, such as Michael Gold (whose *Jews without Money* was the first important novel of the genre), James T. Farrell, John Steinbeck, and other more or less familiar names. But by the mid-thirties this genre's life was about over. The trouble with this subclass of realistic fiction was that it espoused the theory that art is a weapon, that propaganda is art. Here it is apposite to note that the *Marxist Quarterly*, which Irving Howe argues was the most distinguished Marxist journal ever published in this country, began its life in 1937 and by 1938 had ceased publication. But *Partisan Review*, begun in 1936, was a journal of a different color—"off red"—for its founders, Philip Rahv, William Phillips, and Sidney Hook, had by this time shed any sympathy they might once have felt for Stalinism. The events of the thirties were too blatant to be excused; the Moscow show trials of 1936, the Hitler-Stalin pact, the dissection of Poland, and the invasion of Finland dealt staggering blows to most on the left. There would, of course, be a few die hards such as Howard Fast, but for most Jews these were blows to the heart as well as to the head. *Partisan Review*, then, began with dissociation from the American Communist party; yet it held the hope that one could find some other system, a purified version of Marxism, perhaps something associated with Trotsky. But even this pious hope was doomed from the outset, for the times were out of "sync" with class struggle: the dark shadows of totalitarianism undercut these once-sacred categories. Lucy Dawidowicz recalled in her memoir of Vilna, *From That Place and That Time*, that she herself quit the YCL at Hunter College in 1936 when the Communist party, abandoning class against class, approved the united or popular front policy—that is, that "Party members were now directed to establish united fronts with all political forces, whatever their particular positions, so long as they opposed German Nazism and Japanese militarism."[14]

Thus the New York Intellectuals arrived on stage for the last act of both cultural modernism and political radicalism. But what about the third part of Howe's argument, that they also came at the end of the Jewish experience? True, they came at the end of the Eastern European Jewish immigrant experience—but, as we shall see from the essays in this book, that was not the *only* Jewish experience; and as we now see at the close of the twentieth century, there was to be much more to come with regard to the Jewish experience in America.

What is more to the point, however, is the fact that these were the very years that were dealing not merely blows to the heart, but now literal death blows to the Jewish world in Europe and in Palestine. Not only were these the years of the Nuremberg Laws, the Moscow trials, the British White Paper, the report of the Peel Commission urging the partition of Palestine, and the Arab disturbances, but the reports from the ghettos and the camps began to come in. For the ordinary Jew in America, though the crisis was not always immediately personal, it was profoundly communal. And where were these New York Intellectuals during the years of the least comprehensible man-made disaster in human history? Had their lives as "intellectuals" made them any more sensitive to the fate of the community they had rejected, scorned, and even satirized? Despite some of their late claims to an early response, the truth appears to be that the unfolding of Soviet Russian history was more compelling for them than the fate of the Jews. Thus, by the postwar period, in political and intellectual crisis, in disillusionment and instability, the New York Intellectuals turned in three directions. The literary critics shifted to the political center, to democratic socialism and political liberalism, while at the same time embracing America by turning to American literature for its subject: Howe wrote on Faulkner and Sherwood Anderson; Rahv wrote his best essay on Whitman and James called "Palefaces and Redskins"; Trilling wrote on James, but, more the genteel Victorian than either Howe or Rahv, Trilling also wrote on Arnold and Forster; Kazin's best work was his hymn to America, *On Native Grounds;* and Fiedler produced his great celebration of America, *Love and Death in the American Novel.* The social scientists such as Irving Kristol and Daniel Bell, and the philosopher Sidney Hook, mostly turned to the right. In 1952, under the editorship of Elliot Cohen who had left *Menorah Journal, Commentary* became soft on anti-communism and tended to downplay the threat of the demagogue senator from Wisconsin. As for the creative writers—Bellow, Malamud, Schwartz, Rosenfeld, Goodman, and even Trilling with his foray into fiction (together with their disciples Roth and Mailer)—where could they turn? Many turned inward; having been betrayed by the faithless left, and themselves having spurned their Jewish origins, there was no romance for them save self-love. Alienated from their Jewish mothers, estranged from their Marxist fathers, they were orphaned in America. So they sought a system to heal their sickened souls: they found it in Freud, Wilhelm Reich, Karen Horney, and Carl Jung. Mark Schechner writes, "It was in the post-war climate of dis-orientation and regrouping that a few disheartened radicals turned toward psychoanalysis as an alternative to their shattered Marxism. Onetime partisans of the workers' vanguard or the popular front against fascism quietly lay aside their copies of *State and Revolution* to comb through *The Psychopathology of Everyday Life* or the *Function of the Orgasm* for clues to the universal affliction that Karen Horney had called 'the neurotic personality of our time.' "[15] Moreover, their mid-century angst placed these intellectuals acutely at the nerve center of postwar philosophical and literary trends; they were a veritable casebook on French existentialism.

The New York novelists, now under the influence of psychoanalysis, began to reach back into their own Jewish family romances to create that brief moment in the sun for the Jewish American novel, the moment when Malamud's immigrant Jews of Brooklyn in *The Assistant* (like Joyce's Leopold Bloom before them), now stand for the marginality and alienation of all mankind; when Bellow's Augie March announces that he is an American—Chicago born, and in Bellow's later attack on alienation, when the assimilated Jewish academic Moses Herzog—the better to end his severe case of alienation—becomes his own analyst; when Philip Roth escapes from suburban Philistines in *Goodbye Columbus* to his interior, self-abusive refuge in *Portnoy's Complaint*. It cannot be denied, that all these fictions, together with many more, are about Jews—but mostly about the immigrant Jews the New York writers left behind for the non-Jewish Jews they had become. It is an irony, indeed, to read in the *New York Times* obituary for Irving Howe that "Perhaps his most famous book was *World of Our Fathers*, a history of Eastern European immigration to the United States that won the National Book Award in 1976."[16] One is hard-pressed to avoid invoking Cynthia Ozick's now famous dictum "If we blow into the narrow end of the *shofar*, we will be heard far. But if we choose to be Mankind rather than Jewish and blow into the wider part, we will not be heard at all; for us America will have been in vain."[17]

The so-called New York Jewish Intellectuals, however, were not the only Jewish intellectuals active in New York during the critical years of the late thirties and forties. There was another group who read the ominous signs of the times and instantly knew that these were portents demanding drastic action. Without hesitation, this group of Jewish intellectuals rallied to the defense of their fellow Jews in Europe and in the Middle East. These men and women were not nearly so widely lionized, but they were quite as "intellectual" as those who cohered around two journals: *Jewish Frontier* and *Menorah Journal*. And while some writers of the former group, such as Lionel Trilling or Hannah Arendt, published early on in *Jewish Frontier* or *Menorah Journal*, writers from the latter group were not represented in *Partisan Review*. Although the "other" New York Jewish intellectuals were little celebrated by the general American public, that is, Gentiles and non-Jewish Jews, the international Jewish world that had remained within the perimeters of Zionism, Yiddishism, Judaism, and Jewish culture in its infinite variety, respected and revered such names as Hayim Greenberg, Henry Hurwitz, Marie Syrkin, Maurice Samuel, Ben Halpern, Ludwig Lewisohn, and Mordecai Kaplan, among a longer list of influential thinkers.

This is not to suggest that these "other" intellectuals spoke in one voice, not in their politics nor in their Jewishness. Most were Zionists, a few were not; some advocated a binational state, some argued for partition; most argued against *shelilat ha golah* (negation of the Diaspora), one or two argued for it; some were secularists, others were religiously observant; some were immigrants to America, some were born in the United States. Yet perhaps what finally unites this group is what Ira Eisenstein has written about Henry Hurwitz: "He had always been an intellectual Jew, while younger writers and thinkers were, in fact, intellectuals who happened to be Jewish. The difference between the adjective and the noun was at the heart of their disagreement." All the subjects in this volume are intellectual Jews. They were as fully engaged with world politics and the culture of their time as were the Jewish intellectuals: Lewisohn, for example, wrote one of the first analytical books on American literature; Greenberg exchanged views with Mahatma Ghandi; Samuel wrote a rejoinder to Arnold Toynbee; Halpern rebutted Daniel Bell's "Parable of Alienation"; and Marie Syrkin took on Toynbee, Hannah Arendt, and Philip Roth. These "others," in contrast to the *Partisan Review* intellectuals, never self-consciously strove to be "brilliant"; and most of all, they never described themselves as alienated—especially not from the Jewish world. They were nominatively, not nominally, Jews.

I have organized the essays in this book into three groups: Opinion Makers, Men of Letters (as it happens, there are no women in this group), and Spiritual Leaders. As the reader will see, the positions taken by these men and women are by no means identical; they do not espouse a "party line." The first section, "Opinion Makers,"

includes Hayim Greenberg, Marie Syrkin, Ben Halpern, and Trude
Weiss-Rosmarin. All four in this group are associated with journals,
the first three with *Jewish Frontier*, the official organ of the Labor
Zionist movement, the last with the *Jewish Spectator*. As the first
editor of *Jewish Frontier*, Hayim Greenberg was not only the undis-
puted leading intellectual figure in the Labor Zionist movement in
America from the 1920s to his death in 1953, but he was regarded as
a moral force as well. In the words of his friend and colleague,
Marie Syrkin, "one cannot pigeon hole Greenberg as a thinker; the
consistency is one of attitude. His writings reflect the continuous
painstaking struggle of a sensitive and subtle spirit to discover the
ethical bases of action, special or individual."[18] Marie Syrkin had
received a graduate degree in English literature from Cornell University and hoped to become a poet, yet she became associated with
the *Jewish Frontier* at its outset in 1934. The daughter of Nachman
Syrkin, the theoretician of socialist Zionism, she herself went on to
become the doyenne of Labor Zionism, while at the same time
establishing a reputation as a journalist, polemicist, poet, author of
a number of books including the biography of her dear friend Golda
Meir, and as professor of English at Brandeis University. At Brandeis
she was joined by her friend Ben Halpern. After receiving a Ph.D.
from Harvard, then pursuing a career in the Labor Zionist movement, being elected a member of the Jewish Agency Executive, and
becoming managing editor and writing for *Jewish Frontier*, Halpern
was named Richard Koret Professor of Near Eastern Studies at Brandeis. Halpern was revered by both his colleagues and his students
for his civility, accessibility, and sharpness of analytical powers.
The character and full contribution of each of these three interpret-
ers of Labor Zionism and shapers of Zionist thought in America—
Greenberg, Syrkin, and Halpern—are brought to life in essays by
Robert Seltzer, Carole Kessner, and Arthur Goren. The fourth essay
in this section, by Deborah Dash Moore, is devoted to the career
of Trude Weiss-Rosmarin who earned her doctorate in Semitics,
Archeology, and Philosophy at the University of Würzburg in 1931.
She emigrated to America and when she could not secure a position
as a professor of Assyriology, she founded the *Jewish Spectator* in
1935. She also founded the School of the Jewish Woman in New
York City which she modeled after the famous Frankfurt Lehrhaus

where she had studied. No more a Labor Zionist than she was a secularist, her religious traditionalism led her to the position that Judaism and Zionism are co-extensive. Weiss-Rosmarin has been called the most Jewishly learned woman in the world.

Syrkin and Weiss-Rosmarin are the only women included in this volume. This is perhaps due to the fact that the choices they made with respect to their careers in journalism and scholarship were atypical for women of their generation in America. While many American Jewish women made important contributions to Jewish life in the volunteer realm, Syrkin and Weiss-Rosmarin chose the path of professionalism.

The second section of this volume, "Men of Letters," comprises eight men (listed chronologically by date of birth) whose lives were spent in a variety of occupations. The section begins with Morris Raphael Cohen, who was born in Russia in 1880 and emigrated to the United States in 1892. Cohen's story is initially a typical up-from-the ghetto tale of Lower East Side beginnings, but he was to become a legendary professor of philosophy at City College where he acquired a reputation for a probing and electrifying, but pugnacious, style of teaching that intimidated most of his students. Irving Howe, who was his admiring student, describes him as having a "terrifying, sometimes even a sadistic method of teaching, and only the kinds of students that came to Cohen could have withstood it— Jewish boys with minds honed to dialectic, bearing half-conscious memories of pilpul, indifferent to the prescriptions of gentility, intent on a vision of lucidity."[19] Boys, one takes it, like Irving Howe himself. Despite recollections of his ferocious classroom style, Cohen left a legacy of "khochem" anecdotes, testifying to his encyclopedic, razor sharp, analytical mind. What distinguished Cohen from those of his best students who admired him, but went on to join the *Partisan Review*, was that although Cohen was an agnostic or rationalist, as he preferred to call himself, he was a deeply affirmative Jew. Milton Konvitz's essay on Cohen delineates the breadth and depth of Cohen's knowledge of Jewish history and philosophy, of Yiddish and Hebrew, and his decision in the 1930s after Hitler had come to power, to devote himself full-time to the problems of the Jewish people. In 1933 he organized the Conference on Jewish Relations, which in 1955 became the Conference of Jewish Social Studies. After his retirement in 1938 from City College, he devoted almost all of his time to the Conference and its scholarly journal.

Horace Kallen, born in 1882, is probably better known in America today than any of the others in this book because of the current new interest in multiculturalism and American pluralism. Turn-of-the-century America took to its heart Israel Zangwill's image of America as a melting pot, but Kallen, the philosopher of cultural pluralism, put forward the alternative metaphor of the orchestra, in which each instrument has its own timbre and plays its own part, but contributes to the harmony of the whole. Kallen's essayist in this volume, Milton Konvitz, informs us, moreover, that the Harvard-educated Kallen was the first Jewish professor of a non-Jewish subject in a non-Jewish college or university who was intimately and prominently identified with Jewish interests, Jewish concerns, Jewish organizations. He was, in Konvitz's opinion, *"primus inter omnes."* [20]

Ludwig Lewisohn was born in Germany in 1883 and grew up in genteel Episcopalian Charleston, South Carolina. Educated in literature at Columbia University, but denied a Columbia fellowship, he was compelled to teach German rather than English literature at a midwestern university. He began his career as a proponent of a modern post-Victorian American literature, he wrote the first Freudian analysis of American literature, and he became drama critic for the *Nation*. His education in European languages and literature should have made him the cosmopolitan *par excellence,* worthy of inclusion in the *Partisan Review* crowd—but they mocked him. Alfred Kazin, who thought that his own comprehensive exploration of American literature *On Native Grounds* would be the historical corrective to Lewisohn's Freudian *Expression in America,* admired the older critic to some extent, but complained that Lewisohn wrote at a "Wagnerian pitch," and "came to interpret almost sadistically the basic qualities of the literature he sought to elevate. It was not enough," Kazin went on, "for him to write in his autobiography that 'the Jewish problem is the decisive problem of Western Civilization. By its solution this world of the West will stand or fall, choose death or life.'" This was in 1942; but then Kazin was only twenty-seven when he published his remarkable first book. Ultimately Lewisohn traveled the route from assimilation to negation of the Diaspora, from pacifism to militant political Zionism. The story of this conversion is thoroughly recounted in Stanley Chyet's essay.

Henry Hurwitz might have been included among the "Opinion Makers" because, in addition to being the initiator of the Menorah Societies in American universities, he was the founder and editor of the influential periodical *Menorah Journal*. This journal published the work of almost everyone included in this volume, as well as the early writings of some of the New York Intellectuals, most especially Lionel Trilling and later Hannah Arendt. Yet I have chosen to locate Hurwitz among "Men of Letters" because, as we learn from his essayist Ira Eisenstein (who himself edited an important Jewish journal, *Reconstructionist*), among other goals Henry Hurwitz intended his nonpartisan and nonacademic publication to be a new force in modern critical intelligence, to "offer no opinions of its own but [to provide] an orderly platform for the discussion of mooted questions that really matter," and to be "devoted first and foremost to the fostering of Jewish Humanities and the furthering of their influence as a spur to human service."

The name Marvin Lowenthal is perhaps the least known among those included in this volume. If he is remembered at all, it is probably for his pioneer translation into English of the memoirs of Glueckel of Hameln (1932). That, however, was only a minor part of his contribution to Jewish life. Lowenthal, who was born in 1890 to an assimilated Philadelphia German Jewish family, had no particular interest in things Jewish until he became a student and then disciple of Horace Kallen at the University of Wisconsin. There, as Susanne Klingenstein recounts for us in her study of Lowenthal in this volume, he inadvertently stumbled into "mildly Zionist circles," twice winning the Wisconsin Menorah Society essay prize. Henry Hurwitz published Lowenthal's second essay on Zionism in the first issues of *Menorah Journal*. After a fellowship at Harvard where he came into contact with Louis Brandeis, Lowenthal continued his career as a Zionist; at Brandeis's request, he headed up the Zionist Bureau of the Pacific Coast. After a twelve-year sojourn in Europe, where the Rathenau case in Germany revealed to him the virulence of anti-Semitism in Germany and

Eastern Europe, as early as 1923 he began to warn against Hitler. Lowenthal served as representative for Jewish interests at the League of Nations and he wrote a study of the Jews of Germany which "inevitably became a history of anti-Semitism in Germany." In addition to becoming one of Henry Hurwitz's closest associates, Lowenthal went on to write and edit *The Life and Letters of Henrietta Szold*, and to edit and translate *The Diaries of Theodor Herzl*.

In her foreword to *The Worlds of Maurice Samuel*, edited by Milton Hindus, Cynthia Ozick remarks that in her "hungry twenties" she used to "follow Maurice Samuel from lectern to lectern, running after whatever it was I thought I might get from him." Samuel, indeed, was one of the most charismatic intellectual figures in twentieth-century American Jewish life, who became well known to radio audiences for his weekly conversations about the Bible with Mark Van Doren. Born in Romania in 1895, educated in England, and emigrating to the United States in 1914, Samuel made his living as a public lecturer—but that is misleading. An autodidact, he was a scholar, a lover of language and poetry, a writer of fiction and nonfiction, and a spokesman for Zionism. In the essay on Maurice Samuel in this book, Emanuel Goldsmith tells us that although Samuel was not a formulator of Zionist ideology, he was part of Chaim Weizmann's inner circle, collaborating with Weizmann on his autobiography *Trial and Error*. Moreover, Samuel was a passionate promoter of Yiddish, and an expositor of anti-Semitism. In an interesting detail, Goldsmith points out that Samuel discovered from his study of Bible and Jewish history that Judaism had always lacked a sports-fixation, and that it was "characterized by a rejection of sports and the combative ethic which was the result of a moral fixation rooted in the writings of the Hebrew prophets." It also is of some interest to note that in his discussion of the range of Jewish intellectuals in America in *The World of Our Fathers*, Irving Howe bestows special favor on two representatives of the affirmative Jews. "The Zionist movement," Howe writes, "produced some keen English-speaking intellectuals, especially in later years, men like Maurice Samuel and Ben Halpern."[21]

Of all the personalities in this volume, Charles Reznikoff is alone in his total commitment to his true profession as a poet. Despite a degree in law, he never really practiced as a lawyer, and although he was forced to try to earn a living at other enterprises such as writing for a legal encyclopedia, an unlikely stint as a Hollywood scenario reader and writer, and managing editor of the *Jewish Frontier*, his true vocation was poetry. Reznikoff was not an activist; he was an intellectual who spent his days reading, writing, and walking. He was associated closely with the American objectivist school of poetry founded by Louis Zukofsky and whose most famous practitioner was William Carlos Williams. Reznikoff, however, was steeped in Jewish learning, in love with Jewish literature and lore, and many of his poems were permeated with Jewish national and religious awareness. His activism was in his verse, in his lyric poems on Jewish Holy Days, Jewish liturgy, a verse playlet on Rashi, and a long cycle entitled *Holocaust*, based on the Nuremberg trials. His work went unappreciated and unrecognized except for a small group of admirers until quite late in his life, although one perceptive early admirer, Lionel Trilling, wrote in his *Menorah Journal* review of the poet's prose chronicle *By the Waters of Manhattan*, "Mr. Reznikoff's work is remarkable and original in American literature because he brings to a 'realistic' theme a prose style that without any of the postures of the stylist is of the greatest delicacy and distinction. But more important, and by virtue of this prose style, he has written the first story of the Jewish immigrant that is not false." A somewhat later admirer, one who has spent many years as an advocate of Reznikoff's poetry and who became his close friend as well, is Milton Hindus, whose essay in this volume not only provides a sensitive critique of the poetry of Charles Reznikoff, but also chronicles Hindus's own determined personal effort to bring the poet's work to public attention. Hindus's essay is more an eloquent remembrance than a scholarly exposition.

Although the Canadian poet A. M. Klein did not live in New York, I have included him among the "other," the affirmative New York Jewish Intellectuals because he deserves a place in this volume by virtue of affinity of intellect and sensibility. Like Reznikoff, he too took a degree in law, but Klein actually earned his livelihood as a practicing lawyer while simultaneously pursuing a second career as poet and editor of the *Canadian Jewish Chronicle*. As Rachel Feldhay Brenner explains in her essay on Klein, "an examination of A. M. Klein's stature as a Canadian and Zionist intellectual against the coterie of the New York Jewish Intellectuals reveals the irony of inverse symmetry." Brenner argues that Klein "sensed the 'Intellectuals' uneasiness regarding their Jewish origins when he mocked them as 'Americans by disuasion [who] think that by travelling incognito they will be mistaken for royal, or at least New England personages.' Conversely Klein declared that he travels 'on his own passport.' " Klein's passport was boldly stamped Canadian Jew, and he strenuously tried to amalgamate the two traditions in his literary work. Though the symbols and subject matter of his poetry are more often than not derived from Jewish sources—ancient and modern—his stylistic debt is to English poets from the Elizabethans through the imagists. Klein's brilliant novel *The Second Scroll*, published in 1951, has as its theme Klein's own vision of Zionism which asserts that repossession of the land in the post-Holocaust era is ineluctably tied to the history of Jewish exile and the Diaspora. Until quite recently Klein's work has gone virtually unnoticed in the United States. In some part, this may be due to critical neglect by the New York Intellectuals.

The final section of this book is devoted to "spiritual leaders." On the grounds that these were quintessentially intellectuals, I include only three individuals here: Mordecai Kaplan, Milton Steinberg, and Will Herberg—two rabbis and one theologian. One could make the case for other rabbinic figures such as Abba Hillel Silver and Stephen Wise, but the constraints of space, as well as the fact that their extraordinary contributions to Jewish life were more through their charismatic activism than through their achievements as writers and thinkers, has persuaded me to omit them.

Mordecai Kaplan, the ideologist of Reconstructionist Judaism, was arguably the preeminent intellectual American rabbi of his time—and his time extended over one hundred and two years! Born in Lithuania in 1881, he came to America in 1889 and grew up in New York City. He had a traditional Jewish education and received his secular education at City College and Columbia University, where he came into contact with some of the most eminent thinkers of his day who were to influence his ideas about Judaism. Kaplan's lifelong engagement with the redefinition and reinterpretation of Judaism, his formulation of the now famous descriptive definition that Judaism is the evolving religious civilization of the Jewish people, his belief in the possibility of creative Jewish survival in America along with his commitment to the centrality of Israel, his application of American democratic principles to Jewish communal organization, his religious naturalism, his liturgical innovations, his pioneering views on the role of women in Judaism, among an even longer list of his modernist views, are carefully covered in Jack Cohen's essay.

Among the most intellectually gifted of Mordecai Kaplan's disciples was Milton Steinberg. As his distinguished biographer, Simon Noveck, explains, Steinberg was born into a secular socialist family in Rochester, New York, in 1903, but in his teens moved to Jewish Harlem, where he encountered the philosophically oriented thought of Rabbi Jacob Kohn. At City College, he sharpened his philosophical thinking by defending his newly found religious convictions from the logical persuasions of the legendary Morris R. Cohen. After graduating summa cum laude, Steinberg entered the Jewish Theological Seminary where he came into contact with Mordecai Kaplan, whose teaching methods were quite as challenging as Morris Cohen's. From Kaplan, whose interests were more sociologically oriented, Steinberg learned to understand Judaism in more comprehensive terms as a complete civilization. Ultimately, however, he came to be critical of Kaplan's theological views and to engage his teacher in an ongoing debate on such issues as metaphysics, the nature of religion, the problem of evil, and prayerbook revision, among other considerations. Although Steinberg referred to himself as a "religious rationalist" and identified with Reconstructionism throughout his life, his readings in theology and philosophy, his attention to the writings of the European philosophers from Kierkegaard to Sartre, from Barth to Maritain, took him along paths divergent from Mordecai Kaplan. He was among the first of American Jewish thinkers to familiarize himself with postwar Christian theology. Yet, as a pulpit rabbi he was an eloquent philosophical preacher who believed that he had a responsibility to speak out on social problems as well. Steinberg's death at the age of forty-seven deprived the Jewish community of one of its preeminent philosophers.

As indebted to Kaplan in his formative years as Steinberg was, he owed some of his later ideas to his friend Will Herberg, with whom

he discussed the works of several German thinkers and with whom
he shared an interest in theological speculation. Herberg, who was
born in the same year as Steinberg, arrived at his theological position by an altogether different route. Herberg was one of the first
American Jewish philosophers to present existentialist Judaism in
systematic form. As David Dalin tells us in his account in this
volume, Herberg had begun as the quintessential New York Intellectual and became the only ex-Marxist to embrace Jewish theology. At a critical juncture in his personal life he became acquainted
with Reinhold Niebuhr, and, like Franz Rosenzweig, Herberg came
to Judaism only after flirting with conversion to Christianity. As
the alienated New York Intellectuals turned from "the god that
failed" to the substitute faiths of psychoanalysis, socialism, science,
or aesthetics, Herberg turned to God and Jewish existentialism. His
first major work, *Judaism and Modern Man* (1951), was widely
acclaimed by Jewish and non-Jewish scholars from Steinberg to
Niebuhr, but it was completely ignored by *Partisan Review*. Herberg's most important work, *Protestant-Catholic-Jew*, became a
classic in the sociology of American religion. As religion editor
for *National Review*, he became one of the leading figures of the
conservative intellectual movement in post–World War II America.
Will Herberg's influence waned in the last few decades of his life;
yet it would not be surprising to find renewed sympathy for
Steinberg's theology and Herberg's sensitive critique of an American
public life and politics devoid of religious values reemerging in
this last, more religiously and spiritually attuned decade of the
twentieth century.

It is of interest to note that the two groups of intellectuals—the
New York Jewish Intellectuals and the affirmative "other" New
York Jewish Intellectuals—found themselves face to face for the
first time when President Abram L. Sachar brought them together
at the newly founded Brandeis University. Here, in an ironic twist
of American Jewish history, Marie Syrkin, Ludwig Lewisohn, and
Ben Halpern were employed by the same institution as Philip Rahv
and Irving Howe. And it is perhaps of more than passing interest
that, with regard to the essays in this volume, Brandeis University
was a crossroads for more than the three personalities who are the
subjects of study. Milton Hindus, who has written so movingly

about his personal relationship with the poet Charles Reznikoff, became a professor of English at the founding of the university; here he taught in the same department as, and became a close friend of, Marie Syrkin who was married to Reznikoff. I myself was a student of Marie Syrkin and maintained a lifetime friendship with her. Stanley Chyet was a student in the first class at Brandeis where he met and studied with Ludwig Lewisohn, later writing his Ph.D. dissertation about his former professor. Moreover, the essayists in this volume represent several generations of Jewish American scholars. Some of the contributors, though younger than their subjects, knew them personally—sometimes intimately. This is true of Milton Hindus and Charles Reznikoff; Simon Noveck and Milton Steinberg; Jack Cohen and Mordecai Kaplan; Milton Konvitz and Horace Kallen and Morris Raphael Cohen; Arthur Goren and Ben Halpern; Stanley Chyet and Ludwig Lewisohn; and Carole Kessner and Marie Syrkin. The younger scholars in the book may not have known their subjects personally, but they have written about them persuasively and sensitively because they have discovered deep affinity; their subjects have spoken to them across the generations. This can be felt in the essays by David Dalin on Will Herberg, Robert Seltzer on Hayim Greenberg, Emanuel Goldsmith on Maurice Samuel, Deborah Dash Moore on Trude Weiss-Rosmarin, Rachel Feldhay Brenner on A. M. Klein, and Susanne Klingenstein on Marvin Lowenthal. As one of the contributors remarked, "I have fallen in love with my subject." Love, however, does not preclude a balanced view; thus the essays that follow have eschewed hagiography.

Some will instantly observe that the only essays on women in this collection are on Syrkin and Weiss-Rosmarin. Why there were no others prominent enough to include is the subject of a different essay. Suffice it to say here that, in America at this time, Jewish women of ability (sometimes extraordinary ability) tended to carve out places for themselves in the organizational volunteer arena. Hannah Arendt, of course, might have been included, but she belongs with the New York Jewish Intellectuals, not with these "others."

There has been no attempt to regularize style in this volume. Each essay reflects not only the relationship of author to subject, but also the various disciplines of the writers. Poets do not write like historians, literary critics have different linguistic proclivities from journalists, rabbis and academics are not likely to select the same word from the thesaurus.

A final word about the two groups of intellectuals. One must in the last analysis give the New York Jewish Intellectuals their proper due. As independent public intellectuals who wrote for the educated reader, they played a crucial role in the shaping of contemporary American culture. Although they were post-immigrant, they were pre-ethnic; thus they understood their own cosmopolitanism as embracing the openness and inclusiveness implicit in Enlightenment secular rationality. In this they stood opposed to narrow chauvinism, or parochialism. Yet, in a bold assertion, David Hollinger suggests that, in fact, the New York Intellectuals played a critical role in the "*de-Christianization* of the public culture of the United States."[22] If we add to their impressive record that of the "other" New York Jewish Intellectuals, we come closer to writing the story of what may be seen as the most vigorous and fascinating period in American Jewish history.

Notes

1. See especially Alexander Bloom, *Prodigal Sons: The New York Intellectuals and Their World* (New York: Oxford University Press, 1986); Terry Cooney, *The Rise of the New York Intellectuals: Partisan Review and Its Circle 1934–35* (Madison: University of Wisconsin Press, 1986); Russell Jacoby, *The Last Intellectuals: American Culture in the Age of Academe* (New York: Noonday Press, 1987); Alan Wald, *The Rise and Fall of the New York Intellectuals: The Rise and Decline of the Anti-Stalinist Left from the 1930's to the 1980's* (Chapel Hill: University of North Carolina Press, 1987); *American Jewish History* 80 (Spring 1991).
2. Irving Howe, *World of Our Fathers* (New York: Harcourt Brace Jovanovich, 1976), 586.
3. Eugene Goodheart, "The Abandoned Legacy," *American Jewish History* 80 (Spring 1991): 361–96.
4. Irving Howe, "The New York Intellectuals: A Chronicle and A Critique," *Commentary* 46, no. 4 (October 1968): 29. Hereafter called "New York Intellectuals."
5. Ibid.
6. Ibid., 31.

7. Goodheart, "The Abandoned Legacy."
8. Jacoby, *The Last Intellectuals*, 106, 107.
9. "New York Intellectuals," 29.
10. Ibid., 40.
11. Mark Schechner, *After the Revolution: Studies in the Contemporary Jewish Imagination* (Bloomington: Indiana University Press, 1987).
12. "New York Intellectuals," 32.
13. Irving Howe, "An Exercise in Memory," *New Republic* (March 11, 1991): 30.
14. Lucy Dawidowicz, *From That Place and Time: A Memoir 1938–1947* (New York: W. W. Norton, 1988), 18.
15. Cited in Schechner, *After the Revolution*, 50.
16. Richard Bernstein, *New York Times*, Thursday, May 6, 1993, p. D22.
17. Cynthia Ozick, "Toward a New Yiddish," *Art and Ardor* (New York: Alfred A. Knopf, 1983), 177.
18. Marie Syrkin, *Hayim Greenberg Anthology*. Selected Essays and with an Introduction by Marie Syrkin (Detroit: Wayne State University Press, 1968), 17.
19. *World of Our Fathers*, 284, 285.
20. E. R. A. Seligman, for example, was named full professor of economics at Columbia University in 1891, but he was not identified with Jewish causes.
21. *World of Our Fathers*, 599. "New York Intellectuals," 599.
22. David A. Hollinger, "A Response to the Essays of Terry A. Cooney, Eugene Goodheart, and S. A. Longstaff," *American Jewish History*: 381.

PART ONE

Opinion Makers

CHAPTER I

Hayim Greenberg, Jewish Intellectual

Robert M. Seltzer

If an intellectual is a person who lives in the world of ideas, Hayim Greenberg represents the twentieth-century intellectual most at home in Jewish ideas. Caught up in the world of action, Greenberg thought about the destiny of the Jews, about Judaism in history, about the spiritual element in human life, and spoke and wrote of these ideas all his life. Like many intellectuals, he had liberated himself early on from the constraints of tradition. But he drew on the inner resources of having been raised in a coherent world so that there was no agonizing crisis to overcome a chaotic lack of identity, no periodic reinvention of himself to accommodate changing ideological fashions, no torrent of self-revelation to drown out uncertainty and doubt. Like other progressive Jewish intellectuals of his time, he had rejected formal religious observance and orthodox belief. Unlike the "non-Jewish Jews," however, Labor Zionism provided him with a framework to direct his energies in behalf of his people in decades of crisis and, at the same time, this commitment enabled him to think about fundamentals freely without being the stereotypical "free-thinker" of his generation.[1]

There were several waves of Jewish writers, artists, editors, and scholars after 1900 who settled in New York to comprise the "New York Jewish Intellectuals" in the broad sense. Hayim Greenberg belonged to a cohort born and raised in Eastern Europe before the Russian Revolution, at a moment when Russian and Jewish socialism and their non-Jewish equivalents provided an almost messianic sense of immanent transformation. The chains of exploitation and oppression were to be sundered, once and for all, and a great leap forward to the perfection of humankind taken very soon, after the next and decisive battle against the forces of darkness. In the Bund and Zionism this redemptive dream was attached to a Jewish self-discovery that involved a more complex relation to Judaism than merely marching alongside the burgeoning revolutionary parties of late Tsarist Russia. More insistently nonreligious than Western Jews (in this they imitated their non-Jewish contemporaries), Greenberg's Russian-Jewish intelligentsia was far better acquainted with the world of traditional Judaism than were the Western Jewish intellectuals of those decades and more deeply rooted in the Yiddish language and literature and in modern Hebrew culture. The result was an idealism with a tone distinctively its own, at once cosmopolitan and ethnic, universalist and particular.

Forced to grapple with the seemingly endless emergencies of the interwar years, Greenberg was both a defender of his besieged people and of absolute ethical standards. Apart from an unshakable belief in the urgency of the Zionist project, Greenberg upheld until the end of the thirties a dogmatic pacifism like that advocated by Mohandas K. Gandhi, the world-renowned Indian nationalist and spiritual leader. While Greenberg was critical—sometimes devastatingly so—of Jewish attitudes and behaviors, there was no ambivalence about his Jewishness; he balanced *ahavat Yisrael*, love of the Jewish people, with a love of truth and fairness to all. To be sure, there were paradoxes in his life. He devoted his energies and intellect to Zionism during its decades of pioneering fervor, but lived in the Diaspora and loved the land of Russia and the idea of America as much as Eretz Yisrael. A secular Jew, he was troubled by the spiritual vacuum at the heart of modern secularism. A scintillating conversationalist, polished lecturer, and disciplined journalist, he was an intensely private person. Zalman Shazar characterized his reserve: "A certain refined solitude kept him apart and even when he was going with the stream, even when he was at the helm, many had the irrepressible feeling that he was somehow apart and alone."[2] Writing not of himself but unconsciously revealing his own needs, Greenberg refers to "the consoling melancholy of aloneness and self-confrontation."[3] A distinguished public figure and an adroit diplomat (gregarious callings indeed), Greenberg was philosophical, reclusive, and drawn to the meditative way.

Marie Syrkin observed that many of the most perfect and touching of his reflections and anecdotes "share only the eternity of their hearers."[4] Greenberg's literary output represents a fragment of what he created in moments of conversation. Shaping a reminiscence or a fleeting observation into a finished artistic product, he had that rare ability to translate the vagaries of life into symbols of the human condition. Greenberg the story-teller is represented by the "sketches" included in both volumes of the Inner Eye, each episode revealing its own pungent, fresh, ironic meaning: a chance encounter with a Panamanian Indian, a conversation in a Tsarist prison, a stay with inhospitable Karaites in the Crimea, and so forth. A Greek restaurant owner in Atlantic City wonders what will become of his children, detached from their own roots in the corrosive American melting pot. A proud Russian derelict in Washington Square will not deign to accept a cigarette from a Jew, but an Italian lad is more than grateful for the largesse, to the disapproval of a severe nun standing nearby. An "Assyrian" exile from Iraq asks Greenberg if a small piece of land could be set aside in Israel for his persecuted Christian people. And so on.

Greenberg the editor had to expend much of his literary energies on the immediate events of the day, but, a cultivated man of letters, he preferred where possible to develop his subject in the broad historical and ethical perspective, even sub specie aeternitatis. Growing up in a generation dominated by positivism and philosophical materialism, Greenberg knew from his study of literature and theology that these ideologies, together with the anti-ideological vulgarity and materialism of American society, produced an impoverishment of the Jewish soul. Greenberg was susceptible to the lure of transcendence. Moving from Russian to Yiddish to Hebrew to English with fluency and ease, he brought a distinctive type of modern Jewish intellectuality that was at once of the Old and New Worlds to New York Jewry, in what may eventually be seen as its golden age.

Born in the small Bessarabian town of Todoristi in 1889, Greenberg found in the Zionist movement an outlet for his considerable promise early in life. Already at the age of fifteen he was a correspondent at the 1904 Zionist Congress at Helsinki and a sought-after speaker at underground meetings. Zalman Shazar remarked that it was a time when "lecturers" played a unique and powerful role in East European Jewish life: "The lecture halls became spiritual laboratories where the dominant ideas of the time were forged. The law was laid down and defined orally by such masters as Borochov, Syrkin, Jabotinsky, Zhitlovsky, and others who wandered from one city to another and from meeting to meeting."[5] When Greenberg moved to Odessa in 1910, he was noticed in a community famous for its modern Jewish nationalists, Hebrew and Yiddish writers, and cosmopolitan style. He spent the First World War in Moscow on the editorial staff of the Russian-language Jewish periodical *Raszvet*. After the Revolution he was briefly instructor in medieval Jewish literature and Greek drama at the University of Kharkov and then taught at the Kiev Academy. Arrested several times by the Communist authorities for illegal Zionist activities (he protested the government's suppression of Hebrew-language education and tried to rally support for *Habimah*, the Hebrew theater of Moscow),[6] Greenberg was finally permitted to leave the Soviet Union along with a group of Russian-Jewish writers and scholars in 1921. Like many of these emigrés, he was a Social Democrat (the Mensheviks were one of the first parties to be repressed by the Bolsheviks after their takeover of November 1917, along with the Bund and the Zionists). Drawing on first-hand experience, he warned readers in the twenties and thirties of the repression of individual liberties by the Soviet dictatorship and the fundamental immorality of Communist tactics that justified any behavior, however brutal, by genuflecting to the eventual achievement of socialism.

During his three years in Berlin, Greenberg served as editor of *Ha-olam*, the weekly of the World Zionist Organization, and of *Atidenu*, a Zionist monthly. In 1924 he came to New York. At first he edited *Farn Folk* (For the People), the organ of the Zeire Zion movement. When the Zeire Zion merged with the Poalei Zion in 1932, Greenberg was made editor-in-chief of the Poalei Zion biweekly (later weekly) *Der Yidisher Kempfer* (the Jewish Militant), the outstanding Yiddish journal of its day on political and social themes. In 1934 he became editor-in-chief of the Labor Zionist monthly *The Jewish Frontier* and a member of the Central Committee of the Labor Zionist Organization of America. In the thirties and forties, Greenberg came to be regarded as one of the most distinguished guides of a Jewish public highly sympathetic to the ideals of Labor Zionism at a time when this movement attracted a whole panoply of outstanding leaders and spokespeople.

During World War II Greenberg served as head of the American Zionist Emergency Council; later he also became a member of the American branch of the Jewish Agency executive and director of its Department of Education and Culture. At the United Nations in 1947, he played an influential role in winning support for Israel from Latin American delegations and among Asian intellectuals. He died in New York in 1953.

Emblematic of the Yiddish, Hebrew, Russian, and English sources of his style were the instructions Greenberg left for his funeral. There were to be no speeches, only a psalm or two ("103, 23, 42"), chapter 28 of Job in praise of wisdom (to be read in the original, in Yiddish, or in English), a song dear to his wife and him in their youth which had as its text the Russian poet Lermontov's "I Go Out Alone Upon the Road," and, possibly, Chopin's Funeral March. His last will and testament concludes with a statement that could have been in a Hebrew ethical will that medieval Jews left for families and friends:

> There are a number of men and women who brought the light of their souls into my life. To each of them I send my deep blessing. There are also no doubt men and women whom I hurt and to whom I caused sorrow. Of them I ask forgiveness. I sinned not out of love of sin; I was guilty out of weakness and I did wrong without intent to do so.[7]

All his life, Greenberg called himself a socialist. To be a socialist was for many of his generation to believe that democracy be enlarged to its full meaning, to express sympathy for the working class, to seek fundamental reforms in a society that seemed to be permanently polarized between the rich and the poor, the owners of property and the exploited, the rulers and the oppressed. (Writing in 1935 of Marx's thesis that "the friction of class interests in the course of centuries generated the heat needed to turn the wheels of history," Greenberg remarked: "Everyone concedes the validity of the idea.")[8] Yet he devoted some of his sharpest polemics to attacks on the ideological basis of Marxist socialism, seeing in "Marxian philosophy" a false messianism that was a terrible simplification closed off from the subtleties and complexities of reality. Marxism "represents the naiveté of the human race scientifically decked out."[9] Marx's atheism was not an act of courage but a dogmatic optimism that denied everything that Marx could not subsume into his system, in contrast to Nietzsche's braver atheistic despair affirming the tragic individual despite everything. While the Marxists denied the earlier religious precedents of the socialist impulse—Greenberg himself observed that none of the ancient atheists were socialists[10]—they allowed the movement to take on the distorted character of a secular religion: "You are not only atheists, but you have also accepted the "atheistic faith." You have become a church, created a dogma, and established a Vatican.[11]

In a 1936 essay in the form of a letter to a "Communist friend" who called on Greenberg to return to Russia to help build socialism in the USSR, Greenberg accuses the Soviet system of having done evil in the name of good:

> For almost twenty years you have been conducting a system of physical and moral terror for the sake of human happiness; you have been employing the unholy to achieve the holy. Is it so hard to understand that darkness is not the road to light, that dictatorship and paternalism are not the paths to freedom and independence, that terror is no express train to the golden age? Ends and means in politics are analogous to form and content in art. Form in art is not merely technique; means in politics are not merely instruments. The content must be felt in the form. The means must contain the basic elements of the end. When this minimal harmony between ends and means is lacking, we get the stake at which the holy inquisition burns unbelievers to save their souls.[12]

What, then, is the valid essence of the socialist idea? Socialism was not a system that offers an answer to every question that troubles human beings. It was a principle that enhances justice and equality, that affirmed the inherent value of each individual, that rested on freedom of conscience, persuasion rather than brute coercion and the deliberate use of fear. Socialism was not primarily an economic arrangement but a moral goal:

> Under no circumstances can I reduce the goal of socialism to economic equality. I know three institutions where (excluding a small number of officials) economic equality exists: the monastery, the prison, and the army. . . . I do not believe that security and equality can bring man happiness or absolute contentment, but they can bring him something no less important—dignity—a sense of social value and individual worth. Human dignity is the sense and goal of socialism, the only sense and the only goal for which all else is an instrument. Every man, no matter how great or small, must be viewed not as a means to an end, but as an end in himself. This is an elementary truth which is not scientifically demonstrable. Science sees no equality among men; it sees the strong and the weak, the more and the less productive, the bright and the dull—all largely biological evaluations. . . . Without equal worth, there can be no equal rights; without equal rights—no economic equality. . . . Whoever lacks this *a priori* knowledge, has no reason to be a Socialist and cannot be one.[13]

In short, socialism cannot claim that it will abolish suffering, only that it will mitigate *degrading* suffering.

Greenberg's socialism rested on a venerable Kantian rule that all humans be treated as ends, never only as means, and that the guiding principles by which one lives be such that could govern all human action. A blindness to the categorical imperative underlay the Marxist notion of "transitional generations." After the overthrow of capitalism and the establishment of the dictatorship of the proletariat, but before true communism has been attained, a transitional generation had to lay the groundwork for a society organized according to the principle that communal wealth should be allocated "from each according to his ability, to each according to his need." As in the Soviet Union in the late twenties and thirties, workers, peasants, and everyone else were to endure massive self-sacrifice to accomplish this great leap forward. In theory the sacrifice was voluntary, but in fact the sacrifice was extracted without the generation's consent, often at the cost of sheer physical survival. This was the central moral flaw in the Soviet ideological argument.

> There are no transitional generations in history. No individual may be considered as a means to advance the interests of another, because each one is an end in himself. Similarly we must not look upon any generation as an instrument to advance the welfare of another, as

fertilizer on the fields of future history, because in the endlessness of historical development every generation is also an end in itself.[14]

As a student of human nature and a cultured man, Greenberg sought to pinpoint the personal characteristics of the leaders of the Communist movement that explained their propensity to manipulate and destroy. He pointed to Lenin's single-minded, ascetic coldness, fearful of poetry or music because they might seduce him from the revolution. ("All his life he was mortally afraid of looking beyond the horizons prescribed by Marx and losing his faith, of assuming any possibility that our empirical world is irradiated by rays from another, metaphysical world.")[15] Greenberg observed first-hand the self-centered hypocrisies of Leon Trotsky during the Russian Civil War so that, unlike the *Partisan Review* intellectuals, he consistently refused to idealize Trotsky, even after Stalin's agent had killed the exiled Trotsky with an axe:

> Under the impact of the tragic aspects of the murder one is inclined to forget Trotsky's role before his power waned, the sadistic nature of his revolutionism, his initiative in establishing the Cheka [the Soviet secret police] and introducing inquisitorial methods, his approval of mass terror, his theory of revolutionary morality which sanctioned punishment not only of persons who had transgressed against the Soviet government but also of their wives, children, friends, and neighbors (Trotsky's well-known policy of taking hostages), his theory and practice of punitive expeditions against villages and entire districts, the executions he ordered in the army and the mass slaughter in Kronstadt of fellow-Bolsheviks who rebelled against the bureaucracy which Trotsky so energetically and capably established . . .[16]

Perhaps socialism could bring an end to starvation (though Greenberg doubted if it would bring a higher standard of living than capitalism). Nevertheless, there were some hard psychological realities that could never be invalidated by any new order. No regime could exorcise human greed or the will to dominate others that, as Freud (and Nietzsche) argued, had their source in primordial human realities.

Thus, for example, in a 1937 essay entitled "The Avoided Subject," Greenberg asks if socialism will do away with prostitution. Prostitution is older than capitalism, even if capitalism had created a particularly favorable soil for the growth of professional prostitution. Individuals turn to prostitution for subjective as well as objective reasons: " 'One weeps because her soup is thin; another because her pearls are few.' Greed is no less a factor in sexual corruption than genuine need." Needs are relative, and cupidity can not merely be dismissed as "bourgeois degeneration." Indeed, avarice can be a far more powerful craving than poverty. "The urge for 'more,' the yearning for imaginary 'power,' the element of greed, I doubt whether these can be eliminated by instituting plenty. The forms and gradations of corruption may change under a collectivist system. But can corruption itself be eliminated?"[17] Greenberg is dubious. Socialism can clear the way for a new freedom but cannot by itself do away with fear and redeem the human drives for satiety, power, and control.

In his realism, Greenberg resembled George Orwell, who from the late 1930s on began telling his comrades on the Left what they did not want to hear. In his philosophy, Greenberg resembled the neo-Kantian philosopher Hermann Cohen, who was also a socialist and a philosopher of Judaism. Greenberg himself acknowledged an affinity with Eduard Bernstein, though he found Bernstein's revisionist socialism lacked the "moral pathos without which socialism cannot become a social-educational force."[18] Socialism was not a substitute religion but it did derive its energy from an ethical absolute, not from sociopolitical pragmatism.

In 1936 Greenberg wrote, "I am a pacifist and a socialist. I am an opponent of force and a believer in democracy." At this point he was experiencing the most troubling internal tension that can be discerned in his writings: deciding that pacifism was perhaps the wrong way to deal with the Nazi onslaught. Could it be that pacifism was inappropriate not only practically but, more important, inappropriate theoretically?

Like so many who looked back in horror at the carnage of World War I, Greenberg had concluded that military violence, so easily rationalized, was destructive to the soul of all the parties involved. As was the case for many of his generation, Greenberg venerated Mahatma Gandhi. Gandhi was a saint who cared for others, an ascetic who could have withdrawn from worldly concerns, but in-

stead had become a crusader for justice. Greenberg's portrait of
Gandhi is highly idealized; he minimizes the sociopolitical dimension of the Gandhi phenomenon or the psychoanalytic aspect of
Gandhi's self-abnegation.[19] (A hint of a more critical attitude toward Gandhi is Greenberg's remark apropos of a sketch on the
Japanese pacifist Toyohiko Kagawa: "Kagawa belongs to the same
type as Tolstoy and Gandhi, but he is much less complicated. Perhaps this is the reason why he escaped both the pseudo-religious
and pseudo-ethical extremes which mark the Russian artist and
God-seeker and the Hindu moralist and politician. Unlike Tolstoy
and Gandhi, Kagawa is a great admirer of science and technical
progress and sees in them a source of liberation rather than enslave-
ment for humanity.") [20]

Greenberg held that Gandhi "believed that everyday acts and
deeds can be suffused with elements of the Absolute" (which,
Greenberg noted, in a rather understated manner, was "not foreign to Jewish religious tradition"). He extolled Gandhi as an
exemplar of someone who tore down the wall between the everyday, especially politics, and the eternal that is experienced in
religion, ethics, and aesthetics.[21] In particular, Greenberg praised
the Mahatma's efforts to awaken the self-respect of the Indian
untouchables and inculcate a measure of regard toward them
among upper-caste Indians.[22] Greenberg admired, above all, Gandhi's effort to effectuate change through *ahimsa* (nonviolence) and
satyagraha ("soul-force"): a deliberate refusal to cooperate with
the *Raj* so as to force a confrontation with British imperialism
while, at the same time, using only morally pure means to oppose
injustice.

Gandhi's advice to German Jews in the 1930s to practice *satyagraha* in face of Nazi persecution is well known through the Indian's
correspondence with Martin Buber. Greenberg also took public issue
with Gandhi on this matter.[23] Despite the theoretical superiority of
militant pacifism as a moral strategy, Greenberg noted, *satyagraha*
would be completely ineffectual in this context. Unlike the British,
the Nazis had no conscience to which to appeal. "A Jewish Gandhi
in Germany, should one arise, could 'function' for about five minutes—until the first Gestapo agent would lead him, not to a concentration camp, but directly to the gallows."[24] Greenberg rather sar-

donically observed that passive resistance had not been used by any
non-Jewish Europeans under Fascist, Communist, or Nazi control.
The notable exception was a young German member of a Christian
sect known as the International Union of Bible Students, who was
shot in 1939 for refusing to go to the front. In the essay referring to
this man, Greenberg remarked that he cannot recall any *secular* pacifists in Russia during the First World War, although there was a trial
in Moscow of a large group of Tolstoyans who were opponents of the
war on religious grounds.[25] Greenberg reluctantly concluded that
Gandhi's inability to appreciate the tragedy of European Jewry under the Nazi boot was not unrelated to his insensitivity to the moral
claim of the Jewish people to a homeland, suggesting that the latter
was probably derived from political engrossment with an united
Hindu-Muslim front that left Gandhi susceptible to pan-Islamic anti-
Zionist propaganda.

When all was said and done, the political realities of the post-
1933 years exposed the inherent weaknesses of pacifism as a principle. Contrasting the situation of men like himself in 1939 to the
earlier stance of such famous pacifists such as Tolstoy, Romain
Rolland, and Einstein, Greenberg referred to "a certain break that
has occurred in the souls of many pacifists in recent years":

> They can no longer apply their pacifist beliefs to the present world
> situation. This may be so because they no longer think in terms of "I
> and the universe," "I and eternity," but in the narrower terms of "I
> and my generation," "I and my direct historical responsibilities." . . .
> A Nazi victory may allow the evil to rule over an enslaved world for
> many years, for one or perhaps for many generations. And it is toward
> this generation, or these generations, that pacifists feel responsible.
> . . . I still believe fervently that what we usually and incorrectly call
> Passive Resistance could quickly demoralize the totalitarian armies
> and make them incapable of carrying out their functions, and that
> the genuinely human which is also inside them, though it is buried
> under heavy layers of their idolatry, would gradually awaken. But
> passive resistance on any kind of mass scale is today impossible. It is
> both too late and too soon for it. . . . War, every war, is a crime, but
> there are world situations when passivity is a much greater crime.[26]

The consistent universalism that Greenberg expected of Gandhi and
other spiritual teachers, if it were to be truly universal, had to

embrace the claims of Jewish people as well. The Zionist idea, itself based on a moral argument, was a litmus test whether an intellectual dealt only in abstractions or was attentive to the concrete needs of flesh-and-blood human beings. Greenberg's ire was directed especially at the etherialization of the Jews prevalent among well-thinking moralizers and "non-Jewish Jews" who could find no place in their heart for particular Jewish agonies. Thus in 1943 Greenberg published a scathing critique of the philanthropist and book collector Lessing Rosenwald, chairman of the board of Sears, Roebuck and Company and leader of the anti-Zionist American Council for Judaism. Responding to an interview in *Life* magazine with the Saudi Arabian king, Rosenwald had expressed his agreement with Ibn Saud's opposition to Zionism on the grounds that Jews were solely a religious community, that they had long ceased to be a people, and that Judaism's universalism was incompatible with the idea of a Jewish state. Greenberg retorted:

> One might conclude from the tone of [Rosenwald's] composition that landlessness is a blessing bestowed upon his "co-religionists," that Zionists, in their stubbornness, refuse to recognize the beneficent effects of this blessing and are unable to grasp the profound thought that "there is no historical or organic relationship between Judaism as a world religion and national statehood." For a moment one might have thought that before us was a man preaching poverty as a religious tenet, that the Jews were a sort of Franciscan order whose mission it was to live an ascetic life, away from the vanities of the temporal world. But we happen to know something of Mr. Rosenwald's social landscape, enough at least to be certain that neither he nor his associates have much in common with religious asceticism. . . . The fact that there are so many millions of Jews—in Europe, in Asia, in Rosenwald's own America—who identify themselves as a people with a destiny of their own, with the drama of their own history, with common hopes and aspirations for the future, should have given Mr. Rosenwald cause to stop repeating the perverse nonsense on which he and others like him have been brought up. . . . Historically the traditional Jew has never accepted the foolish and basically pathological theory that just because his people has created a universalistic religion—or has been the medium through which that religion has been revealed—that people should disappear from the face of the earth.[27]

Implicit in the sarcasm is Greenberg's conviction that Judaism was a universalistic religion. Maurice Samuel noted, "There was no trace of provincialism or national egotism in his passionate Zionism. He thought of the Jewish people and the Jewish State in terms of universals, so that whatever he said and wrote about our immediate tasks echoed in large stretches of space and time. He had, in human values, what in music is called absolute pitch—the instinctive placing of a note in the absolute and universal scale."[28] If Rosenwald erred by ignoring the ethnic element of Jewishness, most intellectuals of Greenberg's generation, including many of Jewish extraction, erred in conceiving of Judaism as a particularistic culture of a completely different kind from that of the universalistic cultures created by ancient Hellas or medieval Christianity. Judaism was both ethnic and ideational.

Greenberg's most developed analysis of the nature of Judaism and the meaning of Jewish peoplehood, selected to open the first volume of the *Inner Eye*, is entitled "The Universalism of the Chosen People." He began by taking up the usual accusations that Judaism was responsible for racism, that it was primitive and tribal compared to the New Testament, and that, by not engaging in conversion, Jews demonstrated that their notion of election was incompatible with democracy. Unlike Mordecai Kaplan, Greenberg did not advocate eliminating the notion of "Chosen People," but sought to show its intrinsic connection to the ideals of human equality and fair treatment of the stranger.[29] In defense of Jewish loyalties he maintained that "a certain degree of narcissism is requisite for the survival of an ethnic group, just as every man necessarily possesses a measure of egocentricity." The heart of his argument, however, is a historical analysis of the emergence of a universalized Judaism as a result of the inner development of biblical ideas.

First, the promise of the land of Canaan to the Israelites was related to the biblical idea that lands were given to other peoples as well. Second, noting the absence of the racial element present in ancient Greek concepts of the barbarian, Greenberg insisted the status of the resident alien and the stranger in the Bible indicated a reaching out beyond the tribal system, culminating in the universalism of the books of Jonah and Ruth. This, in turn, eventuated in the more explicit universalism of the classic rabbinic writings in which biblical Israel was transformed into *knesset Yisrael*, the Congregation of Israel, in principle open to all humans, regardless of origin.

A discussion of rabbinical attitudes toward mixed marriage and converts to Judaism led him to conclude that the relevant tension over inclusion or exclusion in Judaism was not between particularism and universalism but between liberalism and orthodoxy: "The Jewish people and its religious congregation thus become, to borrow a term employed by Henri Bergson, an open rather than a closed society, a community which is, in principle, prepared to become all-embracing and to welcome all men, regardless of their racial origin."[30]

The historical analysis in this essay follows closely Yehezkel Kaufmann's brilliant work of historical sociology, *Golah ve-Nekhar* (In Exile and Alienhood).[31] Like Kaufmann, Greenberg emphasized the uniqueness of biblical monotheism in contrast to ancient Greek and Persian concepts of divinity and fate. Mature Judaism was essentially universalistic, although historical conditions after the triumph of Christianity and Islam limited the social options open to Jews and precluded conversion on a large scale.

The continuation of this discussion is found in Greenberg's other essays on Jewish survival in the Diaspora. Thus, he observed that during the centuries of Diaspora, Jews did not require a land of their own; despite all the traditional lamentations, perhaps the destruction of the Temple was a liberation, because the Temple could be built anywhere under the invisible roof of the Shechinah.[32] Elsewhere Greenberg rejected with scorn the common accusation that Diaspora Jews were economic parasites, noting the valuable roles that Jews played as economic and cultural middlemen in the lands where they lived. The pride that Jews felt in their election mitigated the outward humiliations they were forced to endure. However badly they were treated, it enabled them to go on living as Jews with dignity and meaning.[33]

How did the universalism of Judaism give rise to the particularism of Zionism? Zionism was a necessity in modern times because the medieval status and the traditional self-conception of Jewry were being subverted by overwhelming forces from without. Zionism was a response to pressures that forced the Congregation of Israel to become something less transcendent and more tangible: an ethnic-national group.

Modern Judaism was being inexorably stripped of the unique, if paradoxical, at-homeness in exile that had characterized Jewry for centuries. "The Dispersion was not just a calamity . . . but also—and perhaps most of all—a dynamic-creative state, a sharp tension against ourselves and against the outside world, perhaps the loftiest mystery that a nation ever made of its life." Now, however, "our misfortune is not so much that we are in *Galut*, as that we [have been] in some degree liberated, released from the *Galut*, from its tension, creativeness, life-shaping mysteriousness."[34] Having for so many centuries given meaning to their lives according to the shape of sacred time, "we grow more and more sensitive to space, to spatial neighborliness with others." Yet, he continued with reference to contemporary anti-Semitism, "instead of us rejecting their space, their space is beginning to reject us." Alternatively, their space threatens to dissolve Jewish identity. The paradoxical combination of the destructiveness of anti-Semitism, on the one hand, and the siren call of assimilation, on the other, explained the purpose of the modern Zionist project:

Instead of Dispersion, history demands of us concentration—again as thousands of years ago, before we were formed as a people: a spatial basis and a spatial frame for further revealing ourself. From this aspect Zionism is a new Genesis, a new grasping point for forming ourselves. It is possible that for such a Genesis the land we call the Land of Israel is not the best, not politically the most convenient, and if history were rationally planned some other country in some other continent might have been more easily the assembly point for Israel. But this is the way it happened. That vitality in us which seeks a Genesis had a familiar address. It let itself be directed not by practical common sense and calculation, but by a historical compass; and the compass led to the Land of Israel. Should we be angry with the compass? Or should we say thank you to it? What is the difference? That is where it led and that is where it will lead—at least within the limits of our epoch.[35]

"*Galut* is an algebraic expression," Greenberg proposed in an address to the World Zionist Congress in Jerusalem in August 1951.[36]

Exile is a variable which differs from land to land and period to period. Reiterating the heart of classical Zionism, Greenberg averred that *Galut* exists where, lacking political or social independence, Jews were subject to the daily pressure of the majority and rely on its goodwill for their continued existence. "Even Israel itself was for many, many centuries, in essence, *Galut*." Certainly for the Jews of the Soviet Union and Islamic countries, exodus from *Galut* was the only solution, Greenberg argued in the early fifties.

Contrary, however, to the position reiterated by Ben Gurion and others at that time, Greenberg insisted that the Jews of the democratic West, and particularly the United States, were not poised for mass emigration, even though they could be viewed as living in *Galut* as well. Individual American Jews might settle in Israel out of love for the country, but not massive numbers out of fear. The notion that Israel would be a refuge to a persecuted American Jewry was nonsense; were America ever to become a land of fascist anti-Semitism, the State of Israel itself would probably not long survive such a disaster. To a Zionist audience in Israel in 1951, he contended that they showed an egregious lack of appreciation of the strengths of American Jewish communal life and the attractions of American democracy. Greenberg called for an intensive program of Jewish education centered, not on Zionism, but on Jewishness, or, as he explained, on "Hebraism."

> I use the word *Hebraism* here not in that polemical sense which in our times signifies an extreme language preference, a purely linguistic shibboleth, but in the same way that I should use such a term, for example as Hellenism. . . . We have every reason to regard Judaism not in terms of a completed plastic "petrification" but in terms of melody; and melody—precisely because the "area" of its existence is time—has in principle an unending continuity. There is always room for possible variations, even for creative mutations, deviations, and complementary contrasts for new experiments upon itself, but such experiments as do not lose their link (their "memory") with the past, and with those forces that created the past. This brings us, willingly or not, to the question of religion. . . . It is quite unnecessary to be religious in a dogmatic or institutional sense of the word, to be orthodox—if I were to use American parlance, I should say it is unnecessary to be a fundamentalist—in order to recognize the insep-

arable significance in our future folk education of the cultural embodiments of the Jewish religious genius.[37]

Did Greenberg want the fruits of religiosity but not religion, as was said of various supporters of the religious revival of the late forties and early fifties? No, because he had a deep appreciation of the spiritual dimension of human existence that subsists under the veneer of militant secularism.

In an address delivered in 1951 to the New York Board of Rabbis, Greenberg expressed apprehension that the religious vitality of American Judaism was atrophied beyond hope. What was the greatest danger threatening the Jewish will-to-live in the Diaspora? He answered that question with another: "What was the secret of our ability to remain firm in our Jewishness during so many generations despite the fact that we were everywhere a minority, and a severely persecuted one at that?" He reiterated that the Jews did not survive as a group because they had a distinct culture or a well-knit social network, but because they were "an exclusive group of believers."

> This is much more than a group sharing common memories (time and environment frequently eradicate group memories and eliminate them as influencing factors); it is much more than blood kinship. In other words, we survived not simply because we were a people—how many peoples did not Jews see go under in the course of their long history, so that not a trace was left of them—but because we were a Chosen People with a special place in the history of the world, and a central position in the destiny of the cosmos as such.[38]

The Jewish people had not been a minority psychologically as long as it saw itself in cosmic perspective as "conspirators" in Providence's plan leading to the eventual End of Days. But in an increasingly comfortable American Diaspora, Jewish conviction has become anemic and peripheral: "Should we now be honest with ourselves, we would be compelled to conclude that today there are in America hundreds of thousands of Jews who are, in the religious sense, not Jews. They are Jews only insofar as they are not Christians."[39] Remarking on someone's proposal that Jews should send missionaries to other peoples, Greenberg noted, "I too think that a people which believes that its religion is an expression of eternal truth is duty bound to proselytize: it must not monopolize the truth for itself but should spread it also among others."[40] However, Jewish missionaries should first be sent to Jews. Even though the road to complete assimilation in America would be an off-again, on-again process, it would eventually take place unless there was a true spiritual awakening along the way.

In an editorial defending Scholem Asch against the accusation that his supposedly Christological novels opened the door for Jews to convert to Christianity, Greenberg maintained that this was hardly the danger that American Jewry faced:

> The problem is not how to armor the souls of American Jewry against Christianity, but how to arouse those souls, how to make them receptive to religion, how to awaken within them the need for values that transcend the utilitarian, the hunger for style in life, for metaphysical experience, for calm exaltation. It is not suicide that threatens us here, but life without vitality.[41]

Judaism needed a new *hasidut* (he explained that he used this term because he had no other) — a new pietism sensing "that man should be less organized, more of a spiritual 'vagabond,' but [also] that within the framework of society there should be room . . . for community."[42] It was the spiritual substance, not the form that mattered. Defending the kibbutzim against Indian critics who argued that they were breeding-places of vulgar materialism and atheism, Greenberg remarked, "I regard their irreligion as true religion."[43] What was needed was a free and open-minded religiosity, not a return to traditionalism. Discussing the separation of church and state (indirectly referring to the pressures to give official status to Jewish religious law in Israel), Greenberg concluded, "That which we describe in our political jargon as a Theocratic State is in the final reckoning an anti-religious and Godless state."[44]

We recall that Greenberg wrote at a time when secularism was still *de rigueur* among Jewish intellectuals. The low repute of religion among the literati was not a Jewish matter, but belonged to the *mentalité* of the general intelligentsia, especially of East European origin. In his remarks to the New York rabbis he delineated five factors which had caused religion to lose its credibility. First, because of traditional religious claims to answer questions outside its province: "Religion is neither able nor called upon to explain the mystery of life." At best religion evoked, "by means of its specific and largely artistic means, the existence of mystery, veneration of it as well as confidence in it." Second, religion had been exploited in the course of history for nonreligious aims. (This was Greenberg the socialist speaking, referring to the way in which religion had been used to bolster systems of power in many societies.) Third, modern technology fostered the illusion that "man is fundamentally not dependent on powers outside himself or above himself." Fourth, "scientism" has engulfed the public, even though the vast majority has no direct knowledge of scientific procedures, resulting in a materialistic conception of reality that dulled the intuitive faculties without which one could not view the world metaphysically or religiously. Fifth, life in the industrial metropolis "deprives man of his capacity . . . for that type of contemplation of the world and of the self which leads man to wonder and amazement." "I am convinced," Greenberg concluded, "that without a removal of the obstacles which stand in the way of what I called contemplation, without a curing of that specific blindness that affects so many people as a result of their fixation on the material and on those problems of the material which can be experimentally solved, there is no room for authentic religious life, and naturally also not for authentic Jewish religious life."[45]

Greenberg was a secular man, unobservant of religious law, certainly not a theologian. But he pointed to the veracity of the religious in a way that is not merely sentimental or vaguely appreciative of the psychological advantages of having faith. He did not spell out fully what he meant, but Marie Syrkin observed that Greenberg was not someone whose written words exceed the individual's personal depth:

> Whatever field he touched on, the *said* was not his all, carefully garnered and given; the *unsaid* was even more—a deep reservoir from which he brilliantly and unexpectedly drew. He did not exhaust himself spiritually. This was especially true of the areas of his most intimate concern, the questions of religion and social ethics. Not

everything had to be stated, made explicit or resolved. There was a secret treasure to be cherished, an untapped wealth of which his writings, whatever their excellence, were luminous intimations.[46]

How to combine a tough-minded psychology, which has made us aware of how easily human beings project their needs onto the cosmos to find comfort in times of distress, with the limitations of theory to explain why anything exists at all. Deliberately unsentimental Freudian theory was for Greenberg a corrective to the utopian illusions of socialism.[47] But at the same time it was a defective account of human motives. A form of psychological determinism, Freudianism reduced all moral demands to a set of mechanisms (in this case sexual instincts), thus cutting the ground out from under actual ethical choice. For all his brilliance, Freud was himself prone to simplistic reductionism and a morally disastrous pessimism.[48] The ethical self-transformation that could not be derived from scientific socialism could not be constructed on Freudian foundations either.

Freud had, of course, dismissed religion as a form of sublimation. For Greenberg, the fruits of sublimation pointed to a dimension which Freud hid from himself in a maneuver which a psychoanalyst might call "denial":

Through sublimating our feelings, inclinations, and energies we compensate ourselves for the losses suffered through obeying the ego or super-ego and depriving ourselves of pleasures for which we yearned. . . . But here we may ask whether the new gratifications which we obtain through sublimation merely fill the place of others and are, in a sense, ersatz pleasures in themselves, deriving their existence from a different plane of our being. . . . If the "sublime" were lacking within us as a special sphere of existence, we could never attain it, and if it were not genuine and a value in itself, it could never become as creative and serviceable as it often appears to be in the realms of religion, science, art, and politics. Freud's description of the processes of sublimation and their results should have led him to a revision of his concept of the superego and to an earnest consideration whether the 'sublime' is merely an end product of certain developments or a basic factor, as elemental as the erotic factor itself.[49]

He concluded that there was ground enough for an intrinsic but nonreductive relationship between the erotic and the moral: the moral element in us might well be erotic, meaning (going beyond Freud) that it was "native to the human psyche and possessing its own unborrowed forces."

Freud's sociology is pessimistic, but there was room to believe that "to the extent that Freud recognized the existence within us of a capacity for erotic devotion and self-identification with others, he must have recognized that the way to a broad altruistic attitude is not impossible in principle."[50] In a critique of Einstein at a conference in September 1940 at the Jewish Theological Seminary of America, Greenberg remarked, "From a certain point of view, religion is probably the most daring attempt to conceive the totality of worldly existence in ethical terms. Fear *plus* Promethean ethical demands on a responsive cosmos—demands which, if met, would put an end to fear—are the foundation of religion."[51] In the history of Jewish thought, therefore, Greenberg represents the recognition by Jewish secularism of its limits and of the intellectual veracity of the sacred.

Traditional Jewish intellectuality has taken three different paths. First, textual exegesis unpacks the Torah as a never-ending fountain of wisdom and insight. In this regard, midrashic and other strategies of interpretation (such as that used by the medieval Jewish philosophers and kabbalists) developed a ramified hermeneutics in which each word, even each letter of Scripture, were hints of ever deeper, ever more profound levels of meaning. Second, Jewish intellectuals have sought to construct ideal systems of order in which needs are reconciled to values. The halakhic systems of the Mishnah, Talmuds, and codes addressed themselves to the establishment of order in the face of potential chaos, as philosophical and perhaps kabbalistic metaphysics respond to the disorder of the world that threatened the rationality of God's creation. A third style is more immediate and mundane: the application of ethical values to the everyday through preaching, responsa, and halakhic decisions. There is a special literary genre, *musar*, which offers ethical instruction, social criticism, and personal encouragement. It is this last category of *musar* writing into which Hayim Greenberg's essays fit.

Moral action was the controlling factor in Greenberg's analysis, not brilliance for its own sake. Thus he observed, in a critique of Martin Luther's theology, that the Protestant reformer never understood that " 'works' without faith, or faith registered in consciousness, are in the final analysis nearer genuine religious life than faith without 'works.' "[52] Greenberg's *musar* was not a verbal pyrotechnics, which is often a hallmark of the intellectual—it was a sense of the right act, in the spirit of Rabbi Simeon son of Rabbi Gamaliel, *lo ha-midrash iqar ela ha-ma'aseh* (not interpretation but doing is the chief thing, *Pirqe Avot* 1:17).

One of Greenberg's best-known editorials was written for the *Jewish Frontier* issue of February 12, 1943, when the rumors of the mass murder of the Jews in Nazi-dominated Germany began to circulate openly among American Jewish leaders:

> The time has come, perhaps, when the few Jewish communities remaining in the world which are still free to make their voices heard and to pray in public should proclaim a day of fasting and prayer for American Jews. No—this is not a misprint. I mean specifically that a day of prayer and of fasting should be proclaimed for the five million Jews now living in the United States. They live under the protection of a mighty republic governed by democratic laws. . . . The vast majority of them have enough food to eat, clothes to wear and roofs over their heads. . . . Nevertheless, they deserve to be prayed for. They are not even aware what a misfortune has befallen them, and if they were to look at themselves with seeing eyes they would realize with shock how intolerable this misfortune is. . . . If moral bankruptcy deserves pity, and if this pity is seven-fold for one who is not even aware of how shocking his bankruptcy is, then no Jewish community in the world today (not even the Jews who are now in the claws of the Nazi devourer) deserves more compassion from Heaven than does American Jewry.[53]

Greenberg bitterly castigates the ineptitude and passivity of organized American Jewry in the face of monstrous knowledge which puts to shame all their organizational and ideological rivalries. Whatever the rights and wrongs of Greenberg's accusation, the voice, because it was not of a rabbi, was all the more authentically a Jewish one.

About Hayim Greenberg, Maurice Samuel explained, "He was a sage; that is, he had a grave and affectionate understanding of man's nature and man's needs. His *sagesse* did not derive from his learning; on the contrary, he had accumulated his vast learning in the practice of his *sagesse*."[54] Greenberg was a classical Jewish moralist who called for a restoration of ethical values in light of a realistic perception of the sins of the age: indifference to the suffering of concrete human beings. Perhaps that is why Greenberg is one of the few mid-twentieth-century Jewish intellectuals who can still be read with profit.

Notes

1. The collected essays of Hayim Greenberg are found in the following books: *The Inner Eye: Selected Essays*, [volume I] (New York: Jewish Frontier Association, 1953); *The Inner Eye: Selected Essays, volume II* (New York: Jewish Frontier Association, 1964); *Hayim Greenberg Anthology*, selected and with an introduction by Marie Syrkin (Detroit: Wayne State University Press, 1968); *Yid un Velt* (1953); *Beytlakh fun a Tog-Bukh* (1954); and *Mentshn un Vertn* (1954). There is also a collection of his essays translated into Hebrew, *Ayin Ro'i* (1958), with an essay on him by Ben Halpern, who worked with Greenberg many years at the *Jewish Frontier*. Among the essays and accounts of Hayim Greenberg are the following: Arnold Eisen, "Out of the Depths: On Hayim Greenberg and Religion" (*Jewish Frontier* [Dec. 1984], 48–50); David Rosenthal, "Hayim Greenberg's Legacy: The World of His Ideas" (*Jewish Frontier* [March/April 1991], 24–32); Sholomo Bickel, *Shreiber fun mayn Dor* (1958), 256–66); G. Kressel, *Leksikon ha-sifrut ha-ivrit ba-dorot ha-aharonim*, (Merhavyah: Sifriyat ha-po'alim, 1965), I, 509 (with additional bibliography); brief notices by Robert Gordis in *Judaism* (2:1953), 99–100; and Mordecai Kaplan in *Jewish Frontier* (Fall 1957). I am grateful for being allowed to read two excellent papers by graduate students: "When Goodness Fails: The Response of Labor Zionism to the Holocaust as Articulated by Hayim Greenberg" by Rosalie K. Bachana of the CUNY Graduate Center and "Reclaiming the Un-personhood of Hayim Greenberg" by Mark A. Raider of Brandeis University.
2. *Inner Eye* II, 15.
3. Ibid., 233.
4. *Hayim Greenberg Anthology*, 19.
5. *Inner Eye* II, 15.
6. In an essay published in 1945, Greenberg described a visit to Romain Rolland in 1924 to ask if he would use his influence to remove the Soviet government ban on Hebrew (*Inner Eye* II, 271–78). The famous French writer demurred. *Habimah* was founded in Moscow in 1917. In 1926 the company left for a tour abroad to New York, Palestine, and Berlin; it finally settled in Tel Aviv in 1931.

7. *Inner Eye*, Frontispiece of vol. II.
8. *Inner Eye* I, 242.
9. Ibid., 243.
10. Ibid., 245.
11. Ibid., 252; see also p. 320.
12. Ibid., 256.
13. Ibid., 254–55.
14. Such sacrifice has to be the free moral choice of volunteers, as in the case of the Zionist pioneers in Palestine, not the result of a government *ukaz* (edict) issued in the name of its victims. Thus, when he was challenged by a Zionist audience as to whether he was denigrating the call to self-sacrifice by the *halutzim* (pioneers), he explained: "I would be an opponent of pioneering in Palestine if the hardships entailed in the rebuilding of a long-neglected country were imposed on Jewish youth from above and against its will, if the pioneers in Palestine were considered fertilizer on the fields of the country so that a later generation might enjoy its roses. But the pioneering in Palestine is a voluntary task freely undertaken by those rejoicing in it" (*Inner Eye* I, 325).
15. Ibid., 264.
16. *Inner Eye* II, 236. "What is most deplorable is the fact that in certain liberal circles Trotsky is still considered an innocent sufferer and, what is more important, is looked upon as a temporarily defeated fighter for all those great values which Stalin so brutally tramples with his despotic boots. But in the final analysis, Trotsky is a good Stalinist and Stalin is not such a bad Troskyist. . . . The clash between the two is not a clash between a Cain soul and an Abel soul, but between two Cains for whom the world is too small to be divided equitably" (ibid., 230–31).
17. Ibid., 169.
18. *Inner Eye* I, 327.
19. One must note, however, that Greenberg's posture before Gandhi seems at times rather self-abasing: "I have read, in the languages familiar to me, all that you have written and there has been no social-religious thinker who has exerted so fruitful an influence on me. If, despite the fact that in various periods I have been stirred to the deeps of my soul by your teaching and your life, I am far from being your disciple or follower, the fault is not yours" (*Inner Eye* I, 219). In all fairness, this tone of adulation may have been heightened because the main essay on Gandhi in the *Inner Eye* was an address delivered at a memorial meeting for Gandhi after his assassination (*Inner Eye* I, 157–61).
20. *Inner Eye* I, 391.
21. Ibid., 159.
22. Ibid., 220.
23. His arguments are most fully developed in "A Letter to Gandhi" (*Inner Eye* I, 219–29) and "An Answer to Gandhi" (ibid., 230–38).

24. *Inner Eye* I, 233.
25. "Without an Army," *Inner Eye* II, 157–63.
26. *Inner Eye* II, 161, 163.
27. "Lessing Rosenwald and Ibn Saud," in *Inner Eye* II, 100–101.
28. *Inner Eye* II, 13.
29. In "The Future of American Jewry," delivered before the New York Board of Rabbis in 1951, Greenberg spoke of chosenness as intrinsic to the Jewish perspective on the world and the Jewish people. Describing a conversation with a "young rabbi," Greenberg remarked, "He regards the existence of the Jewish people as a Divine Drama on a universal scale" (*Inner Eye* II, 62). A few pages later he explains: "Nietzsche once sarcastically remarked regarding Christians: 'Christianity, I have been told all my life, is the religion of salvation. But I know my Christians well and they don't look saved.' I could paraphrase this to read: 'Jews, I have been told all my life, are a chosen people. But knowing my contemporary Jews, they somehow don't look chosen.' Yet it may not be so very important how Jews appear in the eyes of non-Jews; but it is important how they appear to themselves. Our chosenness has become a tradition rather than a living, nourishing faith" (67).
30. Ibid., 56; also 49, 51.
31. There is a direct quote in ibid., 21.
32. "Dispersion and Concentration," in Joseph Leftwich, ed., *Great Yiddish Writers of the Twentieth Century* (Northvale, N.J.: Jason Aronson, 1987 [first published in 1969 as *The Way We Think*], 124–26).
33. "The Myth of Jewish Parasitism," *Inner Eye* I, 62–69. Yehezkel Kaufmann wrote of this theme, but is not cited in Greenberg's essay.
34. "Dispersion and Concentration," *Great Yiddish Writers*, 125.
35. Ibid., 126.
36. "Jewish Culture and Education in the Diaspora," *Inner Eye* I, 70–86.
37. *Inner Eye* I, 83–85.
38. *Inner Eye* II, 65–66.
39. Ibid., 69.
40. Ibid.
41. Ibid., 263. Written in 1948.
42. Ibid., 75–76.
43. *Inner Eye* I, 226.
44. "Church and State—Seven Theses," *Inner Eye* II, 173–89; also "Concerning an Israel Constitution," *Inner Eye* I, 191–209.
45. *Inner Eye* II, 76.
46. *Hayim Greenberg Anthology*, Introduction, 18. Also *Inner Eye* II, 9.
47. "Psychoanalysis and Moral Pessimism, *Inner Eye* II, 132.
48. "Psychoanalysis and Moral Pessimism," *Inner Eye* I, 132–45. Greenberg does not point out that Freudianism, like Marxism, actually smuggles in a strong moral component under the guise of being a disinterested

scientific theory: why, after all, should one want to be a mature human being, liberated as much as possible from unconscious motivations and infantile needs?

49. *Inner Eye* I, 141–43.
50. Ibid., 144–45. One could carry this further and refer to the erotic impulse in a Platonic sense as pulling us toward the idea of the good.
51. Ibid., 125.
52. Ibid., 106.
53. *Inner Eye* II, 193–94.
54. Ibid., 12.

CHAPTER 2

Marie Syrkin: An Exemplary Life

Carole S. Kessner

At the end of her life, Marie Syrkin said, "Today I can write with as much passion about old age as I once could about love."[1] The following verse, from a poem entitled "Of Age," written when she was nearly eighty, is, however, about both love and age:

> Women live longer than men;
> The few that I loved are dead.
> Had I the power to summon,
> Whom would I bring to my bed?[2]

Her question goes unanswered, although there were indeed a few good candidates for the position. But more to the point is the fact that since Marie Syrkin *did* live longer than most of her male colleagues, it left her, in the last decade of her life, having to justify her past as an idealistic polemicist for the Labor Zionist movement, as an apologist for the words and actions of her friend Golda Meir, as an antagonist of the New Left, as a bewildered but vocal adversary of the ascension of Likud, as an unshaken believer in her own interpretation of history in the face of the new revisionist historiographers, and as an idiosyncratic feminist. Doubtless, in her long life of one month short of ninety years—she died on February 1, 1988—she made mistakes; but the significance of her life perhaps lies less in her polemical stances, and, in the assessment of Irving Howe, "more in the kind of life she led, a life committed to values beyond the self."[3]

Marie Syrkin led a life that reads like a gripping novel, full of romance, history, poetry, and action, all quickened by intellect, conviction, and, most of all, wit—both ironic and self-deprecatory. Born in Switzerland in 1899, two years after the First Zionist Congress and six years before the 1905 Russian Revolution, she was the only child of Nachman and Bassya Osnos Syrkin. Nachman Syrkin met his wife Bassya Osnos at the Second Zionist Congress in Basle in 1898, where both were studying medicine. This, their daughter has pointed out, "gives some idea of how far my mother was emancipated."[4] Moreover, in 1898 Syrkin had written his seminal work, *The Jewish Socialist State* (one year after Herzl's *The Jewish State*), in which he expounded his vision of the synthesis of socialism and Zionism; this ultimately would become the program of the founders of the State of Israel. Bassya Syrkin, though a tubercular who would die in America at the age of thirty-six when her daughter was only sixteen, was herself a headstrong revolutionary activist.

To be born the only daughter of two such professional idealists could not be without consequences, both positive and negative. Psychobiography has to take into account the daughter's love-hatred for her father who was an erudite moralist, yet who was possessed of a blazing temperament that vented itself publicly in scathing argument and privately in what his daughter has described as a zealous "dedicated hardship."[5] It would also have to take into account the model of feminist activism and egalitarianism provided by her mother, for Bassya Syrkin held the conviction that women should have independent careers and that they should not be "shackled by men and society and should be free."[6]

One might go so far as to claim that Marie Syrkin's attraction to Golda Meir was influenced by the model of Bassya Syrkin. In the introduction to Marie Syrkin's biography of Goldie Myerson (Golda Meir), published in 1955, the author describes her friend as "the rare type that one might simply describe as the effective idealist. . . . Among the remarkable personalities who created the State of Israel, I met a number of such men and women—individuals who responded to a world in chaos neither passively as "alienated" intellectuals, nor actively as energetic cynics. For me, this translation of belief into life became one of the few sources of moral affirmation in our time."[7]

Notwithstanding Bassya Syrkin's conviction that women should have independent careers, she soon discovered that the birth of her child one year after marriage, the demands of her husband's political life which necessitated frequent moves from one country to another, and concerns for her poor health resulted in the abandonment of her medical studies. But it did not stop her from continuing activities in behalf of socialist Zionism; during the first few years of her marriage, at the time of the 1905 Revolution, Bassya Syrkin twice returned to Russia carrying revolutionary pamphlets in the false bottom of her trunk.

These were years, moreover, when the Syrkins' peripatetic life meant that by the time Marie was ten, she had lived in five countries—Switzerland, Germany, France, Russia, and the United States. The family finally moved to America in 1908 because, as Marie Syrkin herself quipped, "Papa was always getting exiled—so we traveled a lot."[8] By this time she was fluent in five languages—Russian, French, German, Yiddish, and English—which she quickly picked up in school. One might note here that Hebrew was *not* among the languages she learned, despite the fact that when she was a child her father would make sporadic attempts to instruct her in Spinoza in Latin, Marx in German, and the Bible in Hebrew. She later lamented the fact that Hebrew was never to become one of her languages. In her eighties, in a response to a remark by Trude Weiss-Rosmarin that Marie was fortunate to be, after all, the daughter of Nachman Syrkin, she snapped back, "Yes, but one thing he failed to provide me. He did not teach me Hebrew at an age when one could have learned it. It's maddening. . . . That he didn't teach me Hebrew was a serious loss."[9] This lack, she later claimed, was a major reason for her own failure to make *aliya*. The more compelling reason, however, was her refusal to give up joint custody of her child.

Not only was Marie Syrkin an unusually beautiful child, as she was a beautiful mature woman and handsome into old age, but she was exceptionally intelligent and treated as a prodigy by her parents. Yet in these early years, if she admired her parents' dedicated poverty, she did not seem the slightest bit interested in the politics that inspired their chosen financial condition. She was fast developing a passion for romantic poetry equal to her parents' passion for radical politics. Nor did she show any signs that she was to develop a writing style that more often than not would be characterized as acerbic. Her diary for the year 1915, when she was barely sixteen, reveals the usual adolescent propensity for romantic sentimentality, though it also demonstrates an unusually lush and rich vocabulary. The following is an example from the diary:

> All day that sad line from Keats' immortal poem has been ringing in my brain. "Where but to think is verily a vale of tears." This world *is* verily a vale of tears, tears which can never be dried. I find myself continually thinking of W. . . . The remembrance of my dream kiss still burns my lips; I feel sullied, outraged, my whole soul is seared, and yes, I would willingly dream it again and again. The dominant note in my entire being has become the primitive call from man to woman, the first hushed whispering of love.[10]

There is nothing at this stage to suggest that Marie Syrkin would become the "doyenne of Labor Zionism." If anything, her diary suggests that she might become a woman of belles lettres; this is no doubt what would have happened, had she not made a conscious career choice to use her literary gifts in the service of Zionism and the Jewish people. She liked to tell a story about the time, a few years after the death of her mother, when Nachman Syrkin, who disapproved of her literary bent, blazed out at her because he thought she was frittering away her abilities. When she was about nineteen, she happened to be quietly reading a novel by H. G. Wells. The newspapers at that time were full of the exploits of a young woman criminal who had been dubbed "the bobbed-haired bandit." When this female outlaw was not busy committing crimes, she was reputed to have spent her time reading novels. Syrkin, upon seeing his daughter leisurely reading her novel, exploded, "What difference is there between you and the bobbed-haired bandit? She has short hair and you have short hair; she reads novels and you read novels!" It was just at this time, moreover, that Nachman Syrkin remarked somewhat sardonically, "There is a woman in our movement who is a remarkable speaker. I thought you'd be like her." The unnamed woman was, not surprisingly, Golda Meir.[11]

Marie Syrkin's passion for poetry was to inspire her first serious romance, but also it caused a confrontation with her father, for which she would never quite forgive him. The summer after Bassya Syrkin died of chronic tuberculosis, Nachman moved himself and his sixteen-year-old daughter into a couple of rooms in the apartment of some impoverished ladies. He would spend most of the day at the 42nd Street Library, before he went to his meetings at night. Anxious to spare his daughter the loneliness and the unpleasantness of the hot New York summer, Nachman Syrkin sent his daughter off for the season to the Atlantic Hotel in Belmar, New Jersey. It happened to be owned by Syrkin's friend, and it was frequented by the Jewish intelligentsia, so Syrkin felt safe. Although there was a distinct difference between Syrkin's theoretical views in favor of the freedom of women and his overbearing, overprotective, Victorian attempt to control his daughter's life, he nonetheless sent her away for the summer of her sixteenth year.

But the mere delight of a summer vacation away from the hot city was not the real reason for Marie Syrkin's nostalgia for "that fabulous summer."[12] This, it appears, was the precise moment when Nachman Syrkin's daughter was to act on the mixed message that her father had communicated: on the one hand was his general message of independence and equality for the sexes; on the other, was his personal effort to maintain strict control over Marie's activities. She was to decide in favor of asserting her own independence—whatever the consequences; and this would be a lifelong characteristic.

It was during this summer that she met a young man of twenty named Maurice Samuel. He had come to the Atlantic Hotel to visit a friend. Not only was he handsome, and by the sixteen-year-old's standards, an older man, but every poem Marie loved, Samuel knew by heart. He introduced her to the poetry of Francis Thompson (which was to become the subject of her master's thesis at Cornell many years later). The two fell headlong in love, and the intensity of their romance culminated in their elopement in 1917 when Marie was barely eighteen. Maurice was twenty-two; he had enlisted in the army and was about to leave for France. Nachman Syrkin, however, instantly had the marriage annulled, claiming that his daughter was underage. This time he successfully exercised his will, but it resulted in a resentment that his daughter never conquered.

In fact, Marie Syrkin and Maurice Samuel's common interest in Zionism and their activities in its behalf led to a brief resumption of their relationship in later years.

Nachman Syrkin's admonitions notwithstanding, Marie went off to pursue her literary studies at Cornell in 1918 as her father went off to Versailles to represent the socialist-Zionists at the Peace Conference. He wrote to her constantly from Paris, sending her money, warning her about further "affaires de cœur," fussing over her health, and moralizing. On June 12, 1919, after she had written to him that she had just married a young instructor of biochemistry named Aaron Bodansky, Nachman wrote back, "I'm so proud of the nobel [sic] desires which are filling your exceptional soul. Maryetchka, if nobody believes in you, I believe in your talents and your future. Some deep feeling, an intuition, prophesies me that you will develop a nobel [sic] and sublime attitude of life. . . . Read only good inspiring books, every book in its original text, read and re-read every book and try to conceive not only what the great writer has outspoken, but what he has concealed . . ." A paragraph later he writes, "Darling, I understand much your excitement about the change of your name. Of course, I would like very much that you should wear the name Bodansky-Syrkin and write under that name."

Gradually, at Cornell, Marie Syrkin's public commitment to Jewish life and to Zionism began to emerge. While at the university, she had been a member, though not an active one, of the pan-collegiate International Zionist Association. Her merely tangential association with the I.Z.A. is explained in an article she published in the *New Palestine* in 1925, in which she praises the new student movement *Avuka*. In a prose style foreshadowing the sharp ironic wit alongside the roseate idealism that would later characterize her writing, she describes the I.Z.A. as

> a kind of painless dentistry which temporarily filled spiritual cavities of a special nature. . . . A Jewish student of a certain type went to the I.Z.A. meeting to sing the *Hatikvah* when he remembered Zion. To remember Zion in a vague ineffable way, was the chief function of the Zionist student groups. . . . A too platonic love for Zion, rather than a sense of living alliance with a concrete Palestine was the unsubstantial basis on which the I.Z.A. failed to flourish.[13]

In praise of the new Jewish student movement, Syrkin pointed out that the prewar student movement was animated by the desire for conformity and full Americanization; but the new movement arose out of post-mandate conditions and was quickened by the "beat of the *Chalutzim* pickaxes in Palestine." *Avuka* arose when "Zion emerged from the hazy distance of a Utopia to the disconcerting clarity of a reality. To declare oneself a Zionist meant more than merely to sing the *Hatikvah* or bethink oneself of Israel. It was the definite statement of national allegiance. It was also the affirmation of national individuality."[14]

This appears to be the earliest example of Marie Syrkin's Zionist writing. Stylistically it is embryonic Syrkin. In connection with the prose of John Milton, one critic has identified such a style as the rhetoric of zeal;[15] that is, it is a mode that see-saws between extravagant idealism and rapier thrust. Of late, Syrkin has been criticized for having spoken in the language of naive and sentimental early Zionism, but this overlooks the point that such a double-sided rhetorical style is characteristic of the zealous writer from the prophets through John Milton and the polemicists of the sixties. Only the idealist with a sense of high moral purpose can turn the carpet over to expose a rough underside of moral indignation. The cynic has only one texture.

During the early 1920s, Marie Syrkin continued to write her own verse and to translate Yiddish poetry into English. She was, in fact, among the very first to do so. Of course, this was one way of reconciling her love of poetry and her emerging sense of Jewish purpose. By the time she was twenty-four, she had already published translations of the poetry of Yehoash in *Menorah Journal*. These were praised by Yehoash himself. It was with regard to these translations, moreover, that the editor of *Menorah Journal*, Henry Hurwitz, sent her a note asking for biographical data. Syrkin wrote back with the following revealing self description: "As to myself, I am the daughter of Dr. Syrkin and the wife of A. Bodansky who teaches here. I have my B.A. and M.A. from Cornell and, God willing, I may some day get a Ph.D."[16] She never did; but by the time she was twenty-eight, she had such a long list of publications that she was asked to become associate editor of the short-lived publication *Reflex*, edited by S. M. Melamed.[17]

Throughout the 1920s, Marie Syrkin's professional activities were restricted primarily to poetry, journalism, and teaching. Her personal situation—the tragic death of her first son, the birth a few months later of her second son, the death of her father, her separation and subsequent divorce from Bodansky, and her return to New York with her surviving child—necessitated self-support, which she accomplished by teaching English at Textile High School in Manhattan. This was a job that she utterly detested, but which she kept out of economic necessity until 1948. These circumstances, including her marriage in 1930 to the poet Charles Reznikoff, with whom she lived, on and off, until his death in 1976, made anything more than writing a virtual impossibility.

By the early thirties, however, the more urgent the world situation became, the more Marie Syrkin became intent upon doing on-the-spot reporting. In 1933, when she was granted a sabbatical from Textile High School, Syrkin took herself off for the first of her innumerable trips to Palestine. On this voyage, the romance of the *halutziut* seemed more powerful than the news that she heard over the ship's radio about Hitler's edicts. "The Nazi menace," she later reported, "in its initial phase seemed somehow unreal. It was too preposterous; it would blow over."[18] But the great experiment in socialist Zionism sent her into rhapsodic wonderment at the smallest achievement in the kibbutzim of the Jordan and Galilee: "The rapture of a young woman who ran up to me with the first radish grown in her settlement, the hora danced on the Sabbath on the streets of still uncrowded Tel Aviv along whose shores camels slowly made their way,"[19] she waxed eloquent. Today, some may be a bit embarrassed by such "purple prose," but Marie Syrkin was responding ingenuously.

Most Jewish intellectuals (and non-intellectuals) of this period in America and Europe were not especially attracted to the spartan life in Palestine, nor to the Zionist cause itself. They kept their emotional distance. Syrkin, however, returned from her summer visit inspired and eager to work. It was at this time, moreover, that she met Golda (Myerson) Meir, who had come to America both to seek medical care for her daughter and to be a *shlichah* to Pioneer Women. The friendship of the two women was natural and complementary, for as much as Syrkin admired Golda Meir for her rare effective combination of activism and idealism, Meir certainly admired Marie Syrkin for her combination of intellect and idealism. They were, furthermore, both unself-conscious feminists of the same stripe.

After she returned from her 1933 sojourn among the pioneers, Syrkin's career took the signal turn that would propel her into an activist role as commentator, speechmaker, speechwriter for others, witness to great events, and first-hand reporter from the zone of conflict. While maintaining her job at Textile High School, she assumed a position on the editorial board of the newly established journal of the Labor Zionists, the *Jewish Frontier*. The intensity of her commitment to the purpose of this publication is evinced by the fact that for her thirty-five years of editorial service she received no pay. In her capacity as an editor of *Jewish Frontier* she worked closely with the editor, Hayim Greenberg, with whom she had a deep personal relationship.

Among Marie Syrkin's articles in this critical decade were first-hand reports from Palestine on the Arab disturbances, attacks on Jabotinsky and the Revisionists, on the pro-Nazi Mufti, a long stream of articles in praise of the *halutzim* and Youth Aliyah. Among her most prized achievements was her exposé of the Moscow show trials. At the suggestion of Hayim Greenberg, Syrkin read through the six hundred pages of the Russian stenographic typescript of the trials; this resulted in a remarkable full analysis which appeared in the *Jewish Frontier* in January 1937. "By now," she wrote, "everyone is familiar with the set-up":

> The chief figures of the Bolshevik Revolution admit to a collection of crimes among which murder is the most attractive. This wholesale confession is indulged in by all of Lenin's closest associates and collaborators with two exceptions—Stalin and Trotsky. Stalin is in the Kremlin and Trotsky in Mexico, the rest are in their graves or about to repose in them. Just how complete the liquidation of the Old Bolsheviks has been, may be judged from glancing at the membership of the Central Committee of the Communist Party during the crucial years of 1917 to 1920. With the exception of a few who retired from political life, all the surviving members have been shot as counter-revolutionaries—again barring Trotsky and Stalin.[20]

Thus, Syrkin concludes, the defendants' confessions were false and the trials were Stalin's method of liquidating dissent. Today that conclusion does not seem so remarkable, but the writer's insistence that "no service is done to socialism or to Soviet Russia by refusing to face what one conceives to be the truth"[21] was not so easily faced by the Left. And when some believers in the Revolution finally did, it required a complete repudiation not only of Stalinism but of socialism, and then of liberalism as well.

During the war years Syrkin wrote a stream of essays, and poetry too, pressing for the opening of the gates of Palestine, demanding liberalization of immigration quotas; she wrote a speech for Chaim Weizmann to deliver at a Madison Square Garden rally, and articles and speeches for Golda Meir, all the while holding down her teaching job. As detestable as that job may have been, it gave her the raw material for her widely acclaimed book, *Your School, Your Children* (1944),[22] which was a vanguard analysis of the American public school system. In fact she wrote a number of essays on democracy and the schools in *Common Ground*, the official organ of the Common Council for American Unity. It was, moreover, this early interest in the American education system that later led her to speak out against the "politically correct" position in the 1970s on the issues of the black civil rights movement, affirmative action, and their effects on the university. In 1970, at a conference held at the home of the president of Israel on the subject of "Jews Confronting Anti-Semitism in the United States," and again in an article in the *New York Times* magazine, and once more in 1979 in the *New Republic*, Syrkin took the unpopular view among liberals that ethnic proportional representation, which really is racial quota, destroys the merit system and thereby undermines the democratic belief that protection of the individual holds the best promise for meeting the needs of all minorities within a democracy. "The abrogation of individual rights," she asserted, "would mean curtailment of free entrance into the professions and sciences in accordance with ability and intellectual zeal." The implication for Jews, who constitute only 3 percent of the population, she claimed, is that they would be the chief losers.[23]

Perhaps the most celebrated episode in Marie Syrkin's entire journalistic career, and the one she was most proud of, occurred in

1942 when the State Department received a cable from the Geneva representative of the World Jewish Congress to be forwarded to Rabbi Stephen Wise, president of the American Jewish Congress. The message contained the truth about Hitler's plan to annihilate European Jewry. As editors of the *Jewish Frontier*, Marie Syrkin and Hayim Greenberg were invited in August of 1942 to attend a small private meeting of Jewish journalists, where they learned of the perplexing report from Geneva that the mass extermination was already under way. Despite all that they had been aware of for the last nine years, and despite the *Frontier's* continual reportage of conditions in Germany and Europe, the entire group was unable to assimilate this new information. Their immediate response was shock and skepticism. This—in face of the fact that only a week earlier the *Frontier* itself had received a document from the Jewish Socialist Bund which was an account of mass gassings at Chelmno. Later, Marie Syrkin openly admitted that she and Greenberg were unable to assimilate either account, and she confessed that "we hit on what in retrospect appears a disgraceful compromise: we buried the fearful report in the back page of the September issue in small type, thus indicating that we could not vouch for its accuracy. But by the next issue the small staff of the magazine had uncovered enough material so that the truth had to be acknowledged."[24] The October issue was omitted and the November issue appeared with black borders. Syrkin wrote the following editorial remarks:

> In the occupied countries of Europe, a policy is now being put into effect whose avowed object is the extermination of a whole people. It is a policy of systematic murder of innocent civilians which in its ferocity, its dimensions and its organization is unique in the history of mankind . . .[25]

This editorial was the first American report of the systematic annihilation that Syrkin claimed was already in force. It is also a succinct formulation and anticipation of later arguments for the uniqueness of the Holocaust, such as that of the historian Lucy Dawidowicz.[26]

In 1945, when the war was over, Marie Syrkin took the first available ship to the Middle East for another of what she claimed were her "firsts." This time she went to gather material for her book on Jewish Resistance, *Blessed Is the Match*.[27] This was, in fact, the first of the eyewitness accounts of partisans, ghetto fighters, and Jewish-Palestinian parachutists. In this volume of personal interviews, the mother of Hannah Senesch describes her daughter's last days in the Hungarian prison. Marie Syrkin's account of the heroism of the young Hannah Senesch, already a legend in Israel, brought this story to the American public for the first time, and Syrkin's translation of Senesch's poem "Blessed Is the Match" became the authoritative one:

> Blessed is the match that is consumed in
>   kindling flame.
> Blessed is the flame that burns
>   in the secret fastness of the heart.
> Blessed is the heart with strength to stop
>   its beating for honor's sake.
> Blessed is the match that is consumed
>   in kindling flame.

The volume also contained an interview with Joel Brand who told of his negotiations with Adolf Eichmann for the ransom of European Jewry in the famous "goods for blood" episode.

During the 1945–46 sojourn in Palestine, Syrkin had her own personal adventure with underground activity when she was recruited to give the first English-language broadcast over the secret radio of *Kol Yisrael*. She always insisted that, unlike Golda Meir, she herself was not a true activist, that she merely did what she had to do; that is, she put her gift for writing in the service of her moral and political convictions. Perhaps this is why she took particular delight in dramatically recounting her adventure with "undercover" activism. Proudly she would display two books given to her in 1946 by "comrades of the Haganah." The dedication reads: "Receive the blessings of the sons of the homeland for your voice that added color to the announcement of the redemption. When the day comes when the wall of evil crumbles in the storm, your reward will be the opening of the gates."

In November of 1946, in anticipation of the Twenty-Second Zionist Congress which was to be held the following month in Basle, Syrkin published an urgent plea for Partition which she knew would be among the acute issues on the agenda. Zionist leaders were busy aligning themselves pro and con prior to the Congress, and Syrkin felt compelled to make the case for Partition in advance. In words that carry some resonance today, she summed up her argument with a clever twist of a well-known biblical story: "In 1937 partition was called a Solomon's judgement. Today we must perhaps consider that the child is a Siamese twin whose life can only be saved by drastic operation."[28]

The 1946 Zionist Congress was a profoundly emotional experience. Urged by Ben Gurion and Golda Meir, who insisted that that so important was Marie Syrkin's participation in this Congress that they would cover her expenses, she attended the meeting as a delegate of the American Labor Zionist Party. This Congress, the first since 1939, was marked by the twin traumas of loss and reunion. The participants mourned the many delegates of the 1939 Congress who had not survived, and they took bittersweet pleasure in reunion with those who had remained alive. They also met a group of delegates who arrived from the DP camps.

The 1946 Congress was Marie Syrkin's first encounter with displaced persons. Her next experience came in 1947 when Abram L. Sachar, then the director of Hillel, asked her to take an assignment to help screen suitable candidates from among the young survivors in the DP camps for admission to American universities. They would be permitted, under these circumstances, to enter the United States beyond the restrictions of the prevailing immigration quotas.

The assignment was challenging in the extreme, for the job of making "selections" had connotations from the immediate past. Syrkin was warned not to allow herself to be too emotional, but the grim tales she heard from the scores of hopeful applicants from whom she could choose only fifty, from the physically stunted and psychologically scarred young people who looked at her with pleading eyes, tore at her heart.

For a woman who claimed to be without great physical stamina and less than adventuresome, Marie Syrkin's actual activities in these years belied her protestations. After her strenuous stint in the DP camps, she went back to Palestine in the wake of the siege of Jerusalem. Her fears for the life of the nation had been expressed in the poem entitled "David," written at the time of the Arab attack:

Suppose, this time, Goliath should not fall;
Suppose, this time, the sling should not avail
On the Judean plain where once for all
Mankind the pebble struck; suppose the tale
Should have a different end: the shepherd yield,
The triumph pass to iron arm and thigh,
The wonder vanish from the blooming field,
The mailed hulk stand, and the sweet singer lie.

Suppose, but then what grace will go unsung,
What temple wall unbuilt, what gardens bare;
What plowshare broken and what harp unstrung!
Defeat will compass every heart aware
How black the ramparts of a world wherein
The psalm is stilled, and David does not win.[29]

Once back in Palestine immediately after the siege, Syrkin was assigned the task of compiling data for the official report to the United Nations on the flight of the Arabs from Israel and responding to accusations that the Israelis had desecrated the Christian and Moslem Holy Places. She traveled throughout the territory and finally drew the conclusion, derived from personal interviews with clergy and community leaders whom she named, that for the most part the Arabs had responded to the direction of their own leaders, that they were being used by the Arab states as pawns, that the flight was simultaneously a deliberate part of Arab military strategy, and also an uncontrollable stampede which Arab leadership strove unsuccessfully to check when they realized the level it had reached. There had been no Jewish master plan to expel them, and there had been no Jewish plan to desecrate the Holy Places. Moreover, Syrkin argued that "for the Arab, Palestine is a geographic fact, not an historic concept—and a very recent geographic fact, at that."[30] Further, she held that the nomenclature "Palestinian" for the Arab group is artificial and she questioned the existence of Palestinian nationalism as distinguished from an attachment to the hometown. "Village patriotism," she argued, "was made into a national cause."[31] This, she was to argue later in defense of her friend, was the meaning of Golda Meir's oft-quoted remark that "there are no Palestinians."

Syrkin believed in what she regarded as the absolute justice of

Israel's case: that Israel did not appear as a conquering invader and that at the start it believed it could live in peace with the Arabs; that the truncated State of Israel represents a necessary but not entirely just second partition of the original area designated by the Balfour Declaration; and that the state represents the culmination of decades of peaceful settlement sanctioned by international agreements.[32] For these convictions, Marie Syrkin later found herself attacked by the political left and accused of being an apologist for Golda Meir, who held the same opinions.

Yet despite these firmly held beliefs, like her father before her, Marie Syrkin was not doctrinaire. She was quite aware that there was a distinction to be made between the justice of Israel's case and the practical need to work out a solution. She could have enough empathy for those who were suffering to say, "certainly it is true that the Palestinian Arabs left homes and villages dear to them, and no supporter of Jewish nationalism like myself has the right to minimize the intensity or equivalent dignity of Arab nationalism."[33] As recently as April 1988, less than a year before she died, Syrkin said in print that

> Since 1967 the Labor Party and its adherents have argued that no matter how compelling the legal claim to the West Bank as part of the original territory designated for a Jewish homeland may be, and no matter how deep the religious attachments to the biblical patrimony of Judea and Samaria, these considerations had to give way before the danger to the Jewish or democratic character of the Jewish State that would be posed by the incorporation of over a million hostile Arabs. . . . To save the Jewish State from the progressive corrosion of being an occupying power and from engaging the talent and energy of its people in the unhappy task of maintaining formidable military power able to repeat the miracle of victory against monstrous odds, rational avenues towards a truce, if not full peace, should be explored.[34]

At the age of fifty-one, Marie Syrkin began a new career; or, one might say, she was granted the career she had long ago dreamed of. Again at the invitation of Abram L. Sachar, who was now president of the newly established Brandeis University, Syrkin became the first female professor of an academic subject on the faculty of Brandeis. She was appointed a professor of English literature.

It was here, moreover, that the New York Jewish Intellectuals and the "other" New York Jewish Intellectuals came face to face; Marie Syrkin, Ludwig Lewisohn, and Ben Halpern became the colleagues of Irving Howe and Philip Rahv. Though Howe, as Syrkin believed, initially opposed her tenure on the grounds that she was a journalist and not a scholar, and although Rahv complained that she was not an intellectual, remarking sarcastically that she thought *The Great Gatsby* was a book about bootleggers, Howe eventually grew to admire and honor her. He wrote in the special issue of *Jewish Frontier* (January/February 1983) in tribute to Marie Syrkin, "I value [Syrkin's] good humor, I value her self-irony, but most of all, I think of a remark someone once made about Thomas Hardy—that the world's slow stain had not rubbed off on him. There can be no greater praise, and I think it is true for Marie."

While at Brandeis, Marie Syrkin instituted one of the first courses in Holocaust literature and in American Jewish fiction to be taught in the universities. As early as 1966, in an essay in *Midstream*, she argued a point that later would become a commonplace of the genre: "The literature of the Holocaust . . . eludes the usual classification because of the very nature of its theme. The accepted literary categories—novels, plays, verse, essays—are unsatisfactory because they assume a measure of formal achievement to warrant consideration . . ."[35] In *The American Jew: A Reappraisal*, edited by Oscar Janowsky, she wrote a pioneer essay on American Jewish fiction, and a re-evaluation of Henry Roth's *Call It Sleep* when that work was republished in 1964. She wrote in praise of Nellie Sachs and in sharp criticism of Philip Roth's *Portnoy's Complaint*, an attack Roth himself peevishly referred to in his later novel *Professor of Desire*. All the while she continued to write her own verse—two poems were to be anthologized in the *New York Times Book of Verse*, edited by Thomas Lask, an anthology of the best poetry to have appeared in the *Times* between 1920 and 1970.

In 1955 Syrkin published a biography of her dear friend Golda Meir, a memoir of her father, and edited an anthology of the writing of Hayim Greenberg. She continued her polemical arguments in the pages of many journals, taking on such formidable adversaries as Arnold Toynbee, I. F. Stone, and Hannah Arendt; she also debated the latter in a public forum.

When Marie Syrkin retired from Brandeis in 1966 as professor emerita, she returned to New York to resume her life with Charles Reznikoff. In this penultimate phase of her life, she assumed a desk at the Jewish Agency, became the editor of Herzl Press, and was elected a member of the World Zionist Organization. Now sixty-seven years old, she continued to lecture around the country and in Israel, to serve on the editorial boards of *Midstream* and the *Jewish Frontier*, to write for such diverse publications as *Commentary*, *Dissent*, the *Nation*, *Saturday Review*, the *New York Times* magazine, and the *New Republic*. She kept up her periodic trips to Israel, and in 1973 went there to write a major piece for Golda Meir who was now prime minister, and for whom Syrkin had become a speech writer. The article "Israel in Search of Peace" appeared in *Foreign Affairs* in April 1973. She also edited an anthology of Meir's speeches; and after she flew to Israel on the presidential airplane as an official delegate of the United States at the funeral of her friend Golda Meir, she expressed her grief in the following poem, "For Golda":

> Because you became a great woman
> With strong features
> Big nose
> and heavy legs,
> None will believe how beautiful you were,
> Grey-eyed and slim-ankled.
> The men who loved you are dead.
> So I speak for the record.
> Indeed you were lovely among maidens
> Once
> In Milwaukee and Merhavia,
> And sometimes in Jerusalem.[36]

These busy, productive, and personally satisfying post-academic years, however, were to last only ten years. With no warning, on January 12, 1976, after Marie Syrkin and Charles Reznikoff had enjoyed a pleasant dinner together, he complained of indigestion. A doctor was called in and diagnosed a massive coronary. Reznikoff was rushed to the hospital where he died within hours. In her touchingly spare poem, "Finality," Syrkin describes his death and her loss:

Death, the great kidnapper,
Snatched you suddenly
Asking no ransom.
We were at dinner chatting,
He broke in with two gentle, black attendants
and a noisy ambulance.

When I came back before dawn,
The cups were still on the table
And I was alone.

It is interesting to compare this poem with one that Syrkin had written over half a century earlier, after the death of her first-born son. Although, of course, the emotional content is different in kind as well as degree, the curious fact is that some fifty years later, death is once again experienced as a kidnapper.

They should not have done what they did:
The two men with gloves
And faces I cannot remember
Who came to carry you off
Before my eyes.
Silently they seized you,
Kidnappers.
(A hospital dreads the dead.)
They should not have done what they did.[37]

In her last years, Marie Syrkin lived in Santa Monica—a move she had earlier planned to make with Charles Reznikoff. Here she would escape the rigors of New York City living and be closer to her sister, her son, her grandchildren, and great-grandchildren. From here she continued to write on political issues, to keep up with current ideas and events, to publish a collection of her essays, *The State of the Jews*, and to publish a volume of her own poems, *Gleanings: A Diary in Verse*. In her final years, she would continue to confound her critics on the left and right, first by signing the first *Peace Now* statement, and then, by resigning after its first issue, from the board of *Tikkun*.

To the very end Marie Syrkin remained the consummate pragmatic idealist. Aware of current trends in historiography, she asserted, two weeks before her death on February 1, 1989, that those who now proclaim that the "myth" of Israel is dead are mistaken. Israel, she maintained, is an exemplar of what *can* be done. "Even if it lasts only forty, fifty, years, what that State achieved can never be erased because it shows the potential of idealism. . . . The adaptation of the dream to realities is merely the price of survival."[38]

Notes

1. Marie Syrkin to Carole Kessner, January 1989, unpublished interview.
2. Marie Syrkin, *Gleanings: A Diary in Verse* (Santa Barbara: Rhythms Press, 1979), 13. Hereafter called *Gleanings*.
3. Irving Howe, "For Marie," *Jewish Frontier* (January/February 1983): 8.
4. Marie Syrkin, personal interview.
5. Marie Syrkin, *Nachman Syrkin: Socialist Zionist* (New York: Herzl Press, 1961), 153.
6. Ibid., 60.
7. Marie Syrkin, *Way of Valor: A Biography of Goldie Meyerson* (New York: Sharon Books, 1955), 7. Syrkin's attitude toward the stance of the New York Intellectuals is reflected in her reference to "alienated" intellectuals.
8. Marie Syrkin, personal interview.
9. "Marie Syrkin and Trude Weiss-Rosmarin: A *Moment* Interview," *Moment* 8, no. 8 (September 1983): 40.
10. Marie Syrkin, *Diary*, March 28, 1915–June 4, 1915. This quotation is from the entry on March 29, 1915. On April 10, she identifies "W" as Weinstein.
11. Marie Syrkin, personal interview.
12. Syrkin's characterization of that summer was made when she was eighty-eight.
13. Marie Syrkin, "The New Youth Movement," *The New Palestine* (August 14, 1925): 140.
14. Ibid.
15. Thomas Kranidas, in his essay "Milton and the Rhetoric of Zeal" *TSLL* 6 (1965): 423–32.
16. Unpublished letter, dated May 23, 1923, from the Marie Syrkin–Henry Hurwitz Correspondence, American Jewish Archives, Cincinnati, Ohio.
17. According to Charles Madison in *Jewish Publishing in America: The Impact of Jewish Writing on American Culture* (New York: Sanhedrin Press, 1976), 226, *Reflex* was started in 1927. "In the early issues the articles were of current interest and written by journalists and scholars who were in the limelight or who later attained prominence. Among them were Alexander Goldenweiser, Moses Gaster, Marie Syrkin, S. A. Dub-

now, Isaac Goldberg, Franz Oppenheimer, Maximilian Harden, and Maurice Samuel."

18. Marie Syrkin, *The State of the Jews* (Washington, D.C.: New Republic Books, 1980), 2.
19. Ibid.
20. Reprinted in *Jewish Frontier* (January/February 1983): 23–27.
21. Ibid.
22. Marie Syrkin, *Your School, Your Children* (New York: L. B. Fischer, 1944).
23. Syrkin, *State of the Jews.*
24. Marie Syrkin, "What American Jews Did During the Holocaust," *Midstream* 84, no. 8 (October 1982): 6.
25. Ibid.
26. Lucy Dawidowicz, "The Holocaust Was Unique in Intent, Scope, and Effect," *Center Magazine* (July/August 1981).
27. Marie Syrkin, *Blessed Is the Match* (Philadelphia: Jewish Publication Society, 1947).
28. Marie Syrkin, "Why Partition?" *Jewish Frontier* (November 1946), reprinted in *State of the Jews*, 80.
29. Syrkin, *Gleanings*, 70.
30. Marie Syrkin, "The Arab Refugees," *State of the Jews*, 128.
31. Marie Syrkin, personal interview.
32. Ibid.
33. Ibid.
34. Marie Syrkin, "Doublespeak about Israel," *Congress Monthly* 55, no. 3 (March/April 1988): 11.
35. Syrkin, *State of the Jews*, 297.
36. Marie Syrkin, "For Golda," *Jewish Frontier* (November/December 1984): 13.
37. Syrkin, *Gleanings*, 92–93.
38. Marie Syrkin, personal interview.

CHAPTER 3

Ben Halpern: "At Home in Exile"

Arthur A. Goren

From 1936, when he entered Jewish "communal civil service," as Halpern himself put it, until his death in 1990, an emeritus professor of modern Jewish history at Brandeis University, Ben Halpern devoted a major part of his intellectual energies to examining the American Jewish condition. He approached the task with the skills of the professional historian and sociologist. But he was no less the socialist Zionist ideologue, duty-bound to link intellectualism with activism: ideological discourse, conducted with rigor and intellectual integrity, was a requisite for furthering the cause. Analysis was meant to lead to deeds.[1] From 1943 to 1949, he was managing editor of the *Jewish Frontier*, a member of the Labor Zionist Organization's executive committee, and from 1949 to 1956, the associate director of the Jewish Agency's Department of Education in New York. After entering academic life—in 1956, as a research associate at Harvard University's Center for Middle Eastern Studies, and then, in 1961, moving to Brandeis—Halpern continued his communal activity as a Zionist publicist and lecturer and, in 1968 for a term, as a member of the executive of the World Zionist Organization.[2]

His inquiries into contemporary Jewish affairs, like his scholarly work, flowed from a classical Zionist reading of Jewish history. *Galut*, the millennial experience of exile and distinguishing mark of the Jews, was the key for understanding Jewish survival. "In the system of Jewish ideas," Halpern wrote in 1956,

"Exile" is the *inalienably* Jewish idea, the most intimate creation of the Jewish people, the symbol in which our whole historical experience is sublimated and summed up. All the meaning "Exile" has flows straight from Jewish history, and it gives our history, our being, and our identity as a people its meaning. Live under the sign of Exile—your life as a Jew is an ever-present tension. Cut the idea out—and you cut out memory, identification, and drive, substituting a dull adjustment."[3]

Zionism was the secular revolt against *Galut*. It replaced the mythical hope of messianic redemption with the actual rebuilding of a sovereign nation. (Halpern, it should be noted, recognized the paradox of the anti-historical attitude of secular Zionists who were bent on expunging the *Galut* experience from the "authentic" history of the Jews.) The revolt against *Galut* also demanded, Halpern declared, an individual commitment to participate personally in the collective effort to rebuild the homeland.

For Halpern, America, too, was Exile. True, it was the most benign of all the diasporas. Unlike European Jewry, American Jews never wrestled with the question of emancipation. They did not have to win it by proving that they deserved it. Political equality, separation of church and state, and acceptance of the newcomer were established principles of the Republic before Jews arrived in any numbers. Nevertheless, Halpern argued, there was an ideological and historical barrier that prevented and prevents the full acceptance of the Jew. Culturally, America was a Christian country, and neither Christian Americans nor American Jews, no matter how tenuous their religious ties, could cast aside the theological and folk legacies that defined the separateness of the Jew. In this respect, America was no different from other diasporas.

In *The American Jew: A Zionist Analysis*, which appeared in 1956, Halpern presented his fullest and most systematic examination of American Jewry. The book established Halpern as perhaps the most acute critic of American Jewish thought. Based on articles that had appeared mostly during the previous ten years, *The American Jew* coincided with the Zionists' victorious "revolt against the Galut." The struggle for statehood, the establishment of Israel in 1948, and the first years of the "ingathering of the exiles," provoked an intense, introspective, and often acrimonious debate among

American Jewish leaders and intellectuals. Questions of self-defini-
tion were intertwined with an uneasiness over the implications of a
sovereign Israel for the Jews of the Diaspora. The debate was, in
fact, a many-sided one: veteran Zionist leaders of the Jewish state
calling for American Zionists and American Jewish religious thinkers to accept Israel's centrality; American religious leaders and
non-Zionists disputing Israel's claim to hegemony in the Jewish
world but differing among themselves in their understanding of
the relationship. In *The American Jew*, Halpern bypassed the sur-
face debate over primacy of place. Instead, he focused on the ideologies that presumed an American Jewish exceptionalism ("America
is Different")—from Reform Judaism to Americanized Zionism—
and that posited the viability of a creative Jewish community comfortably at home in America. He tracked down the explanatory
theories: Will Herberg's notion of the religious parity of Protestantism, Catholicism, and Judaism; Horace Kallen's America as a federation of ethnic groups ("cultural pluralism"); and Modecai
Kaplan's eclectic "organic" Jewish community ("Judaism as an
evolving religious civilization"). Halpern argued that the American
Jewish idealogues, eager to tailor an ideology of Jewish group identity to fit the American norm—a norm essentially Protestant in
form—offered prescriptions that produced a pale replica of an
authentic "Jewishness." An interpretation of Judaism or Zionism
that "lobotomized" the idea of exile from its ideology was a recipe
for transforming American Jewry—a process well under way—into
a vacuous and sterile cult devoid of Hebrew culture or Jewish
roots.[4]

Of all the American Zionist thinkers, Halpern was, in a sense,
the most un-American. One can, in truth, place him within the
European *halutz* tradition, the movement founded by the socialist
Zionist pioneers who settled in Palestine between 1905 and 1924
(the second and third *"aliyah"*) to create a self-governing, socialist
"society of workers." Yet Halpern, Boston born and Harvard educated (A.B. 1932 and Ph.D. 1936), assimilated that tradition growing up in America. He viewed the doctrine of *halutziut*, indeed,
experienced it, through the lenses and sensibilities of a second-
generation American Jew. In this essay I argue that the *halutz* idea
was the decisive influence in molding Halpern's value system and

ideological credo. No less important: Halpern was not alone in this social and intellectual experience.

In significant ways, he was prototypical of scores of young Jews who in the 1930s and early 1940s were distressed by the deteriorating situation of European Jewry and the rising anti-Semitism in America fanned by an expansive Nazism. But unlike others on the left, they were also troubled by the estrangement of their generation from Jewish life which was either bent on a career or enamored of the cosmopolitan Left. They harbored, one should emphasize, an immense empathy for America. Educated in public schools, attending or recently graduated from university, they were absorbed with American culture and politics. As democratic socialists, they criticized the inequity of the economic system, social discrimination, and racial prejudice. Numbers of them, about a thousand in a dozen cities, banded together in the Young Poale Zion Alliance, the youth affiliate of the Socialist Zionist movement.[5] A few, planning to live in kibbutzim or other labor settlements in Palestine, joined Hechalutz, the organization responsible for training would-be *halutzim*. The Young Poale Zion also established a youth movement, *Habonim* (The Builders), whose educational goal was living a socialist Zionist life in Palestine.[6] For a brief but decisive period, Halpern participated in these developments. As we shall see, the socialist Zionist movement provided the cultural and social habitat where he honed his beliefs and intellectual interests into a full-grown ideology that remained unchanged for the rest of his life. Two other factors were crucial in laying the foundations of Halpern's intellectual world: the culture and values he grew up with at home, and the Jewish education he received, especially at the Hebrew Teachers College. The three—home, Hebrew studies, and the socialist Zionist youth movement—meshed with extraordinary harmony, as they did in the case of hundreds of other Labor Zionist families.

Halpern's parents, Zalman and Fannie, were Poale Zionists before they emigrated to America, his father in 1902, and his mother in 1905. In fact, members of Zalman's family settled in Palestine, a sister in 1910 and his parents and another sister in 1925. The family came from Bialystok in the Grodno province of the Russian Pale, an industrial city of some forty thousand Jews, which by the turn of the century was a center of social and political ferment. Besides the Jewish socialist Bund, there were active Zionist groups, among them socialist Zionists, and anarchist cells. Zalman, who received a traditional education and studied for a time in a yeshiva, broke with Orthodoxy and moved in anarchist and Poale Zion circles. On his arrival in America he tried farming for a brief period in up-state New York, before settling in Boston where relatives had preceded him. Fannie grew up in the small town of Ostrino, in the province of Vilna. She was active in the underground self-defense units that the Poale Zion organized at that time. Family lore has it (the Halpern children grew up with such stories) that Fannie smuggled pistols from place to place, traveling freely with the "yellow card" of a prostitute during the revolution of 1905. The Halperns married in Boston in 1911. Ben was born the next year and two brothers followed.[7]

Socially and culturally, the elder Halperns belonged to a network of like-minded Labor Zionists. The branches of the Poale Zion, its auxiliary fraternal order, the Farband (the Jewish National Workers Alliance), and, beginning in the mid 1920s, the Pioneer Women, offered the camaraderie of a common cause and common needs. Literary evenings, lectures by visiting dignitaries, often from Palestine, and political activity (mainly competing with the anti-Zionist Left for public support), intertwined with the round of fund-raising affairs. There were bazaars, balls, "benefit" concerts to support the movement's cultural and educational activities in America, and an annual "third seder" sponsored by the "Gewerkshaften" (Histadrut) campaign on behalf of the labor movement in Palestine. Although devoted Labor Zionists, the Halpern were not doers. Fannie was as active as her frail health allowed. Zalman, a quiet man, was busy running his shop of tailor's trimmings. For the Halperns, the Jewish education of the children was of special importance. They chose not to send them to the Labor Zionist afternoon school, the *folk-shule*, with its radical orientation and emphasis on the Yiddish language. Instead, they chose another afternoon school, Hatikvah, because it offered an intense modern education in Hebrew. (The mark of a modern Hebrew school was its emphasis on language, teaching *"ivrit b'ivrit,"* all instruction in Hebrew.) The decision reflected the Zeire Zion strand in Labor Zionism, with its emphasis on a Hebrew cultural renaissance. Zalman was proficient in the language. Samuel, Ben's youngest brother, recalls the occasion his father was called to school because of his son's irregular attendance. Father and teacher began conversing in Hebrew. Engrossed in the joy of speaking the language, both men forgot the purpose of the summons, to Samuel's great relief.[8]

In 1925, Halpern began his studies in the high school department of the Hebrew Teachers College. He completed the three-year course and continued another four years in the college division, graduating in 1932. Simultaneously, he completed Boston Latin School and Harvard College.

The years Halpern attended the Hebrew Teachers College were especially auspicious ones in the college's history. The first dean, Nissan Touroff, had been one of the leading educators in Palestine in the years 1907–1919 before he emigrated to the United States. A zealot for the revival of Hebrew culture, Touroff assembled a faculty of like-minded teachers. All instruction was, of course, in Hebrew. Advanced for the time was the inclusion of Jewish history, modern Hebrew literature, and sociology in the curriculum, in addition to the traditional subject matter. When Touroff left the college, the year of Halpern's arrival, Samuel Perlman succeeded him. Perlman had settled in Palestine in 1914, and during the war years directed a school in Alexandria for children of the refugees expelled from Palestine by the Turks. For several years before coming to the United States he was one of the three editors of the World Zionist Organization's Hebrew weekly, *Haolam*, published in Berlin, and collaborated with Zev Jabotinsky in issuing the first historical atlas in the Hebrew language. Perlman also translated Heine's prose work into Hebrew. Students at the College recalled his courses in modern Hebrew literature as "the very best literary-critical courses many of us had anywhere." Perlman also lectured on Rembrandt, accompanied by slides, "where we learned all about chiaroscuro in Hebrew." He spoke Hebrew in a *sefardic* accent, rare for the time, and taught songs which he had brought with him from Palestine. Other Touroff appointments were Jacob Newman and Yishai Adler who taught Bible and Talmud. Both had lived in Palestine for extended periods. Nathan Ben Nathan taught history and sociology, and introduced his students to the work of Arthur Ruppin, the Jewish demographer and head of the Zionist colonization bureau in Palestine. A Young Poale Zionist student of his remembers Ben Nathan agreeing to lead a study group on Ber Borochov, the Marxist Zionist theoretician. The college also provided a public platform for eminent figures, from the Hebrew poet Shaul Tchernichovsky, to the Labor Zionist leader and head of the Political Department of the Jewish Agency, Hayim Arlosoroff.[9] The historian, Frank E. Manuel, who graduated from the college two years before Halpern, characterized the milieu at the college as "aesthetic nationalism . . . tarbut [Hebrew culture] nationalism." Manuel, like Halpern, was an undergraduate at Harvard at the same time that he studied at the college (and went on to get his Ph.D. at Harvard). "I found Hebrew Teachers College," he remarked, "more stimulating than Harvard College."[10]

By the time Halpern reached graduate school he had acquired a well-rounded humanistic Hebrew education. (In later years, he published translations of several short stories and a novel by the Israeli writer Hayim Hazaz, and some perceptive essays of literary criticism.) During the years when he was simultaneously a student at Hebrew Teachers College and an undergraduate at Harvard he read the four volumes of Yehezkial Kaufmann's Golah Ve-Nekhar (Exile and Estrangement), a socio-historical study of the Jews that appeared between 1929 and 1932. Halpern was profoundly influenced by Kaufman's grand theme that Jewish group consciousness was forged by an ideological identity (the adoption by the Israelites of a monotheistic faith). This primordial event and its historical consequences imposed upon the Jewish people a minority status in perpetual conflict with the Gentile world. It was here that Kaufmann found the essence of the idea of Exile and the obstacle to (or safeguard against) assimilation.[11] Halpern was persuaded by Kaufmann's methodology, no less than by his conclusions. Sociology, or more precisely, historical sociology, became the requisite tool to probe the problematics of Jewish survival. This he proceeded to do at Harvard.

Halpern pursued his graduate studies in sociology at a time when Talcott Parsons was the dominant figure in the field at Harvard. Halpern's interest in Jewish history also brought him close to the eminent Jewish philosopher, Harry Wolfson, with whom he studied as well and under whose supervision he wrote his dissertation. Not surprisingly, his choice of a dissertation topic, "Certain Sociological Aspects of the Jewish Problem in Christian Europe Prior to the 19th Century," was the sum total of his intellectual and ideological concerns. Historians, he noted in his introduction (paraphrasing Max Weber), "select their problems with reference to the issues debated in their own time." True or not as a general statement, it was the point of departure of his own thesis. What concerned Halpern were those "sociological aspects of Jewish life which throw light . . . upon the origin of the contemporary Jewish Problem." The "Jewish Problem" in that sense appears at the beginning of the nineteenth century when "the existence of the Jews became problematical to themselves." In Germany, advocates of radical reforms arose and proposed a new basis for living among the Gentiles, breaking with the tradition of Jewish separatism. To understand this momentous break with the past, Halpern undertook to examine the history of accommodation and conflict between Jew and Gentile and within the Jewish community, in the pre-modern era.[12]

With a Harvard doctorate in hand, Halpern's decision not to pursue an academic or professional career is, on first sight, inexplicable. In fact, Halpern's mentors in the sociology department had forewarned him that being Jewish virtually precluded an academic appointment. But his aspirations were also of a different order. Graduate studies were part of a process of self-understanding. They had enabled him to probe the history and fate of the Jews and their culmination in Zionism. Now, there was the personal conclusion to be drawn, to act upon one's beliefs. This notion of a moral imperative—to realize Zionism by "going up to the land," *aliyah* to *Erez Yisrael*—found its most impassioned expression in the writings of Yosef Chayim Brenner and A. D. Gordon, both of whom called on Jewish youth to abandon Galut and join them in building—in the literal, physical sense—a new and just society in Palestine. Both men left a powerful impression on Halpern. They joined myth and ideology: the myth of the metamorphosis of the individual *halutz* rooting himself in the ancestral soil; and the ideology of a collective will laying the groundwork for political and social redemption.[13]

The imperative to act upon one's beliefs—*hagshama atzmit* (self-realization)—was not only a matter of ideology. It was rooted, as well, in the moral climate of family. In a rare autobiographical sketch, Halpern recalls how from earliest childhood his parents expressed their contempt for the careerist. The "carierist"— only the Yiddish pronunciation carried the full import of the word for Halpern—were Jews "who junked their scruples and standards in a single-minded scramble for promotion and power." Approvingly, his father recollected how his forebears, who were learned enough to hold rabbinical positions, shunned the rabbinate, abiding by the Talmudic injunction, "Thou shalt not make of thy learning a spade wherewith to dig." In principle, his parents' generation condemned the flow of Jews into the learned professions. "That was the time when troops of near-sighted intellectuals roared at dozens of Jewish meetings nightly, demanding that the Jews become farmers, plumbers, anything, but not doctors, lawyers, and salesmen." Reality was otherwise. "The older generation agreed that except for a few who might go to Palestine as pioneers, most would have to make out as best they could in the urban, industrialized countries of the west." Nevertheless, his parents could not make peace with "the blithe American credo that to 'succeed' was the purpose of living."[14] What the *halutz* movement did is redefine what success was.

The *halutz* ideal never found fertile ground in the United States as it did in Poland. One element within the Young Poale Zion espoused the ideal and produced a small stream of *halutzim* who went to Palestine. Hashomer Hatzair (the "Young Guard"), a youth movement left of the Young Poale Zion which educated its members to the single purpose of living in one of the movement's kibbutzim in Palestine, had similar results. Members of both movements, as well as unaffiliated individuals, belonged to Hechalutz, which was charged with preparing would-be pioneers for life in Israel. Between 1931 and 1939, about two hundred Americans completed their training and went to Palestine as *halutzim*. The attrition rate was high. As many as half returned unable to make the adjustment to physical labor and communal living and unable to overcome the social and cultural estrangement they felt.[15]

While making preparations for *halutz* training, Halpern came to the attention of Golda Myerson (Meir), a member of the executive of the Histadrut and at the time on a fund-raising tour in the United States, and Enzo Sereni, the emissary assigned by the Histadrut to direct the affairs of Hechalutz in America. Sereni, a charismatic educator, descendent of an old Italian Jewish family, and a founding member of Kibbutz Givat Brenner, convinced Halpern to become the executive secretary of the organization. In the fall of 1936, Halpern, newly married, moved to New York with his wife, Gertrude, and immersed himself in movement work.

Some of the responsibilities suited him: preparing educational material (among other projects, translating for publication a weekly summary of important articles appearing in the Hebrew press in Palestine), writing for the movement periodicals, and lecturing and leading discussion groups of Hechalutz and the Young Poale Zion.[16] Working with Sereni—the impetuous, provocative Italian intellectual—fit Halpern's own staunchly independent mode of thought. In a portrait of Sereni, written in 1945 in his memory, when Sereni's death was confirmed—he was dropped by parachute into northern Italy in 1944 on a British intelligence mission, captured by the Germans, and tortured to death in Dachau— Halpern captured the verve and iconoclasm of the Italian *halutz*. He recalled his friend Shlomo Grodzensky's description of Sereni's arrival in America nine years before. Just off the boat "the sturdy little Italian" immediately asked whether it was true that there was a vogue for Marxism in America. When Grodzensky reluctantly confirmed the fact, Sereni responded "with glee." "Excellent! You know, I'm a first-rate expert in arguing Zionism from a Marxist basis." When asked if he believed in Marxism, outraged, Enzo shot back: "What do you think I am, a simpleton, to believe in such vulgar banalities?" Sereni also raised the problem of Jewish-Arab collaboration at a time when it was all but ignored. He criticized the positions held both by the Labor Party in Palestine and by Hashomer Hatzair. In early 1937, *Jews and Arabs in Palestine: Studies in a National and Colonial Problem* appeared. Sereni collected a number of factual and interpretive essays by prominent Labor Party figures and included a long, controversial essay of his own, "Towards a New Orientation." Halpern helped in the final editing of the volume and participated in the debates that followed.[17]

Other responsibilities he had in Hechalutz proved irksome, and he displayed little interest or talent for them. This was the case with internal politics, particularly the factionalism between the competing youth movements within Hechalutz and their Palestinian sponsors, and the persistent problem of finances, in no small measure exacerbated by Sereni's free-wheeling approach. (Sereni returned to his kubbutz in the spring of 1937, leaving Halpern with the financial problems.) Especially troublesome were the chronic deficits of the training farms and the threats of foreclosure. On one desperate occasion, Halpern turned to Louis Brandeis for help. The justice invited him to his summer home on Cape Cod. During the interview, Halpern explained that Hechalutz had used funds entrusted to it by its members for their *aliyah* to cover the most pressing debts. Now the organization had to make good on these funds. Halpern, who enjoyed telling the story, quoted Brandeis, "Young man, as a judge, I should warn you that you have committed a felony. As a Zionist, I will give you my personal check covering the money drawn on the *aliya* accounts." (In one retelling, the check was for $10,000, and in another it was for $20,000.) [18]

Despite the onerous side of his responsibilities, this brief period of movement work was an exhilarating one. The leadership circle he became part of provided a stimulating home where educational and political issues were thrashed out. The movement took stands on domestic and international issues; it attacked the popular front tactics of the Communist Party within and without the Jewish community and youth sector; it discussed the policies of the trade union movement and the Socialist Party; and it examined the intellectual and cultural currents in American Jewish life. Contact with visiting kibbutz, Histadrut, and Labor Party dignitaries from Palestine, as well as with the elder statesmen of the American Labor Zionist Organization, gave the group a sense of importance. But surely the most gratifying consequence of these years was the comradeship that evolved—and that has remained intact—among these young men and women, in their twenties at the time, who shared a common ideology and common aspirations, and whose upbringing was so similar. [19]

The majority of the group Halpern joined in the fall of 1936 were first-generation, native-born Americans. Like Halpern, nearly all came from Labor Zionist homes and had received a Hebrew education that included the literature of the Hebrew revival, or had attended the movement's own Yiddish folk schools with their radical-secular approach to Jewish history, tradition, and Zionism. Minneapolis is a striking example of the Hebrew school track. Labor Zionist parents sent their children to the community Talmud Torah whose teachers were Hebraists and Poale Zion sympathizers. The school sponsored Hebrew-language clubs and boasted a Hebrew-speaking branch of the Young Poale Zion. For its size, an extraordinary number of its graduates became active in the Labor Zionist movement, entered Jewish communal service, or settled in Palestine. New York, Philadelphia, Baltimore, Chicago, Cleveland, and Detroit had schools with a Hebrew cultural orientation similar to that of Minneapolis and most had institutions like Boston's Hebrew Teachers College which were attended by Labor Zionist children. In these cities, the Labor Zionists also established a network of Yiddish folk schools whose teachers belonged to the movement. Graduates, it was presumed, would become active in the Young Poale Zion and provide leaders for Habonim. Often Labor Zionist parents took the initiative in organizing local Habonim chapters by raising the funds to support a salaried organizer. They were the main financial backers of the Young Poale Zion-Habonim summer camps which were founded in the 1930s, served on the camp committees, and sometimes filled in as cooks and administrators.[20]

The problem that preoccupied the group during the mid-1930s centered on ways of revamping the organization to attract an acculturated generation of American Jewish youth. Much thought was given to method and structure. A detailed program was drawn up, introducing scoutcraft, music, and recreational activities into the local clubs. A monthly magazine for young people was launched, and the summer camps, modeled after the kibbutz, were expanded. Through these means, by imparting a concern with Jewish history, contemporary Jewish affairs, Zionism, and the halutz ideal, the youth movement endeavored to win over young people to the cause. In 1935, Habonim was established for these purposes, and in 1940, it supplanted the Young Poale Zion Alliance.[21]

Method was linked to ideology. How was one to reconcile the new emphasis on educating for halutz life in Palestine with the adult movement's commitment to Diaspora work? Labor Zionism, seeking to appeal to a broad spectrum of American Jews (the founding of the Jewish Frontier in 1934 is the clearest indication), increasingly stressed its dedication to creating a rewarding Jewish life in America, and it reaffirmed its duty to support progressive causes in America. The organization aspired to a mass following. Could the youth movement of the Poale Zion, by its very nature selective and moralistic, offer its members a choice, each of equal worth, between building a creative American Jewish community or fulfilling the ideals of the *halutz* by going to Palestine?[22]

Halpern agreed with the majority of the leadership in rejecting equality of status for Diaspora and Palestine (a point we will return to). The *halutz* ideal was central. But there was a prefatory question to address. How effective would the new educational techniques be in "making *halutzim?*" Halpern was skeptical. He was uncompromising in his belief that there were no short cuts. At the conference of Young Poale Zion-Habonim leaders in August 1937, he discussed the qualifications required of the would-be *halutz*. One had to know Hebrew. One had to have acquired a knowledge of the philosophy of the *halutz* movement through the writings of Gordon, Brenner, Hayim Nachman Bialik, the national poet, and others of the second *aliyah*. "We are forced to live a life that demands self-reliance, moral responsibility for everyone else," he remarked. "This spirit requires the sort of training that our revolutionary parents who looked at a careerist as someone despicable, might have had. According to the Jewish ideal there are more important things than trying to get ahead of the others."[23] Towards the end of his remarks he was even more direct about the inner-directed, organic process of growing up Labor Zionist that led, logically, to the decision to live in Palestine. "All these things can be taught to people not so much by YPZA [Young Poale Zion Alliance] activity, but by going to Talmud Torath, folk shuln, or by living in a home that is still imbued with the revolutionary tradition of one's parents. It is only necessary to make this explicit by reading and learning about Gordon, Brenner, Bialik, who were brought up in this manner."[24]

There were few, then, who would choose the way of the *halutz*. In a sardonic piece written the same year, "In Defense of the American Chalutz," Halpern described "the process of making chalutzim" as "the recreation of the fanaticism which easy-going America dissolves." Fifteen years later and five years after the establishment of

Israel, Halpern, still holding to his earlier views, remarked that Zionism, when taken seriously, resulted in dissatisfaction with the superficiality of Jewish life in America and ultimately to *halutziut*. The "push" came from the "sharp sense of the inadequacy of American Jewish life" and the unwillingness to accept compromises and paths of least resistance. The "pull" sprang from the expectation of building an ideal Zion. However, this very type—the rebel, "devotees of the absolute," Halpern called them—who found it insufferable to accept inane compromises in America, would surely find the reality of Israel difficult to accept as well. This was the great problem of *halutz* education, to merge the ideal Israel with the contemporary reality. "Only if contemporary Israel is seen through and accepted as a society in embryo and a community with potentialities for building toward the envisioned ideal, can the chalutz movement hope to bring American Jews to Israel and help them strike roots there." [25]

The context of these later remarks is important. Halpern was reacting to the controversy David Ben Gurion had ignited with his call for mass *aliya* from America. Israel desperately required the skills and spirit of young American men and women. Ben Gurion insisted that the *halutz* movements be by-passed. Their educational methods were too slow and their results meager. He favored a direct, massive appeal to the idealism of Jewish youth. Thousands would answer the call, he was convinced. Halpern responded: "The only way in which American Jews are brought to emigrate to Israel was personal conversion, the sense of calling of the chalutz, in one form or another, to a greater or smaller degree." Once more he repeated his early stand, "The youngsters who come naturally within the orbit of [the halutz youth] movements are the children of the parents who are themselves actively resisting the pressures of accommodation: orthodox Jews, devotees of secular Jewish culture, Hebrew or Yiddish. They are necessarily few." [26]

Another element in the evolving Young Poale Zion-Habonim ethos was especially important for Halpern's ideological system and moral outlook. In its formative years, Habonim adopted a unique position on the question of *aliyah*. Speaking to a conclave of youth movement leaders in 1937, Halpern explained that a Habonim member was "not bound by a decision of the organization to join

Hechalutz." In the case of Hashomer Hatzair, on reaching the designated age, the member declared his or her intention to go on *aliyah*
and went to *hachshara* (agricultural training) or was forced to
leave the movement. Habonim gave its members "the freedom of
going and coming and a certain leeway in the movement to criticize
and to improve [it], as well as an opportunity to be disappointed—
and yet not tragically disappointed."[27] Thus the organization had
room for members who, for one reason or another, did not go on
aliyah, or who went and returned. In good time, these "graduates"
would join the Poale Zion, mitigating the confrontation feared by
some between a Palestine-directed youth movement and its
America-centered parent organization.

The result of *aliyah*-oriented nonexclusiveness was a tolerance
and sensitivity for the individual. In 1959, on the twenty-fifth anniversary of the founding of Habonim, Halpern explained the full
import of this ethos. "A chalutz movement is essentially committed
to the immediate, personal realization of ultimate and maximum
objectives." Habonim began with an acceptance "of the duty of
aliya, but with a method of free choice; the result of which was
that *aliya* had to spring not only from early indoctrination and the
discipline of an organization, but also from the resolution of one's
own problematic personal and social situation." This did not exist
in the classical *halutz* movements, nor in the European Zionist
parties or their American or Palestinian extensions. These movements sought to maintain "party discipline," or "kibbutz discipline," or "ideological collectivism." Ambiguity and ambivalence
were unacceptable. For Halpern, the dogmatic was unacceptable.
Doctrinaire education and sectarianism were the dangers. An
"open," democratic *halutz* movement, which respected the right of
the individual to find his or her way, was less militant and demanding, perhaps, and, possibly, less effective than its European or
Palestinian prototypes. But it was more moral and caring, concerned with means no less than ends. In this manner these young
American Jews grafted an American strain on a foreign trans-
plant.[28]

The permissiveness of the Habonim *halutz* ethos led to an appreciation for the problems of Diaspora living and, in particular, for
Jewish life in America. If the *halutz* ideal implied *shlilat ha'galut*

[the negation of *Galut*], even of the American *Galut*, then it was to be negated with empathy. Striving to maintain Jewish life in the *Galut* was not to be disdained. For those who never left the *Galut* or left it and then returned, and Halpern was one of the latter, there was the ambivalent, paradoxical prescription, "At Home in Exile," the title of Halpern's first essay on his thesis that America was *Galut*.[29]

The essay appeared in the January 1943 issue of *Furrows*, a new monthly published by Habonim. Launched in November 1942, *Furrows* had a dual purpose: to maintain ties with the increasing number of members who were joining the armed forces, and to reach young Jewish adults awakened by the war to the plight of the Jews. Akiva Skidell, the founding editor who had served as the executive secretary of the Young Poale Zion during its transition to Habonim in the late 1930s, describes the informal editorial board that ran the monthly. Skidell consulted most frequently with Halpern and Shlomo Grodzensky, the managing editor of the Labor Zionist *Yiddisher Kempfer* and in the 1930s the editor of the Poale Zion's monthly *Newsletter*. Both helped select the articles and wrote for the journal themselves. After Halpern became managing editor of the *Jewish Frontier* in the spring of 1943, he continued to write for *Furrows*.[30]

Four years had elapsed from the time he completed his term as executive secretary of Hechalutz until he took over the *Frontier*. In late 1938, he and Gertrude sailed for Palestine and settled in Kibbutz Givat Brenner. Farm labor proved difficult for him, and communal life was dissatisfying for Gertrude. To compound matters, his health deteriorated. Gertrude returned to the United States just as war broke out in Europe. Halpern followed, arriving in New York at the beginning of 1940. He freelanced, doing research for the American Jewish Committee on Jewish resettlement, editing the American Jewish Congress's biweekly, and serving on the editorial board of the *Jewish Frontier* until he was appointed managing editor. The hope of settling in Palestine—and then in Israel—remained, and there were extended stays in Israel, once for an entire year with Gertrude and their two sons.[31]

"At Home in Exile" had its genesis in a talk to a Habonim leaders' seminar in December 1942, but the published version was clearly intended for a broad public. In his appraisal of the state of American Jewry, Halpern singled out the "Jewish survivalists," particularly the Reconstructionists and cultural pluralists, for reproof. True, both rejected assimilationism and "were not even afraid of a Jewish state in Palestine." Nevertheless, despite these commendable positions, the survivalists had charted a false and dangerous path. Their ideal, to be at home in America, had bound them to a "minimalist program," one driven by considerations of accommodation. In such matters as Jewish education, for example, the survivalist-integrationists rejected the day school as the desired mode of education, and in matters of communal organization they acquiesced in the feeble, voluntaristic polity that was proving to be so ineffectual at a time of unprecedented peril to the Jews. Such policies hardly reflected a society intent upon creating a permanent, self-sufficient Diaspora community. The spiritual leaders had defined Jewish identity in religious terms that were dictated by their compatibility to the American way. How could such a strategy produce a lasting, authentic culture in America? "We cannot see any hope for a permanent, distinct Jewish culture in America," Halpern wrote, "nor do we care to see it. Being much attached to Jewish values we are that much in exile." (Four decades later, Halpern adamantly restated his view: "no true Jewish culture but only a cult can be sustained in America.") [32]

This was not all. An even more compelling reason for rejecting "at homeness" and accepting the yoke of exile was the mortal peril confronting the Jewish people. "It can be rescued, collectively, and—the tragic necessity of our very days—individually, only in its own land. Until *the people* is firmly and safely planted at home, we Jews in America cannot allow ourselves the dear luxuries of being at home." Halpern concluded his essay with a Herzlian flourish: "Collectively we cannot be at home here, individually we must not, until our people has a home to itself and to all its suffering sons. For American Jewry exile is not a fact only, it is a duty."[33]

For Halpern, the mere fact that integration into American society determined the thinking of the survivalists was proof that Jews were, in truth, not at ease in America and hence not at home. But overshadowing ideological arguments and sociological analysis were the horrendous events that by the end of 1942 were certified as true. With the mass destruction of European Jewry proceeding unabated, there was but one moral way for individual American Jews to respond to the fate of their people: intuit Exile and share, at least vicariously, the common fate of the Jewish people. Only such a mentality could produce the single-minded, unswerving dedication to transforming the Jewish homeland into a sovereign state, the sole salvation for the Jewish people.

"At Home in Exile" provoked a number of responses. The most notable, by Eugene Kohn, a founder of the Reconstructionist movement and the managing editor of its journal, appeared in the March 1943 issue of *Furrows*. In "Is It Our Duty to Remain Maladjusted?" Kohn rejected Halpern's fears "that if Jews make themselves at home in the diaspora they will not feel the imperative urgency of securing the collective survival of the Jewish people through the establishment of a Jewish commonwealth in Palestine." The Reconstructionists had made "Zionism an essential plank of their platform and pinned their hopes for Jewish life in the diaspora mainly on the achievement by Jews of majority status and statehood in the national home." But more telling for Kohn, the notion of "exile" when applied to American Jews was meaningless. American Jews had overwhelmingly chosen America over Palestine and were participating individually and not merely as a group in the social, political, and economic life of the country. Under these circumstances, he countered with Mordecai Kaplan's well-known thesis that only by stressing the religious character of Jewish civilization was it possible for the Jewish people to survive in the Diaspora.[34]

Halpern's rejoinder, "How to Observe the Commandment of Exile," appeared in the same issue. A philosophy of *Galut* survivalism carried to its logical conclusion, Halpern insisted, threatened Jewish unity. It would circumscribe the Jewish interests of a particular Diaspora community to its own locale. Jewish survivalists might by sympathetic to Palestine as a refuge for their co-religionists and as a future cultural center from which they would be able to draw inspiration. But if one seriously believed in the Diaspora, such a center was only a frill. ("There is already enough of a Jewish community in Palestine to provide folk dances and social ideas for Jewish center programs," Halpern quipped.) The logical result of Diaspora Survivalism, therefore, would be "to take no more interest in Palestine than a benevolent non-Zionist, who is not afraid of the Jewish State bogeyman."

How then should one observe the commandment of Exile? Becoming a *halutz* was "the crowning obligation." But there were also other concrete *mitzvot* to be performed while in Exile. One must learn Hebrew. One must thoroughly assimilate a considerable knowledge of Jewish tradition and "develop the instinct for its active application which will be required in Palestine." True, only a handful would actually perform the ultimate duty of being a *halutz*, Halpern admitted. But this was the case with other *mitzvot* too. Personal obligations or countervailing circumstances might stand in the way of *aliyah*. "The dangerous thing was to deny the obligation to do so. One was still bound to *opzurichtn golus*," the Yiddish expression of observing Exile as a rite and a penance.[35]

Halpern's diction resonated with the religious accents of a traditionalist. Years later, following the appearance of *The American Jew*, critics challenged his ideology of *Galut* as irreconcilable with his uncompromising secularism. Halpern reaffirmed his view that the religious tradition *was* the primal influence in shaping the collective ethos. In his analysis, a uniquely Jewish "symbol-set" of their own historical civilization formed the basis of Jewish solidarity. These "symbols" and "myths," which the secular Zionists transmuted into ideology, were intrinsic to the national culture. Indeed, it was he, Halpern, advocate of redemption, rather than his religious critics, who insisted on the integrity of the "symbol-set."[36] Thus, while the vocabulary of Exile and Redemption carried religious accents, for the secularist Halpern it meant above all *ahavat yisrael*—the monogamous love of Israel—and the precept to strive to fulfill that love in building the homeland. With great vehemence Halpern rejected the various schools of non-Orthodox Judaism. Their spiritual leaders manipulated the tradition and reduced Jewish peoplehood to denominational rites. "The attempt to redefine Judaism as a cult, to make it over into an intelligently engineered curriculum for training in piety, to reduce it to the scale of experience of no more than the contemporary synagogue, . . . constitutes an assault upon our past."[37]

During the years between the early formulation of his "at home in exile" ideology in 1943 and the considerable agitation his critique of American Jewry provoked in 1956, Halpern was occupied with Jewish public affairs as contributor and editor of the *Jewish Frontier*. Alternating between stridently polemical essays and academically precise articles, he wrote on the plight of European Jewry, the politics of rescue, the communal struggle for power within American Jewry, social and economic developments in Palestine, the fight for a Jewish state, and the early years of statehood. Halpern also commented on affairs in general: the 1943 race riots in Detroit and Harlem, freedom of speech and human rights issues, and the plight of democratic socialism. He evinced a singular regard for black-initiated activism. In November 1947, at the height of the United Nations debate on the Palestine partition plan, Halpern paired that issue with African American demands for equal right. In an article titled "The Destinies of Jew and Negro," he observed that at the very moment the United Nations was considering "Palestine and the Jewish question," it had also accepted a petition presented by African American leaders appealing, in the words of the statement, for "redress" for the "denial of human rights . . . to citizens of Negro descent in the United States." Different as the circumstances were, Halpern wrote, "under which Dr. Abba Hillel Silver [representing the Jewish Agency] and Dr. W. E. B. Dubois [representing the National Association for the Advancement of Colored People] appeared at Lake Success, and different as the outcome of their visits may prove to be, the essential problems of American Jews and American Negroes, which ultimately explain both these appearances, are strikingly similar." Both groups, as he was to write in *The American Jew*, were "the classic American minorities," the two major unassimilable communities in America. The similarities and contrasts that Halpern found in comparing American Jews with African Americans enabled him to explain the different causes of that "unassimilability" and thereby define the limits of American pluralism. (In the 1960s and 1970s Halpern addressed the phenomenon of "Black Power"—"I fully understand the Negroes who adopted the slogan"—and confronted the deterioration of Black–Jewish relations and Black antisemitism.) [38]

As managing editor under Hayim Greenberg, Halpern was the workhorse of the *Frontier*'s editorial board, translating from Yiddish and Hebrew and writing editorials and book reviews in addition to the stream of signed contributions. Among the cognoscenti, the *Frontier* earned the reputation of being the most perspicacious journal of Jewish opinion. Occasionally it attracted intellectuals outside of its own circle, Carl J. Friedrich, Paul Goodman, Hannah Arendt, Daniel Bell, and Will Herberg, for example.

Halpern and his associates apparently gave some thought to winning over the young New York Jewish Intellectuals. The chasm that had separated the various sorts of socialist-cosmopolitans from their Jewish ideological adversaries, the socialist Zionists, during the 1930s had narrowed. The oft-described account of the trek from cosmopolitan radicalism to patriotic liberalism was well under way. With it went a newly acknowledged sensitivity to one's Jewishness and a tentative search for its meaning. Halpern's attitudes, thinking, and training placed him in an admirable position to address these Jewish intellectuals. Like them he was an American-born child of immigrants who had won the highest award the academic track offered. (Being a Bostonian, it was straight Harvard rather than its proletarian New York version.) Like his New York peers, Halpern was a confirmed secularist, and his ethical socialism approximated the social liberalism of the reformed Marxists. ("The social principle of mutual responsibility," Halpern remarked, "rather than the economics of distributive justice, represents the core of my socialist concerns.") Moreover, Halpern's devastating criticism of the shallowness of Jewish communal life was also shared by the "other" Jewish Intellectuals. But the most promising entrée to their turbulent world, where the radical certainties of the 1930s lay in ruin and the newsreels of the death camps forced them to confront their Jewishness, was through the idea of alienation.[39] In the plethora of writing that began appearing in the mid-1940s on the theme of alienation, Daniel Bell's "Parable of Alienation," published in November 1946, is of special significance. Its importance lies in the essay's own intrinsic value and Bell's place among the young Jewish intellectuals. No less notable was its publication, followed by Halpern's response a month later, in the Labor Zionist *Jewish Frontier*.[40]

At the time, the twenty-seven-year-old Bell was teaching at the University of Chicago. Born on the lower East Side of New York to Yiddish-speaking parents (his father died when he was an infant),

Bell joined the Young People's Socialist League at thirteen, attended a socialist Sunday school, became a staff-writer for the *New Leader* in 1939 and its managing editor in 1941.[41] The parable Bell offered was an analysis of Isaac Rosenfeld's autobiographical novel, *Passage from Home*.[42] Its theme was the prodigal son. "In the original," Bell wrote, "the prodigal son returns home, his quest revealing to him that home, the concreteness of family love, is the greatest truth. Rosenfeld's retelling of the story has a modern ending. The Jew cannot go home. He can only life in alienation." Bell quoted several passages from the novel describing the warmth of Jewish family life (the Passover seder), and the attractiveness of the old religious fervor (witnessing the protagonist's grandfather in the course of a discussion with a fellow *hassid*). But in the end, on the most elementary level, seeking reconciliation with his father ("My only hope had been to confess that I did not love him, to admit I had never known what love was or what it meant to love, and by that confession to create it"), the protagonist fails, the breach between the generations too great to be bridged. "At this point," Bell wrote, "manhood begins. At this point, in a true *bar-mitzvah*, begins the assumption of alienation."[43]

What was the young Jewish intellectual, now on his own, to do? He faced a society whose basic values—distorted by "the narrowing of the area of free moral choice" and particularly by pervasiveness of the "stilted forms of mass organization and bureaucracy"—had produced a "rawness, vulgarity, mass sadism and senseless sybaritism, the money lust and barbaric extravagances." But joining the organized opposition was impossible. For it meant accepting "the ambiguities of motives and interests" inherent in group action. As an intellectual, duty-bound "to maintain a critical temper," he could only live without dogma and without hope.[44]

Nor was it possible to return home, deep as the impulse was. ("We identify as Jews, the definition being derived from our specific immigrant roots," Bell granted.) The Yiddish immigrant world had faded and could not be recreated. All that was left for authentic Jewish intellectuals was the "hardness of alienation, the sense of otherness." And with it came a special critical faculty: "an unwillingness to submerge our values completely into any 'cause' because of the germ cells of corruption which are in the seeds of organization."[45]

And Zionism?—a necessary afterword, considering the periodical in which his essay was appearing. The Zionists offered a haven for prodigal sons, Bell wrote. But emotionally, Zionism and nationalism voided the special quality of being Jewish. "The whole world is our world; we were born in its ghettos and have a special place. Each man has his own journey to make and the land we have to travel is barren."[46]

Halpern began his reply with a comment on the rash of articles and symposia on being Jewish which were appearing in various magazines. The "gruesome unfolding of the Hitler story" had stirred Jewish intellectuals to face their Jewishness. What shocked and saddened him was how poverty-stricken and vacuous the "Jewishness of our day" appeared, even in the most objective and the most sensitive of their accounts. The single positive note relating to Jewish life in Bell's essay—his empathy with Rosenfeld's warm-felt remembrance of Jewish family life—Halpern found utterly superficial. But more distressing was Bell's verdict that Jewishness inheres almost exclusively in the family. Hence, when the son or daughter can not return home, for they no longer speak the language of the elders, alienation was almost inevitable. What Bell completely ignored, Halpern argued, was community. "The reconciliation with the family must always make its way through the community, finding there again threads of the same tradition that had been woven into family ties now irrevocably cut." Through "the incoherent 'community' of the disinherited"—"the academy of alienated intellectuals"—as Halpern put it, there could be "no return to the family, to the 'concreteness of love,' or to any historic continuum."[47]

The alienated Jewish intellectuals faced a more basic question. "In this frightful time for Jews, how, without cynicism, can I regain my community with the suffering and the heroic of my people? How, without romanticism, can I love them concretely once more—and thus truly recapture for myself once more an integral personality, love?" It was a problem which not only affected intellectuals, but was at the root of all efforts to "reconstruct" the Jewish community.[48]

Halpern led Bell through an analysis of the role traditional Jewish intellectuals had played in Jewish history. They had formulated the Jewish stand in Exile and guided the alienation of the Jewish people from their Gentile environment. In this way, the Jews permanently maintained an ideological opposition to the ruling ideas and lived by their own scale of values, historic time, sacred calendar, and history. "It is because of this, as you note in your essay," Halpern declared, "the Jews were so plainly seen to be *whole*, though radically alienated: because of this strong ascendancy of the intellectuals and their close integration with the people." The ancestors of the present generation of alienated Jewish intellectuals had forged an entire community that had gloried in its "integral alienation."[49]

And today, in America, what of the efforts to "reconstruct" the Jewish community? Such a community, Halpern well understood, could not possibly appeal to the estranged intellectuals. They would perceive the attempts to "naturalize" Judaism—to divest it of its alienness and reinterpret ancient themes so that they appear identical with the contemporary values of democracy and progressivism—to be a derivative, unauthentic endeavor. Such a community could not be the home that provided the love the alienated wanted.[50]

Only authentic Zionism remained. To consider it, Halpern realized, required overcoming the trauma of the disillusionment with all political movements Bell's sort of intellectuals had experienced in the 1930s and 1940s. "We have gone through a very purgatory of social education in our century, and one of the chief devils stoking the fires has been the demon of intellectual theocracy—the Ideocrat," Halpern wrote. "Movements have been organized around ideas with a ruthless consistency and single-mindedness quite equal to anything in the history of the Church Militant." Halpern understood why the new generation of intellectuals recoiled from *any* commitment to action. And yet, were there not

> ways of action and types of commitment by which the independence of the spirit need not be sold out? As a first modest contribution towards the quest, let me propose the thesis that loyalty to a dogma is a tyranny which suffers only slaves in its realm; but loyalty to one's fellow-men—and, first of all, to the concrete, particular aggregation of fellow-men who have the precise responses which meet the acts and fill the deeper expectations by which each of us defines his true personality—can be a compact of love and freedom, preserving the independence of the individual and of the spirit.[51]

Ironically, in later years the group of Jewish intellectuals Bell was so prominent a member of was given the appellative, "the Family," a three-generation intellectual family. It was, as its members will attest, a cantankerous one, marked by feuds, splits, hostility, and broken marriages.[52] It is worth noting, in comparison, the congruence between biology and ideology in the families Halpern and his fellow young Poale Zionists came from, where the children credited the parents for the values and beliefs they held, and the generations shared a common vision and passion. In part this community of families explains the poignancy of Halpern's invitation to the Daniel Bells to join his loving family of socialist Zionists. Merely to make this observation is to demarcate the wall that separated next of kin, and that only occasionally and then only in part would be breached in the years ahead. One is reminded of Halpern's firmly held view as a young exponent of *halutziut. Halutzim*, the "fanatics of Jewish survival," were the products of homes where the love of the Jewish people was absorbed through the tradition, Hebrew literature, and the law of moral accountability. For those who remained in their homes in America, or went and returned, there was the arduous "commandment of Exile" to fulfill.

Notes

I want to acknowledge with appreciation Gertrude Halpern's graciousness and candor in responding to my questions about her husband Ben in the course of interviews at her home in Brookline, Massachusetts, in the spring of 1990, 1991, and 1992. Samuel Halpern of Kfar Blum, Israel, Ben's younger brother, provided family details and insights in two extensive telephone interviews. A number of Ben Halpern's close associates from the Labor Zionist movement provided me with lively accounts of movement life and answered specific questions about Halpern. They are: David Breslau (Jerusalem), Saadia Gelb (Kfar Blum), Nachum Guttman (New York), Jacob Katzman (New York), Moshe Kerem (Gesher Haziv), Eddie Parsons (Kfar Blum), Shirley Lashner Shpira (Jerusalem), Yechiel Sasson (Kfar Blum), and Akiva Skidell (Kfar Blum). Frank E. Manuel and Saul Cohen offered valuable insights into the Hebrew Teachers College. Arnold Schutzberg (Cambridge, Massachusetts) helped me locate some of the materials. Maurice Tuchman, the librarian of the Hebrew College in Brookline, Mass. called my attention to sources relating to the early years of the college. I want to thank the following persons for their critical reading of a draft of this paper: David Breslau, Zvi Ganin (Beth Berl College), Ezra Mendelsohn (Hebrew University), Deborah Dash Moore (Vassar College), and Akiva Skidell.

A grant from the Lucius N. Littauer Foundation facilitated the research in Israel.

  1. Ben Halpern, Curriculum vitae, n.d.; Paul Mendes-Flohr, "The Intellectual and Zionism: An Appreciation of Ben Halpern," *Jewish Frontier*, 51 (November/December 1984): 43–47.
  2. Marie Syrkin, "Ben: A Personal Appreciation," in *Essays in Modern Jewish History: A Tribute to Ben Halpern*, edited by Frances Malino and Phyllis Cohen Albert (Rutherford, N.J.: Herzl Press Publication, Fairleigh Dickinson University Press, 1982), pp. 9–12.
  3. Ben Halpern, *The American Jew* (New York: Theodor Herzl Foundation, 1956). All citations are from the reprinted edition with a new preface and postscript (New York: Schocken Books, 1983), p. 100.
  4. Ibid., pp. 70–96.
  5. I have used socialist-Zionist, Poale Zion ("Workers of Zion"), and Labor Zionist Organization interchangeably.
  6. See articles by Moshe Cohen ("First Steps"), Saadia Gelb ("The Founding Convention"), and David Breslau ("Under Fire"), in *Arise and Build: the Story of American Habonim* (New York: Ichud Habonim Labor Zionist Youth, 1961), pp. 1–18, 31–37.
  7. Syrkin, "Ben," pp. 7–8; Gertrude Halpern, Samuel Halpern interviews.
  8. Gertrude Halpern, Samuel Halpern interviews; for an evocative memoir of a Labor Zionist family, see Jacob Katzman, *Commitment: The Labor Zionist Life-Style in America, A Personal Memoir* (New York: Labor Zionist Letters, 1975). Katzman describes Labor Zionist social life in Chelsea, Massachusetts, an immigrant suburb of Boston, during the same years Halpern was growing up in Roxbury, a Boston neighborhood quite similar to Chelsea. Katzman also attended the Hebrew Teachers College.
  9. Alef Lamed Hurwich, "L'toldoth beyt hamidrash l'morim d'boston," *Sefer Tourof*, editors Yitzhak Zilberschlag, Yochanan Twersky (Boston: Hebrew Teachers College Press, 1938), pp. 104–8; Yaacov Neuman, "Reyshit avodato shel Tourof b'Erets Yisrael (Zichronot)," ibid., pp. 98–103; Aryeh Leib Hurwich, *Zichronot m'chanech ivri*, vol. 2 (Boston: Bureau of Jewish Education, 1960), 172–83, 211–30; *Sefer hashana-alef shel talmidey beyt hamidrash l'morim d'boston*, edited by first graduating class (Boston, 1925), p. 113; "The Family Remembers" [alumni reminiscences], *Hebrew College Bulletin*, 5, no. 4 (June 1975): 18–27; "The Alumni," *Hebrew Teachers College: Register (1954/1955)*, pp. 39–61; Jacob Katzman interview.
 10. Frank Manuel interview.
 11. On Kaufmann's influence, see Mendes-Flohr, *Jewish Frontier*, pp. 45–46; Sharon Muller, "The Zionist Thought of Ben Halpern," *Judaism*, 27

(Summer 1978); 365–67; Edward S. Goldstein, "ATentative Intellectual Profile," in *Essays in Modern Jewish History*, pp. 298–304.

12. Benjamin Halpern, "Certain Sociological Aspects of the Jewish Problem in Christian Europe Prior to the 19th Century," (Harvard University, Ph.D. dissertation), pp. i–iii, 1–4.

13. Ben Halpern, "Letter to Joseph Alsop," *Midstream*, 20 (February 1976): 4; Yehudah Reinharz informs me that Halpern stated to him that it was common knowledge at Harvard that departments of sociology were closed to Jews. See Halpern's review of *A. D. Gordon: Selected Essays* which was privately published in Boston in 1938, "Aaron David Gordon," *Jewish Frontier*, 5, no. 3 (March 1938): 22–24, and "Aaron David Gordon," ibid., 14, no. 4 (April 1947): 17–20.

14. Alexander Lurie [Ben Halpern], "The Ugly Word 'Careerist,' " *Jewish Frontier*, 10 (November 1943): 26–28.

15. Nahum Guttman, "Hechalutz in America," *Arise and Build: The Story of American Habonim* (New York: Ichud Habonim Labor Zionist Youth, 1961), edited by David Breslau, pp. 26–31 Yehudah Riemer, "Haʾaliya haʾkhalutzit mitzfon amerika bʾrayshit shnot ha-30," *Hatzionut*, 17 (1991): 121–40; *Labor Zionist Handbook* (New York: Poale Zion Zeire Zion of America, 1939), pp. 136–43.

16. Halpern's column, "In the Homeland," a summary of information culled from the Hebrew press, appeared regularly in the bi-weekly *Labor-Zionist News Letter*, which was edited by Shlomo Grodzensky. For a sampling of his signed articles see: "The Right of Class Struggle," *Labor-Zionist News Letter*, 3, no. 3 (May 21, 1937), 10–31 (defending the sit-down strikes); "Colonization, Old and New—A Review," *Labor-Zionist News Letter*, 3, no. 4 (June 4, 1937), 10–16; (on the wave of new settlements and the Arab uprising); "Reconstructionism," *Labor-Zionist News Letter*, 3, no. 6 (July–August, 1937), 24–27 (a critique); "20 Years of Hechalutz," *Labor-Zionist News Letter*, 3, no. 10 (January 15, 1938), 3–5; "The Price of Freedom," *YPZA News and Views* (Bi-weekly Bulletin for Members of the Young Poale Zion Alliance), 4, no. 6 (January 9, 1939), 6–10 (comparing the Soviet Union with Nazi Germany).

17. Ben Halpern, "Enzo," *Furrows*, 4, no. 2 (December 1945), 14–17; Ruth Bondy, *The Emissary: A Life of Enzo Sereni* (Boston: Little, Brown, 1977), pp. 136–51.

18. Saadia Gelb, Akiva Skidell, Nachum Guttman interviews. Twice, Halpern related the story of the visit to Brandeis to the author. Professor Zvi Ganin recalls Halpern telling him about his trip to Brandeis's home on Cape Cod to gain Brandeis's financial support.

19. Akiva Skidell interview; David Breslau, "Under Fire (1936–1940)," in *Arise and Build*, pp. 31–37. Among the Palestinian labor leaders who visited the United States during this period and showed special interest in the Young Poale Zion were Golda Myerson, Zalman Rubashov (Sha-

98   ARTHUR A. GOREN

zar), Berl Katznelson, Israel Meriminski, and Yosef Baratz. Ben Zion
Appelbaum (Elan), an "alumni" of the Young Poale Zion who settled
in Kibbutz Afikim, was an envoy to the movement between 1936 and
1938. Of the American leaders, Hayim Greenberg, who frequently participated in meetings of the youth leaders, was especially influential.

20. Nachum Guttman, "Talmud Torah Tales," *Jewish Frontier*, 58 (Novem-
ber/December 1991): 28–30; Saadia Gelb, Nachum Guttman, Yechiel
Sasson, Moshe Kerem interviews; Samuel Dinin, "Twenty-five Years of
Teacher Training," *Jewish Education*, 7 (January–March 1935): 25–33;
see "Mosdot hakhinukh ha'ivri," in *Sefer Hayovel*, pp. 249–311, for
brief accounts of the teacher training schools established in New York,
Philadelphia, Chicago, Baltimore, and Cleveland; Rivka Harmati,
"M'khanekh b'aspaklariya shel t'kufa: trumato shel H. A. Friedlander
l'khinukh ha'yehud b'Artzot ha'brit," (unpublished master's essay, In-
stitute of Contemporary Jewry, Hebrew University, 1986), pp. 29–86.
For a case study of the involvement of Labor Zionists in furthering
youth activities, see Yehuda Rimer, "Youth Movement and Adult
Sponsorship: The Relations of American Habonim and Poale Zion as
Revealed in the Papers of Joseph Gootman, Cincinnati" (manuscript).
I want to thank Dr. Riemer of the Yad Tabenkin Institute, Efal, Israel,
for making his unpublished paper available to me.

21. Merkaz [national executive] Habonim, "Habonim Prospectus," in *Arise
and Build*, pp. 18–22; "This Issue," ibid., 23–26.

22. Baruch Zuckerman, "Problems of Our Youth Movement in America";
Jacob Katzman, [response], September 1934, in "Ideological Development of Habonim (Documents 1922–1957), prepared for 25th Convention, December 1957 and revised January 1958 (Habonim Labor Zionist
Youth, mimeographed), pp. 2–8.

23. *YPZA News and Views*, 3 (October 1, 1937): 2–3.

24. Ibid., p. 4.

25. Ben Halpern, "In Defense of the American Chalutz," *Hechalutz*, 5
(February 1937): 27; ibid., "The Problem of the American Chalutz,"
Forum for the Problems of Zionism, World Jewry and the State of Israel,
1 (December 1953): 50–51.

26. Ibid., p. 51.

27. *News and Views*, October 1, 1937, p. 2.

28. Ben Halpern, "Habonim and American Zionism," *Jewish Frontier*, 26
(December 1959): 16–18; reprinted in *Arise and Build*, pp. 247–51.

29. Ben Halpern, "At Home in Exile," *Furrows*, 1, no. 3 (January 1943):
6–9.

30. Akiva Skidell interview.

31. Syrkin, "Ben," pp. 12–14; Gertrude Halpern interview.

32. Halpern, "At Home in Exile," pp. 7–8; Ben Halpern, "Exile and Redemption: A Secular Zionist View," *Judaism*, 29, no. 2 (Spring 1980): 177.

33. Halpern, "At Home in Exile," p. 9.

34. Eugene Kohn, "Is It Our Duty to Remain Maladjusted?" *Furrows*, 1, no. 5 (March 1943): 13–17.
35. Halpern, "How to Observe the Commandment of Exile," *Furrows*, 1, no. 5 (March 1943): 19–20.
36. Ben Halpern, "Exile," *Jewish Frontier*, 21, no. 4 (April 1954): 6–9; Halpern, "Exile and Redemption," p. 180.
37. Ben Halpern, "Apologia Contra Rabbines," *Midstream*, 2, no. 2 (Spring 1956): 19.
38. Ben Halpern, "The Destinies of Jew and Negro," *Jewish Frontier*, 14 (November 1947): 19–23; *New York Times*, October 12, 1947, p. 52; *New York Times*, October 24, 1947, p. 9; *An Appeal to the World: A Statement on the Denial of Human Rights to Minorities in the Case of Citizens of Negro Descent in the United States of America and an Appeal to the United Nations for Redress*, edited by W. E. Burghardt Du Bois (New York: National Association for the Advancement of Colored People, 1947); Halpern, *The American Jew*, pp. 46–59. For the 1960s and 1970s see Halpern, "Negro–Jewish Relations in America: A Symposium" (Comment), *Midstream*, 12 (December 1966): 44–47; Halpern, *Jews and Blacks: The Classic American Minorities* (New York: Herder and Herder, 1971); Halpern, "A Program for American Jews," *Jewish Frontier*, 38 (November 1971): 12–18.
39. Alexander Bloom, *Prodigal Sons: The New York Intellectuals and Their World* (New York: Oxford University Press, 1986), pp. 141–57; Terry A. Cooney, *The Rise of the New York Intellectuals: Partisan Review and Its Circle* (Madison: University of Wisconsin Press, 1986), 225–50; Halpern, "Exile and Redemption," p. 178.
40. Daniel Bell, "A Parable of Alienation," *Jewish Frontier*, 13, no. 11 (November 1946): 12–19. In a footnote (p. 18), Bell remarked that in addition to Isaac Rosenfeld, whose novel, *Passage from Home*, he discusses in the article, others dealing with the theme of Jewish alienation were: Saul Bellow, Paul Goodman, Delmore Schwartz, Clement Greenberg. A month before Bell's article appeared, Irving Howe discussed Rosenfeld's novel in an essay entitled "The Lost Young Intellectual: A Marginal Man, Twice Alienated" (*Commentary*, 12, no. 4 [October 1946]: 361–67).
41. Job L. Dittberner, *The End of Ideology and American Social Thought: 1930–1960* (Ann Arbor, Mich: UMI Research Press, 1979), pp. 156–72, 309–25, 332–35.
42. In the first part of the essay, subtitled "The Alienation of the World," Bell discussed the alienation concept, drawing on Max Weber, George Simmel, Karl Marx, and Thorstein Veblen; he entitled the second section, "The Alienation of the Jewish Family," and then presented the parable under the rubric, "The Alienation of the Young Jew" (Daniel Bell, "A Parable of Alienation," *Jewish Frontier*, 13, no. 11 [November 1946]: 12–16).

43. Bell, "Alienation," pp. 16–18.
44. Ibid., p. 18.
45. Ibid., 19.
46. Ibid., p. 19.
47. Ben Halpern, "Letter to an Intellectual," *Jewish Frontier*, 13, no. 12 (December 1946): 13–15.
48. Ibid., p. 16.
49. Ibid., p. 17.
50. Ibid., p. 17.
51. Ibid., pp. 17–18.
52. Norman Podhoretz, *Making It* (New York: Random House, 1967), pp. 109–36; Daniel Bell, *Winding Passage: Essays and Sociological Journeys, 1960–1980* (Cambridge, Mass.: ABT Books, 1980), pp. 127–37; Ben Halpern, "Ha'vikuach lim'oravutah shel ha'inteligentsia ha'yehudit-amerikanit b'vikuach b'ad v'neged ha'kamat ha'm'dina," *Hatziyonut*, 14 (1989): 89–105.

CHAPTER 4

Trude Weiss-Rosmarin and the *Jewish Spectator*

Deborah Dash Moore

Trude Weiss-Rosmarin arrived in New York City in 1931. In her early twenties and recently married, she already possessed considerable intellectual credentials: academic, educational, and political. She came from Germany hoping to launch a career in semitics; instead she became an independent intellectual, intimately associated with the equally independent monthly, the *Jewish Spectator*. She founded the *Jewish Spectator* and edited it until her death in June 1989. For four decades beginning in the mid-1930s, Trude Weiss-Rosmarin participated actively in New York's Jewish cultural life. An intellectual with fierce opinions and a biting pen, she carved for herself a niche as the gadfly of Jewish organizational politics. But she also opened the pages of her magazine to a wide array of opinions and she consistently nurtured young, aspiring literary talents. A passionate devotion to Judaism ran through her editorials and articles. Judaism was probably her first true love and one she never abandoned, although her understanding of what Judaism required changed over time. Trude Weiss-Rosmarin's passion for Judaism informed her Zionism, her politics, her cultural vision, her interpretation of religion, and her feminism. It was her prism to refract the world around her.

As one of the "other" New York Jewish Intellectuals, Trude Weiss-Rosmarin stands apart on a number of grounds. First, she was a woman. As a woman she decided to pursue both motherhood and a career, perhaps symbolically signified in her choice of a hyphen-ated name. Second, she was a religious traditionalist. As a young woman she believed in the tenets of Orthodox Judaism; later she ceased to observe many Jewish religious practices but she never became a secularist.[1] Third, she was an editor of an independent—unaffiliated and unsubsidized—magazine. Exactly how she man-aged to keep the *Jewish Spectator* afloat during the more than fifty years of her editorship is not clear. During the early years the *Spectator* carried a significant amount of advertising;[2] Trude Weiss-Rosmarin also lectured extensively and undoubtedly used some of those monies to support the monthly;[3] finally, reparations pay-ments after World War II probably helped.[4]

Weiss-Rosmarin also shared many characteristics of the "other" New York Jewish Intellectuals. Like most of them, she was born abroad but became an American Jew. She was a Zionist, albeit more of a cultural than a political Zionist. She adopted the essay as the characteristic vehicle for her opinions. Although she wrote many books, most reflected the essay structure. She possessed a deep and extensive knowledge of Jewish sources, traditional and contemporary. Her writing is studded with citations to Talmud and midrash, medieval and contemporary philosophy, ancient and modern Hebrew literature. She was an engaged intellectual, moving in and out of Jewish organizational life. She was also an educator, a believer in the power of education. She used both the written and spoken word to teach. She was, like her peers, an excellent and dynamic speaker. Like them, too, she had faith in the word, its ability to inspire action, to change behavior. She held high cultural standards before American Jews and challenged them to aspire to reach these standards. Yet despite the absence of evidence to sus-tain her vision, she never completely gave up hope.

In the context of this volume it is appropriate to focus upon three discrete facets of Trude Weiss-Rosmarin: those elements of her biography that limn a portrait of the making of a Jewish woman intellectual; her founding of the *Jewish Spectator* in New York City and its development into the format that characterized it for roughly fifty years; and her response to the central issues animating the "other" New York Jewish Intellectuals—Zionism, the future of American Jews, and the destruction of European Jewry.

Trude Weiss was born in Frankfurt on June 7, 1908, the daughter of a prosperous wine merchant.[5] In interviews almost eighty years later, she describes her parents as "religiously" Jewish but not "culturally" so.[6] Presumably, they were culturally German and, as good bourgeois, subscribed to that German Jewish faith in a universal "bildung" so insightfully described by George Mosse.[7] They worshiped in an elegant, "civilized" Orthodox synagogue, that had a "luxurious women's gallery, with a dressing room to leave your coat and a beadle in a splendid uniform."[8] Its modern Orthodox rabbi and staunch believer in the congruence of Judaism and "bildung," Nehemia Anton Nobel, advocated Jewish women's right to vote and hold office within the Jewish community.[9] Trude recalled her eagerness to see the charismatic rabbi preach, which produced her first sense of discrimination because she was a woman. "I would go down to the first row, and invariably the beadle would yank me back. And I knew that if I were a boy, I'd have been downstairs, and perhaps even been able to shake the rabbi's hand."[10]

But Trude Weiss was a rebel at an early age. In 1917 she went to an afternoon meeting at the home of a friend and immediately was "speared" as a new member of the Blau-Weiss. This German Zionist youth movement emphasized hikes and Jewish cultural activities. Describing the attraction of the Blau-Weiss, she indicates the appeal of coeducational equality. "There was hora dancing which I'd never seen before, and singing of Zionist songs, boys and girls together." Shortly afterward, Trude began attending a Zionist Hebrew school, "which was also with boys and girls together, and I had a wonderful teacher, Yosef Yoel Rivlin," at the Hebraische Sprachschule, a "non-establishment school."[11] The experience of equality was a heady one. Trude was a good student, excelling in her Hebrew studies and receiving recognition for her efforts. Eager to make *aliya* and join a kibbutz, she ran away from home and school in 1922–23 to join a *hachshara* near Berlin. Her efforts to train as a pioneer ended with a severe case of pneumonia and six weeks at home recuperating.[12]

Failure as a *halutz* did not scotch Trude's rebelliousness. When her parents refused to pay for a tutor to make up the lost school year, she left home again and found employment as director and teacher of a Hebrew language school in Duisburg. Not too extraordinary, except that she was only sixteen or seventeen at the time and she organized the school herself. Using her earnings to pay for a tutor, Trude took her final exams ahead of her class. But she did not neglect her Jewish learning. She studied the classical Jewish texts, including Talmud. Many years later she recalled how one professor would ask her and the other woman in the class to leave the room when sexual matters were discussed in the text.[13] She also studied at the Freie Jüdische Lehrhaus, the Frankfurt school established by Franz Rosenzweig in 1920. In retrospect, she remembers its "spirit" of Jewish learning as an inspiration. The Lehrhaus closed in 1926 and Trude entered university studies first at the University of Berlin, 1927–28, then at Leipzig, 1929. Finally, at Würzburg she received her doctorate in semitics, archeology, and philosophy in 1931. Her dissertation, later published, dealt with "The Mention of Arabia and the Arabs in Assyrian-Babylonian Texts." She was twenty-two years old.[14]

Here is a portrait of the Jewish intellectual as a young woman, a rebellious young Jewish woman. In interviews Trude admits that she was "a black sheep," a "dropout," "a runaway," but she sees her rebellion in the context of post–World War I German Jewry. "We were of that generation of young German Jews who discovered Judaism and were intoxicated . . . with it."[15] She was also among the first generation of women to enter university in Germany. If she rebelled against her parents' formal religious Judaism, she embraced Zionism and Jewish culture. The former constricted her as a woman, the latter liberated her. The former found expression in home and synagogue, the latter flourished in school and the world of ideas. Trude linked feminism with Zionism and the world of ideas and allowed one to inform the other. She rejected the patriarchal, familial Jewish piety of her parents and its German culture. She married Aaron Rosmarin, a Russian Jewish scholar, four years her senior. Upon receiving her doctorate she and her husband went to America.

"I wanted to teach Assyriology," Trude Weiss-Rosmarin admitted.[16] America, the land of opportunity, promised more than Germany where she would have received the lowest rank of an unsalaried instructor. But America in 1931 was in the depths of the

Depression. Universities were firing faculty, not hiring.[17] Although Weiss-Rosmarin wrote to Cyrus Adler and other leading scholars of semitics, she failed even to obtain a part-time academic appointment. Unsuccessful in finding employment, she created her own job. She repeated her Duisburg experiment, albeit with an important difference. In October 1933 she founded The School of the Jewish Woman, under the auspices of Hadassah.[18]

Weiss-Rosmarin designed the School, located on the Upper West Side of Manhattan at 251 West 100th Street, as a model of adult Jewish education, inspired in part by Rosenzweig's Lehrhaus. The School attracted both married and single Jewish women. It offered a diploma for Sunday School teachers and "alertness credit" to public school teachers.[19] Regular radio broadcasts, monthly gatherings of a B'not Torah League and bi-monthly lectures-teas-dances of a Young Folks League (to which men were invited) helped spread the message. As she later admitted, "my feminism in those days was intellectually oriented."[20]

An early pamphlet on "Jewish Women and Jewish Culture" confirms her recollection.[21] Weiss-Rosmarin, like the Jewish feminists of the 1970s, begins with the two contradictory Talmudic statements: "Every man is obliged to teach his daughter the Torah" versus "Whoever teaches his daughter Torah is as if he teaches her obscenity." Recognizing that the latter has become "the slogan of the masses," she observes that "this world was and still is essentially the world of man. Our society is made by men and not by women. Men have always been the legislators; and it is therefore not surprising," she concludes, "that they favored their own sex." But the modern world is changing. Men have to earn a living and have no time to see their children let alone to educate them. That responsibility has shifted to mothers. Weiss-Rosmarin then argues that Jewish culture has preserved the Jews, that cultural assimilation is fine provided it does not weaken Jews' allegiance to their own culture, and that a cultural crisis exists today: "the desertion of our culture by the Jewish people of our generation." This crisis is much more dangerous than Nazism and the only way to overcome the threat is "to instill love and affection for Judaism in the young generation." The best way to reach that goal is "to teach them what Judaism really is." Weiss-Rosmarin had enormous confidence in Judaism, its attractiveness and ability to compete with contemporary cultures in the modern world.

This is where women—mothers and mothers-to-be—enter. They need to learn that they have failed their children if they only send them to Hebrew school. Perhaps remembering her own rejection of religious education, she declares that "to send the child to Hebrew School is not enough." Mothers must know enough themselves to supervise their children's Jewish studies. "Children are not so eager to go to Hebrew School in the afternoon at the time when their Gentile friends are out at play. They might also ask their parents, 'Do you know Hebrew?' And hundreds and thousands of mothers cannot answer this question without losing respect in the eyes of their children. If you want your children to grow up as educated Jews," she concludes, "you yourself must become educated." Finally, Weiss-Rosmarin appeals to the modern woman who no longer needed to work, whose days were filled with leisure time, the same women who joined Hadassah and other women's organizations. She urges them to find "a center for their personality" by concentrating "their powers upon one point, upon Judaism."

Weiss-Rosmarin centered her educational curriculum around Hebrew, the language of past Jewish literary treasures and the tongue of the contemporary cultural renaissance in Palestine.[22] The School of the Jewish Woman offered eight levels of Hebrew instruction. Hebrew was the key to the study of Bible, Talmud, and liturgy. As an intellectual feminist, Weiss-Rosmarin promoted the study of the liturgy, learning the meaning and history of the prayers, "to stimulate attendance" of women at synagogue. The curriculum also included classes in Jewish history and philosophy, and in Jewish customs and ceremonies.[23] Weiss-Rosmarin tried to impart through the School the same Jewish education she had struggled to obtain, starting with her passion for Hebrew, and then continuing with Tanakh, Rashi, Jewish history and philosophy. Jewish women had been short-changed and Weiss-Rosmarin saw education as the remedy. Not only did she run the school, she taught there, as did her husband. In 1937, the school's faculty also included Rabbi Philip Alstat, who taught Jewish history and problems in modern Jewish life, Jonah Schneidman and Morris Skop—both of whom taught

Hebrew—and Israel Knox, who gave a class in Yiddish.[24] None of the faculty received a regular salary.[25]

After two years of successful and stimulating classes, Weiss-Rosmarin introduced a new vehicle of education: a newsletter. "News from the School of the Jewish Woman" first appeared in November–December of 1935. It announced that as the School had "grown from humble beginnings to become one of the best known and largest institutions of Jewish adult education, so we hope that our News Letter will eventually develop into a regular magazine of high literary standing."[26] Weiss-Rosmarin was not lacking in ambition and ideals. Her hopes for the newsletter took a mere three months to materialize. In February 1936, the fourth issue of the newsletter appeared as the *Jewish Spectator*. By April the *Spectator* was advertising that it was mailed to the Jewish teachers in all the New York City public and high schools and that it reached "the JEWISH WOMAN of medium and ample means."[27] By May the magazine had acquired its cover listing the titles of articles and had grown to twenty small-format pages. It continued to grow, reaching forty-two pages by July. Thereafter the number of pages fluctuated, with issues as large as fifty pages during the winter months.

Characterizing itself as "a typical family magazine, with a special appeal to the woman," the *Jewish Spectator* bore little resemblance to the typical family magazines of the period.[28] From the beginning its hard-hitting editorials addressed the most pertinent issues of the period. The April editorial, for example, roundly condemned Columbia and Yale for their participation in the celebration of the 550th anniversary of the founding of Heidelberg University. It compared the event to the 1936 Olympics—a chance to lure intellectuals, instead of athletes, to Germany to inculcate them with Nazi propaganda. The editorial praised the firm rejection of the German invitation by the University of Virginia as a fitting expression of the democratic heritage of Thomas Jefferson.[29] The magazine assumed that Jewish women were engaged and committed, concerned with the state of the Jewish world as well as with their homes and families.

However, the *Jewish Spectator* did include a number of familiar features targeted at a female audience. Among these were an advice column, "The Clinic of Personal Problems" in which Dr. B. L. Wise-

man answered letters sent by readers, and condensations of great
novels. The first issues also carried a page of jokes, news from The
School of the Jewish Woman, and a test your IQ made up of questions from Jewish history and philosophy. By the second year, the
Spectator regularly published poetry, original short stories, articles—often on topical, religious, historical, or biographical subjects, and condensations of a novel. In addition, its standard features included several editorials, an historical column, "It
Happened to the Jews," a section of brief book reviews, and Hebrew
Wisdom in translation (a second translation feature called "From
the Sea of the Talmud" was tried briefly in 1937, as was a special
page, "Ludwig Lewisohn's Page"). In February 1939 the *Spectator*
introduced a "Juniors' Library" of four pages for children. These
were added upon the request of readers.[30] Most of the *Spectator's*
pages were devoted to literature: poetry, short stories, serialization
of novels, and biographies of writers.[31] The magazine also rarely
failed to publish at least one woman author each month (in addition to Weiss-Rosmarin's monthly essay), although often the contribution was some verse and not an article or story.

Looking at the Anglo-Jewish press in 1937, only a year and a
half after the successful start of the *Jewish Spectator*, Trude Weiss-
Rosmarin concluded that the pitiful condition of the weeklies
stemmed from their character. "For there is so little of real interest,
of vital and important material printed in them, that one can but
marvel that there are still Jews who are willing to spend a few
dollars a year for them," she observed. Now, at the point of an
"historical transition" from Yiddish to English, the Anglo-Jewish
papers had "a chance to become powerful instruments of public
opinion." All that was needed was a change in editorial policy, a
willingness to publish good fiction, some poetry, "a few worthwhile
utterances by distinguished personalities . . . or perhaps some Talmudical quotations," together with an end to harping on two topics—anti-Semitism and fascism.[32] Weiss-Rosmarin's confidence in
the effectiveness of her prescription can be read as a blueprint for
the *Spectator*. She assumed that at this "unique moment" it would
be possible to capture an English-reading audience who wanted to
keep up with Jewish life but, due to ignorance of Yiddish, had lost
the connection provided by the Yiddish press. The appearance of

several new Anglo-Jewish magazines in the mid-thirties suggests the accuracy of Weiss-Rosmarin's perception.[33]

Because it emerged out of The School of the Jewish Woman, the *Jewish Spectator* quickly developed an audience, initially composed largely of women.[34] Its original place in American Jewish publishing derived as much from its distinct audience as from its editorial posture.[35] The *Spectator* represented a blend of Jewish political and literary writing; its politics were Zionist and democratic, its aesthetic was contemporary and moral but hardly modernist. The monthly assumed an intelligent readership, but not necessarily an educated one. Unlike the *Menorah Journal*, it did not appeal exclusively to the college-educated; unlike the *Jewish Frontier*, it did not voice the perspective of a movement (i.e., Labor Zionism); unlike the *Reconstructionist*, it did not articulate a radical religious posture. Yet the *Spectator* shared much in common with its peers, these three important American Jewish English-language magazines. The *Spectator* aspired to transmit the best contemporary Jewish culture, it espoused political Zionism and saw Jewish politics through Zionist eyes, and it was committed to Judaism as a religion and to a pluralist American Jewish community. Most importantly, it never lost sight of women, their rights, their roles, their responsibilities, their concerns, their values. Undoubtedly, the *Spectator* articulated a woman's position because Trude Weiss-Rosmarin served as associate editor.[36] Her husband, the editor, assumed the prerogative of men.

In 1936, Weiss-Rosmarin's contentiousness led to the first of a number of crucial separations. "Differences in policies," produced "the withdrawal of Hadassah" from The School of the Jewish Woman, despite the "real contribution" made by Hadassah through the School. Hadassah's minutes mention the quality of the program, its ability to meet the needs of women, the teachers chosen for personality as well as scholarship, and the convenient hours for study.[37] But working with Weiss-Rosmarin was difficult. "I ignored them," Weiss-Rosmarin admitted many years later regarding Hadassah. "I'm not such an angel when it comes to dealing with organizations."[38] Two years later, in 1938, she gave birth to her son, Moshe. "I didn't permit myself to interrupt my professional schedule," she recalls. Since her husband wasn't interested in taking care of the child, she "worked in order to support a maid and a nursemaid." Looking back she argued that her decision to spend all of her earnings on proper care for her child "was a wonderful investment." Had she "taken off four or five years to take care of him myself, I would really have suffered major professional damage."[39] The School for the Jewish Woman did not survive, however. It closed in 1939; the start of World War II put its feminist educational goals on permanent hold.

Weiss-Rosmarin turned her attention exclusively to the *Jewish Spectator*, her new classroom. (In February 1938 the monthly began publishing under its own auspices, rather than that of the School, and moved its offices downtown to West 40th Street.) She had already launched a successful speaking and lecturing career in 1936.[40] The freedom that came from continuing to write and to lecture proved to be crucial. Five years after the birth of her son, Weiss-Rosmarin was divorced. Her husband accepted a position as the director of education for Mizrachi and she moved up to sole editor of the *Jewish Spectator*. From 1943 until her death, the *Spectator* was her pulpit and her classroom.

In the November issue, Weiss-Rosmarin eagerly took the opportunity to assess her editorial stewardship. Reflecting on "Our Ninth Year," rather than waiting for the tenth, she wrote: "We are always ready for a good fight, provided the cause is worth fighting for. And we are not committed to any political camp or party line." Instead, she mused, "we have criticized and praised, according to our best lights and not on account of political motives, orthodox, conservative and reform organizations and leaders . . ." However, not infrequently, such independence put her and the *Spectator* "in opposition to 'the best people' and the pillars of Jewish society." Weiss-Rosmarin then lists those things she was very proud of and would continue to value: "We have plugged along under our own power—without subvention and patrons. We have never (really *never*) 'skipped' even a single month . . ." Finally she articulates the *Jewish Spectator*'s creed: "Eretz Israel, Hebrew, a thorough Jewish education for every child, the integrity of Judaism as a living force of life distinct and independent from any other faith and culture. Our main concern is JEWISH SURVIVAL," she concludes, "and so we judge all communal and individual Jewish efforts from the viewpoint of their survival value."[41]

Writing from the viewpoint of Jewish survival was exceptionally arduous and discouraging during the Second World War. For the first three years of the war, before the official United States' confirmation of the Nazi extermination of European Jews, her editorials and essays emphasized the importance of Judaism. Weiss-Rosmarin even argued that the future of Judaism took precedence over the future of the Jews and she criticized the preoccupation of American Jewish organizations with fighting anti-Semitism. Jews survived because they had something to live for: one God, one mankind, one justice and universal peace. These ideals of Judaism were embodied in the ritual law and Jewish ethical teaching. Weiss-Rosmarin taught that Judaism "encompasses life as a whole. It supplies a regimen as well as a philosophy for each and every moment. . . . It blends religion, national feelings, cultural aspirations and the hopes for a better future into an inseparable wholeness of purposeful holiness."[42] Such optimism could not be sustained by 1943.

The January issue, with a black border, announced the horrible news. The extermination of European Jewry dominated the editorial pages of subsequent issues: Too Late, A People in Mourning, A Stab in the Back, What Now, Tortured Jew?, A Jewish Call to the Conscience of the United Nations, The Curse of Complacency.[43] In the last editorial, Weiss-Rosmarin returned to the theme of Jewish survival. How to explain the extraordinary complacency of American Jews who watch the slaughter of their brethren as they watch others being martyred, with no special pain of bereavement, she asked. And she answered: "the tragic complacency and indifference of millions of American Jews in the face of the worst Jewish disaster and tragedy ever are due to the fact that these people . . . no longer are capable of feeling and reacting as Jews." Because American Jewish leaders have harped on politics, on Jewish rights, on fighting anti-Semitism, the masses have no sense of solidarity. Due to the neglect of Jewish education, "we have brought up a generation of American Jews that is innocent of any adequate knowledge of the implication of Jewishness." American Jews have lost the poetry and passion of Judaism.[44]

A year later, anticipating the imminent end of the war, Weiss-Rosmarin linked the slaughter of five million Jews to Jewish survival. "The millions of Jews who have died in the last ten years have left us a sacred trust," she wrote, "to work indefatigably for Jewish survival and the continuity and fruitful growth of our Jewish culture, the eternal and human, yet also distinctly national-religious culture, by which Western civilization of the democratic kind has been nurtured."[45] The unfolding Holocaust required that American Jews "assume the burden and shoulder the responsibilities of the five millions whose lives were snuffed out by the nazis."[46] Weiss-Rosmarin proposed ten Jewish New Year's resolutions, beginning with "I shall become a member of the local synagogue where I usually attend High Holidays services;" it included sending children to Hebrew School or parochial school if possible, subscribing to a Jewish periodical, reading Jewish books, buying Jewish art, listening to Jewish music, and it concluded with a statement of personal responsibility in the face of the Holocaust.

> I shall be conscious of the fact that due to the overwhelming losses of the Jewish people in the last ten years I no longer have the right to regard myself as a mere individual. I shall keep in mind that I must take the place of at least one other Jew, who died without fulfilling his Jewish tasks and destiny.[47]

The goal was to insure Jewish survival; the task belonged to all American Jews.

Weiss-Rosmarin did not limit her response to the destruction of European Jewry to a program of personal responsibility for Jewish survival. She bitterly attacked the United Nations for their repeated betrayals of the Jews, she lashed out at the revival of anti-Semitism in Poland, England, and France during and after the war, she called repeatedly for realistic rescue efforts, and she supported vehemently the opening of Palestine to the surviving remnant, the abrogation of the White Paper of 1939, and the establishment of a Jewish state. She even addressed the issue of guilt. "In assessing the guilt of the nazis, let us not forget that all of us are to a certain extent accomplices to their crimes," she cautioned. "We Jews of the Western democracies are guilty of not having been more vociferous and zealous in pleading the case of German and Austrian Jewry prior to

1939 and our Christian neighbors are guilty of having dismissed our reports as 'horror tales.' "[48] Yet each time she also returned to the theme of Jewish survival. Although she recognized that "from a survivalist perspective American Jewry numbers about half a million at best rather than five and a half million," she neither tired of addressing that minority nor yielded in her use of hyperbole. "I do not hesitate to state emphatically," she wrote in 1945, "that one Hebrew class is more important for Jewish survival than all Jewish political conferences and conclaves."[49]

Preoccupation with Jewish survival colored Weiss-Rosmarin's response to the Jewish survivors, their plight in the displaced persons camps, and the Zionist solution to their desperate situation. Though she called it "tragic," she concluded that "there is no future for the Jews in Europe."[50] The only future lay in Eretz Yisrael. Yet Weiss-Rosmarin rejected partition. Zionism stood above realpolitik, above appeasement.[51] She saw Zionism and Judaism as "coextensive and synonymous." Judaism embraces "the sum total of the religious-national culture of the Jewish people."[52] Zionism was not less; it certainly could not be reduced to "refugeeism." Even as the United Nations prepared to vote on the recommendations for partition, to establish a Jewish and an Arab state, Weiss-Rosmarin voiced her opposition.[53] She wanted a state from Dan to Beer-Sheba, not to solve the pressing problems of the current generation but for future generations. Zionism was the path of Jewish survivalism; Zionist leaders could not sacrifice the future for the sake of the present refugees. Writing "on the threshold of the Jewish State," Weiss-Rosmarin stepped back to assess the costs: "To relinquish seven-eighths of its territory is a sacrifice no people has ever been asked to make. It is a sacrifice comparable in magnitude only to the sacrifice of six million Jewish lives . . ."[54] Only if the Jewish state could rescue not merely the DPs, but North African Jews and Yemenite Jews and bring them to the Homeland, would partition be worthwhile. There would still be *Galut*, and at best only 20 percent of the world Jewish population would live in the state, but if the yishuv would serve as the spiritual center for the dispersion, then the loss of territory would be justified.[55]

As Weiss-Rosmarin anguished over the costs of partition and the horrible facts of war, she also anticipated the new Jewish world.

Writing as a survivalist, she accepted the fact of *golah;* it can be neither negated nor affirmed. She looked to the past to determine the proper relation between a Jewish state and a dispersion and came up with four principles. The first affirms the equal human importance of *golah* and yishuv. The second states the supremacy of the land of Israel over other countries as a place to live. The third declares the spiritual superiority of Jews living in the Holy Land and the fourth outlines responsibilities of the *golah* to the yishuv. These include monetary support and submission to the yishuv's spiritual authority. Weiss-Rosmarin then suggested several contemporary equivalents to ancient practices, including a tax on each Jew (as opposed to charity) to build identification with the Jewish state and such modern versions of pilgrimage as vacations and summer camps in Eretz Yisrael.[56] "The Jewish world of tomorrow will have a political center of gravity," she prophesied. "It will have a unified cultural-religious base, anchored in the Jewish State. . . . The Jewish world of tomorrow will be dichotomous . . ."[57] Both the center and the periphery will have the right to live and prosper, each will be interdependent.

Where did American Jews fit in this Jewish world of tomorrow? Weiss-Rosmarin hesitated. In 1947 she wrote:

> As to American Jewry, even the most enthusiastic believers in its survival potential and its ability to substitute partially at least, for the loss of European Jewry, know that Voloshin and Slobodka cannot be transferred to American soil, just as little as American Jewry will be able to produce Hebrew and Yiddish writers comparable to those who firmly established modern Hebrew and Yiddish literature over the past five or six decades.[58]

Weiss-Rosmarin concluded that "under the most favorable circumstances, the quality of American Judaism will be preservative rather than creative." Did this mean that America was *galut?* Again, Weiss-Rosmarin hesitated. In 1951 she returned to the subject in response to David Ben Gurion's whirlwind tour of the United States and his provocative challenge to American Jews to settle in Israel, or at least to send their children. Rejecting the arguments of Jacob Blaustein, president of the American Jewish Committee, that America was not *galut,* she admitted nonetheless to believing "that there is a future for Jews in America." Yet her *"belief* in America" clashed with her *"knowledge* of Jewish history." Comparing America with Germany, she wondered out loud "whether I am not caught in the same illusion that blinded the German Jews."[59]

Given her analysis, Weiss-Rosmarin logically concluded that "America *is* Galuth . . . because the American Jew *must* be a Jew, even when he does not want to be a Jew." She rejects various alternatives, including the Reconstructionist one of living in two civilizations. Such a formula stunts the Jewish civilization, forcing it to conform to the accepted norms of American culture. However, Weiss-Rosmarin was not prepared to take the next step and negate *galut*. Instead, she pauses to observe that most people muddle along and that only an elite is capable of acting on the basis of spiritual insight, especially when that involves both physical and economic sacrifices. Since catastrophe was not about to overtake American Jewry in the foreseeable future, few American Jews would come to Israel. How, then, should Zionists cope with such a reality? Not "by pouring fire and brimstone on those who squat by the flesh-pots of America." Instead, "in order to be a Jew and remain a Jew outside of Israel one must be sensitive to the subtle undertones of Jewishness and accept the difficulties of the Galuth situation . . ."

> Jewish continuity in the dispersion therefore calls, first of all, for the recognition that Jewish survival is embattled and, secondly, for the determination to insure Jewish continuity by means of strengthening its base and foundation: Jewish distinctive separateness.[60]

Ultimately, Weiss-Rosmarin argues, "the very awareness of Galuth makes for Jewish survival while its absence inevitably results in Jewish extinction."

The article drew a response from Israel Schen, editor of the *Zionist Newsletter*, the official organ of the Jewish Agency. Weiss-Rosmarin thought that the issue was important enough to reprint his answer to her analysis in the *Spectator*.[61] After praising her for her analysis showing that America is *galut*, Schen then questioned her refusal to negate *galut*. "Does she really believe what she wrote?" he asked increduously. She condemned American Jewry "to a kind of spiritual purgatory of indefinite duration without even the hope of ultimately ending that unhappy state." If denying that America is *galut* is tantamount to saying American Jews have been redeemed—obviously an untruth—one cannot avoid the issue merely by saying America is *galut* and leaving redemption for the indefinite future. Hence, Schen concludes, Weiss-Rosmarin, like other Zionist intellectuals in the Diaspora, lacks the moral courage of her own convictions.[62]

Although Weiss-Rosmarin did not reply, feeling that her initial essay was enough of an answer, Schen's attack continued to rankle. Two years later, as the organized American Jewish community was preparing for the celebration of the three hundredth anniversary of Jewish settlement in America, she published a long essay acknowledging Schen and retracting her earlier argument. Weiss-Rosmarin defiantly titled it "America Is Not Babylonia!" After briefly surveying the history and cultural productions of American Jews—a history that demonstrated how America consumed its Jews—Weiss-Rosmarin comes to the central falsity of the comparison of American Jewry with Babylonian or any other creative Diaspora Jewry. "Everywhere the Jews lived *in* the respective country of their *exile*, but were not *of* it," she explained. By contrast, "American Jews are proud of being fully and unconditionally part *of* America." Even theories of cultural pluralism assume that a group preserves " 'another language,' *in addition* to English, and 'another culture,' *in addition* to our common and shared American culture . . ." Such a formulation yields to the seductiveness of America. As long as American Jews have "neither an understanding nor sympathy for the frame of mind of the *mipney hukkos hagoyim* legislation," that sets Jews apart just to be different, the chances for creative Jewish survival in the United States are "nil." The problem, Weiss-Rosmarin argued, was that Jews love America, with all their heart and soul.

Thus the true comparison to be drawn was with Alexandrian Jewry and German Jewry. Both groups relinquished their own language, as American Jews did. Both read the Bible in translation—if they read it at all. Both produced scholarship that argued for the congruence of Judaism with Hellenism and Germanism, respectively, just as American Jews saw a kinship between Hebraic values and American democracy. Here was the crux of the problem:

American Zionists insist that "America is not Galuth"—and they are right. We do not know what tomorrow will bring, but certainly today America is home, genuine and beloved home, of close to six million Jews. They are *of* America as all Americans and resent, and justly so, any intimation that they are not like all Americans. For they are— they really are Americans, even in their unconcern about the future, *their* future in America.

The negation of the *galut* sounds nonsensical to American Jews, Weiss-Rosmarin now recognized, because their own living reality refutes it. American Jews "are convinced that they shall succeed in keeping America as their home, for ever and ever." And they even think that they will write another Babylonian Talmud. Unfortunately, the evidence of Jewish history refutes their optimism. At most, American Jewry will write another Alexandrian and German chapter of Jewish history. Because American Jewry is American, "through and through," it will never produce another Talmud. "Babylonian Jewry was never Babylonian. This is the difference— and this difference will determine the future of American Jewry," she concludes.[63]

Ironically, in reaching her pessimistic assessment of the future of American Jewry, Weiss-Rosmarin denied the alienation and sense of being a stranger—marks of a *galut* existence—that she previously saw in American Jews. Instead, their very feeling of at-homeness foretold their dismal destiny. Yet Weiss-Rosmarin did not abandon American Jews. She remained that all too common anomaly: an American Zionist. In her case, her commitment to traditional Judaism and her insistence on seeing Zionism as the affirmation of Judaism—the solution to the problem of Judaism as much, if not more, than the solution to the problem of the Jews— mitigated the irony.

Weiss-Rosmarin never tired of quoting Solomon Schechter's phrase about "falling in love with everything Jewish."[64] To fall in love, as she had done and as she tried to inspire others to do, one didn't need to live in Israel. It helped, of course, but the passion of Judaism could touch Jewish souls even in the Diaspora. This passionate love affair with everything Jewish set Weiss-Rosmarin apart from those alienated, nominally Jewish, New York Intellectuals. It determined her intellectual agenda as much as the intricacies of

left-wing politics shaped their concerns. It guided the editorial policies of the *Jewish Spectator* and gradually changed the readership
of the magazine. By the early 1950s, Weiss-Rosmarin counted close
to one thousand rabbis among the *Spectator*'s subscribers, a figure
that pleased her. No longer speaking just to women in New York
City, the *Spectator* addressed the male, Jewishly committed elite.
And Weiss-Rosmarin, through her lectures and her magazine, assumed a singular place within that elite. In the process she helped
to expand the boundaries of the world of the "other" New York
Jewish Intellectuals.

Notes

I would like to thank Seth Kemil for his valuable research assistance.
1. Interview with Robert Bleiweiss, 5 May 1991.
2. In 1940, for example, an average of 8 to 12 pages out of 50—15 to 25
   percent—were devoted to advertisements.
3. A sample of her lecture schedule, for the first two weeks of December
   1946, ran:
   Dec. 1– Boston, Yeshiva Lubavitz,
   　　　 2–New York City, West Side Institutional Synagogue,
   　　　 3–Brooklyn, Women's Division, American Jewish Congress,
   　　　 4–Springfield, Mass., Sisterhood dinner,
   　　　 6–Brooklyn, Bensonhurst Jewish Community House,
   　　　 8–Richmond, Virginia, Jewish Book Month,
   　　　 10–Perth Amboy, N.J., Congregation Shaarey Tefilah,
   　　　 11–Boston, Hadassah,
   　　　 12–Cincinnati, Forum of the Friends of Hebrew Culture,
   　　　 13–Cincinnati, Avondale Synagogue,
   　　　 14–Cincinnati, an Oneg Shabat at Avondale Synagogue,
   　　　 15–Birmingham, Alabama, Jewish Book Month communal event.
   And this was before extensive airplane travel! *Jewish Spectator*, 12
   (December 1946): 6. Hereafter cited as *JS*.
4. Interview with Robert Bleiweiss, 5 May 1991.
5. There is no good biography of Trude Weiss-Rosmarin. The brief entry in
   the *Universal Jewish Encyclopedia* contains some information. More
   valuable are the essays published in *JS*, 54 (Fall 1989): 6–18.
6. Estelle Gilson, "Trude's a Holy Terror," *JS*, 54 (Fall 1989): 7. This profile
   originally appeared in *Present Tense* in 1978.
7. George L. Mosse, *German Jews beyond Judaism* (Bloomington: Indiana
   University Press, 1985), 3–8.

8. This interview in *Moment* of Trude Weiss-Rosmarin and Marie Syrkin contains valuable reminiscences. *Moment* (September 1983): 37–44; quote on 38.
9. Shulamit Magnus, "A Decade of Writing on Modern German Jewry," MS, 11–12. In 1922 Nobel preached that Judaism and Goethe had much in common, namely, "a serene world view and the belief that every religion was an artistic creation." Mosse, 46. Weiss-Rosmarin later decisively rejected such a linkage of Judaism and *Bildung*. See her essay on Goethe in *JS*, 14 (August 1949).
10. *Moment*, 38.
11. Ibid., 38; Gilson, 7.
12. *Moment*, 40; Gilson, 7.
13. The recollection described by Elliot B. Gertel, "My Friend, Trude Weiss-Rosmarin," *JS*, 54 (September 1989): 13.
14. *Moment*, 40; Gilson, 7–8.
15. Gilson, 7.
16. Ibid., 8.
17. Frederick Rudolph, *The American College and University: A History* (New York: Vintage, 1962), 465–66.
18. Gilson, 8.
19. "Alertness credit" was given by the New York City Board of Education to public school teachers for certified courses taken. Accumulation of enough "alertness credit" resulted in a salary increment. The School of the Jewish Woman received a charter from the State Board of Education in 1936. *JS*, 1 (May 1936): 27.
20. *Moment*, 39.
21. Trude Weiss-Rosmarin, *Jewish Women and Jewish Culture* (New York: School of the Jewish Woman, n.d., 1936?). The following paragraphs are drawn from this pamphlet.
22. The finances of the school were covered in part by tuition, $2.00 per course plus $1.00 registration fee, and by subsidies of $100 each paid by the cooperating organizations, which included Hadassah, Ivriah, the Women's League of United Synagogue, and the New York Section of the Council of Jewish Women. Hadassah National Board, Minutes, 8 January 1936; Archives of Hadassah.
23. Weiss-Rosmarin, *Jewish Women and Jewish Culture*.
24. *JS*, 2 (January 1937): back cover.
25. *JS*, 1 (January 1936): back page.
26. This is the first issue of *JS*. *News from the School of the Jewish Woman*, 1 (November–December 1935).
27. *JS*, 1 (April 1936): back page.
28. *JS*, 1 (April 1936): back page.
29. "Columbia & Yale vs. Thomas Jefferson," editorial, *JS*, 1 (April 1936): 1.
30. *JS*, 4 (February 1939): 7; the "Junior Library" ran from 26 to 28.

31. In April 1939 *JS* invited its readers to rank its features in order of preference. These were listed for ranking: "Short Stories, The Latest Jewish News, Poems, Editorials, The Novel of the Month [a condensation], This Is a Good One, Test Your I.Q., Books in Brief, Articles on World Events, Articles on Jewish History, Articles on Jewish Customs and Ceremonies, Juniors' Library, Articles on Judaism and Philosophy, Readers' Correspondence, Hebrew Wisdom, Sports, Serials, Articles on Outstanding Personalities." *JS*, 4 (April 1939): 4.
32. Trude Weiss-Rosmarin, "Taking Stock of the Anglo-Jewish Press," *JS*, 2 (July 1937): 12–13.
33. For example, the *Jewish Frontier* in 1934 and the *Reconstructionist* in 1936, followed several years later by *Contemporary Jewish Record*, the predecessor to *Commentary*.
34. This observation is based on the published letters to the editor. A majority were women. In addition, *JS* occasionally promoted and announced bulk subscriptions to women's groups, especially Hadassah. See a particularly charming letter from Else Hirschmann, age 11, who was a "Star saleslady" among the "ladies who sit and walk with their babies on Riverside Drive . . ." *JS*, 2 (April 1937): 47.
35. *JS* published close to three hundred authors during its first four years, a suggestion of its diversity. See index in *JS*, 4 (October 1939): 44–46.
36. Weiss-Rosmarin appears on the masthead in May 1939.
37. Hadassah National Board, Minutes, 8 January 1936; Archives of Hadassah.
38. Gilson, 8.
39. *Moment*, 39.
40. See advertisement in *JS*, 1 (October 1936): back page.
41. "Our Ninth Year," editorial, *JS*, 9 (November 1943): 6, 27. Emphases in the original.
42. Trude Weiss-Rosmarin, "Some Observations on Jewish Survival: Israel is the Future of Mankind—This is the Secret of Its Survival," *JS*, 6 (January 1941): 7–9; quotes on 7.
43. See the editorial pages, Topics on the Agenda, *JS*, 9 (January, February, March, April 1943).
44. "The Curse of Complacency," editorial, *JS*, 8 (April 1943): 4–5.
45. Weiss-Rosmarin developed this theme in numerous essays on Judaism. For example, see the series, "Jews Are Liberals," running from May 1939 through August 1939, or "The 'Four Freedoms' in Judaism," beginning in April 1942 and running through August 1942 in *JS*.
46. "The Voice of Our Brothers' Blood," editorial, *JS*, 9 (July 1944): 6.
47. "The New Year and the Tasks Ahead," editorial, *JS*, 9 (September 1944): 4.
48. "Buchenwald and Treblinka," editorial, *JS*, 10 (May 1945): 5–6.
49. Trude Weiss-Rosmarin, "A Strategy for American Jewish Survival," *JS*, 10 (May 1945): 23.

50. "How Many DP Jews?," editorial, *JS*, 12 (January 1947): 5.
51. "Realpolitik," editorial, *JS*, 12 (January 1947): 5.
52. "Zionist Education," editorial, *JS*, 12 (January 1947): 6.
53. See also her earlier editorial rejecting partition, "The Twenty-Second Zionist Congress," *JS*, 12 (December 1946): 4–5. "We shall never be partners to an agreement involving the renunciation of even one foot of sacred Eretz Israel earth," she wrote.
54. "On the Threshold of the Jewish State," editorial, *JS*, 13 (November 1947): 4.
55. "Periphery and Center: We and the Jewish State," *JS*, 13 (January 1948): 8–9.
56. Trude Weiss-Rosmarin, "Periphery and Center: We and the Jewish State," *JS*, 13 (January 1948): 8–9, 29.
57. Trude Weiss-Rosmarin, "Periphery and Center: We and the Jewish State," *JS*, 13 (February 1948): 25.
58. "On the Threshold of the Jewish State," editorial, *JS*, 13 (November 1947): 5.
59. Trude Weiss-Rosmarin, "Is America 'Galuth'?," *JS*, 16 (January 1951): 7. Emphasis in the original.
60. Ibid., 7–11. Emphasis in the original.
61. This was not that unusual for Weiss-Rosmarin. She often gave space in the magazine to responses to her editorials which she felt deserved a hearing (e.g., representatives of Orthodox day schools who wanted to answer her call for cooperation).
62. "A 'Galuth Negator' Has the Floor," editorial, *JS*, 16 (June 1951): 5–7.
63. Trude Weiss-Rosmarin, "America Is Not Babylonia!" *JS*, 18 (March 1953); the essay was reprinted by The Institute for Jewish Youth Leaders from Abroad (Machon Le'Madrichei Hutz La'Aretz), 1–8. Emphases in the original.
64. Trude Weiss-Rosmarin, "Falling in Love with Everything Jewish," *JS*, 7 (October 1942): 6–8.

PART TWO

Men of Letters

CHAPTER 5

Morris Raphael Cohen

Milton R. Konvitz

Morris Raphael Cohen and Horace M. Kallen were, I submit, the two most intensely Jewish thinkers, not only of their time, but in the entire sweep of American history. One difference between them is that Kallen began his Jewish activity early in life and early in the twentieth century, while Cohen, two years his senior, began his Jewish activity in the early 1930s. Each of them was a professor of philosophy in a non-Jewish institution of higher learning at a time when very few Jews had appointments on college or university faculties, and each identified himself with Jewish interests and causes. The American Jewish community recognized in each of them great symbolic value as Jewish intellectuals who had won recognition as equals among American thinkers.[1] Each was a non-conventional, non-traditional philosopher, for, instead of concentrating on metaphysics and epistemology, they devoted their genius to the contributions that critical thinking can make to individual and social problems in law, science, politics, ethics, international relations, religion, ethnicity, and other matters that tangibly affect the lives, sufferings, and hopes of people and nations.

Cohen was born on July 25, 1880, in Minsk, chief city of Belorussia. His father made a poor living as a presser. His parents were Orthodox, observant Jews, after they settled in New York, as they had been in Russia. In 1935 Cohen wrote about his father:

In all I knew of my father he conformed to the old conception of a saint. He was kindly, sympathetic, just in all his dealings, and never harming anyone, pained at the presence of any injustice or inequities, and always hoping for the triumph of good causes.[2]

Of his mother, Cohen wrote that she was the faithful and devoted companion of her husband for sixty-seven years, that she had a remarkable and vigorous intelligence, and that all the dreams of his life, all the long communings with himself, were directly or indirectly connected with her and were endowed with some of her tenacious vitality.[3]

It was his maternal grandfather, however, who most profoundly influenced his early life. Between the ages of seven and ten Cohen lived with him in the city of Nesvizh in Belorussia, where Isaac Elhanan (Spektor) was rabbi and where Rabbi Josef Baer Soloveitchik was born, as was also Solomon Maimon, a city with a yeshivah, a Hebrew school, a kindergarten, a Yiddish school, and a Zionist society.[4] His grandfather was a tailor with a modest Jewish education. During those three years Cohen attended a *heder* six days a week, generally from eight o'clock in the morning until after six, and yet, he remarked, his main education came from his grandfather. It was from his lips that he first heard the name Aristotle, and the name Maimonides (abbr. Rambam), and of Napoleon's campaign in Russia. It was in his grandfather's home that Cohen found a copy of a Hebrew version of Josephus, which he "devoured" and which gave him a taste for history that he never lost. Without the three years with his grandfather, Cohen wrote, "I could not have acquired the moral and intellectual interests which have been controlling in the course of my subsequent life." Cohen, years later, remarked that his grandfather's ascetic life had influenced his temperament "even more than my philosophy." On the day in 1890 when he was to take the train back to his parents in Minsk, Cohen wrote many years later,

I was awakened by my grandfather kissing me good-bye. I was overcome with keen anguish that never, never would I see him again. The tears rolled down my cheeks before I knew it. Compared to my mother, he had been a hard taskmaster. But he had been the center of my life during three formative years of young boyhood and I realized even then, as I have more fully since, that he had laid the foundation not only of my intellectual development, but of that inner superiority to worldly fortune which is the essence of genuine nobility, spirituality, or as I prefer to call it now, the truly philosophic life.

It was walks and talks with his grandfather in Nesvizh that first stimulated Cohen's imagination about the world and history, that "gave a special zest to reflections on law and ethics which form the substance of Orthodox Hebrew education. His talks to me about Maimonides and the Book of Cusari [by Judah Halevi] stimulated an interest in the philosophy of religion that has never waned."[5]

He returned to his parents' home in Minsk, where he remained for the following two years. In the Hebrew schools that he attended, in Minsk and in Nesvizh, he studied Bible with Rashi's commentary, and Talmud, especially the Tractates Baba Kama and Gittin. His study at the *heder* was supplemented by study with a tutor engaged by his mother. Years later he wrote that "the Talmud had been my first teacher."[6]

In 1892 his family emigrated to the United States. His father had made the crossing of the Atlantic alone several times before in efforts to save enough money to take his family with him. The first time his father came to New York he arrived with a bundle containing his tallit, tephillin (prayer shawl and phylacteries), some underwear, with eighty-five cents in his pocket, and he had no one awaiting him—no relative, no friend.[7] Years later Morris Cohen wrote of his parents, immigrants in a strange land, as persons "who were of that heroic generation that tore up their roots in their old homeland, and unaided and with no equipment other than their indomitable faith and courage, built new homes in this land and raised up children who have made invaluable contributions to the life of this country . . ."[8]

The family moved into a three-room apartment on the corner of Broome and Norfolk Streets on the Lower East Side of Manhattan. Life was difficult. The father worked as a presser when employment was available, and Morris Cohen tried to help out with after-school jobs selling newspapers or working at a soda fountain adjacent to a pool room operated by his brother. He was always eager, he wrote, "to lighten the burdens of my parents."[9] He once wrote that he would have liked to have lived over again the first fourteen years of his life; that in his fourteenth year he had "gained consciousness." He read avidly; in 1897 he made a list of seventy-three cloth-bound and seventy-seven paperback books that he had read. While still in his teens he read extensively in history, including Gibbon, Mommsen, Green's *History of the English People*, Milman's *Notes on Roman History*, Freeman's *Ten Great Religions*, Marcus Aurelius, Ibsen, *Imitation of Christ*; the textbook that influenced him most, he wrote, was Meyer's *General History*, but it was Gibbon that made a more enduring impression on his thinking than any of the books he read in his courses.[10] During that seedtime he thought that he would like to become a teacher or a journalist.[11]

In September 1895 he entered City College, from which he was graduated with a B.S. degree in 1900. He took courses in French and German, history, English, zoology, logic, and mathematics. He was especially impressed with the course in French literature, with the poetry of Racine and Corneille, with Molière, Voltaire, and Victor Hugo; he read John Stuart Mill's *Logic*, and books by Comte, Herbert Spencer, and George Herbert Palmer. He had not abandoned his interest in Jewish history and religion—he read Graetz's *History of the Jews*, and books on the higher criticism of the Bible. He read histories of Egypt and of Assyria and Babylonia. He was especially interested in pre-Socratic philosophy, and read Plato's *Parmenides* and Aristotle's *Metaphysics*, as well as Hegel's *Encyklopädie*.[12]

During his years as an upper-classman at CCNY, however, Cohen's chief intellectual interests were centered at the Educational Alliance on the Lower East Side more than at his college. In 1889 a number of Jewish cultural agencies amalgamated and formed the Hebrew Institute. Four years later the name was changed to Educational Alliance, of which Isidore Straus was president. Its Aguilar Free Library and reading room were stacked with Yiddish, Hebrew, English, and Russian books and periodicals. The lectures offered there by Sholom Aleichem, Zvi Hirsch Masliansky, and other well-known literary and religious speakers attracted as many as thirty-seven thousand persons a week. There were English language classes, naturalization courses, preschool classes, literary and civic clubs, music and drama classes, art exhibits and a children's orchestra. There was also a synagogue and a religious school.[13]

Cohen frequented the Aguilar Free Library as soon as he learned to read English. But when he was eighteen he discovered at the Educational Alliance a person who was to have a decisive influence on his life and thought, Thomas Davidson.

Davidson, identified as a philosopher and wandering scholar, was born in Scotland in 1840. In 1866 he moved to Canada and taught school in Toronto; then he went to Saint Louis, wandered off to Boston, and at last reached New York and attached himself to the Educational Alliance. In a book about him published seven years after his death, he is described as follows:

> His learning was encyclopedic, and his culture almost universal. A great linguist, he had a knowledge of philosophy in all its branches that was amazing . . . but he was so humble and altruistic that very few of his friends and acquaintances knew what treasures were stored within his brain and heart. More than any of the nineteenth century thinkers known to fame, he lived and toiled for other people, and from first to last had no thought of himself.

As we shall see, Cohen readily agreed with this estimate of the man. Davidson lived modestly and made his meager living by private teaching, tutoring, lecturing, and writing. He spent more than half of each year in leisurely study and frequent long visits in Europe. In London, he established the Fellowship of the New Life, of which the Fabian Society was an offshoot.[14]

In the fall of 1898 Davidson conducted a class at the Educational Alliance on Saturday evenings. With some misgivings and hesitation, Cohen started to attend these lectures and found them to be, to his amazement, interesting. After one of the sessions Davidson met Cohen and said to him: "You have a fine mind. You ought to cultivate it." "It was," Cohen later wrote, "years since anyone had paid me such a compliment." It was not long before Cohen thought of Davidson as his beloved teacher, and the teacher thought of Cohen as his son whom he would like to have adopted. In his autobiography, Cohen wrote:

> To me, as a youth of nineteen, Davidson had been a father, a guide into fields where he thought my highest possibilities lay, and an

inspirer of efforts which became my life's passion. . . . None of us who were touched by his spirit can ever forget his heroic devotion to the pursuit and expression of truth as he saw it "in scorn of consequences" or his magnificent disdain for worldly goods whenever he might serve the spiritual needs of those with whom he came into contact. None of us can ever forget the teacher who showed us that there are values of character which remain when all else decays and that theirs is the enduring victory.[15]

It was Davidson who made Cohen study Latin, and who directed him to reading Hume's *Treatise on Human Nature*, and Kant's *Critique of Pure Reason*. Is it any wonder that when Cohen was sixty-three years old he referred to Davidson as one who had been "a light of my life and of my intellectual development"?[16] Davidson also introduced Cohen to Tennyson, Dante, and Goethe, in each of whom Cohen maintained an interest to the end of his life.

In 1889 Davidson bought a farm near Keene in the Adirondacks, where he spent eight months of the year (the other four months December–March he was in New York at the Educational Alliance). He called his place Glenmore, and in the summers of 1889 and 1900 he conducted a school of philosophy there that attracted William James, John Dewey, Felix Adler, Stephen S. Wise, W. T. Harris (a leading American Hegelian philosopher), and other scholars and thinkers. Davidson invited Cohen to come as his guest, and there Cohen met and established friendships with persons who were significant for his intellectual life. In the fall of 1900 Davidson was operated on for cancer and died at the age of sixty. Nine years after Davidson's death, Cohen wrote: "Davidson got hold of me when my soul was parched and all its zest for life gone. Through his personal friendship he opened the wells of life within me . . . the remembrance of my personal relation with him is enough to bear me up for a lifetime."[17] The extent and depth of Davidson's significance for Cohen may in part be measured by the fact that Cohen made annual pilgrimages to Davidson's grave at Glenmore; the last such visit was in August 1941, when Cohen was sixty-one.[18]

One additional important fact with respect to the Davidson-Cohen relationship needs to be mentioned. Immediately after Davidson's death, Cohen and other young students who had been attached to him decided that it was imperative that the work that

Davidson had started at the Educational Alliance be continued. They therefore established the Breadwinners' College. There were to be no degrees, no credits, no teachers' salaries, but adult education offered to all takers. (No school with such an objective was in existence in New York at the time; the New School for Social Research was opened in 1919.) Cohen was for some years principal or chairman of the executive committee. There were classes in Latin, French, German, algebra, ancient history, modern history, and other high school-level courses, as well as college-type courses such as those on the Book of Job, on philosophy, and on the philosophy of history. In addition the college (also called the Davidson School) organized clubs, Sunday outings, and a summer camp for weekends and holidays. The attractiveness of the school is indicated by the fact that in 1902–3 there were 783 students in the classes, and that altogether in that year close to 1,400 persons benefited from its program. The Breadwinners' College continued for eighteen years, until 1918, its program in a way taken up by the New School for Social Research, with which Cohen became identified as the school's first lecturer and where he taught a weekly course for many years.[19] Among its lecturers and teachers were, besides Cohen, leading scholars and thinkers including Charles M. Bakewell, W. T. Harris, John Dewey, Edwin R. A. Seligman, and William Allan Neilson.[20]

It was Thomas Davidson who inspired Cohen to devote days and years to the Breadwinners' College. In May 1900 Davidson wrote to his students in New York:

If you found a Breadwinners' College now, and make it a success, you may live to see a copy of it in every city ward and in every country village. . . . A little knot of earnest Jews has turned the world upside down before now. Why may not the same thing—nay, a far better thing—happen in your day, and among you? Have you forgotten the old promise made to Abraham,—"In thee and in thy seed shall all the families of the earth be blessed"? You can bring the promise to fulfillment if you will. A little heroism, a little self-sacrifice, and the thing is done.[21]

William James had wanted Harvard to appoint Davidson a professor of philosophy—"a kind of Socrates, a devotee of truth and lover of youth, . . . a contagious example of how lightly and humanly a burden of learning might be borne . . . his influence among students would be priceless. . . . I think that in this case, . . . Harvard University lost a great opportunity." [22] Harvard's loss, however, was Cohen's gain, and a gain for workers and society; for the college, as Cohen wrote, helped "to transform [Jewish] shirtmakers into teachers, physicians, biologists, . . . engineers . . . heads of settlements." [23] And it helped to move Morris Cohen into intellectual and spiritual adulthood, and into making him the great teacher and great Jew that he was.

After receiving his B.S. degree from City College in 1900, for two years, 1902–4, Cohen was a graduate student in philosophy at Columbia. At the same time he taught mathematics at Townsend Harris Hall, City College's preparatory high school. In 1904 Felix Adler (who had founded the Ethical Culture movement in 1876) arranged for Cohen to go to Harvard on a $750 fellowship. He studied at Harvard for two years and received a Ph.D. in 1906. His dissertation was on Kant's theory of happiness. In his second year at Harvard his roommate was Felix Frankfurter, who graduated from City College in 1902. During that year Cohen was in poor health, and Frankfurter, who was a law student, looked after him. They became lifelong close friends. At Harvard Cohen studied under William James and Josiah Royce. He later noted that James was his best friend (a photograph of James was on a wall in the Cohen apartment, and he named his younger son for James), and that Royce was his best teacher, one after whom he wanted to model himself. During his second year, from his close relationship with Frankfurter, Cohen developed an interest in law and legal philosophy that remained with him all his life. Royce frequently mentioned Charles S. Peirce, and Peirce, too, became a lifelong interest of Cohen's, eventually leading to Cohen's pioneering work on behalf of Peirce in editing *Chance, Love, and Logic: Essays of C. S. Peirce* in 1923. While at Harvard, Cohen organized a branch of the Ethical Culture movement.

He left Harvard with letters of recommendation from William James, Royce, George Herbert Palmer, and Ralph Barton Perry. He also had such letters from Felix Adler and William T. Harris. No one could have started out to look for a first position as a teacher of philosophy with better recommendations. Yet he found no open door, no welcome. In those early years of the twentieth century, philosophy and religion were closely tied at almost all colleges and universities, and religion meant, of course, Christianity. Cohen went to Townsend Harris Hall to teach mathematics. He was, naturally, unhappy, frustrated, and despondent. Fortunately, in June 1906 he married Mary Ryshpan, who sustained his spirits (as she did until her death in 1942, predeceasing him by five years). At last, in 1912, after a wait of six years, Cohen was appointed assistant professor of philosophy at City College. Before his appointment Cohen published articles and reviews in leading philosophical journals and conducted classes at the Davidson School.

It was as a great teacher at CCNY that Cohen won fame among philosophers and intellectuals. In 1921 he was promoted to full professor. Until his retirement in 1938, after twenty-six years of teaching philosophy, he taught many young men who themselves became professors of philosophy when restrictions on the appointment of Jews became less severe. These former students of Cohen constituted a veritable galaxy of American philosophers; they included Ernest Nagel, Sidney Hook, Lewis S. Feuer, Joseph T. Shipley, Paul Weiss, Joseph Ratner, Daniel J. Bronstein, Philip P. Wiener, Herbert Schneider, Morton White, Milton Munitz, Leo Abraham, and others; Cohen estimated that at CCNY he taught a total of some fifteen thousand students.

Cohen's method of teaching, in his day, was not of the conventional sort. He was not tied down to a textbook and student recitations, nor did he rely on lectures, but used the Socratic method of questioning the students to elicit a latent idea, directed toward the establishment of a proposition. In his autobiography Cohen explained that he resorted to the Socratic method because when he started to teach philosophy he had found himself devoid of the gift of verbal fluency. As the years passed, perhaps it was in the early 1930s, Cohen felt that his method of teaching had lost some of its sparkle, due to his declining physical energy and to the growing size of his classes, as well as the distraction of outside activities (especially his involvement with Jewish activities); he was questioning less and resorting more to lecturing. He was very critical of

his own lecturing, for he feared that "lecturing would unconsciously beget an easy omniscience and satisfaction with apparent
or rhetorical truths. No man, no matter how critical, can stand up
before a class and refrain from saying more than he knows." [24]

Cohen was well aware that his method of teaching by raising
questions and demolishing answers had created the widely held
opinion that he was merely negative, destructive. He readily
pleaded guilty to the charge. When a student ventured to complain
that Cohen was merely critical, he responded: "You have heard the
story of how Hercules cleaned the Augean stables. He took all the
dirt and manure out and left them clean. You ask me, 'What did he
leave in their stead?' I answer, 'Isn't it enough to have cleaned the
stables?' " [25] Cohen wrote that he had learned from Davidson not to
succumb to the natural urge to remake God and the universe in
one's own image. Davidson, he noted, had made it a rule of his life
to quarrel with those who agreed with him, and to have as his
favorite students those who most radically differed from him. "Why
should I assume," Cohen wrote,

> that my own convictions represented the summit of wisdom in philos-
> ophy or anything else? It seemed to me a more important service in
> the cause of liberal civilization to develop a spirit of genuine regard
> for the weight of evidence and a power to discriminate between
> responsible and irresponsible sources of information, to inculcate the
> habit of admitting ignorance when we do not know, and to nourish
> the critical spirit of inquiry which is inseparable from the love of
> truth that makes men free. [26]

Cohen had also acquired a reputation for being acerbic in class
as he commented on what students said. At the time of his retirement in 1938 the magazine *Time* referred to Cohen as "a modern
Socrates with an acid tongue." [27] The testimony of Cohen's former
student, Professor Richard B. Morris, of Columbia University, well-
known American historian, was, however, that "perhaps two percent of Cohen's students were rankled by his acerbity. For most of
us, to be corrected by Socrates seemed neither a surprise nor a
disgrace. He cracked down on the fakers. But to the responsive
students he was encouraging and generous." [28]

In October 1927, over a thousand persons gathered at the Hotel As-tor to honor Professor Cohen by marking his twenty-five years of teaching at City College (including his years at the college's preparatory school). Professor Felix Frankfurter was toastmaster. Among the speakers were Professor Nathan R. Margold, of Harvard Law School, a former student; Dean Frederick J. E. Woodbridge, under whom Cohen had studied philosophy at Columbia; Dr. Judah L. Magnes, president of Hebrew University (which had opened in 1925); Judge Julian W. Mack; Bertrand Russell; Frederick B. Robinson, president of City College; and John Dewey. There were letters from Justice Holmes, Dean Roscoe Pound, Benjamin N. Cardozo (then chief judge of the Court of Appeals of New York), and others.[29]

Eight years later, at the age of fifty-seven, Cohen retired, for reasons of health and because he wanted more time for writing, and more time for the Jewish activities that he had started in the early 1930s.

When Cohen was twelve years old, he overheard a conversation between his father and an acquaintance. The latter challenged Abraham Cohen to prove that there is a personal God. To this challenge Mr. Cohen could only reply: "I am a believer." "This," Cohen later wrote, "did not satisfy my own mind. After some reflection I concluded that in all my studies no such evidence was available. After that I saw no reason for prayer or the specifically Jewish religious observances."[30] However, since he lived with his parents in their home, he continued to comply with religious requirements until he was nineteen years old.

Cohen was an agnostic, or what used to be called, especially in England, a rationalist. He would not, however, think of himself as an atheist. "Those who called themselves atheists," he wrote,

> seemed to be singularly blind, as a rule, to the limitations of our knowledge and to the infinite possibilities beyond us. . . . Those of my circle who rejected religion *in toto* seemed to me to be casting away the ideals that had sustained our people through so many generations. . . . In this some of us lost sight of the larger view that Thomas Davidson had taught, that we have no right to break away from the past until we have appropriated all its experience and wisdom, and that reverence for the past may go hand in hand with loyalty to the future, "to the Kingdom which doth not yet appear."[31]

Cohen lived up to the mandate to appropriate from the past all its experience and wisdom. He studied the Bible and other Jewish classics all his life. While a graduate student at Harvard, he studied with Professor George Foot Moore, an authority on comparative religion and author of the highly regarded, magisterial three-volume work *Judaism in the First Centuries of the Christian Era* (1927). And Cohen accepted for himself Santayana's definition of piety as "reverence for the sources of one's being."[32] He wrote that it is to be regretted that most Jews had "lost contact with the traditional substance of Jewish education." It is important, he wrote,

> for a Jew living in a predominantly non-Jewish world to understand the actual history of his own people. . . . In other words, to lead a dignified, self-respecting life, a Jew must know the history of his people, not merely in the Biblical period, . . . but also in the Talmudic and more recent historic eras.[33]

The Hebrew Scriptures, he wrote, "never ceased to grip me," and when he was depressed and had little energy for study or writing, he found the Bible and biblical criticism "most absorbing reading."[34]

Although firmly an agnostic, Cohen wrote that his studies of the great religions had led him to see that ritual is a primary fact in human experience. For himself, he wrote,

> the ancient ceremonies that celebrate the coming and going of life, the wedding ceremony, the *b'rith*, and the funeral service, give an expression to the continuity of the spiritual tradition that is more eloquent than any phrases of my own creation. The ritual may be diluted by English and by modernisms, but the Hebraic God is still a potent symbol of the continuous life of which we individuals are waves.
>
> Like vivid illustrations in the book of my life are the prayers of my parents, . . . and the celebration of the continuity of generations in the Passover services in the home of my parents and in the homes of my children. And though I have never gone back to theologic supernaturalism, I have come to appreciate more than I once did the symbolism in which is celebrated the human need of trusting to the larger vision, according to which calamities come and go but the continuity of life and faith in its better possibilities survive.[35]

In 1928–29 Cohen undertook the chairmanship of a project called the Talmudic Library. Together with Professor Chaim Tchernowitz (Rav Za'ir), of the Jewish Institute of Religion (later joined to Hebrew Union College), he had a plan to prepare and publish an encyclopedia that would make the Talmud intelligible to general readers, but the time was apparently not ripe for this venture. It attracted the support of Professors Moore, John Dewey, Roscoe Pound, and other leading non-Jewish scholars, but not enough enthusiasm among Jewish scholars. The idea is currently being implemented by the Israeli *Encyclopedia Talmudica* and by the work of Adin Steinsaltz.

The breadth and depth of Cohen's knowledge of Jewish history and philosophy can easily be seen in his profoundly scholarly essay on "Philosophies of Jewish History,"[36] published in 1939. The essay shows his knowledge of practically all the great masters of Jewish life and thought: Philo, Rashi, Maimonides, Joseph Karo, Graetz, Dubnow, Zinberg, Elijah Gaon of Vilna, Hermann Cohen, Claude Montefiore, Nachman Krochmal, Leopold Zunz, Abraham Geiger, Zacharias Frankel, Ahad Ha' Am, and many others—not to mention the Bible, the Talmud, and the Apocrypha. It is an essay with encyclopedic sweep and yet it has depth and a personal touch and spirit. Only a master scholar could have written the essay.

As a boy living in Minsk, Cohen became an avid reader of Yiddish novels, and his fondness for Yiddish was sustained throughout his life. He read a Yiddish newspaper. "I owe a good deal of my education," he wrote, "to the Yiddish press. It taught me to look at world news from a cosmopolitan instead of a local or provincial point of view, and it taught me to interpret politics realistically, instead of being misled by empty phrases."[37] The Yiddish press, he noted, prepared millions of Jews to take a worthy part in American civilization and promoted the self-respect to which they were entitled because of their character and history. Furthermore, he gave credit to the Yiddish press—perhaps because it had no army of reporters to dig up sensational news—for emphasizing things of permanent, rather than ephemeral, interest. "It tried to give its readers something of enduring and substantial value."[38]

On the question of Zionism, however, Cohen listened to a differ-

ent drumbeat. He was not a Zionist. Just as he opposed assimila-
tionism, so, too, he opposed the separatism that Zionism implied.
While he greatly admired the *halutzim* who reclaimed the soil of
Eretz Israel, opposed the restrictions on Jewish immigration and
land ownership in Palestine imposed by the British government,
and supported the establishment and development of the Hebrew
University, he felt repulsed by the idea that the establishment of a
Jewish state would necessarily mean discrimination against non-
Jews. In any case, he felt that Zionism was a distraction of Ameri-
can Jews from the problems they faced at home.

But while Cohen was not a Zionist, he was not an anti-Zionist.
Zionism, he wrote in 1945, "has served a high purpose," it has
"rendered the supreme service of increasing men's self-respect . . ."[39]

Cohen fitted the Jews and his own awareness of himself as a Jew
into his philosophy of pluralism and the desirability of cultural
diversity—a philosophy that he shared with Horace M. Kallen. He
rejected the notion of nationalism that pervaded Europe, a narrow
nationalism that contrasted with American federalism and the idea
represented by the motto *E pluribus unum.* America has been settled by many different peoples, and each has made its contribution
to a common civilization. Why, then, he asked,

> should not the Jews contribute their specific gifts? The idea that all
> immigrants should wipe out their past and become simple immit-
> ations of the dominant type is neither possible nor desirable. . . .
> All great civilizations have resulted from the contributions of many
> peoples, and a richer American culture can come only if the Jews,
> like other elements, are given a chance to develop under favorable
> conditions their peculiar genius.[40]

In another context he wrote: "Why should not the Jews contribute
their specific gifts in the way of enthusiasm for the arts, for social
idealism, as well as their peculiar love of intellectual life for its
own sake?"[41]

In the spring of 1933, when Cohen was fifty-two years old, he began
to think of retiring from teaching. In 1931, with the help of his son
Felix, Cohen's *Reason and Nature,* and in 1933 his *Law and the*

Social Order, had been published, and soon there was to be published *An Introduction to Logic and Scientific Method* (1934) by Cohen and his former student Professor Ernest Nagel. He had been a regular contributor to the *New Republic* from its very conception in 1914; he wrote for it some forty review essays, as well as editorials, some of which were later incorporated into his books.[42] His health was precarious. He could retire, he wrote, with the feeling that what he had to contribute to philosophy would not perish with him. This gave him a sense of relief. But he did not contemplate, for his remaining years, days of idle reveries. No, he wrote,

> With this sense of relief, I could look about me to see what, if anything, the meager offerings of a logician could contribute to the future of my people here and abroad and to the cause of human freedom, with which the fate of the Jew has been so intricately bound for so many centuries.[43]

In 1933 Hitler had come into power. It was no time to merely dabble in Jewish affairs; the dangers loomed large. Cohen decided to devote his major efforts to the problems that the Jewish people faced. From a part-time Jew, Cohen was moving to become a full-time Jew.

When he considered his own intellectual equipment and the things that he could best do, Cohen decided that his contribution would best be to research and the application of the scientific method to some basic Jewish interests and needs. Anti-Semitism was rampant and was threatening the very life of the Jewish people. But how much was really known about the causes and nature of anti-Semitism? As he looked about him, Cohen saw the Jewish people hopelessly divided over ideology, religion, Zionism, capitalism and communism, and other issues. It seemed to him "that the only possible basis of unity was the basis that gives unity to the disagreements of scientists, a common acceptance of the need for demonstrable knowledge, based on nonpartisan scholarly studies." In any case, he wrote,

> it seemed worthwhile to try to mobilize intellectual forces for a study of the present and prospective situation of the Jewish people. . . . Human knowledge and understanding may not enable us to solve all

the problems of the Jew in an unjust world, but abandoning the effort
to understand the underlying causes and to avoid foreseeable errors is
intellectual cowardice.[44]

To realize this objective, Cohen, with the help of Alvin Johnson,
convened a meeting in June 1933 at the New School for Social
Research. It was attended by some of Cohen's old associates from
the days of Thomas Davidson: lawyers, scholars, doctors, econo-
mists. Out of this meeting there was organized, a few months later,
the Conference on Jewish Relations (which in 1955 became the
Conference on Jewish Social Studies).

The Conference was publicly launched in 1936 at a meeting
presided over by Albert Einstein and addressed by Cohen, Harold
Laski, and Professor Salo W. Baron, who was closely associated with
Cohen in this activity. At the conclusion of the meeting, an appeal
for funds was made by Henry Morgenthau, Sr. The organization was
conceived as one that would be directed by scholars for scholarly
objectives. It was felt that the research would help in the struggle
against Nazi propaganda that was being widely spread throughout
the world. But beyond this immediate need, there was also the need
for reliable data on Jewish population, the economic composition
of the Jewish people, and other relevant aspects of Jewish life.

The Conference launched a number of projects. A major one was
the publication of the scholarly quarterly *Jewish Social Studies* in
in 1939, which marked its fiftieth anniversary in 1989. Cohen was
its first editor, as he was also the first president of the Conference.
Baron was vice president, as were also Professor Harry A. Wolfson
of Harvard, Professor Edward Sapir of Yale, and Dr. Israel Wechsler,
a famous neurologist. The Conference was not intended to be a
propaganda agency or anything other than a research bureau. Several offshoots of the Conference were the Jewish Occupational
Council and the Jewish Cultural Reconstruction, which was in
charge of salvaging and redistributing manuscripts, books, artistic,
cultural and ritual objects looted by the Nazis from Jewish communities and individuals.

After his retirement from City College in January 1938, Cohen
devoted almost all his time and energy to the Conference and its
scholarly journal. At the same time many colleges and universities

tried to induce him to come as a lecturer or a visiting professor, and he accepted a limited number of the offers, especially from Harvard and the University of Chicago, but always on a restricted schedule that would leave him time for Conference work. His health was poor but he kept pushing himself, and he was always worried and concerned that he was not doing enough in the face of the monumental needs of the Jewish people.

With the help of his son Felix, also published in Cohen's lifetime were his *Preface to Logic* (1944), *Faith of a Liberal* (1946), and the book that Cohen thought of as his *magnum opus, The Meaning of Human History* (1947). Nine additional books were published posthumously.

In 1990, more than forty years after his death in 1947, seven of Cohen's books were in print, and the Conference on Jewish Social Studies and the journal *Jewish Social Studies* were still in existence. Morris Raphael Cohen, a man frail in health, a man with a sad face and subject to despondency, a man who came as an immigrant at the age of twelve and who for many years suffered physical and spiritual deprivation, a scholar and teacher whose first book was not published until he was fifty-one years old—although he was universally recognized as a leading philosopher and thinker—was elected president of the American Philosophical Association (Eastern Division) in 1929, perhaps the first Jew to have been given this honor. Cohen's life and work touched the lives of countless people—his former students who themselves became philosophers; jurists, like Justice Holmes and Felix Frankfurter, Jerome Frank and Nathan Margold; Jewish scholars; and Jewish communal workers—it has been given to few persons to leave a legacy so rich, so abundant and variant.

Notes

1. See chapter 6 in this volume for my essay on Kallen.
2. *A Dreamer's Journey: The Autobiography of Morris Raphael Cohen* (Boston: Beacon Press, 1949), 282. Hereinafter this book will be referred to as *Autobiography*.
3. Ibid., 283.
4. *Encyclopedia Judaica* 12: 967. The Jewish population in 1897 was 4,700,

which was 55 percent of the total population.

5. *Autobiography*, 32, 33, 35, 39, 40, 57, 165. See also Leonora Cohen Rosenfield, *Portrait of a Philosopher: Morris R. Cohen in Life and Letters* (New York: Harcourt, Brace & World, 1948), 157. This excellent biography will hereinafter be referred to as *Portrait*.

6. *Autobiography*, 235.

7. Ibid., 13.

8. Ibid., Foreword.

9. Ibid., 58.

10. Ibid., 91; *Portrait*, 10, 11, 12, 14, 20.

11. *Portrait*, 6.

12. *Autobiography*, 93; *Portrait*, 12.

13. *Encyclopedia Judaica*, 12: 1093.

14. *Memorials of Thomas Davidson: The Wandering Scholar*, collected and edited by William Knight (Boston: Ginn, 1907), 13–14. See also *Dictionary of American Biography* (New York: Charles Scribner, 1930–31), vol. 3, pt. 1, p. 95 (article by Chas. M. Bakewell); M. R. Cohen, in *Encyclopedia of Social Sciences* (New York: Macmillan, 1931) 5: 10. See also, Thomas Davidson, *The Education of the Wage-Earners* (Boston: Ginn, 1904), edited with Introduction by Chas. M. Bakewell.

   For a bibliography of Davidson's publications, see *Memorials of Thomas Davidson*, 235–38.

15. *Autobiography*, 121–22.

16. Ibid., 108, 281.

17. *Portrait*, 54.

18. Ibid., 52.

19. Ibid., 144.

20. Ibid., 55. For William James's tribute to Davidson, see *Memorials of Thomas Davidson*, 107, and James, *Memories and Studies* (New York: Longman, Green, 1924), 73.

21. *Portrait*, 60.

22. William James in *Memorials of Thomas Davidson*, 111–12.

23. *Portrait*, 62.

24. *Autobiography*, 158.

25. Ibid., 146.

26. Ibid.

27. *Portrait*, 157.

28. Ibid., 96.

29. *A Tribute to Professor Morris Raphael Cohen, Teacher and Philosopher* (New York: Published by the Youth Who Sat at His Feet, 1928).

30. *Autobiography*, 69–70.

31. Ibid., 215.

32. Ibid., 229.

33. Ibid., 230.

34. Ibid., 231.

35. Ibid., 218.
36. The essay was published in the first issue of *Jewish Social Studies*, 1 (1939): 39. It is reprinted in one of Cohen's posthumously published books, *Reflections of a Wondering Jew* (Boston: Beacon Press, 1950), 53.
37. *Autobiography*, 219.
38. Ibid., 220.
39. Ibid., 226.
40. Ibid., 220.
41. *Reflections of a Wondering Jew*, 33.
42. *Portrait*, 429.
43. *Autobiography*, 236.
44. Ibid., 240–41.

CHAPTER 6

Horace M. Kallen

Milton R. Konvitz

For about a half-century, Horace Kallen occupied a special—for many of these years, a unique—place on the Jewish scene in the United States. For he was not a professional Jew, not a rabbi, not a professor in a rabbinical seminary, not a scholar who made a specialty of Judaic study, not eminent among Jews by reason of the high office he held in a Jewish organization. He was the first Jewish professor of a non-Jewish subject in a non-Jewish college or university who was intimately and prominently identified with Jewish interests, Jewish concerns, Jewish organizations.[1] While widely recognized and honored as a thinker, philosopher and psychologist, Kallen devoted much of his time and thought to Jewish problems and influenced Jewish educators, communal workers, rabbis, and Jewish public opinion. In some ways he served as a role model emulated by his peers and many younger men and women, who looked to him for guidance and direction. In all these respects Kallen had no predecessor, and, regrettably, no successor. In American Jewish history he carved out for himself a very special place. He was, by reason of that very special place, *primus inter omnes*.

Kallen was born on August 11, 1882, in Berenstadt, a town in the German province of Silesia (now Poland). His parents were Jacob David and Esther Rebecca (Glazier) Kallen. His father, who had emigrated from Latvia, studied at a yeshiva and was an assistant rabbi in Berenstadt. As a foreigner, Rabbi Kallen was expelled from Germany and emigrated to the United States. When Horace Kallen was five years old, his father returned to Berenstadt and moved his wife, Horace, who was the eldest child, and two daughters to the United States, where he became rabbi of an Orthodox congregation in Boston. Rabbi Kallen (the original family name was Kalony-mous, the name of many medieval Jewish families) was a scholarly man; at the time of his death in 1917 he left some manuscripts that have remained unpublished. The son was close to his mother, who died in 1928, but was alienated from his father, whom he remem-bered as a domineering father and husband. For many years father and son were estranged, but when his father was on his deathbed, Horace Kallen sat beside him for a fortnight until he died. During those two weeks parent and son achieved a reconciliation, and on the wall of his study Professor Kallen had a framed photograph of both his parents.[2]

Rabbi Kallen apparently tried to keep his son from attending a public school and to teach him at home, but when the truant officer threatened Rabbi Kallen, he sent Horace to an elementary school. The boy also attended a *heder* for his Jewish studies; and after school he sold newspapers, to help support the large Kallen family, for in due course there were eight children. The father wanted the son to follow in his footsteps, but Horace rebelled and at times ran away from home. Professor Kallen remembered his years through elementary and secondary schools as very troublesome. The rebel-lion was not only against his father, but also against the father's religion. Although reconciled to his father in the latter's last days, he did not sit *shiva* nor say *Kaddish* for him. His estrangement from Judaism as a religion was never overcome.

When he was eighteen years old, Kallen entered Harvard College, and in 1903 received his B.A. *magna cum laude*. His years as an undergraduate were perhaps the most important for his intellectual and spiritual development. His interest in philosophy, however, had started while he had been still living at home, where one day he discovered among his father's books a copy of Spinoza's *Ethics* and the *Tractatus Theologico-Politicus* in a German translation. These books excited his eager mind. As a freshman at Harvard he took a philosophy course with Santayana, and as a junior a course with William James. James especially influenced him; both the person and his teaching had a lifelong impact on Kallen.

In addition to William James, another Harvard professor greatly influenced Kallen. That was Barrett Wendell, whose field was American literary history. Kallen took a course with Professor Wendell in his sophomore year, a course in which Wendell tried to expose and evaluate the Hebraic elements in American literary and political thought and institutions. Kallen tried to close his mind against this teaching but in private conversations with his argumentative student the professor won out, and Kallen began consciously and eagerly to reclaim and to identify himself with his Jewish background and inheritance, with Jewish culture, and with the Jewish people. He continued, however, to reject Judaism as a religion. This was the beginning of Kallen's commitment to agnosticism, Jewish secularism, Jewish culture, Zionism, Hebraism, cultural pluralism.

After graduating from Harvard, Kallen became an instructor in English at Princeton, where he remained for two years. When his contract was not renewed, it was intimated that had it been known he was a Jew, he would not have been appointed in the first place.[3] He then returned to Harvard as a graduate student and wrote his Ph.D. dissertation under the direction of William James. He received his degree in 1908, and remained at Harvard for the following three years as a lecturer and teaching assistant to James, Santayana, and Josiah Royce, the three philosophical giants who made Harvard's philosophy department world-famous. During this period Kallen in 1907 received a Sheldon fellowship that made it possible for him to travel to Europe, where he studied under F. C. S. Schiller, noted pragmatist at Oxford, and attended the lectures of Henri Bergson in Paris. Kallen then taught philosophy and psychology at the University of Wisconsin from 1911 to 1918, but resigned over an issue of academic freedom. During his years at Wisconsin, Kallen published three books: a study of James and Bergson, *The Structure of Lasting Peace*, and and the book that has had the longest life, *The Book of Job as a Greek Tragedy*, published in 1918. It was in those years, too, that Kallen published his articles in the *Nation* (in 1915) that represented the first formulation of his philosophy of cultural pluralism, and it was in those years, too, that he became involved in Zionist thought and affairs.

In 1919, as the New School for Social Research was being established in New York, Kallen was invited to become a member of the founding faculty, joining Alvin Johnson, John Dewey, James Harvey Robinson, Thorstein Veblen, and other famous scholars. He readily accepted the invitation and remained at the New School for over a half-century.

Kallen was not cast in the mold of a conventional philosopher. He was too greatly interested in political and economic movements, in civil liberties and civil rights, in the labor movement, in the consumers' cooperative movement, to allow himself to become completely absorbed in the life of a detached, self-isolated thinker.[4] High among his interests were Zionism, Jewish education, adult education, Jewish culture, pragmatism, the philosophy of pluralism, art and aesthetics—indeed, of Kallen it may be truly said that nothing human, no human concern, was alien to him. The institutions that he helped found or that he supported to his last day—the American Jewish Congress, the American Association for Jewish Education (which later became the Jewish Education Service of North America), the Jewish Teachers Seminary—Herzliah, the Farband Labor Zionist Order (later the Labor Zionist Alliance), the Rochdale Institute, the New School for Social Research—were for Kallen sacred treasures, and this showed where his heart lay.

Who were the persons who had influenced Kallen? In 1935 he wrote that the paramount influences were William James, George Santayana, Barrett Wendell, F. C. S. Schiller, Edwin B. Holt,[5] and Solomon Schechter. In later years he added John Dewey, Louis D. Brandeis, and Edward Everett Hale.[6] On the walls of his study at home were portraits of Goethe, Jefferson, William James, Santayana, John Dewey, Hale, Judge Julian Mack,[7] and Solomon Schechter, in addition to the photograph of his parents.

As we have said, when Horace Kallen enrolled as a freshman at Harvard College, his feelings towards Judaism and Jewishness were more than negative, they were feelings of hostility, of total rejection. But Professor Barrett Wendell "converted" him to Judaism— albeit not to the religion of his father, Rabbi Kallen, but to the heritage of Jewish culture, thought, and values, to a positive feeling of membership in the Jewish people, an openness to being Jewish and to the Jewish experience. Like Heine, Kallen felt as if he had never really left the Jewish community and that his "conversion" was only a restoration of his sight.

Before long, Kallen discovered Zionism and threw himself into Zionist activity. In 1902 Solomon Schechter came to the United States to become head of the Jewish Theological Seminary, and soon after meeting Schechter, young Horace Kallen came to think of him as his "revered friend and teacher." Three years after his arrival in the United States, Schechter stated that Zionism was a great bulwark against assimilation; he supported religious and spiritual-cultural Zionism, and despite opposition from leading members of the board of trustees of the Seminary, he opened the institution to Zionism and attended the eleventh Zionist Congress in Vienna.

To understand Kallen's early and lifelong devotion to Zionism, it is necessary to see it in the context of his broader philosophical stance, of which Zionism was, for him, a prime example and the application of his philosophy to his own life and his own living values. And so we shall at this point consider his philosophy of cultural pluralism.

In his first formulation of cultural pluralism, in 1915,[8] Kallen had in mind only the ethnic groups to which Americans belonged, and he thought of this membership as something which the individual could not easily shed. The ethnic group was a *Gemeinschaft*,[9] a natural, not a voluntary, community. While a person could cease to be a citizen or a member of a church, or cease to be a carpenter or a lawyer, he could not cease to be a Jew or a Pole. A man, he wrote, cannot change his grandfather. Later, however, Kallen came to think that while a person cannot change his or her grandparents, he or she can, indeed, reject them—as many have done.[10] All associations, he thought, ought to be voluntary; a person ought to be able to reject the fact that he or she is a Jew or a Pole—that membership in a group should be by "contract" and not by "status."[11] But Kallen continued to believe that participation in one's ethnic group and in its special culture has great significance for a person's self-identity, sense of worth and dignity, and for the person's full human development.

While Kallen held fast to a belief in individualism, he contended that no individual is merely an individual. "States, churches, indus-

Hayim Greenberg.
(Courtesy *Jewish Frontier*)

Marie Syrkin.
(Courtesy American Jewish Archives)

Ben Halpern.
(Courtesy Gertrude Halpern)

Trude Weiss-Rosmarin.
(Courtesy American Jewish Archives)

Horace M. Kallen.
(Courtesy American Jewish Archives)

Morris Raphael Cohen.
(Courtesy American Jewish Archives)

Ludwig Lewisohn.
(Courtesy American Jewish Archives)

Henry Hurwitz.
(Courtesy David Hurwitz)

Marvin Lowenthal.
(Courtesy American Jewish Archives)

Maurice Samuel.
(Courtesy American Jewish Archives)

Left to right: A. M. Klein, Saul Hayes, and Monroe Abbey celebrate the publication of Klein's novel, *The Second Scroll*. (Courtesy Jewish Public Library, Montreal)

Charles Reznikoff.
(Courtesy Milton Hindus)

Mordecai M. Kaplan.
(Courtesy Reconstructionist Rabbinical College)

Milton Steinberg. (Courtesy American Jewish Archives)

Will Herberg. (Courtesy Drew University Archives)

tries, families are organizations, not organisms," he wrote, and added:

> They are associations of men and women occurring not because they inwardly must, but because an outward condition calls for control or manipulation which individuals cannot accomplish alone. There are no social institutions which are primary, which are ends in themselves, as individuals are ends in themselves.[12]

The elemental term in every union, in every association, wrote Kallen, is "the individual, in his indefeasible singularity."

Although Kallen held fast to this belief in individualism, he was ready to admit that, he said,

> he knew of no instance . . . of an individual building his personal history solely by himself, from himself, on himself; feeding, so to speak, on nothing but his own flesh and spirit and growing by what he feeds on.[13]

Kallen's individualism was not, therefore, "rugged individualism," not narcissistic or solipsistic; rugged individualism was only a case of extreme selfishness; when invoked as an ideal, it can only defeat defensible individualism. For inherent in individualism, as understood by Kallen, is the principle of cooperation—but cooperation that is voluntary, cooperation that does not replace the primacy of the individual with the primacy of the state or society.

In 1909 Israel Zangwill's *The Melting Pot* was published, and the play had a long run on Broadway. Its theme—later rejected by Zangwill himself—was that "America is God's crucible, the great melting-pot where all the races of Europe are melting and re-forming." The melting-pot idea was the the pervasive, dominant view of the Protestant establishment. Immigrants were expected to shed their religious and cultural baggage at Ellis Island or as soon after their arrival as possible. This was the meaning of the "Americanization" process. Jews who had settled in the United States in the nineteenth century accepted this conception of what the American Idea intended. Jews and all other immigrants were to become "assimilated," homogenized. To them any other way meant segregation, and segregation meant that the ghetto would be transferred to America—a dangerous and repulsive idea.

It was against this ideological background that Kallen promul-
gated the idea of cultural pluralism and his version of the American
Idea. Kallen rejected both assimilation and segregation, and
pointed to the Declaration of Independence, the Constitution, the
Emancipation Proclamation, Lincoln's Second Inaugural Address,
Washington's Farewell Address, and Jefferson's First Inaugural as
the basic documents expressing the American Idea,[14] the essence of
which is that the purpose of freedom is to guarantee *the right to be
different*—not to abolish differences, but to sustain and enhance
them. But different individuals, and the different groups that they
compose, are not to isolate themselves but to cooperate one with
another. Differences were to be "orchestrated." The motto "*E pluribus unum*" does not mean just "*unum*," just oneness (the melting-
pot idea), nor does it mean just "*pluribus*," each individual and
each group, each ethnic or racial or religious group, each culture,
existing separately, rigidly segregated. No, the ideal means that the
diversity exists but all the diversities are a union, just as an orchestra is a union of diversities.[15]

Kallen gave this conception of cultural pluralism or the American Idea many different expressions. This is how he expressed it in
an essay in 1942:

> In affirming that *all* men are created equal, and that the rights of *all*
> to life, liberty and the pursuit of happiness are *unalienable*, it [the
> Declaration of Independence] accepts human beings as they are, with
> all the variety and multiplicity of faith, of race, of sex, of occupa-
> tions, of ideas, of possessions; and it affirms the equal right of these
> different people freely to struggle for existence and for growth in
> freedom and in happiness as different. . . . The American way of life,
> then, may be said to flow from each man's unalienable right to be
> different . . .[16]

This understanding of the American Idea, said Kallen, translates
in the political order as equal suffrage, and as government by the
people and for the people—all people; in the economic order it
means free enterprise; in religion, freedom of conscience; in the arts
and sciences, freedom of inquiry, of research, of expression. It
means freedom of association into sects, parties, corporations, trade
unions, fraternal orders, and many other voluntary associations.[17]

Now, the national being rests upon the cooperative and competitive relationships of these diverse voluntary associations. And the members of these associations have each of them multiple associations. A member of the Bar, for example, is at the same time a citizen, a family member, a member of a church or synagogue, member of a political party, a social club, an alumni association, and so forth.

> Each [membership] is a different way of his being together with other people. He is the bond which unites the societies with one another. . . . His relations are not fixed by status; they are not coerced, . . . but are liquid and mobile. This mobility of relationships is what gives its characteristic quality to the national living. Of this quality [of national living] the consummation is Cultural Pluralism. For its diverse and ever-diversifying members are united with one another in and through their differences, and the singularity of our culture is the orchestration of those manifold differences—*e pluribus unum*— into the common faith . . .[18]

Throughout his many years, Kallen applied, and kept on applying, the fact and ideal of cultural pluralism to American Jewry. He saw American Jews as constituting a group that, in the mix that is the American nation, is

> one more variety in the dynamic whole, is, like the addition of another taste or sight or sound, an enrichment, a contribution to abundance, spiritual and material. If against the assimilationist the American spirit affirms the right to be different, against the segregationist it affirms the right of free association of the different with one another.[19]

In addition, the Jewish group has a special claim of priority, for, Kallen noted, the American community was established through the Hebrew Scriptures, a fact that contributes heavily to "the singularity of the Jewish psyche," and he quoted the judgment of the historian William E. H. Lecky that "the Hebraic mortar cemented the foundations of American democracy." And Kallen added one more attribution: that the Jewish community, as every other composing the American nation, "serves as a psychological locale for voluntary social experimentation, for invention and discovery,

[and] as such involving more limited risks than a national-wide adventure would." In this way American Jewry has made its contribution to employer-employee relations, to philanthropy, to education, to literature and the arts. Such and other contributions represent both an Americanization of Jews and also an enrichment of the American way; thus "American Jewish living" is in a healthy symbiotic relationship with all other forms of living, "whose interaction orchestrates the Union we call America, and whose combined utterance is the American spirit."[20]

This philosophy of cultural pluralism as applied specifically to American Jews can be valid, said Kallen,

> only for those Americans whose faith in democracy is a fighting faith, and for those American Jews who are resolved to stand up in the armies of democracy as the democratic faith requires, freely and boldly as Jews.[21]

As we have noted, Kallen agreed with Lecky that "the Hebraic mortar cemented the foundations of American democracy." What is Hebraism? In an essay written as early as 1909,[22] Kallen contrasted Hellenism and Hebraism. For the Greeks, he wrote, the essence of reality was an order that was immutable and eternal. For the Greek mind, change was unreal and evil; the universe was static. Hebraism, on the contrary, saw reality as flux, change, dynamic and functional. Kallen thought that the Book of Job was the most representative book of Hebraism, and he never tired of quoting from it the cry of Job: "I know that He will slay me; nevertheless will I maintain my ways before Him." In his commentary on this cry Kallen tried to encapsulate the essence of the Hebraic Idea:

> The very act of maintaining one's ways may render the slaying impossible. To believe in life in the face of death, to believe in goodness in the face of evil, to hope for better times to come, to work at bringing them about—that is Hebraism. Whether Biblical or Talmudic, that is the inner history of Jews, from the beginning to the present day—an optimistic struggle against overwhelming odds. That is Hebraism, but it is the Hebraism, not of childhood and innocence; it is the Hebraism of old age and experience. It is a vision of the world that has been tested in the furnace and [has] come out clean.[23]

Kallen saw Hebraism in the philosophy of William James, whose pragmatism defined an idea or thing by what it does. Ideas are true if they lead to successful fruition, if they endure, if they have survival value. And Kallen saw in Bergson "the most adequate exponent" of a "tested and purified philosophic Hebraism." For Bergson change and not immutability was real, and such a finding, in which the dynamic, and not the static, is real, was for Kallen "the essential finding of Hebraism."[24]

In his writing early in the twentieth century Kallen attacked Reform Judaism for denying the particularity of Judaism and stressing its universal elements and teachings, for, he contended, "Particularity, as opposed to universality, is the essence of life and power. The most universal thing is the deadest. . . . Hebraism is a life and not a tradition; . . . a concrete and particular mode of behavior, not a formula." Hebraism and Judaism are not "dead unalterable 'universals.' " Contending against the early leaders of Reform Judaism, Kallen maintained that "What really destroys the Jews is what 'universalizes' them, what empties their life of distinctive particular content and substitutes void phrases to be filled with any meaning the social and religious fashion of the day casts up." Because it is particularistic, individualistic, and not universalistic in its basic metaphysical and general philosophical forces and tendencies, the essence of Hebraism is plastic and fluid, and so compatible with science and accommodating "to every pressing human need."[25]

This particularism, as it relates to the Jewish people, Kallen, early in his life, translated into Zionism. In an article published in 1910 Kallen wrote "I am a Zionist." And he elaborated: "I look toward the concentration and renationalization of the Jews." "I am committed," he wrote, "to the persistence of a 'Jewish separation' that shall be national, positive, dynamic and adequate."[26]

Within the context of his concern with Hebraism and Zionism, Kallen contended that eighteenth-century liberalism had overstressed and exaggerated the idea of the isolated individual; that liberalism had failed to see that individuality is not attained at birth but is something that one needs to achieve; that all persons in their beginning depend on a society. Genuine liberalism, he argued, requires for the group, for the races and nationalities, the same freedom of development and expression as that required for the individual. Indeed, insofar as this freedom is required for the individual, it must be required for the group, for races and nations are "the essential reservoirs of individuality."

Through national freedom, the Jewish people would be able to render service to mankind, and for this the Jewish people need to have their national home in Palestine. The Jew, Kallen contended, will not win emancipation as a human being, as an individual, unless he first wins it as a Jew, and "the prerequisite to liberation of the individual is the liberation of the group to which he by birth belongs." Thus Zionism demands "not only group autonomy, but complete individual liberty for the Jew *as Jew*."[27] Enlightenment failed the Jew because it offered him liberty as an individual provided he ceased being a Jew. Zionism corrects this misconceived proposal; it offers the Jew complete individual liberty, not as an abstract human being, but as a Jew. While the Enlightenment offered to remove all inferiorities, it also removed all differences. The Enlightenment was, thus, a kind of melting pot; it was based on the misconception that equality had to mean identity or similarity. It failed to recognize the idea that there can be equality based on the right to be different.

It should be apparent that all the essential ingredients of what came to be known as cultural pluralism were already the constituents of what Kallen called Hebraism and what he had recognized as Zionism. On the published record, it seems that Kallen had arrived at cultural pluralism through his thinking about himself as a Jew and what meaning and significance his Jewishness should have for him. It was in an essay on "Judaism, Hebraism, Zionism," published in 1910, that Kallen wrote:

> Culture . . . constitutes a harmony, of which peoples and nations are the producing instruments, to which each contributes its unique tone, in which the whole human past is present as an enduring tension, as a background from which the present comes to light and draws its character, color, vitality.[28]

Here one sees the metaphor of the orchestra, the harmony that was the orchestration of differences.

Thus it was that, by some invisible complex process, there fused in Horace Kallen's mind ideas that had made their way into it from the Hebrew Scriptures, from William James, Barrett Wendell, Louis Brandeis, Herzl, Moses Hess, Thomas Jefferson, James Madison, Solomon Schechter, Thomas Paine, and Ralph Waldo Emerson— strange bedfellows; yet in his mind all were on friendly speaking terms, so that they all became harmoniously orchestrated; they came in separately but came out as cultural pluralism, as the American Idea, as Hebraism, as Zionism. Kallen could have said, quoting from T. S. Eliot's "East Coker," "In my begining is my end."

Reflecting upon his own intellectual development, in 1933 Kallen wrote: "It is upon the foundation and against the background of my Jewish cultural milieu that my vision of America was grown." It is not that he saw Zionism through his vision of America; the order was the reverse: he saw America through his vision of Hebraism, Zionism. He read the Declaration of Independence against his memory of the emancipation of the Israelites from Egyptian slavery. In the parental Kallen household, he wrote,

> the suffering and slavery of Israel were commonplaces of conversation; from Passover to Passover, freedom was an ideal ceremonially reverenced, religiously aspired to. The textbook story of the Declaration of Independence came upon me, nurtured upon the deliverance from Egypt and the bondage in exile, like the clangor of trumpets, like a sudden light. What a resounding battle cry of freedom![29]

Zionism to Kallen did not, however, mean the negation of the Diaspora. He wanted Jewish life and Jewish ideals to flourish and flower in America no less than in Israel. And the key to the future of a Jewish life, wherever Jews make their home, is Jewish education. For the last forty years of his life Kallen, therefore, worked closely with leading Jewish educators, with Samson Benderly, Ben Rosen, I. B. Berkson, Israel S. Chipkin, Alexander M. Dushkin, Judah Pilch, Oscar Janowsky, A. P. Schoolman, and Emanuel Gamoran. He attended countless meetings and conferences, traveling everywhere to lecture and exhort on behalf of Jewish education. At times it appeared as if it was his life's mission. And whenever an opportunity presented itself, he tried to explain what teaching the

Jewish tradition should mean and be. He did not mean that Jewish schools should teach the history and thought of the Jewish past as the pastness of the past. No, tradition is a process, an ongoing activity, and activity in the present changes the past. A person or group *makes* his or her or its past, and so the past is constantly remade, and in this way the tradition becomes a *living* tradition. Thus the Bible can be a part of my past, a part of my tradition, only because it is a part of my *present* life.

Kallen never tired of teaching this lesson; he formulated it in countless ways. A typical statement is the following from a book published in 1956:

> The word [tradition] means, literally, carrying on, a continuous on-going—but a carrying on, or ongoing, as any person's life goes on, not changelessly, but as a process of changing, where the old phases both continue in the new and are altered by the new. Self-preservation, whether of an individual or a group, is this process wherein the past endures only as it lives on in the present and future, and lives on only as it is changed by them.[30]

People say they cannot change the past. But Kallen would ask: "What else is there to change? What else is the present but the past changing?" "A living culture is a changing culture."

It should be noted that Kallen did not view Hebraism as an isolated phenomenon. In the United States Hebraism is to be a part of Americanism. The Jew is to be a Jewish American person. In an essay written in 1955, Kallen explained the union or fusion or interplay as follows:

> Such consummations are beyond the reach of the individual iso-late and alone. They require a home-centered community with its traditions of language, diet, worship, feasting and fasting, play and sport, expressive and representative arts, all carrying forward communal remembrance, beliefs, works and ways. . . . Their communication by the generations is what sustains the communion which holds the altering community together. They are what *Jewish* in *Jewish American* signifies. They thrive best when supported by a free trade with their peers of different communal cultures, assimilating and hence transfiguring what they get in exchange, and again communicating the new life-form of their changing and growing old culture to their non-Jewish neighbors, and receiving theirs in return. The social

orchestration which this intercultural exchange consummates actualizes the American Idea and gives the culture of the American people the qualities that Whitman and Emerson and William James and Louis Brandeis celebrated.[31]

Horace Kallen referred to himself as a humanist, a temporalist, a pragmatist, an instrumentalist, and to his philosophy as Cultural Pluralism, Hebraism, as the Hebraic Idea, as the American Idea. Perhaps all these terms ought to be strung together, linked by hyphens. "The hyphen," he wrote, "unites very much more than it separates."[32] Kallen was perhaps the most hyphenated American thinker, and so he lived more abundantly, more richly, more freely, and to whomsoever and whatsoever he was linked he gave abundantly, richly, freely. That his influence is lasting is borne out by the fact that in 1990, some sixteen years after his death in 1974, seventeen of Kallen's book were in print.

In the last quarter of the twentieth century, however, both the melting-pot idea and cultural pluralism were under attack from forces that preached and practiced "otherness"—not assimilation, not pluralism, but ethnicity; that ethnic, racial, and cultural differences are not bridgeable. And this reactionary ideology has worldwide ramifications, for everywhere there is a recrudesence of tribalism, regional chauvinism, and blazing nationalism. One cannot foresee when, if ever, these forces will have dissipated their strength. Meanwhile, there is a struggle between the children of light and the children of darkness; but struggle, Horace Kallen taught, is an indispensable quality of all life, human no less than animal—we struggle, he wrote, if only so that we may go on struggling, for that is life.

Notes

1. Morris Raphael Cohen came on the Jewish scene, as an activist Jew, some twenty to twenty-five years after Kallen. See chapter 5 in this book for my essay on Cohen.
2. The biographical facts are based on a long interview with Kallen by me and the late Dorothy Kuhn (Mrs. Adolph S.) Oko, in August 1964, at Truro, Mass. The interview was later made part of the oral history collection of the American Jewish Committee. The biographical facts

are also based on many conversations and on an extensive correspondence between Kallen and the author. The interview and correspondence are at the Documentation Center, School of Industrial and Labor
Relations, Cornell University, Ithaca, N.Y.

3. Cf. Ludwig Lewisohn, *Upstream: An American Chronicle* (New York:
   Boni & Liveright, 1922).
4. See Sidney Hook and M. R. Konvitz, eds., *Freedom and Experience:
   Essays Presented to Horace M. Kallen* (Ithaca, N.Y.: Cornell University
   Press, 1947), Preface, viii.
5. Edwin B. Holt was an American psychologist, author of *The Concept
   of Consciousness* (1914), *The Freudian Wish* (1915), and other works.
6. Edward Everett Hale was the son of Nathan Hale and nephew of Edward Everett; a Unitarian clergyman, author of the famous short story,
   "The Man without a Country"; and active in civil improvement and
   philanthropic work.
7. Julian W. Mack (1866–1943), from 1913 to his retirement in 1941 was
   judge of the U. S. Court of Appeals; a pioneer in work on behalf of child
   welfare and on the problem of juvenile delinquency; a Zionist leader,
   president of the Zionist Organization of America and president of the
   first American Jewish Congress in 1918; and a member of the Harvard
   University Board of Overseers for eighteen years.
8. "Democracy versus the Melting Pot," *Nation* 100 (Feb. 18, 25, 1915):
   190–94, 217–20. Reprinted in *Culture and Democracy: Studies in the
   Group Psychology of the American Peoples* (New York: Boni & Liveright, 1924), hereinafter referred to as *Culture and Democracy*.
9. Cf. Ferdinand Tönnies, *Gemeinschaft und Gesellschaft* (1887).
10. *Culture and Democracy*, 94, 122, 123.
11. Cf. Sir Henry Maine, *Ancient Law* (1861).
12. *Individualism, an American Way of Life* (New York: Liveright, 1933),
    142.
13. *Culture and Democracy*, 181.
14. Kallen, "The National Being and the Jewish Community," in Oscar I.
    Janowsky, ed., *The American Jew: A Composite Portrait* (New York:
    Harper & Bros., 1942), 270, at 277.
15. Ibid., 280.
16. Ibid., 278.
17. Ibid., 279.
18. Ibid., 280–81.
19. Ibid., 283.
20. Ibid., 284.
21. Ibid., 285.
22. The essay is reprinted in Kallen, *Judaism at Bay* (New York: Bloch
    Publishing, 1932).
23. Ibid., 13.
24. Ibid., 14.

25. Ibid., 39.
26. Ibid., 33.
27. Ibid., 116.
28. Ibid., 37.
29. Ibid., 7.
30. Kallen, *Cultural Pluralism and the American Idea* (Philadelphia: University of Pennsylvania Press, 1956), 23.
31. *Jewish Social Service Quarterly* 32 (Fall 1955): 27.
32. *Culture and Democracy*, 63.

CHAPTER 7

Ludwig Lewisohn: A Life in Zionism

Stanley F. Chyet

Ludwig Lewisohn, Berlin-born, South Carolina–raised, was at most twenty-one when he came to New York in the fall of 1903 to study literature at Columbia University. His years in the city—interrupted by lengthy sojourns elsewhere in the United States and in Europe—saw him undertake a long, difficult journey back to his German and Jewish origins, fall in and out of love with three or four women, father a son, achieve fame as a literary and drama critic, as a translator and even as a novelist, become the apostle of Goethe and Hauptmann and Rilke, of Herzl and Buber, and make an extraordinary contribution to a still emergent and precarious American Zionist movement.[1]

The young Lewisohn very much exemplified Veblen's notion of "renegade Jews," a gifted intellectual who had become "a naturalised, though hyphenate, citizen in the gentile republic of learning" and exhibited "at the best . . . a divided allegiance to the people of his origin." The criticism Lewisohn produced, even in middle age, much of it for the liberal weekly the *Nation*, had little to do with specifically Jewish concerns and a great deal to do with the struggle for a modern, post-Victorian literature in America. That body of criticism—*The Modern Drama* (1915), *The Spirit of Modern German Literature* (1916), *A Modern Book of Criticism* (1919), *The Drama and the Stage* (1922), *The Creative Life* (1924), *Cities and Men* (1927)—impressed his younger contemporary Alfred Kazin as "a force for progress." Kazin credited Lewisohn with "greater cultivation than any of his fellow critics save Van Wyck Brooks" and honored him for his belief "in the highest purpose of expression." Not that Kazin's admiration was unqualified: Lewisohn was given to "a rhetoric of exaltation"; he put everything "a little too grandly." Still, "no critic had ever insisted so strenuously on the need of precise study of the basic facts underlying art as a spiritual vocation."

It is our loss that a generation after his death Lewisohn's impact on American letters, so compelling in its time (his *Expression in America* [1932] was probably the first attempt at a Freudian account of American literature), has left behind few traces. Scarcely more, it would seem, can be said for his Zionist reputation—and one suspects it is this last oblivion Lewisohn would have deemed most demeaning. Veblen had also written that the emancipated Jew was, in his intellectual life, "likely to become an alien," but "spiritually he is more than likely to remain a Jew."[2]

Lewisohn would have appreciated the eulogy given him in 1956 by the *Jerusalem Post*, which memorialized him as "the first great American literary spokesman for the Zionist movement." Two decades earlier, in 1935, he had offered a most interesting third-person account of himself: "Never except in his confused and misled twenties" had he been "as alienated from his people as he had often been assumed," and even then, in turning his back on Judaism and Jewishness, he had not been able to escape "a recurrently evil conscience." To be sure, Lewisohn was forty in 1922 when the autobiographical *Up Stream* made its first appearance, and *Up Stream* does not quite support the contention of 1935 either as to the date of his return or the limits of his disaffection. "Slowly, in the course of the years," he had allowed in *Up Stream*, "I have discovered traits in me which I sometimes call Jewish. But that interpretation is open to grave doubt." The Modern Library edition of *Up Stream*, issued four years later, added a footnote: "No longer (1926)" was "that interpretation . . . open to grave doubt." Still *Up Stream* would somehow remain for him a source of discomfort; he would insist on dismissing it as "comparatively unimportant," though years later he listed it, a trifle inaccurately, among his "specifically Jewish books."[3]

In *Roman Summer* (1927), really the first of his Jewish novels, he had a Jewish character speak ruefully of "our eternal longing for the Gentile world." That "longing" may be what Lewisohn wanted to deny in himself when he miscalculated his Jewish "rebirth" and misrepresented the character of *Up Stream*. Perhaps for this man whose parents had felt themselves "Germans first and Jews afterwards" and "had assimilated, in a deep sense, Aryan ways of thought and feeling," this man who as an immigrant youngster in South Carolina had hungered for the identity of "an American, a Southerner, and a Christian," for him, the struggle to be free of what was alien, to grasp what was his own, could never be looked upon as won. But during the early 1920s, when he had already entered on his fifth decade, Lewisohn found a way to make his struggle if not less urgent, at least less desperate.[4]

As early as 1915, it appears, Lewisohn had begun addressing meetings of the fledgling Menorah Society at the Ohio State University, where he served as a member of the German Department faculty. His dearest friend, the non-Jewish poet William Ellery Leonard, contributed what might be called a proto-Zionist poem to the inaugural number of the *Menorah Journal* in 1915, but Lewisohn himself could still speak in 1916 with approval of "the Jew who has discarded his archaic Orientalism." Something may have been stirring in him, but it would be more than a few years before he could give voice to it.[5]

In May 1923, Lewisohn and his employer, Oswald Garrison Villard, the editor of the *Nation*, went to Boston to speak at a Harvard University Menorah Society banquet. Lewisohn later summarized his speech in *Mid-Channel* (1929), another of his autobiographical volumes:

> I besought the young men who filled the hall to be themselves, to follow their inner law as human beings and as Jews, to consider profoundly what each was meant to be and to be that—that and nothing else, to kill the fear-born ape that lives in almost every human breast and to follow the absolute command of inner oneness.

The German Zionist leader Kurt Blumenfeld, who had won Albert Einstein for the Zionist cause, was present that evening. He had come there "without particular expectations," though he knew of

Lewisohn as the author of *Up Stream* and the *Nation*'s celebrated
drama critic, but as Lewisohn spoke, Blumenfeld heard ideas which
he himself might have expressed.[6]

Lewisohn was not yet able to speak of his "Jewish soul, the
eternal unresigned and Messianic," but Blumenfeld could have had
little cause to doubt that he had found for Zionism another "useful
member and co-operator." Had not Lewisohn been "hoping for Jewish Jews, united for Jewish purposes deeper than charity, more
serious than anti-defamation campaigns"? Blumenfeld would not
need to press him. Lewisohn was already on "a road of thought that
inevitably met his own." Through the German visitor, Lewisohn
soon met Chaim Weizmann, who made a powerful impression on
him. Weizmann, he wrote admiringly, was "both mystic and practical man, dreamer and hard-headed money-gatherer at once." Lewisohn would have his disagreements with Weizmann, but would
always be conscious of him as a man who could engage "one's
affection and loyalty."

Weizmann suggested to Lewisohn that he undertake a journey
abroad and write a series of articles for the *Nation* "on the Palestinian experiment of colonizing Jews upon their ancestral soil." Villard gave his blessing, and so Lewisohn embarked on that enterprise
which would enable him to "seek . . . the facts of our Jewish fate"
and to write his first unequivocally Jewish book, *Israel*, the fervent
Zionist report he published in 1925.[7]

Israel was a lovely, melodic, empyrean sort of book, the utterance of a man who had discovered in himself a love for the abraded
contours of a land and an identity. Again one thinks of Veblen's
willingness to see in the Zionist effort "an idyllic and engaging air."
In the ghettos of Poland, Lewisohn had come upon Jews "filthy,
starved, oppressed," yet clinging heroically "to that strange eternal
thought that they are, in the words of the Torah, a kingdom of
priests and a holy nation." Then, going on to the Palestine mandate, to "the mauve . . . or golden hills," he came upon "stones
hewn and graven once by the hands of men, . . . by the workmen of
Israel, built and always destroyed." He could read in them "the
chronicle of conquest upon conquest," of defeat and ruin, but not
that alone, for Palestine made him alive now to "the immortal

spirit that broods here despite a hundred conquests . . . the spirit that, in this evening of time, has brought us here again." It was, he saw, "a small land and a poor land. Yet . . . not so small or so poor but that, as in ancient days, it can give birth to ideas that mankind will not willingly let die."[8]

The Zionist viewpoint Lewisohn formulated in the course of this pilgrimage to Europe and Palestine deserves some comment. It was, to begin with, a religious expression—not, to be sure, in any orthodox or pietist sense ("Neither Rabbinical rigidness nor Chassidic mysticism . . . has any saving power," he declared in *Israel;* he was "glad to see the citadel of orthodoxy a ruin today"). It was religious in its awareness that "spiritual facts and values alone are permanent." Lewisohn did not fail to speak of the achievements of modern socio-economic institutions like the Keren Hayesod, the Histadrut, and Solel Boneh, and he was duly impressed (and, invincible individualist that he was, sometimes filled with "misgiving and dismay") by what he saw of the *halutzim* (the "pioneers") in their communes and collective farming villages as they went about their labor of building up the Land: "But greater than the task is the spirit of the task and the example of it. And that spirit and that example belong even now to the permanent possessions of all men and are becoming 'part of our lives' unalterable good. . . .' " Only a man endowed with what Kurt Blumenfeld would call a *religiöse Begabung,* a gift for religion, would have seen what Lewisohn saw: "Palestine has healed thousands of souls, it has spread the sense of national and human dignity to the remotest regions of the dispersion; it has given us recognition as a people and a place in the councils of the nations. It is self-recovery; it is salvation." One cannot place too much stress on Lewisohn's sense of Zionism as a salvationist force. Lewisohn had become a *maggid,* an evangelist. He was avid to save souls, to save them with the good news of the redemptive possibilities of the Zionist effort. Zionism was nothing less than a path to redemption. "If we fail we fail the world, we fail ourselves. . . . We dare not and we cannot fail." That is no secular Zionism. In its time, it is likely to have had few parallels, but among them would be poems in Uri Zvi Greenberg's *Anacreon* collection of 1928.[9]

Lewisohn, it is worth noting, cared nothing at all for "the normalization of the position of the Jewish people"; he distrusted that Zionist vision which longed for the emergence in Jewish Palestine of "the lovely primitive lyric cry, the simplicity of the folk-song"; he divined in such a vision "the romantic muddle-headedness, the false cultivation of the primitive . . . characteristic of the . . . patriotic nationalist in all countries," something from whose blandishments people had to free themselves "if human life is to be worth living at all." Lewisohn had no wish to solve, he wanted "to affirm the Jewish problem and, by being and remaining emphatically what we are, [to] transcend the reactionary nationalist . . . everywhere in the world."[10]

This last leads one to another salient feature of Lewisohn's newfound Zionist faith, the passionate insistence on pacifism, on a spiritual nationalism, which in those still relatively innocent, pre-Nazi years he believed utterly at one with the work of *Judaea rediviva*. Long before his discovery of Zionism, he had committed himself to—and, during World War I, suffered for—the conviction that "there is . . . no certain effectiveness but in an abstention from all force." In Zionism, he saw no rejection of that stance; he saw its affirmation. What was it Zionism offered "all the world" if not "the first example of a national community that exists, in the old, eternal words of Zechariah, not by might, not by power, but by the spirit"? History had chosen the Jews "as the example of a people of peace, a people without power, a people by the force of the spirit alone." Zionism would demonstrate that "there can be a people that is never an enemy of any other people, that is never held together by the possession or the hope of power, that has . . . represented for centuries, and represents now, a type of nationalism that may be the hope of a barbarous and warlike world." Jews, "by the constant example of [their] pacifist and spiritual nationhood," would "help to remold the concept nation itself and at last consciously function correctly and so fulfill [their] mission among the peoples of the earth."

Pacifism and Judaism—they were virtually synonymous: "The memory of war . . . is hideous and unnatural to the soul of Israel." Jews had "as a people outgrown the delusions of force and war," so that "the modern Jewish renaissance" was "absolutely pacifistic," uniting "the possibility of Jewish cohesion with friendliness toward all mankind." The Jew would "as a normal self-expression of his Jewishness" hold it his duty "to resist war and the call to war and the propaganda of war to the uttermost," and would "build up in Palestine a state that abstains from power, that knows nothing of rivalry, that will suffer injustice rather than seek to share political responsibility, a state that shall not only restore the preserved of Israel, but be a light to the Gentiles." A state? Clearly, Lewisohn had in mind no nation-state in the ordinary sense. Zionism would build in the Land of Israel not a sovereign state but an exemplary society. And it would be a bi-national society. The word is not his, but the bi-nationalist idea was very much alive in his consciousness. Through the instrumentality of the Zionist Organization,

> the scattered Jewish people . . . is building up the land and founding a new and fruitful civilization in it at its [Jewry's] own expense, and without the slightest desire or hope of exercising political power. We desire to possess the land creatively and not in terms of power and force and dominance. A constitution will be drafted in time. Under it we expect equal rights with Arab and Christian. No more. For all that we bring to the land we ask no no more than equality with the people of continuous residence in it.

Even Judah Magnes never gave more eloquent expression to the bi-nationalist idea. Lewisohn indeed felt himself so drawn to bi-nationalism that, in "the continued Christian or Mohammedan possession of the memoried places of the land"—the cave of Machpelah at Hebron, the Temple Mount in Jerusalem, Jericho, Shechem—he could see "a not unwelcome symbol of our national mood and our national aspirations." In this aristocratic doctrine, *Judaea rediviva* did not mean "the exercise of force and the exertion of power"; it meant "quite literally" turning "a poisonous desert into a garden," "a green and irrigated land, a land of parks and pools, a land of mountain gardens and of hillside-fields, of blossoms of the almond and the orange everywhere, vineyards on all the southern slopes and of palm groves to the rim of the desert." "The future is here, the forest coolness of days to come."[11]

But the Arabs were here, too, those "people of continuous residence" in the Land. Lewisohn is unlikely to have had a very sure grasp of Palestinian history at the time. Perhaps he did not realize that Jews, too, if not in impressive numbers, were to be found among "the people of continuous residence," or that the Arabs included recent immigrants from elsewhere in the Levant, immigrants attracted to Palestine by the economic development the Land had been experiencing since the initiation of Jewish resettlement and the efforts encouraged by the British Mandatory authorities. Still, he did not deceive himself about Arab enthusiasm for bi-nationalism. He understood very well that bi-nationalism was at best a Jewish and not an Arab aspiration. "The problem of the Arab population is our most serious one," he conceded. The Arabs would "inevitably" be a minority in the Land "tomorrow," but today they were the majority. Not untypically, they were "fanatical and hostile," but their rights were "clear and indestructible." Arab antipathy, their inability to "reach the level of our economic and political thinking," their reluctance to be conciliated, these were, after all, comprehensible enough:

> the Arab cannot, in the nature of things, believe in our sincerity since to him, . . . it seems axiomatic that those who have power of any sort should use it, that intelligent minorities should seek to oppress or to stamp out those who are different . . . and fewer than themselves.

Even the undeniable technological and medical benefits brought to Palestine by Zionism would not suffice to dispel Arab distrust. Nonetheless, the Jews had to "be deterred by no hardship from carrying out [their] duty toward the Arab population with perfect patience, serenity . . . unfaltering good-will." What better opportunity would Zionists have to bear witness to "the divorcement of nationalism from power"?[12]

Lewisohn's Zionist faith as propounded in *Israel* was for him no mere question of philosophical preference or spiritual yearning. A letter he addressed to the *Nation* from Vienna, in September 1925, makes that very plain. The American Jewish Joint Distribution Committee had proposed a campaign to raise $15 million, a sum which, in large part at least, was to be used to resettle Jews in the Soviet Crimea. Lewisohn felt it his "duty to protest . . . with all possible urgency against the investment of one penny of Jewish money anywhere except in Palestine. No more disastrous, no more tragic error could be made." He wished to impugn no one's "conscious good faith," but: "I assert that there is no hope in Europe," and that included the Soviet Union, which could never number him among its admirers. His travels had convinced him that the future held only pogroms in store for European Jewry, and it did not matter whether the regime was "a red tyranny or a white." European Jews were everywhere in danger of being "slaughtered, buried alive, crucified, shot." It was perfectly clear to him: "To spend one penny on keeping a Jew in Eastern or Central Europe is to subsidize murder. Palestine . . . is the only hope, the only duty, the only salvation." [13]

Lewisohn would remain in Europe for nearly a decade. He would be able firsthand to watch the crisis in European Jewry deepen, to see his grim prophecy move toward fulfillment. He had for some time been preternaturally sensitive to the "pretense within pretense and self-deception within self-deception" of the assimilated, "emancipated" Jews of Western and Central Europe. Now he was increasingly oppressed by their refusal to recognize that they stood in Europe like the protagonist of his story "The Romantic," the tragic Baron Tamaczvar whose "love was not wanted. . . . He was a stranger. To be a stranger was his doom." What seemed to Lewisohn most ominous, however, was the omnipresent confirmation of Christianity's failure "as a curb upon pagan barbarism and as a guide of the good life in the age of science and of the industrial revolution." As he put it in *The Island Within* (1928), the first of his novels devoted wholly to Jewish themes: "The Christian rabble still held itself superior. . . . Nor had the actual slaying, the actual martyrdom, ever ceased. Yesterday in Russia, today in Rumania, tomorrow where?"

By 1930, Lewisohn sensed that Germany's "national state of mind" was "at work breeding future wars." Only a few years later, by the time *The Permanent Horizon* (1934) and *Rebirth: A Book of Modern Jewish Thought* (1935) appeared, it had become necessary to face not only the "rigid barbarism and slavery" of the Soviet regime, but also "the stern facts of the German terror." The old gods were wakeful once again. "At this hour in history, which is marked by a pagan revolt against Christianity, there seems less hope than there was only a few years ago. . . . There is no hope for the Jews in

a pagan world. For they are that world's evil conscience and gnaw-
ing worm of the soul." It was, he thought, "wholly logical" that the
Nazis "should repudiate Christianity *in toto* as a loathsome Jewish
invention." No comfort was to be taken in the Soviet Union; Hitler
was merciless to Jews, Stalin equally so to Judaism:

> Today, in this year 1935, two-thirds of the Western World has re-
> lapsed into pagan barbarism and only, or almost only, in France and
> Britain and America are there left any profoundly sincere Gentile
> Christians and liberals, any men and women who have put aside
> the old pagan Adam of their ancestors and accepted the ethos first
> proclaimed by the teachers and prophets of Israel. Hence the Jew is
> once more plunged into all the horrors of a pagan world, . . . which
> . . . wreaks upon him more brutally than ever its evil conscience for
> having twice and in a twofold manner betrayed the faiths it professed
> and crucified its Christ.

All this promised a diluvian time. Genocide had yet to cross Lewisohn's mind; even after World War II had begun, he still expected
Jews, if only a (rather sizable) remnant, to survive in the Reich
itself, but the Jewish people would surely need a sturdy ark to ride
out the flood. That ark was none other than Zionism.[14]

The world, the outward world at least, had changed crucially
since Lewisohn's first sight of the Holy Land in the mid-1920s. Had
his view of Zionism changed, too? Fundamentally, it had not, except that now Zionist goals had to be pursued with far greater
intensity, for now it was palpable fact that Jews confronted "a
mounting world conjuration against the very life of Israel." He
continued in the mid-1930s to believe what he had asserted in the
late 1920s, that "the affirmation of nationalism in a spirit of love
and peace through economic co-operation [was] the only rational
ideal of the next few centuries." Zionism, he never doubted, was
that brand of nationalism, not one of "the pagan nationalisms of
rivalry and hatred and war." Jewish nationalism was not to be
compared with "the other nationalisms that fill the world . . . with
their arrogance and lust after power." For "Jewish nationalism . . .
issues from a moral instinct and a moral vision for ever separate
from the life of the pagan and all its works." Even as Hitler prepared
the Nürnberg Laws, Lewisohn demanded of the Jews that they rec-

ognize themselves as "conscious bearers of one of the world's great spiritual civilizations," and on that basis claim their "rights . . . as a people in the land of [their] fathers."[15]

Piety, it is clear, had come to mean more to him now. In earlier years, he had tended to shy away from Jewish orthodoxy as "a web of intellectually indefensible formalism," but that had all been before "the great study" to which, one learns from *Mid-Channel*, Lewisohn gave himself in Europe on his return there from Palestine. As early as 1931, in *The Last Days of Shylock*, he depicted Shylock recoiling in a genuinely pious way from an involuntary "dream of pride and vengeance. He had better betake himself to prayer; it was more fitting for an Israelite. He would pray for wisdom, which alone prevailed from time to time over the cruelty of the heathen." And the young Gabriel Weiss, in *Trumpet of Jubilee* (1937), when depression assaulted him,

> slipped into the synagogue for *Mincha* prayer. He knew what he needed—to reaffirm the fate of such a being as he was in such a universe as this; to re-embrace his kind of humanity; to be strengthened against the temptation of sloth and flight. He sought to concentrate all the forces of his young and troubled being and chanted not without a tear gathering under his lid yet not falling, *"Emeth v'emunah khol-soth v'kayam alenu. . . .* Truth and faith is all this and established for us." . . . *Emunah*—that which is trustworthy, that which does not change and on which the soul can lean, that which is so *alenu*—for us. He was tranquil when he came home for dinner.

In *The Answer* (1939), essentially a garnering of excerpts from the weekly syndicated column "The World's Window" he had produced for the American Jewish press during the 1930s, Lewisohn declared himself "a conservative nationalist Jew with a *yarmelke* ready in his pocket and a *mezuzah* on each door of his house." That was a far cry from his feeling a decade earlier that it would be "overemphasis" to affix a mezuzah to the door of his Parisian apartment. January 1938 found him addressing a United Palestine Appeal meeting at Washington's Mayflower Hotel. He spoke "as an American liberal," he assured his audience, but: "I do not desire that my other convictions be forgotten. I am religiously a conservative Jew; metaphysically I am very 'rightist'; I am, if you like, a radical

Zionist, hoping for the liquidation of the greater portion of the diaspora. . . . But indeed I think these convictions wholly harmonious with those of a liberal."[16]

He still held to bi-nationalism. In *Trumpet of Jubilee*, he gave his hope an especially imaginative form, a projection into the future in which a Zionist devotee is made to exclaim:

> You've read and heard how once the Arabs feared and hated us? They don't any longer. In the long run they were convinced by the rightness of our intent. We struck no blow. We never retaliated. We went on doing good. It worked. In the long run it worked. Goodness works. Justice works. In Eretz Yisrael [the Land of Israel] . . . there is neither hunger nor ignorance, neither rivalry nor hatred.

Gabriel Weiss, the novel's hero, pictures "a human caravan in which each was himself and no man desired his human brother to be aught but what he was, aught but what God had made him; . . . a humanity in which groups had not desired any to be subject to another or to become another."

Lewisohn was more explicit in his journalistic efforts. In one of "The World's Window" columns, written as anti-Jewish riots were erupting in Palestine during 1936, he argued that "a bi-national British dominion or neutralized state . . . on both sides of the Jordan would, through the work of Jews, enhance the prestige of the Arabs by virtue of their very collaboration in such a state." In another column, written after the Arab riots had grown into an armed rebellion, he urged the Jewish need for establishing a modus vivendi with the Arabs. "We must seek to convince [them] that we are honorably planning a bi-national State and that even when we constitute a majority of the population the Arab will be as free and self-determining, as much at home as are the French Swiss . . . within the predominantly German Swiss Republic." Palestinian Arabs had "an undoubted right" to "the assurance that Arab and Jew in Palestine will be as French and German in Switzerland." As late as the eve of World War II, in the *Answer*, he continued to press for "a Dominion of two nationalities, Jewish and Arab . . . within the British empire."[17]

Chiefly it was Lewisohn's attachment to pacifism that suffered radical alteration as the Nazis made ready for war. In 1936, he had still rejoiced in Zionism as a "pacifist and religious national movement," but *Trumpet of Jubilee*, published only a year later, foresaw a time when even pacifists would be impelled to recognize "the necessity for immense armies and navies . . . as frontier guards" against neo-barbarism. By the fall of 1938, with the sad farce of the summer's Evian intergovernmental conference on refugees burning in his mind and with Austria and the Sudetenland and Spain and Ethiopia abandoned to Nazi or fascist hands, he had turned his back on pacifism: "*The war will come.* Jews, Zionists, pacifists—we live . . . in a world we never made. It is a predominantly pagan world . . . which, evidently, can be cleansed only by fire. . . . The cleansing war will come." But in November 1938, it was the Nazi *Kristallnacht* pogrom which came, and in May 1939, Great Britain's White Paper, severely curtailing Jewish immigration into Palestine, and now Lewisohn spoke as he would never have believed it possible for him to speak: "I will not say in the German manner that necessity knows no law. No Jew, thank God, will ever say that. But I will say that a great people will not consent to perish in order that a handful of semi-barbarians may satisfy their arrogance and a shifty and frightened government indulge in chicanery." Perhaps he relented a bit thereafter, for in June, on the eve of the Zionist Organization's forty-second convention, he urged it on the readers of his "Watchman" column in the *New Palestine* that support for Jewish Palestine was "a task as far as possible removed from any pagan or warlike activity," that Zionists were "the proponents . . . of the most vital and . . . the most moral and universal cause now before mankind." At length, however, nearly four months after the German assault on Poland had inaugurated World War II, he felt himself constrained to admit:

> For once war has brought and has, despite immeasurable cruelty and suffering, continued to bring a gleam of hope, a beginning of healing of the soul if not of the body of mankind. If nothing else, it has helped the Western World to throw off the miasma of fear and irresolution that was stifling the spirit of mankind. At least now we can act.

It was an "empty pacifism" that had brought civilization to the brink of ruin and decay. The time when "an abstention from all force" could be thought the best therapy for mankind's ills, and

when Zionist goals and pacifist goals could be seen as complementary, if not indeed identical—that time had all too manifestly
passed.[18]

Something else appeared to have passed with it, or at least been
much eroded, namely Lewisohn's sensitivity to Arab fears of relega-
tion to a subordinate status. How that erosion came about is not
hard to understand. "The state of the world and, above all, . . . of
the Jewish people," he wrote in December 1939, "is so ineffably
grievous that even the stoutest heart quivers." He saw his people
"being destroyed by savages." How right Herzl had been: " 'If ever
they will leave us in peace for three generations! But they never
have.' Nor ever will. . . . There is not the slightest guarantee that
they ever will." Earlier that year, even before the outbreak of war,
he had tried to explain his sense of the Jewish reality:

> For the sake of the [liberal Protestant journal] *Christian Century* and
> other friendly enemies let me say: We have loved and served the
> lands and peoples and languages and polities of our dispersion. We
> find it heartbreakingly difficult to spread the Zionist truth because
> the majority of Jews love their adopted lands and countrymen too
> deeply and too well. But the great and tragic answer is: Nowhere has
> our love been returned. Nowhere has it been even wanted. Nowhere
> in the deepest sense have *we* been wanted. Nowhere, therefore, de-
> spite our uttermost striving and love and sacrifices, have we been at
> home. Negation of the Galuth [Diaspora] is needing to go home.

One must add to all this an insight of his into the nature of the
Nazi regime: "Those who burned the synagogues [of Germany] and
tortured innocent people to death [on *Kristallnacht*] cannot retrace
their moral steps. Their will has receded to a lower level. And since
life on all levels is dynamic, the wicked must become more
wicked." He can have had, in February 1939, no foreknowledge of
the *Endlösung*, Hitler's "Final Solution," but somehow was tor-
mented nonetheless by a presentiment of Auschwitz! That is why he
could pronounce the Jewish cause "the last touchstone of Western
civilization. No, this is not arrogance. It is cold fact. The Jewish
people has been made . . . symbol and sign of the perishing liberties
and decencies of the West." Now Lewisohn could bring himself to
dismiss the Arabs of Palestine as "semi-barbarians" and insist that
the "only solution" to the Arab problem was "peaceful collabora-

tion on the part of the Arabs with the civilization we are building."
It was sheer desperation which induced him to endorse for Arabs
precisely what he had long since spurned for Jews, an inevitably
servile assimilationism.[19]

Had Lewisohn repudiated his belief that "no man is good enough
to rule another [and] no majority is good enough to rule a permanent and permanently different minority"? He would never display
antagonism to "the simple Arab people," the *fellahin* and Bedouin,
whose "deep conservatism" he accounted a not "wholly unamiable
characteristic." He could even concede that the Palestinian Arabs
possessed "a genuine nationalist movement and a genuine fear of
Jewish dominance," but seized as he was even before the Nazi
Blitzkrieg by anxiety over the fate of the Jews in Nazi-occupied
Europe as well as those in Palestine, he was driven to the judgment
that the "Arab problem" had "become babble," that though Jews
had "clean hands as far as Palestinian Arabs [were] concerned,"
they did "not even need those clean hands [which were] a special
and a unique offering . . . upon an eternal altar of humanity"; in
short, that Zionist development in the Land needed "no defense
and no justification." His foreboding had persuaded him that no
attention should be paid Arab remonstrations: "The life of the Arab
people is not at stake. The life of the Palestinian Arab is not at
stake. . . . But the life of the Jewish people is at stake." Nor had
Lewisohn patience left for "the rather dreadful British use of the
words and concept of fairness," for "what is fairness to the possible
occupants of empty empires is not fairness to a landless people
threatened with extermination."[20]

In general, the war and the ever bleaker prospects it entailed for
European Jewry made for a more aggressive, more militant Zionist
stance on Lewisohn's part. No more would he be heard to advocate
a Zionism divorced from political power. Within Zionism, "within
the Zionist Organization," he agreed, "there must be no desire for
power, office or honor [and] no personal aims," but certainly, indeed "necessarily," Zionism was "to be highly organized, to create
an instrumentality by means of which to transmute" the Zionist
idea "into life and into action." The function of Zionism, he contended now, was "to politicize the Jewish people," to transfigure
that people into one willing its own life, "and a will to life is and

must be . . . a will to political power." That is what preoccupied
him as the world slid into war. After Evian and *Kristallnacht*, he
could not doubt that "in the quite ultimate sense the antithesis for
the entire Jewish people [was] one . . . between a greater Zion
instantly reborn or decimation, degradation, death." The struggle
for Zion required "a political act . . . an uprising of American Jewry
through increase in Zionist membership." American Jews had to be
convinced somehow to "arise . . . and by a political act of overwhelming power and directness say to the world: Palestine is ours;
the Jews of Central and Eastern Europe are ours and not the play-
things of any brute who chooses to void his venom on and through
them."

More: "The whole matter is political; the defense of the Jewish
people must be a political act. The task of the Jewish people, if it
would survive, is by some means to make itself into a political
power and so a counterweight to the political power of the Arabs in
what is necessarily today a game of power." Of course he was not
unaware of the distance he had come, the extent to which events
had compelled him to modify his assumptions: "It is a great pity
that we must stoop to the world's level of brutality and that our
cause can not reasonably prevail by virtue of its inherent truth
and right."[21]

But, the world being what it was, every Jew had a "minimum
duty," "to take an affirmative moral attitude toward his people and
that people's function within the history of our time." He was
"tempted to write—a belligerently affirmative moral attitude."
Lewisohn himself could not be reproached for want of such an
attitude and he would not shrink from publicizing it on innumerable occasions, both in his writings and in the frequent addresses he
was called upon to deliver in various American communities. After
Evian and *Kristallnacht* and his realization of how indifferent the
world was to the Jewish plight, he urged his people "to insist not
only on Palestine in the meaning of Cis-Jordania [West Bank], but
in the meaning of Transjordania." On this point, he would not
compromise; the Jews had to "re-occupy Palestine on both sides of
the Jordan"; more, to "demand to the utmost limit of the lands
available, from the Mediterranean to the Twin Rivers [that is, to
Iraq], the liquidation of the Galuth." That was now his goal: to

bring an end to the Jewish dispersion. He knew very well, of course, that its fulfillment lay, if at all, in the distant future, but one had to overlook no opportunity "to turn the Jewish people into a Zionist people; into a people that at last has learned its lesson . . . the lesson of the negation of Galuth as a form of human life." One had to press forward unrelentingly to win "the Jewish people's conscious assent to its manifest destiny." Jews would have to be taught to forget "the stupid self-lacerating malice of the materialistic interpretation of history"; they would have to be taught that "man makes history. Man is at the core of the dynamism of the historic process. Heroes and heroic people will their destiny."[22]

The left-wing pacifist of earlier years had been transformed into a right-wing militant, but his militancy was not confined to extravagant pronouncements about Jewish destiny. It was revealed also in an unwillingness to see in anti-Zionism anything but an "impenetrable dishonor of the human psyche," an inability to perceive anti-Zionist Jews as meriting any designation but that of "the frightened and the servile and the death-dedicated." But it was in particular against "what was once Christendom" that his militancy asserted itself most astringently. Christianity always commanded Lewisohn's respect in that he could never overlook its Jewish provenance; regrettably, it had never been potent enough to overcome paganism, but as an instance of spiritual striving (had it not produced souls like his friends Thomas Mann, Archibald MacLeish, Reinhold Niebuhr, Carl Hermann Voss, Pierre Van Paassen?) it was far from despicable. But *Christendom* was worthy of a profound contempt, which only grew in ferocity as it became increasingly evident how much success Hitler had enjoyed in his war against the Jews. Lewisohn could not look away from what Jews had been, and were being, made or allowed to suffer within the confines of Christian civilization. Why had Christendom "been able morally to endure what Hitler did in 1933"? Why had the "world" (but he meant the Christian world) said "unanimously" at Evian in 1938: "We want no Jews"? "Where were [the millions of Jesus' followers] in the great Christian democracies of the West when the extermination of the Nazarene's people was going on?" The Christian West had "let the Jewish people be destroyed; without a quiver they saw the foulest crime in all history done."

He had hoped that some of the Jews under the Nazi heel would survive, two or three million at least. Alas, *fuit Ilium*. As the Soviet armies moved west, it became evident that Jewry would emerge from the war "at best totally impoverished, infinitely more stricken both physically and morally than [Churchill's Britain or] any people in the long and somber history of this sorry human race." And "yet no act of restitution, reparation or justice seems even to hover on the farthest horizon."[23]

Christendom had nothing of worth to teach Jewry. There was but one thing of value Jews could gain from the Christian world, recognition of their right to "an undiminished and undivided Eretz Yisrael." Christendom owed this to the Jews, for whose martyrdom it bore so immense a guilt. "Nothing that the Jewish people asks of Christendom can be too much. Nothing it asks can be illegitimate. . . . To mention Arab interests or colonial policy . . . in the face of our martyrdom is as insolent as it is shameless." These were not mere effusions on his part; they were not mere propaganda, but a species of heartfelt polemics. Not only in the *New Palestine*, which he edited from November 1944 to June 1947, but in the novel *Breathe upon These* (1944), he bespoke his scorn for the Christian conscience which had exhibited itself in the SS *Struma* disaster of 1941, when more than seven hundred refugees, denied entry into Palestine, had perished in the Black Sea. He had written *Breathe upon These*, he told the Zionist leader Abba Hillel Silver, because he believed it urgent to address "to the Christian world the great necessary . . . accusation of the Jewish people." Rabbi Silver read the book in manuscript and advised Lewisohn not to publish it; publication of a novel reviving the *Struma* affair, he feared, might offend the British government and thereby injure the Zionist cause, but Lewisohn rejected the rabbi's advice. He did not believe Jews could "afford [the] luxury" of accepting injustice in silence: "The crime committed against us" was too painfully "unique and monstrous." It was an emotion he gave voice to again and again in the novel, at one point with extraordinary wryness when he had his main Jewish character, the refugee Erich Dorfsohn, remark: "If I wanted to be cynical I'd say that, looking at human nature after all these Christian centuries, Pontius Pilate's reputation is worse than he deserves." If it was Lewisohn's fate to see Christian civilization lurch violently into unimaginably grotesque moral chaos and squalor, he felt himself under no obligation, even to the Zionist cause, to conceal his disgust.[24]

As the Axis tide ebbed, Lewisohn realized that the struggle for Jewish rights in Palestine could be expected only to intensify, that now even more than before, with the war's end in sight, it was needful to Zionize Jewry, above all American Jewry. He thought it well then to sum up his understanding of Zionism in a series of four "Letters to a New Member" of the Zionist Organization. These appeared in the *New Palestine* during the winter and early spring of 1945.

The Zionist Organization, he wrote, represented those who were "determined not only that Israel is to be redeemed but that, through Israel's redemption, some good shall finally spring from the chaos and the moral horrors of this age." What was "the center and the core of the liberating truth" Zionism embodied? It was "the recognition of the uniqueness of Jewish history and destiny." Only a Zionist analysis could explain the lamentable vulnerability of European Jewry during World War II, the fact that while other powerless groups, the Danes, for example, had been able to survive the German occupation, mass graves were all that remained of the Jews. To Zionists, the cause was evident: the Jews, unlike the Danes, "were neither together nor at home." They were "helpless . . . in the alien streets of alien places," and "what did we die of but our homelessness?" But the Jews had not recognized their homelessness soon enough, which pointed up the anomaly at the heart of the Jewish experience in Central and Western Europe: "Here were people who felt safe, at one with their environment, deeply at home, and who were . . . on the very edge of the abyss." For this, Lewisohn held the nineteenth-century Emancipation responsible. The sponsors of "the so-called Emancipation" had thought that, "if Jews were left alone, oppressed and restricted in no way, they would blandly disappear." Europe had "never wanted the Jews as Jews," had "never wanted to liberate the Jews as Jews."

It was worse than that. In the course of the nineteenth century, virtually "every people, great or small," had begun clamoring "for racial and cultural and linguistic homogeneity within its national borders," and what were the Jews to do? "To live at all, [they] had to adopt these various passions, or seem to adopt them," and thus they "lived lives ever more false and brittle and precarious." In the end, "everywhere and always surly acceptance was replaced by cruel repudiation," which would have left Jewry "utterly without hope or health or human dignity, except that the Eternal . . . had already prepared a remedy." That remedy was, of course, Zionism, but how many had seen Zionism as such in time to save themselves? The false blandishments of the Emancipation had blinded them to the truth that "modern anti-Semitism . . . arose with and during the emancipation and must consequently be very deeply connected with it." This was "the truth which meets with so much inner resistance on the part of men not brave enough nor clear-minded enough to face things as they really are." It was scarcely a new truth; "wise and sensitive spirits" like Moses Hess had perceived it during the mid-1800s, but Hess's *Rome and Jerusalem* of 1862 had been "almost totally neglected." It took the enormities of the twentieth century to confirm Hess's preachments and to establish beyond doubt what the rebuilding of Jewish life in the Land of Israel meant: "For once in history a political act will be a moral act and security and redemption will be one."[25]

The last decade of Lewisohn's life witnessed first the bloody spectacle of Zionist conflict with the British and then, after the establishment of an independent Jewish republic, war with the neighboring Arab states, and at length the new state's consolidation and internal growth. It was also a decade whose first three years involved painful collisions with leaders of the Zionist Organization of America over his editorship of the *New Palestine*. Subsequently, however, from 1948 on, he faced a far less bruising challenge, membership on the faculty of the newly founded Brandeis University. For all the *Sturm und Drang* of those years, his Zionist standpoint appears to have changed relatively little after the "Letters to a New Member" of 1945. He no longer argued for a total negation of the Diaspora; it was its "transformation . . . into something other and better" that he hoped for now. Lewisohn did, however, make increasingly explicit what had long been at least implicit in his conception of Jewish life, the virtual identity of Zionism and Judaism (and by Judaism he meant now something markedly traditionalist).

In December 1947, with Soviet-Western relations growing more and more problematic, with Palestine lapsed into an interregnum of anarchy, and the United States government wavering in its support for partition, he tried to explain "the frightful confusion and moral deterioration" which, it seemed to him, had become universal: "Deeper even than its moral deterioration" were "the confusion and the aimlessness" of the world. As he saw it from a perspective which owed more than a little to W. B. Yeats and T. S. Eliot, "the democratic forces have no passion and no force . . . because they have no steady and direct aim, an aim which must always have a metaphysical, a religious sanction to validate it." Not long thereafter Lewisohn went on to adumbrate this theme in *The American Jew: Character and Destiny* (1950), his last important Jewish book.[26]

Even the winning of Jewish sovereignty, he asserted in *The American Jew*, had not solved the problem of " 'emancipated' Jews with blurred Jewish memories," who now, with the struggle for a Jewish state won, "were thrown back upon their original Jewish emptiness," that meant, "upon a human emptiness," as he construed it. The "problem of the contemporary Jew" was "one problem, the problem of his total and affirmative re-Judaization," and here Lewisohn envisaged a purely religious solution: "The necessary survival of the Jewish people, which has already survived so many peoples and so many empires, and the survival of that people as the manifest expression of God's will in history—such is at once our Judaism and our Zionism, one and indivisible." He would not be content with a State of Israel which was "merely another state among the states of the pagans"; the State of Israel had to be "in some sense we cannot yet discern . . . a kingdom of priests and a holy nation." And Jewish life in America? "The measure of American Zionism will be the measure of American Judaism. Authentic Jews are and must be Zionists," for Zionism, he insisted sententiously, is "that central aspect of the Jewish faith . . . that the Jewish people, the suffering servant of mankind described by the prophet, must survive as a religio-ethnic entity . . . [in] the historic process determined by the Divine Will."[27]

The founding by the Modern Orthodox "Mizrachi" Zionists of Bar-Ilan University at Ramat Gan, or at least the laying of the projected school's cornerstone in the summer of 1953, offered Lewisohn an opportunity to formulate what it may not be improper to designate his *envoi*. In a speech which he prepared for the occasion, though his affairs in the United States would prevent him from visiting Israel to deliver it, he addressed himself to the Jewish share in "the long crisis of mankind." The Jewish people was "the living incarnation, even in sin . . . of God and his Law, of form, cosmos, obedience," but "idolatrous slave-states"—the Nazi Reich, the Soviet Union—could not endure the incarnation and were impelled to attempt its annihilation. "The destruction of so vast a proportion of the living Jewish people is a description, a definition, of the nature of the human crisis." That was terrible enough, but even more wounding was the fact that Jews had been and were being spiritually as well as physically victimized, so that "thousands of Jews, especially . . . intellectuals, joined in the nihilist rebellion against the foundations of human civilization . . . and helped to gnaw away the rock upon which alone their feet could stand." Even in the Jewish State there was the threat of "this pseudo-humanitarian apostasy," but "no one not wholly bereft of historical vision or historical insight will imagine that the [State of Israel] can serve its function either as a nation or as a factor among the nations, unless it houses a people that will be in the deepest sense a different people, a *goy kaddosh*"—in biblical language, a holy people. More, "unless the people of the State are Jews, Jews in the classical sense, and unless the State is a Jewish State, whose continuity with the whole of Jewish history is unhurt and unbreached, unless that is so, all the aspirations toward Zion and all the blood and tears and all the generosity and selfless effort of many generations will be in mortal danger of having been almost in vain."

And so in the end it came to theology. Did it come also to theocracy? That question eludes a definite answer. Man's freedom, Lewisohn had willed himself to believe, consisted "exclusively in his choice of a Law which he shall obey and that this Law must be, in different senses for different groups, but supremely for the Jewish people, the Law of God." Still, Lewisohn did not or would not indicate how "this end of a wholly Jewish State" was to be attained. He might have used the occasion of the founding of a Mizrachi-sponsored university to urge the virtues of Israel's official rabbinical establishment, but all he would permit himself was the observation

182 STANLEY F. CHYET

that he had an awareness "of the very troublesome problems [involved], such as . . . the crucial problem of adjusting the necessities of a contemporary commonwealth into the framework of hallachic [traditional Jewish religio-legal] structure."[28]

Lewisohn's approach to Zionism from the publication of *Israel* to the appearance of *The American Jew*, a span of twenty-five years, seems rather remarkably consistent when one considers how different the world was in 1950 from what it had been in 1925. Lewisohn, of course, spoke in the idiom of his generation, an idiom which often enough attributed to leadership an exalted glow, made much, however unassertively, of "the white man's burden," and entertained notions of "heroism" and "destiny." Even so, it was scarcely a "Nietzschean" Zionism that Lewisohn advocated; it owed everything to the classical morality of the West. Irwin Edman had not been so wide of the mark in 1929 when he perceived in *Mid-Channel* a "union of Hellenism and Talmudical Judaism" and in Lewisohn's morality an "attachment to . . . the golden thread of Greece, the silver thread of Judea." Not a "Nietzschean" but, if anything, an "Arnoldian" tendency may be said to have informed Lewisohn's Zionist ponderings; he was naturally drawn to the Matthew Arnold who had regarded "the final aim of both Hellenism and Hebraism, as . . . man's perfection or salvation." Even after the horrors of the *Endlösung* had become common knowledge, Lewisohn could write, "The dream and the redemption of Eretz Yisrael are pure. . . . Revenge and triumph do not enter in." Lewisohn always saw "authentic" Jewry, in particular the Palestinian community, as exemplary of the best in Western civilization. Zionism, as he conceived of it, constituted no radical departure from the values of the West; on the contrary, it affirmed and reaffirmed those values: "our hands are the only clean hands in the world."[29]

Lionel Trilling marched to a different drummer; he stigmatized Lewisohn's passionate advocacy of "Jewish self-realization" as a neurosis fostering "a willingness to be provincial and parochial." But in speaking so Trilling misrepresented the man who attacked "an intense Jewish parochialism" as productive only of "tight unilluminated little groups" with "no vision beyond their boundaries," a man who thought in terms of "the classical liberties and tolerance of civilized mankind" and could declare praiseworthy a Zionism which was "not sentimental, nor based upon small loyalties, however honorable." Lewisohn's "provincial" conception of Zionism was of "a movement of the creative word and the persuasive act, a movement founded by men of letters, fostered and spread by them." He had, it is true, long wished to see the development of a "psycho-mythological history of the Jews," and it may be argued with some cogency that his work almost unfailingly evinced a "psychomythological" *Tendenz*, but that is hardly identical with a spirit of provincialism.

Primarily, of course, what did change in Lewisohn's Zionist commitment between 1925 and 1950—indeed, the change had been accomplished by 1938—was his abandonment of bi-nationalism and pacifism. These were casualties of Hitlerism. As the Nazi menace intensified, Lewisohn was no longer able to preach a force-eschewing Zionism; now the Zionism he urged on his readers was unashamedly aggressive, as he felt it had to be if Jews and Jewish Palestine were to survive the machinations of their enemies. But it was never, it could never be, a violent, militaristic Zionism he preached. Lewisohn plainly agreed with the Irgunists and Sternists in their insistence that the Jews were entitled to both banks of the Jordan, but he would never countenance the terrorist tactics they permitted themselves; terrorism was to be "unequivocally condemned" as "stupid, criminal, futile, unJewish." He would never countenance pagan solutions; "Jewish event must remain Jewish or it will serve neither the Jew nor the world," he had written in 1938 (when the "terror in Palestine" was primarily of Arab inspiration), and he was to persist in that view through all the Mandatory provocations of the 1940s.[30]

It would be a mistake to conclude that Lewisohn's Zionist professions were innocent of ambiguity. His Zionism was emphatically not the "utopian fantasy" Elmer Rice imagined it to be in 1933, Hitler would see to that, but Louis Kronenberger's admittedly polemical insinuation a decade later that Lewisohn displayed in his work no "spontaneous Jewishness" should not be too quickly set aside. Was there something to it? Coevals of Lewisohn, like Henry L. Mencken and Fred T. Marsh, would have said, yes. Mencken, in reviewing *Mid-Channel*, had taken it on himself to warn astutely, if mercilessly, that "the repatriated and reconditioned Jew . . . is still bound to be more or less uneasy. He . . . is still a man living in a world of defeats and frustrations, and they pursue him into his Schul quite . . . relentlessly." Marsh observed a few years later, on the publication of *An Altar in the Fields* (1934), that where Lewisohn's salvation was concerned, "almost he protests too much," and "one wonders whether he . . . is truly so happy in Zion."[31]

How "happy in Zion" was he? Lewisohn's first journey to Palestine, in the 1920s, produced not only *Israel*, but also the short story entitled *Holy Land*, which on one level at least may be read as a cautionary tale asserting that Jews alone could hope to survive the fierce realities of the Land and reclaim it for a viable future; neither the Arabs, hopelessly primitive, nor the Christians (at any rate Western Christians), constrained to shape for themselves a purely mythic Holy Land, had any genuine stake in a living Palestine. On another level, however—a level suggested by the fact that Jewish characters, the narrator perhaps excepted, are at most secondary or even tertiary in the story—one may be forgiven for asking whether Lewisohn was not expressing an inability of his own to identify with the Land (as distinct from the Diaspora effort to revive the Land).

The Palestinian Jewish settlement is at best tangential in *Holy Land*, as also in the later tales *The Last Days of Shylock* (1931) and "By the Waters of Babylon" in *This People* (1933). For all his Zionist ardor from 1925 on, Lewisohn never fashioned a story which represented Palestinian Jewry as a tangible presence rather than as something seen, whether physically or spiritually, from afar. Arthur Levy, in *The Island Within*, documents his newfound Jewish identity by going off to aid the Jews of Rumania, not Palestine; Dr. Weyl, in *An Altar in the Fields*, believes "we . . . bitterly need . . . [an] ancestral land and speech," but is nonetheless on his way back to Cincinnati; Gabriel Weiss and his mother, in *Trumpet of Jubilee*, seek refuge not in Palestine, but in the United States, and when Gabriel finally announces his intention of leaving America to join "in the defence of Eretz Yisrael," it is near the end of the novel, but it is with his life and experience in America that *Trumpet of Jubilee* has dealt; the Dorfsohns' son, in *Breathe upon These*, has settled in Palestine, but the Dorfsohns themselves appear permanently located in America; Jerome Goodman, in Lewisohn's last novel, *In a*

Summer Season (1955), is proud of his son, who is preparing himself for *aliyah*, but Jerome himself, though "secretary of [his] local Zionist District," seems to have no thought of quitting the Diaspora. This is all rather remarkable when one takes account of the commitments which Lewisohn urged Jews to take on themselves in his nonfictional writings about Zionism. It is startling to find him, in a review of Meyer Levin's realistic novel *The Old Bunch* (1937), charging Levin with "Jewish self-contempt and self-laceration" and even with "violent Jewish self-hatred," though in *Yehuda* (1930) and later in *My Father's House* (1947) Levin was at pains to depict the Palestinian community, and with undeniable beauty, as a vivid and central actuality, something Lewisohn never achieved or even attempted in any of his novels and stories. (He did relent some years later and express esteem for Levin's "delicacy and sensitiveness.") [32]

What is one to make of these ambiguities? To some degree, they probably reflect the circumstance that Lewisohn's Zionism was essentially reactive, to what he called the "harsh music of reality," the deceptions and broken promises of the nineteenth-century Emancipation, the corruptions, distortions, and "dreadful diseases" of the Diaspora and not least, of course, the atrocities of Hitlerism and Stalinism. It was to escape and to combat all these that he had espoused the Zionist cause, and espoused it with utter sincerity. The Baltimore rabbi, Charles A. Rubenstein, who in 1936 intimated on the evidence of *Up Stream* that Lewisohn had "landed in the lap of Zionism on the rebound," may have come within sight of the truth, though it was not a little foolish and malicious of him to "suppose" in public that Lewisohn had "gained in [his] translation to Eretz Israel what a hard-boiled world would call material advantage," and Lewisohn was really quite charitable in replying that Rubenstein did not "know what a conviction is nor how it is arrived at . . . that the idea, as Heine said . . . , takes us and lashes us into the arena, whether we like it or not, and that we could not stop to count gain or loss if we would."

"Rebound" or "reaction" may very well have figured in Lewisohn's immersion in Zionism. But the conversion, if that term is proper here, was powerless to annul this reality: so embedded in his sensibilities was the life of the Diaspora, and so resistant to erosion were his connections with the cosmopolitan life of the West, that the life of Jewish Palestine and the State of Israel could be fiercely, passionately admired, but never embraced, and thus never rendered in his fiction with any sort of amplitude. In a non-fictional, auto-biographical book like *Israel*, Lewisohn was able to communicate a quite exhilarating sense of the Land and the Jewish possibilities of the Land, but *Israel*, for all its indisputable charm and exaltation, was ultimately a work of immensely superior journalism, not a work of the unfettered imagination. Lewisohn himself perhaps sup-plied a key to the riddle when he stated in the *Nation* during the mid-1920s that "Europe is delicious; Europe is adorable. . . . Only, for us [American expatriates], this is diversion not life, rest and not art. . . . No one can create out of a life that he has to perceive consciously. In this matter all must be instinct or . . . have become instinct." Substitute "the Land of Israel" for "Europe" and the riddle is less of a riddle.[33]

The fact is that Lewisohn could never be entirely certain of victory in the struggle to liberate himself from what he termed "the deep human dishonor of alienation from faith and folk" he had known in his earlier, Methodist-South Carolina years. In that strug-gle, Zionism would become for him a mighty weapon. There may have been a touch of *faute de mieux*, but the core of his Zionist aspiration was something quite different, the reaching out for a swelling personal faith, a personal soteriology. When Lewisohn said, as he so often did, that all roads led to Zion, he did not say it regretfully or invidiously; he said it with a decisiveness, a surety, which was as close as he could ever come to triumph. But for him, to be quite accurate, no road led to Zion, though all roads led to Zionism. Zionism, not Zion, was his liberation. Almost from the beginning he had known that he would never settle in Zion ("Never, I dare say, shall I be able to dwell upon that earth," he wrote in *Mid-Channel*), but he would live in Zionism. The ache of the past, the fear-born ape in his breast, the desperate ills of homelessness, these would nevermore hold him in their stern grip. In the post-war world he had an altered sense of American life, too: he came to feel that American Jewry, instead of disappearing, should be "re-Judaized" and America redeemed thereby from "the traditional hopeless area of exile." The State of Israel, he believed, could not be safe unless—and here he expected American Jews would play an important role—America continued as "the very bastion and defense of human liberty" and avoided crashing "into slavery and chaos."

It seems undeniable, as he believed, that his return to Jewish loyalties and his espousal of Zionism had "isolated [him] as an American man of letters," so that he had "risked and probably lost the illusory satisfaction . . . there is in posthumous fame." Had he regrets or second thoughts?

> I have lost the world, present and future. Have I gained the Jewish people? Have I gained their support and their memory? Time will show. If my choice had to be made over again, I would make the same choice. And that would be no virtue in me. For, being what I am, believing as I do, I could make no other choice. You remember the old saying of Buffon: the style is the man. I add an even deeper and truer one: The choice is the man.[34]

Notes

1. See Lewisohn's autobiographical volumes: *Up Stream: An American Chronicle* (New York: Boni & Liveright, 1922); *Israel* (New York: Boni & Liveright, 1925); *Mid-Channel: An American Chronicle* (New York: Harper & Bros., 1929); and (with Edna M. Lewisohn) *Haven* (New York: Dial Press, 1940). See also Lewisohn, ed. and trans., *Goethe: The Story of a Man* (New York: Farrar, Straus, 1949); Lewisohn, ed., *Theodor Herzl: A Portrait for this Age* (Cleveland: World Publishing, 1955); S. F. Chyet, "Ludwig Lewisohn in Charleston," *American Jewish Historical Quarterly* 54 (March 1965): 296–322; Chyet, "Lewisohn and Hauptmann," *Proceedings of the Sixth World Congress of Jewish Studies* (Jerusalem: World Union of Jewish Studies, 1975) 2:205–13; Seymour Lainoff, *Ludwig Lewisohn* (Boston: Twayne, 1982).
2. Thorstein Veblen, "The Intellectual Pre-eminence of Jews in Modern Europe," in *The Portable Veblen* (New York: Viking Press, 1949), 474, 478 (Veblen's essay dates from 1919); Alfred Kazin, *On Native Grounds: An Interpretation of Modern American Prose Literature* (Garden City: Doubleday, 1956), 153, 205–7 (Kazin's book originally appeared in 1942).
3. *Jerusalem Post*, Jan. 1, 1956: 3; Lewisohn to Abba Hillel Silver, Jan. 1, 1946, and to Irving Miller, July 18, 1946 (American Jewish Archives, Cincinnati); Lewisohn, ed., *Rebirth: A Book of Modern Jewish Thought* (New York: Harper & Bros., 1935), 274; *Up Stream*, 125; ibid. (New York: Modern Library, 1926), 146; Lewisohn, *The Answer* (New York:

Liveright, 1939), 339; Lewisohn, "A Panorama of a Half-Century of American Jewish Literature," *Jewish Book Annual* 9 (1950–51): 4.

4. Lewisohn, *Roman Summer* (New York: Harper & Bros., 1927), 185; *Up Stream* (1922), 17, 77.

5. Henry Hurwitz to Lewisohn, April 20, 1915; May 5, 1917; July 11, 1917; July 16, 1917; May 10, 1921; June 3, 1921; October 10, 1921; February 1, 1923; February 7, 1923; May 15, 1923 (American Jewish Archives); Lewisohn to Hurwitz, February 4, 1923, and to Robert C. Rothenberg, May 4, 1923 (American Jewish Archives); Chyet, "Ludwig Lewisohn: The Years of Becoming," *American Jewish Archives* 11:132; *Haven*, 38; W. E. Leonard, "Menorah," *Menorah Journal* 1 (January 1915): 20–22; *Up Stream* (1922), 125; Lewisohn's introduction to Georg Hirschfeld, *The Mothers* (Garden City: Doubleday, 1916), xiii.

6. *Mid-Channel*, 46, 48–49; Hurwitz to Lewisohn, May 15, 1923 (American Jewish Archives); Kurt Blumenfeld, *Erlebte Judenfrage* (Stuttgart: Deutsche Verlags-Anstalt, 1962), 154.

7. *Mid-Channel*, 20, 52–54; *Menorah Journal* 10 (December 1924): 497; *New Palestine*, December 1, 1939: 4; Blumenfeld to Lewisohn, May 8, 1953 (American Jewish Archives); Chaim Weizmann to Lewisohn, May 21, 1949 (American Jewish Archives).

8. *The Portable Veblen*, 468; *Israel*, 100, 132, 147, 156.

9. Ibid., 84, 158, 181, 199, 204–6, 212; Blumenfeld, *Erlebte Judenfrage*, 155; *Nation*, September 16, 1925: 301–2.

10. *Israel*, 158, 217–18, 248.

11. Ibid., 71, 145–49, 209, 237, 247–48, 252, 254–55; *Up Stream* (1922), 234.

12. *Israel*, 144, 238–39, 248.

13. *Mid-Channel*, 55; *Nation*, October 7, 1925: 385–86; *American Jewish Year Book* 27 (1925–26): 58–60; H. Goldberg to Felix Warburg, October 2, 1925 (American Jewish Archives).

14. *Mid-Channel*, 106; *Nation*, May 3, 1933: 493–94; *Jewish Times* (Baltimore), January 3, 1936: 17; Lewisohn, *Adam: A Dramatic History* (New York: Harper & Bros., 1929), 97; *Menorah Journal* 10 (November–December 1924): 497; *Harper's*, November 1930: 702; Lewisohn, *The Island Within* (New York: Harper & Bros., 1928), 341; Lewisohn, *This People* (New York: Harper & Bros., 1933), 197; *Post* (Charleston, S.C.), January 17, 1931; *Rebirth*, xviii, xx, xxv, xxvii; Lewisohn, *The Permanent Horizon: A New Search for Old Truths* (New York: Harper & Bros., 1934), 49; *New Palestine*, June 28, 1940: 16.

15. *Rebirth*, xxviii, xxx–xxxii; Lewisohn, "The Collapse of Assimilationism," in M. W. Weisgal, ed., *Theodor Herzl: A Memorial* (New York: New Palestine/Zionist Organization of America, 1929), 263.

16. *Israel*, 257; *Island Within*, 342–42; *Mid-Channel*, 236, 259; Lewisohn, *The Last Days of Shylock* (New York: Harper & Bros., 1931), 160–62; *The Answer*, 158; Lewisohn, *Trumpet of Jubilee* (New York: Harper & Bros., 1937), 219; *New Palestine*, January 28, 1938:4.

17. *Trumpet of Jubilee*, 238, 261, 306; *Jewish Times*, July 17, 1936: 4; ibid., October 2, 1936: 2; *The Answer*, 117.

18. *Atlantic Monthly*, January 1936: 60; *Trumpet of Jubilee*, 258; *New Palestine*, October 14, 1938: 4; ibid., January 13, 1939: 4; ibid., May 26, 1939: 6; ibid., June 23, 1939: 4; ibid., December 29, 1939: 4, ibid., February 23, 1940: 4.

19. *New Palestine*, April 14, 1939: 4; ibid., November 24, 1939: 5; ibid., December 22, 1939: 4; ibid., February 3, 1939: 4; ibid., February 17, 1939: 4; ibid., March 17, 1939: 4; ibid., November 3, 1939: 4.

20. Ibid., January 29, 1938: 4; ibid., December 9, 1938: 4–5; ibid., February 24, 1939: 4; ibid., December 22, 1939: 4; ibid., March 8, 1940: 4; *Haven*, 242–43; *Jewish Times*, November 29, 1935: 29.

21. *New Palestine*, January 27, 1939: 4; ibid., March 8, 1940: 4; ibid., April 19, 1940: 6; ibid., February 10, 1929: 5; ibid., March 8, 1940: 4.

22. Ibid., December 2, 1938: 5; ibid., March 17, 1939: 4; ibid., March 24, 1939: 6; ibid., April 14, 1939: 4; ibid., September 12, 1939: 6; ibid., November 24, 1939: 4; ibid., May 17, 1940: 4; ibid., May 24, 1940: 4; ibid., September 11, 1942: 7–8; *Jewish Mirror*, June–July 1943: 5–6.

23. *New Palestine*, December 23, 1938: 4; ibid., December 26, 1941: 10; ibid., February 20, 1942: 18; ibid., May 21, 1943: 10; ibid., August 18, 1944: 480; ibid., January 1, 1945: 6; ibid., March 28, 1945: 4; ibid., November 16, 1945: 47; ibid., December 31, 1945: 4; ibid., July 12, 1946: 2; *Rebirth*, xx, xxiii–xxvii; *Trumpet of Jubilee*, 94–95, 258; Lewisohn, *Breathe upon These* (Indianapolis: Bobbs-Merrill, 1944), 175, 187, 191, 195.

24. *New Palestine*, January 8, 1943: 8; ibid., July 28, 1944: 4, ibid., October 27, 1944: 9; ibid., November 30, 1944: 5; *Breathe upon These*, 132–41, 151–59, 161, 171, 174–79, 185, 188, 192, 195; Lewisohn to A. H. Silver, December 7, 1942, and January 12, 1943, and Silver to Lewisohn, January 7, 1943 (Silver Archives, Cleveland).

25. *New Palestine*, January 19, 1945: 84; ibid., February 16, 1945: 120; ibid., March 17, 1945: 147; ibid., April 13, 1945: 175.

26. Lewisohn to A. H. Silver, January 1, 1946, and April 8, 1947, to Emanuel Neumann, June 16, 1946, and June 28, 1948, to Irving Miller, July 18, 1946, and to Israel Goldstein, April 18, 1947 (American Jewish Archives); Lewisohn, *The American Jew: Character and Destiny* (New York: Farrar, Straus, 1950), 159; *New Palestine*, December 26, 1947: 4.

27. *American Jew*, 160, 162–65.

28. S. F. Chyet, "Ludwig Lewisohn—On the Founding of Bar Ilan University," *Michael* 3 (Tel Aviv: Tel Aviv University, 1976): 336–39.

29. *New Palestine*, October 14, 1938: 4; ibid., October 21, 1938: 5; ibid., February 17, 1939: 4–5; ibid., March 17, 1939: 4; ibid., June 9, 1939: 4; ibid., June 23, 1939: 4; ibid., October 20, 1939: 4; ibid., December 1, 1939: 4; ibid., May 3, 1940: 4; ibid., June 7, 1940: 4; ibid., June 16, 1940: 10; ibid., March 3, 1944: 276; ibid., April 30, 1945: 4; ibid., May 28,

1948: 5; *Nation*, June 5, 1929: 672; *Answer*, 101, 305; *Israel*, 137–38, 252–53; *Trumpet of Jubilee*, 306–7; Lewisohn, *An Altar in the Fields* (New York: Harper & Bros., 1934), 271; *Island Within*, 343; *Haven*, 245; *Breathe upon These*, 147–48; Lewisohn, ed., *Among the Nations* (Philadelphia: Jewish Publication Society, 1948), xvi–xvii; *American Jew*, 168–69. See also Lewisohn, "A Study of Matthew Arnold," *Sewanee Review* 9 (1901): 442–56, and 10 (1902): 143–59, 302–19.

30. *New Palestine*, September 9, 1938: 6; ibid., November 11, 1938: 4; ibid., November 25, 1938: 4; ibid., October 27, 1944: 9; ibid., November 17, 1944: 28; ibid., August 29, 1947: 4; *Contemporary Jewish Record*, February 1944: 17; *Jewish Times*, November 8, 1935: 2; ibid., November 27, 1936: 2; Lewisohn to Emanuel Neumann, June 16, 1946 (American Jewish Archives).

31. *Nation*, May 17, 1933: 557; *Contemporary Jewish Record*, February 1944: 21; *American Mercury* 6 (1929): 380; *New York Herald Tribune Books*, February 25, 1934: VII-7.

32. *Island Within*, 344; *Altar in the Fields*, 271; *Trumpet of Jubilee*, 326; *Breathe upon These*, 47, 199; Lewisohn, *In a Summer Season* (New York: Farrar, Straus, 1955), 149, 185. See Lewisohn's *Holy Land* (New York: Harper & Bros., 1926), which first appeared in *Harper's*, October 1925: 523–27. See Lewisohn on Levin in *New Palestine*, May 31, 1940: 4; *Jewish Mirror*, November 1942: 36; and *Jewish Book Annual* 9 (1950–51): 7.

33. *New Palestine*, November 10, 1939: 4; ibid., April 12, 1940: 4; *Jewish Times*, September 25, 1936: 9; ibid., October 16, 1936: 2; *The Answer*, 339–40; *Nation*, October 14, 1925: 423.

34. *New Palestine*, September 9, 1938: 6; ibid., October 7, 1938: 4; ibid., December 2, 1938: 4; ibid., September 26, 1939: 4; ibid., February 9, 1940: 4; ibid., April 12, 1940: 5; ibid., January 19, 1945: 84; ibid., April 12, 1946: 182; *Mid-Channel*, 49, 93; *Jewish Times*, October 16, 1936: 2, 30; *The Answer*, 340–42; *American Jew*, 124–25, 173–74.

CHAPTER 8

Henry Hurwitz: Editor, Gadfly, Dreamer

Ira Eisenstein

The tens of thousands of Jews who reached these shores at the beginning of this century, "yearning to breathe free," did not find a *goldene medinah*. The adults struggled to make a living; and the children were aware of the fact that, in the eyes of their peers, they were strangers, who came without culture or knowledge of the civilized canons of behavior. The young people, to be sure, soon made their way in this land, and many of them, Henry Hurwitz included, made it to colleges and universities. (He had arrived in the Boston area, with his parents and sisters, in the early 1890s.) In 1904, Hurwitz was admitted to Harvard. But most of these students were by no means happy with their newly elevated status.

Horace Kallen, a contemporary of Hurwitz, wrote, some years later:

> I am inclined to think that feelings of inferiority and insecurity, together with resentment at the condition which bred them—'Jewish self-hatred' as it came to be called—was at work in the few Jewish college students of my day. It consisted of the effort to keep one's Jewish derivation and Jewish connections below the threshold of visibility; even, wherever possible, to dissociate oneself from them altogether.[1]

Professor Harry Wolfson described this state of mind as one of "escaping Judaism."[2]

Hurwitz had no intention of escaping Judaism. In fact, he was determined from the start to lead a renaissance of Judaism through the

191

zeal and energy of fellow students who felt as he did. In a loving portrait of his mother (published posthumously) Hurwitz reveals his
deep attachment to Jewish learning in the Litvak tradition of dedication to study, inspired, it appears, by this wonderful woman. He
studied *Humash* and *Rashi* and *davened* every day in pious devotion.

He writes of Bella Wolfson Hurwitz:

> She doubtless abetted my early zeal for piety and praying (as a boy I
> *davened* to beat the band from rising up in the morning to lying down
> at night, enough for a lifetime). Later she sought to moderate my
> excesses in praying and fasting and certainly when I gave up all
> rituals and praying and fasting, no syllable of reproach came from
> her, nor can I imagine that her affection was in the least abated . . .[3]

Obviously, young Henry experienced neither the indifference of
ignorant parents nor the harsh demands made upon young people
by fathers and mothers whose rigidity turned their children against
Judaism altogether.

At Harvard, Hurwitz was deeply impressed by men like William
James, George Santayana, and others of that brilliant faculty, who
opened up to him a new world, broader, more humane, more universal. It is not surprising that Hurwitz was dazzled by this array of
educated men, even though he had already been exposed to Latin
and Greek in high school. So, while he stopped *davening* and fast-
ing, he retained his passion for the intellectual life and his love of
Judaism, dedicating himself to the task of transposing his inherited
Jewish learning into the key of Jewish humanism.

In 1906, Hurwitz and a band of earnest classmates organized
what they called a Menorah Society "for Hebraic Culture and Ideals." It was an act of *hutzpah* and imagination which was destined
to change the face of Jewish intellectual life in the United States for
many years to come.

By 1913, eleven Menorah groups had been formed; and the Intercollegiate Menorah Association was established, with Henry Hurwitz as the "chancellor." In 1915, the *Menorah Journal* was
launched.[4]

The impressive format and contents of this first issue presaged the
extraordinary career of this magazine. Never before had a cultivated and eloquent presentation of Judaism been made on the level

of the *Journal*. I can testify to the fact that, as a student at Columbia College from 1923 to 1927, I found little inspiration in the then available Anglo-Jewish periodicals like the *American Hebrew*. Of course, learned journals were appearing, like the *Jewish Quarterly Review*; but for the non-academic Jew there was nothing to read. The appearance of the *Menorah Journal* had the same effect upon my sense of Jewish pride in the twenties that the establishment of the State of Israel in 1948 had for me and so many others.

The first issue (January 1915) contained articles by (among others) Louis D. Brandeis, Harry Wolfson, Joseph Jacobs, Max L. Margolis, and greetings from Richard Gottheil, Kaufman Kohler, Judah L. Magnes, and other distinguished Jewish personalities. As time went on some of the most talented writers and thinkers appeared for the first time in the pages of the *Journal*.[5]

In December 1917, the Menorah Quinquennial Convention took place, in New York. The program included addresses by distinguished scholars; but, significantly, it also brought to the delegates a concert of Jewish music, an address by Ernest Bloch, and readings from the French-Jewish poet Edmond Fleg. Included also was an evening of Jewish drama, with works by David Pinski and Sholem Asch. To top it off, there was an exhibit of works by Jewish artists.

The program of the convention reflects the broad interests which Hurwitz insisted was essential to an understanding of the Jewish creative spirit. Long before the now-popular phrase "Judaism as a Civilization" was coined by Mordecai Kaplan, Hurwitz translated that concept into a living program for the intellectuals of his day.

The broad scope of the Menorah movement had been articulated at the very beginning, when its purposes were outlined in the first issue of the *Journal*:

> Conceived as it is and nurtured as it must continue to be in the spirit of the Menorah idea, the *Menorah Journal* is under compulsion to be absolutely non-partisan, an expression of all that is best in Judaism and not merely some particular sect or school or locality or group of special interests, fearless in telling the truth; promoting constructive thought rather than aimless controversy; animated with the vitality and enthusiasm of youth, harking back to the past that we may deal more wisely with the present and the future; recording and appreciating Jewish achievement, not to brag but to bestir our-

selves to emulation and to deepen the consciousness of *noblesse oblige*, striving always to be sane and level-headed; offering no opinions of its own but providing an orderly platform for the discussion of mooted questions that really matter; dedicated first and foremost to the fostering of Jewish "humanities"; and the furthering of their influence as a spur to human service.

For a few years, from 1917 to 1923, Hurwitz issued a modest *Menorah Bulletin*, addressed primarily to members of the various Menorah societies, in which he articulated his strong convictions about the role of students. In October 1922, he wrote, "To be born a Jew is sheer accident; but what a glorious opportunity for fight, for faith, for achievement. The great Jewish heritage we glibly speak of, that is not yours by right of birth; it is yours only as you earn it, enhance it. . . . It is a matter of understanding, of free intellectual discovery and conquest, of the pursuit of studentship."

On later occasions Hurwitz gave utterance to his mature vision of a renewed Judaism: "I cannot conceive of Judaism as a religion in the conventional sense," he wrote in 1946. "I like to think of Judaism as humanity heightened. . . . Jewish religion is indivisible, all-penetrating, coextensive with the whole of life. The segregation of sanctities, prayers, commandments, the so-called religious feelings and attitudes into a church or church-imitating synagogue is offensive to me."[6]

"The elixir of (this) intellectual and spiritual fusion," he wrote in his final years, "I would call Humanist Judaism. It is to my own mind the Judaism of the modern, enlightened Jew who willingly, nay gladly, accepts himself as a Jew, but with the intellectual honesty and moral integrity of scientific man. And humanism, as I conceive it, embraces the poetic and mystical in life as well as the prosaic-rational."[7] "[Judaism] is a heritage of depth and versatility, a historic culture, fenced in and hugged close during times of darkness and dispersion, but a life to breathe free and intermingle with the general culture in times and countries of freedom, as in America today."[8]

From the start, Hurwitz was keenly aware of the need to infuse the Jewish spirit into all aspects of Jewish life, especially the communal institutions which, until then (1918), and for quite a while after, were manned by professionals who had little or no interest in

Jewish spiritual or cultural survival. He therefore urged students as-sociated with Menorah societies to enter Jewish communal service. In the *Menorah Bulletin* of March 1918, he announced that arrange-ments had been made with the New York School of Jewish Commu-nal Work to admit students who wished to enrich their knowledge of Judaism. Open lectures were also set up with Samson Benderly, Mor-decai Kaplan, and others. These lectures dealt with the reinterpreta-tion of Judaism and the reorganization of the synagogue.

This attempt to Judaize Jewish communal work anticipated by many decades the establishment of institutions for training Jewish communal workers; and it also pioneered in the effort to relate these studies to universities, a practice now widely accepted.

While Menorah societies proliferated, Hurwitz became aware of a weakness in their program. He had published Menorah syllabuses and pamphlets on various themes ("The Jew in the Modern World," "Introduction to Jewish History," "Jewish Factors in Western Civili-zation," etc.). But it became evident that these efforts were not always taken seriously. Students did not prepare; the invited speak-ers did all the work. Hurwitz prophetically recognized that the only way to get students to study was to have courses given at the universities themselves, for credit. Indeed, a proposal to introduce Jewish studies in the university came from the Columbia Menorah as early as 1918.

In the *Menorah Bulletin* of winter 1923, in an article entitled "Menorah Fundamentals," Hurwitz again urged the introduction of Jewish studies into the universities: He warned that "so long as Jewish studies are confined more or less to sectarian schools and theological seminaries, and are left mostly in the hands of the clerical profession, whether Christian or Jewish, who naturally bring their special bias to bear upon the interpretation of the mate-rial; as long, that is to say, as Jewish learning fails to command an integral place in our general American institutions of learning, where liberal studies are offered—just so long will Jewish learning, in our conception, remain in a state of suppression and sterility."

In 1927 Hurwitz launched an ambitious program. He convened a Menorah Conference. The theme of the Conference was "The Spiri-tual Situation of the Jew in America." The *Jewish Daily News* of

New York described it as a "turning point in American Jewry." Hurwitz himself regarded it as a milestone. "It was the first such assembly ever held in America, presaging new forces and directions for the future." Directing attention to the "paucity of ideas and content" in what passes as "Jewish education," were such speakers as Professor Mordecai Kaplan, Professor Julian Obermann, Professor Isaac L. Kandel, and others. To help fill this need, Hurwitz, in his Report on the Conference, proposed the establishment of a Menorah Foundation. "Through some such enterprise we can develop a Jewish education worthy of the name for adults no less than for children and youth. . . .

"We need not wait for any endowments to compare with that of the Rockefeller or Carnegie or Sage Foundations. . . . We can start on one or another section of our fields, with Jewish history or in the various aspects of modern life and problems, religious, social, political, economic, as friends are attracted to finance specific lines of inquiry."[9] An ambitious project indeed.

Spurred on by the support of his projects, which had grown, Hurwitz, in January 1928, was able to fulfill a long-standing desire, to change the *Journal* from a bi-monthly to a monthly, believing it to be a response to a new force in American Jewish life; the force of modern critical intelligence.

> In the broadest sense, the quest is a spiritual quest, a religious one. . . . The task is to find a modern spiritual sanction for the Jew's persistent distinctiveness even in the present time of individual religious and moral freedom on the one hand, and mass standardization on the other. . . .
>
> The distinction between clergy and laity, between religious and secular—these distinctions are not Jewish. If persisted in they can only bring added confusion, ill feeling, sterility in our Jewish spiritual life. It is for us to reassert the Jewish conception of the wholeness of human life. The whole is religious and must be sanctified. It cannot be divided into sacred and profane. And the whole life of ours must be humanistic, seeking the good in man in this world, in the free but disciplined cultivation of all human faculties and quests.[10]

The *Journal* was riding high in the late twenties. The January 1928 issue contained material by Charles A. Beard, Lion Feuchtwanger, Louis Golding, Clifton Fadiman, Lionel Trilling, an inset of sculptures by Jacob Epstein, and a frontispiece of Reuven Rubin's portrait of Ahad-Ha'am. And in 1929, Hurwitz announced the "establishment of the Menorah Association for the Advancement of Jewish Culture and Ideals, comprising the Intercollegiate Menorah Association, the Menorah Educational Conference, The *Menorah Journal*, the Menorah Summer School and the Menorah Foundation (when endowed)." An impressive array of distinguished names was appended to the announcement, forming a board of governors and an executive council.

Hurwitz was ready with major projects to be undertaken by the Menorah Foundation, for example, the "preparation of a History of the Jews since the year 70, comparable in method and spirit to the *Cambridge Modern History*." Hurwitz concluded his January 1929 article, "For Jewish Culture," with these words: "So now, with this enlarged scope and form of general organization, inviting all thoughtful men and women to membership in the Menorah Association, and urging . . . upon possible Maecenases the great and beautiful potentialities of the Menorah Foundation—the Menorah movement proceeds in its twenty-third year of quest."

Soon after, in March 1929, a dinner at the Biltmore Hotel in New York was given by wealthy supporters, including Lucius N. Littauer, Joseph Pulvermacher, S. W. Straus, and others, and the formation of the Menorah Foundation was announced. This glowing event was probably the peak of Menorah's influence. Hurwitz was full of hope for a glorious future.

Unfortunately, the Crash of that fall, 1929, and the persistent Depression ensuing, were major factors in the slow but steady decline of Menorah's fortunes.

There were, however, at least two other factors at work. One was the establishment of the Hillel Foundations by B'nai B'rith. This fraternal body had become interested in Jewish students, particularly those who were not members of Jewish college fraternities. In 1923, Hillel began providing centers for Jewish activities, and manning them with full-time salaried rabbinical leaders. In addition, the programs of these Hillel Foundations usually appealed to the broadest interests of the students, which were not always study and serious discussion. Menorah could not compete.

The second factor in the decline of the movement was the internal dissension caused by members of the editorial board who were of Marxist inclination, who tried to politicize the movement. A long and acrimonious struggle took place, involving on the one hand the managing editor, Elliot Cohen, and some of the writers he had attracted, and on the other Henry Hurwitz.[11]

In brief, the Depression had turned many Jewish intellectuals away from specifically Jewish concerns to the problems of economic and political change. During the 1930s, the Soviet Union was widely regarded as the model for future societies. Henry Hurwitz, however, while a liberal Democrat (he voted for Roosevelt and later for Stevenson), considered this new development a diversion from his original purpose in establishing the *Journal*. He had always been an intellectual Jew, while these younger writers and thinkers were, in fact, intellectuals who happened to be Jewish. The difference between the adjective and the noun was at the heart of their disagreement. After the June 1931 issue came out, Elliot Cohen left the *Journal*, and took away with him the group who became responsible, in part, for the establishment of the *Partisan Review* and other leftist publications. Cohen himself was not involved in *Partisan Review*; however, he was to become the founding editor of *Commentary* (1945).[12]

The net effect of these events was the financial impoverishment of the Menorah movement. A new group, known as the Friends of the *Menorah Journal*, was set up to improve the situation: "It is hoped that the financing of the *Menorah Journal* will be to put it on a solid and adequate basis. From there it is hoped to go on to adequate financing of the other activities of the Menorah movement, including the School." (This is from a memorandum most probably written by Hurwitz, date uncertain.) Obviously, Henry Hurwitz still expected to proceed with his ambitious plans.

With no serious prospect of enlisting support for his favorite projects, Hurwitz, from time to time, articulated his dream of a Menorah College for Jewish Culture and Social Science, which would bring together a society of Jewish humanist scholars, culture historians, men of letters, and social scientists. In a post-war article, appearing in spring of 1946, Hurwitz recalled that, twenty years before, in the February 1926 issue of the *Journal*, he had urged "A

Foundation or a School for Jewish historical studies." The need for such a school, he believed, was by now greater than ever.

In that 1926 article, "Watchmen What of the Day?", he had outlined the broad scope of such a College: the Talmud, Jewish law, government and Jewish philosophy, Jewish biography, Western Jewish literature, Jewish art, present Jewish conditions.[13]

Although the first issue of the Journal had stated that the magazine would be "offering no opinions of its own but providing an orderly platform for the discussion of mooted questions that really matter," Hurwitz, writing under the name of Zakkaius,[14] bitterly denounced "the tragic course of British Empire" from Balfour down to Bevin, and described the "challenge to Zionist leadership" caused by that British betrayal of high hopes in Palestine. This outspoken polemic was in the winter 1947 issue. Hurwitz also pointed to shortcomings in the American Jewish Conference which had been convened in 1943 to consider the next step in the Jewish future after the war. The demand by the Conference that a Jewish state be set up was, said Hurwitz, ill-timed and unwise.

"By insisting on the demand for a Jewish State immediately, the political Zionists who controlled and stampeded the Conference overreached themselves and blasted the fair flower of Jewish unity on the stalk." He was referring to the withdrawal from the Conference by the American Jewish Committee, B'nai B'rith, and the Union of American Hebrew Congregations. Hurwitz stressed the "necessity for Jews and Arabs to go along together, to cooperate for common welfare in joint government in the country." Bi-nationalism, proposed by Henrietta Szold of Hadassah, Judah Magnes of the Hebrew University, and others appealed to Hurwitz, despite the fact that the vast majority of Jews saw little prospect of enlisting the cooperation of the Arabs.

It would be unfair to judge Hurwitz as being unrealistic. The fact is that the American Jewish Conference was equally unrealistic. Having lived through this turbulent period, I can testify that, while our hearts told us that a Jewish state was desperately needed, our minds whispered to us that we were "as those who dream." Hurwitz had the courage to challenge the majority; he was on the losing side, but that was not uncommon in Hurwitz's career.

Hurwitz battled on. In autumn 1949, he took the Establishment to task for pursuing "Jew Business" instead of Judaism. He called for a Reformation, to replace the bureaucrats who did not care about Judaism, and the laymen who did not scrutinize what the bureaucrats were doing. He denounced the big salaries, the secret budgets, perpetrated by the "defense agencies" (like the Anti-Defamation League, and the American Jewish Committee).

Obviously the issue of a Jewish state was by then moot; the state existed and he certainly did not wish to turn the clock back. But he never lost sight of his ultimate objectives, to see that the basic needs of American Jewry were met through the allocation of adequate funds for religious, cultural, and educational purposes. Hurwitz was certainly right in these contentions and goals; and time has vindicated him. Today the central agencies do provide a larger percentage of funds to the causes he espoused, partly because of his and others' protests, partly because American Jewry has begun to mature.

In the spring of 1952, Hurwitz addressed himself to the MacIver Report. Professor Robert M. MacIver had been commissioned by the Joint Commission of B'nai B'rith and the Anti-Defamation League, as well as by the American Jewish Committee, to study how best to reorganize the resources of American Jewry, so as to serve its interests more efficiently. The Report was pleasing to Hurwitz in many ways, especially since it decried the overlapping and waste in these organizations which he had been criticizing. His hopes were once again raised that the Menorah ideals might experience a revival.

While the fortunes of the movement did not improve, Hurwitz redoubled his efforts to send a message to American Jewry. In a major essay, entitled, "Israel: What Now?" (Spring-Summer 1954), he analyzed the various problems confronting the new state. The Arab problem was the most pressing, according to Hurwitz, and Israel was not meeting it properly. Accommodation between Arab and Israeli "transcends Zionism, and non-Zionism and anti-Zionism. . . . The present task before us all . . . is to join hands in fostering the social-revolutionary elements among the Arabs, and the liberal, non-chauvinist elements among the Israelis." Hurwitz pleaded with Israel not to "bring [your] country down to the moral level of the Arab States." He saw the dangers of continued conflict.

Today we may appreciate how prescient he was, though his program might seem not to have been practical.

In 1958 Hurwitz spoke before a Philadelphia audience, dealing with the theme, "Judaism in this Nuclear Age."[15] He pleaded again for a humanistic Judaism, one that was neither nationalistic nor supernaturalistic. What is needed, he said, was a modern Yavneh, to spread the spirit of Judaism. This should become the vocation of Jews in the nuclear age. "What then gives to Humanist Judaism today its specifically Jewish character? I would answer: the great Jewish heritage of experience and expression throughout the ages— an incomparable legacy of spirit and intellect, if we would but adequately study and comprehend it. . . . A new reception of the Jewish heritage is now required."

With a tenacity worthy of his dreams, Henry Hurwitz, in what was to be his final article (Autumn-Winter 1959), called upon American Jewry to consider the problem of "Heritage and Allegiance." He outlined the scope of the heritage; he analyzed once again Zionism, anti-Zionism, and non-Zionism; he raised the question of "Where True Allegiance Resides"; and he concluded with a bold proposal for a Menorah Collegium.

He seems not to have been the least discouraged by previous failures, nor by the possibility that he might not survive more than two years after this effort. With undiminished zeal he excoriated the excessive pre-occupation with fund raising and the failure of the intellectuals to direct their talents toward the enrichment of Jewish life and thought. Hurwitz again pleaded for a renaissance of Jewish culture: "An uncultured Judaism, without some fair perception of its history and evolution, its thought and literature and institutions, such a Judaism, be it ever so pious, tends to degenerate into vacuous generalities or phony mysticism and emotionalism."[16]

The end came on November 19, 1961, in his seventy-sixth year. Hurwitz died in New York, mourned by those who had worked with him in his various efforts to transform the face of American Judaism. Marvin Lowenthal, one of Hurwitz's closest associates, said in his eulogy that Hurwitz "while satirizing or castigating the blunders and follies of the passing scene, would nevertheless serve as the herald and champion of constructive, affirmative ideas. [He] always [said] 'yes' to whatever promised a richer, deeper and more Jewish future for our people. . . . [He would] seek out and encourage creative minds within the whole compass of the Jewish world. The *Journal* which Hurwitz created contained in its tables of contents an all but complete directory of leading Jewish writers, thinkers, and artists, American and foreign, brought to the attention of its fortunate subscribers . . . , all of them, in the vision of Henry Hurwitz, exponents of Jewish Humanism."

What manner of man was Henry Hurwitz? In stature he was short but imposing. His broad moustache gave him the look of a foreign diplomat. When he addressed an audience, no matter how small, he waxed oratorical. I believe that a clue to his character can be detected in this incongruity of style and circumstance: He was so passionate about everything he did and said that he usually failed to recognize the reality before him.

Indeed, his whole career reflected a certain detachment from harsh facts. At the beginning it was fortunate that he was not deterred by being virtually alone, except for a small coterie who cared about Jewish culture and ideals. He proceeded to organize the few students available to establish the first, and then several other, Menorah societies. The broad indifference to his purposes did not affect him. He operated on the wonderful notion that what ought to be can be. If he had not believed this he would never have embarked on his remarkable career as publisher, organizer, gadfly, and dreamer.

He was fiercely independent, spurning attractive offers to bring Menorah under the aegis of any other organization. This too was a commendable trait; but he was sufficiently aloof from the realities of Jewish life that he failed to realize the hopelessness of enlisting many generous supporters to his program so long as he remained an outsider, as far as the Establishment was concerned.

The fact is that eventually he did have to turn for help to donors whose anti-Zionist position was so alien to the spirit of the time. When Zionist fervor was at its height, Hurwitz accepted assistance from members of the American Council for Judaism, the ideologically anti-Zionist group. His friendliness toward men like Lessing Rosenwald tarred him with the pitch of anti-Zionism, to the detriment of his cause.

For a long time his was a lone voice. His stress on Jewish culture sounded strange to his contemporaries who, if they thought about it at all, identified Jewish culture with the *shtetl* of Eastern Europe (which hardly rated as culture at all in their eyes). The literature, art, music, and philosophy of the Jewish heritage cried out to be released from their anonymity. Hurwitz heard that cry.

But the Establishment was either focused upon the synagogue or on the physical needs of Jews here and abroad. From 1917 on, shortly after Hurwitz had founded the *Menorah Journal*, European Jewry suffered terrible pogroms, and money was constantly being funneled to their aid. The support that Hurwitz sought for his cultural program had to be ignored. Only very few aficionados responded.

That is not to say that Henry Hurwitz's analysis of the needs of American Jewry was faulty. The decades since his passing have demonstrated that if his plans had been carried out, Jewish life would today be richer and more creative. Unfortunately he did not realize that even the most authentic proposals would not be accepted from one who constantly attacked the Establishment, its faulty priorities, and its short-sightedness. Like the prophets, he was right but failed to persuade his own age.

His contributions were, nevertheless, considerable. First, he left behind a treasury of literary works, not only his own but those he inspired, which can be read today with enormous interest. The writers whose first or early appearance in print was in the *Menorah Journal* were thankful to him for opening the pages of that prestigious journal to their work.

Second, he was influential in popularizing the idea that Jewish studies belonged on the university campus. Menorah influence and the friendship of the Hurwitzs with Mrs. Linda Miller, played a role in her benefaction that established the chair in Jewish History, Literature and Institutions at Columbia University, in memory of her husband, Nathan. The chair was held long and brilliantly by Salo W. Baron.[17]

Hurwitz called attention to the importance of cultivating Jewish students. While his method was perhaps too bookish and academic for most, he made American Jews conscious of the terrible consequences of neglecting the student population.

Henry Hurwitz died without achieving all he had hoped to achieve; but his faith in the future of Jewish civilization has been taken up by those who believe that the humanistic approach to Judaism is the only one which can lead to new creativity. To be sure, he never anticipated the resurgence of Orthodoxy; but those who agree with him are confident that, in a more propitious time, more American Jews will pursue his dream of advancing Jewish culture and ideals as he envisaged them.

Notes

1. Horace M. Kallen, "The Promise of the Menorah Idea," *Menorah Journal*, Valedictory Issue, Autumn/Winter 1962.
2. Harry Aurstyn Wolfson, "Escaping Judaism," *Menorah Journal*, June and August 1921, and reprinted in *Menorah Pamphlets*, No. 2, New York, Intercollegiate Menorah Association (1923).
3. Henry Hurwitz, "A Mother Remembered," *American Jewish History Reprint*, September 1980, Vol. 12, No. 1 (manuscript discovered by the author's son, David Lyon Hurwitz, in Menorah Archives).
4. For a full account of the history of the Intercollegiate Menorah Association, see Jenna Weissman Joselit, "Without Ghettoism: A History of the Intercollegiate Menorah Association, 1906–1930." *American Jewish Archives*, Cincinnati, Ohio, November 1978.
5. An impressive list of authors, artists, and composers is contained in the "Third of a Century Index, 1915–1948, "*Menorah Journal*, Summer 1948, Vol. 36. , No. 3.
6. Henry Hurwitz, "My Faith as a Jew," an address delivered at the Jewish Theological Seminary, in New York, May 1946. It was published posthumously in *Judaism*, Fall 1967.
7. Henry Hurwitz, "Judaism in this Nuclear Age," an address delivered in Philadelphia, October 1959, and published in the Autumn-Winter 1959 issue of *Menorah Journal*.
8. Henry Hurwitz, "Heritage and Allegiance," Autumn-Winter 1959, *Menorah Journal*.
9. *Menorah Journal*, February 1927. The participants in the Conference constituted a veritable "Who's Who" in Jewish life; to mention but a few: Irwin Edman, Abram Sachar, Louis Finkelstein, Maurice Samuel, and Chaim Weizmann.
10. Editorial in *Menorah Journal*, January 1928, inaugurating the new monthly schedule.
11. Correspondence and other papers documenting this rift are found in *American Jewish Archives*, Cincinnati, Ohio.

12. See Alan M. Wald, "The Menorah Group Turns Left," *Jewish Social Studies*, Summer-Fall 1976. It is a detailed but biased account of their schism. See also *The Unpossessed*, by Tess Slesinger, Feminist Press, Old Westbury, N.Y. (published originally by Simon and Schuster, New York, in 1934).

13. Hurwitz thought of himself as a twentieth-century disciple of Leopold Zunz. In an article appearing in the 1922 issue of the *Menorah Journal*, highlighting the significance of the centennial of the founding of the *Zeitschrift für die Wissenschaft des Judentums*, Hurwitz characterizes that journal as the "Menorah of a century ago."

14. Rabbi Yohanan ben Zakkai was one of Hurwitz's heroes.

15. *Menorah Journal*, Vol. 46, Nos. 1 and 2.

16. *Menorah Journal*, Vol. 47, No. 1, Autumn-Winter 1959.

17. See in this connection, Ruth Hurwitz's "Linda R. Miller: A Memoir," *Menorah Journal*, Autumn 1937.

It is worthy of note that Henry Hurwitz enjoyed a happy married life with his wife, Ruth (née Sapinsky), who was a faithful companion for many years, through good times and bad. They had two sons, Henry Hurwitz, Jr., and David Lyon Hurwitz. The latter was of invaluable help to the author in the preparation of this essay, for which he offers grateful thanks.

CHAPTER 9

"Not the Recovery of a Grave, but of a Cradle": The Zionist Life of Marvin Lowenthal

Susanne Klingenstein

This difference, among others, may be apparent—the Christians sought the recovery of a grave; the Jews, of a cradle.
—Lowenthal, "Zionism," 1914

To contemporaries, the year 1917 had an almost messianic quality. The outbreak of the Russian Revolution promising in its wake the establishment of a just society, the disintegration of the multinational empires releasing their subjected peoples into independence, and the declaration of the "Fourteen Points" by President Wilson aimed at preserving the world peace raised in Europeans extraordinary expectations. Although Jews have always had reason to be cautious when the world felt the birth pangs of the Messiah, the events of that remarkable year suffused with new vigor those who concentrated their hopes on a sliver of land on the eastern edge of the Mediterranean. America's entry into the First World War on the side of the allies made it more difficult to supply Jewish settlements in Palestine with much needed goods; but the publication of the Balfour Declaration (8 November) and the liberation of Palestine from Turkish rule on the day when General Allenby modestly set foot in Jerusalem (6 December), appeared to bring the dream of a Jewish homeland, if not a Jewish state, closer to realization. The languishing Zionist movement in Europe and America gained in prestige through the victory of the principle of self-determination in Europe and the Balfour Declaration, and large sections of the Jewish people were swept up in a wave of idealism and a flurry of political activities.[1]

It is characteristic of Marvin Lowenthal that he did not share the easy optimism of his fellow Jews. In 1916, at the age of twenty-six, he had been appointed by Louis Brandeis to serve as director of the San Francisco bureau of the Provisional Executive Committee for General Zionist Affairs (PZEC). World events had somewhat facilitated Lowenthal's Zionizing task among the recalcitrant Jews of California, and by the end of 1917, it seemed indeed as if the Zionist vision he was peddling might provide, if not the right answer to the Jewish Question, then at least a workable solution to a pressing Jewish problem. But the last page in Lowenthal's 1917 pocket diary reveals more clearly than any of his chatty letters to parents and friends his personal assessment of the situation. On that last page he penciled the words of a Yiddish song, "Fregt di velt an alte kashe." The world's answer to the "old question," the plight of the Jews, is a non-committal tral-la-la.[2]

Today, the skeptical, courageous Lowenthal is familiar to us mainly as the translator of the seventeenth-century *Memoirs of Glückel of Hameln* (1932), and perhaps as the compiler of the *Life and Letters of Henrietta Szold* (1942) and editor-translator of the *Diaries of Theodor Herzl* (1956). But he was also an accomplished writer. He first became known with his intellectual Baedecker of Jewish Europe and North Africa, *A World Passed By* (1933), and his history *The Jews of Germany* (1936). Moreover, he was an astonishing connoisseur of European literature. In 1935 he compiled from Montaigne's essays *The Autobiography of Michel de Montaigne*. Lowenthal's major achievement, however, is not as immediately visible as a book on the shelf, but no less important, and that is his continuous involvement in activities for the Jewish people, his visibility as a Jewish intellectual at a time when it would have been easier and more profitable to disappear into America.

Lowenthal was not pushed into a Jewish life by his parents. He was born in 1890 in Bradford, Pennsylvania. His father was a jeweler there and, like his mother, of German Jewish descent. The

family belonged to Bradford's Reform Temple where Marvin became
a bar mitzvah in 1903, but was not familiarized with the traditional
obligations of observant Jews. His letters home, which he dis-
patched almost daily while away on vacation or at college, talk of
theater going on Friday nights, of feasting on "ham-and-lettuce
sandwiches," of secretarial work on Saturday morning; and they
close affectionately but indiscriminately with a "Happy New Year"
in October or a "Merry Xmas to you all" in December.[3]

Marvin did not go to college right away. From 1905 to 1911 he
worked in the store of Leon Feuerbach in Bradford, which he left as
his assistant manager to enroll at the University of Wisconsin in
Madison in February 1912. Although the college registrar gave Lowenthal a rough time because of his advanced age (he was twenty-
one) and poor credentials, and would admit him only as a Special
Adult Student, the long delay proved exceedingly fortunate.[4] It
allowed Lowenthal to skip a semester so that he could catch up
with the class of 1915 in the fall of 1912; but, more importantly, it
allowed him to become the student and friend of Horace Meyer
Kallen who was to have a lasting influence on Lowenthal's life.

Kallen did not arrive at Madison until the fall of 1911. Three
years after receiving his doctorate from Harvard University in 1908
and a year after the death of his revered mentor William James in
1910, Kallen had managed to cut himself loose from his beloved
alma mater. He finally accepted an instructorship in philosophy
and psychology at the University of Wisconsin. Kallen was then in
the midst of developing his theory of cultural pluralism which
helped him to solve the dilemma of being (committedly) Jewish
and a fervent American. He would later claim that in order to be a
functioning member of a culturally pluralist society like America
one had to belong to one of the smaller groups constituting the
larger community. It followed that a firm commitment to Zionism
(such as Kallen's own) was not contradictory to being a loyal
American, because, according to Kallen's theory, in order to be an
American one had to be ethnic.[5] In those years, 1911 to 1913, Kallen's reasoning helped persuade Louis Brandeis, who had been cam-
paigning for Woodrow Wilson, that he could very well be an active
Zionist too, because, far from being unpatriotic, a double commitment was in fact quintessentially American. Brandeis, cautious as

ever, began to study Zionist materials in 1912, but during the crisis of 1914 was ready to take over the leadership of American Zionism.[6] His decision had an immediate effect on Lowenthal's career.

As soon as he had settled into the college routine Lowenthal took some tentative steps into American Jewish life and inadvertently stumbled into mildly Zionist circles. On 12 May 1912 he writes home that he is at work on an essay about "the Jews in the American Revolution," and five months later he reports, "Just won a prize of One Hundred Dollars on my history essay . . . in a contest offered by the Wisconsin Menorah Society. One Hundred Bones! Not bad, eh?" That was a lot of money for Lowenthal who was paying two dollars a week in rent and who had just accepted a job in the ticket office of the local theater that paid four dollars a week for sixteen hours of work.[7] But winning the contest would have larger significance than easing his strapped circumstances. The prize, sponsored by the Chicago merchant Julius Rosenwald and administered by a faculty committee chaired by a professor of English literature, was on the one hand the most important literary prize at the University of Wisconsin, and on the other part of the consciousness-raising campaign of the Menorah Society. This intercollegiate Jewish organization was founded by Henry Hurwitz (assisted by Horace Kallen) at Harvard in 1906. Its goal was, in Mark Krupnick's formulation, "to promote Jewish ideals and learning among Jewish college students so as to offset the negative effects of American anti-Semitism. By demonstrating the interest and dignity of the Jewish past, the Menorah movement encouraged its members to accept and identify themselves as Jews."[8]

Winning the prize was for Lowenthal, who was then planning to become a journalist, predominantly a literary achievement. But he soon began to feel that the prize came with an unspoken obligation. On 4 November 1912 the same Lowenthal who was barely able to sit through a Rosh Hashanah service attended his first Menorah meeting, paid his dollar, enrolled himself as a member, and promised to read his paper some time. He was more condescending than serious, an attitude which was soon to change under Kallen's influence.

On 6 October 1912, two days before he learned that he had won the prize, Lowenthal told his parents that he now took two meals a day in Lathrop Hall, a place "largely patronized by professors." He shared a table with "4 sons of Abraham . . . and 2 Germans." Among the former he counted Horace Kallen. His Boston manners struck the "Pennsylvanian backwoodsman" as very peculiar indeed. On 1 November 1912 he wrote to his parents: "Before I go any further, I want to mention Dr. Kallen who is a regular at our table. He is a tall, well-built, handsome man (Jewish) packed with philosophy. English by birth, a grad[uate] of Harvard, he strikes one at first as effeminate. This impression is increased by the fact that he carries his handkerchief up his shirt-sleeve, and talks in a soft, gentle voice, with broad 'a's of the 'bawth-tub' soc[iety]. But without doubt, he is the wittiest man at the table, especially in the matter of nonsense and puns."[9]

Kallen, of course, was born in Germany (in 1882), but he had been brought to Boston at the age of five when his father, originally from Latvia, was expelled from Germany as an alien Jew.[10] Growing up in Boston Kallen came to defy his father's authority, abandoning his observant Judaism for a cultural Jewishness, and to acquire New England speech and manners, and at Harvard a thorough training by America's leading philosophers, William James, Josiah Royce, and George Santayana. From November 1912 until Lowenthal's graduation, Kallen, who "alas—does not mix well with the girls," imparted to his young friend his knowledge of philosophy, commitment to Zionism, and addiction to tea. Lowenthal discovered quickly that Kallen was quite a "macher" and a widely respected man "even if he does keep his pocket-handkerchief up his sleeve and talk in an extremely high-brow fashion when he is not punning atrociously. He is a firm Zionist and raves beautifully thereon." He persuaded Marvin to come with him to a Zionist convention in Chicago although his student would much rather have gone home for the same money. Lowenthal liked Chicago and his introduction to Julius Rosenwald (whom he put down as "fat" and "simple"), but did not find himself "favorably impressed with Zionism as it is." Nor did his encounter with Henrietta Szold at one of Kallen's afternoon teas in November 1913 win him over. "I enjoyed her company pretty well," he reports to his parents, but "an intellectual woman with a 'cause' always in tow never appeals to me."[11]

Rather than throw in his lot with the Zionists and the Menorah crowd, he decided to join a literary club, The Stranglers, in November 1913. It was his last attempt at escaping the inevitable, the Jewish future for which Kallen was educating him. 1914 was the year of Lowenthal's maturation. A number of factors combined to give him a sense of direction. He was getting seriously involved with a young Russian Jewish woman, Sylvia Mardfin, whom he would marry in 1918; he was exempted from military drill and from participating in a war that he considered a madness and bestial insanity; and his sincere intellectual and personal devotion to the exotic Kallen, who was part of the world Lowenthal aspired to, began to transform his values.

Early in 1914 Lowenthal was "reading up on Zionism," and soon at work on another Menorah prize essay on that subject. He was confident that he would win. He also told his parents about another discovery: "I am sorry . . . that . . . I had to sail into Reform Judaism, which, it seems to me, has tried to sit on two stools at once with the usual result." This was Kallen's position. He abhorred Reform Judaism because it abstracted "ideas like the Unity of God and the Brotherhood of Man from their distinctive roots in Jewish history." Kallen was convinced that "sects and dogmas pass [while] ethnic groups and cultures endure." Therefore he thought Reform Judaism a dead end; it tried "to thin the richness of Jewish existence to the verbal tenuousness of a few unproved dogmas and to substitute for concrete Jewish living the anatomical horror of . . . 'Jewish science.' " As the return to the concrete Jewish living of observance, the Orthodoxy of his father, was not an option for Kallen, "Zionism became a replacement and reevaluation of Judaism which enabled me to respect it."[12] Lowenthal followed him exactly on this path.

Lowenthal's essay "Zionism" won the Menorah Prize (May 1914), and when the *Menorah Journal* was founded a year later, it was published in the April and June issues of 1915. Lowenthal's "Minutes in Colonial Jewry" followed in April 1916. Thus began his long affiliation with the single most important cultural journal for American Jewish intellectuals before the founding of *Partisan Review* in 1934.

These publications may have been the avidly desired break for the budding journalist, but his mentor Kallen had another career in

mind for him. In the fall of 1914 American Zionism experienced an
enormous upsurge. The declaration of war on Serbia and the onset
of active hostilities a few days later threw the international Zionist
movement into a state of total disarray. At that moment, the hesi-
tant Louis Brandeis committed himself to lead the American Zionists by becoming chairman of the newly established PZEC on 30
August 1914. Internationally, his notorious efficiency reassured the
ruffled European leaders of the movement. Domestically, Brandeis's
decision ennobled Zionism for many American Jews who had associated it with an Eastern European Jewry they disdained. Although
Reform Judaism still wanted no part in it, Zionism was now an
acceptable preoccupation for America's upper-class German Jews.
They, in turn, increased its prestige and attracted new members.
That suited Brandeis well, who rallied the Zionists with his battle
cry "Men! Money! Discipline!" [13]

The effects were felt almost immediately in Wisconsin. Kallen's
Zionist paperwork increased; he rented a typewriter and employed
Lowenthal as his secretary. At the same time he urged his disciple
to take a course in public speaking and insisted that he apply for a
fellowship at Harvard University. That would not only place him
in an outstanding philosophy department but also in the center of
an effective social network of Zionists to which Kallen, Brandeis,
Hurwitz, Jacob de Haas (a former aide of Herzl's, now editor of
Boston's major Jewish newspaper), and many others belonged.

When the answer from Harvard came in the spring of 1915, Lowenthal was elated and dismayed. He informed his parents: "I
received word from Harvard that I was appointed a University
scholar, with a stipend of $150. This will just pay my tuition fee. I
will be compelled to borrow $500 to see me through a year there.
Kallen has offered to raise it for me, but I told him that I guess the
family could manage it. . . . Of course, there is honor in receiving
the scholarship, and all that—but nothing very substantial." Lowenthal's disappointment was softened by Kallen's success in securing for him "two commissions for articles for the 'New Republic'
(who pay 2 cents a word)." The New Republic, just founded in
November 1914, was already all the rage among the young, highly
cultured and politically awake intellectuals. Then, as now, the
magazine had strong ties to New England, particularly to Harvard,

and Lowenthal hoped that if the editors liked his work he might get "a permanent job with them writing articles while at Harvard—and maybe eventually getting on the staff." Furthermore, the Wisconsin Zionist group, which Lowenthal now chaired, decided that he should be "assigned to work as Zionist secretary for Mr. Brandeis!" He saw this, rightly, as a tremendous opportunity, "worth many times more than a year's expense at college." However, he was pained that Harvard's puny offer forced him to borrow from his parents. Yet to Cambridge he must go. The vista of a world populated by excellence that Kallen had unfolded before his eyes proved stronger than the shame incurred by giving up his financial independence.[14]

Lowenthal arrived in Cambridge in September 1915 to pursue his master's degree. He enrolled in seven courses, among them "Symbolic Logic" with Josiah Royce, "Philosophy of Nature" with Edwin Holt, and "Philosophy of Religion" with William Hocking. For the latter he wrote an unusual thesis, titled "Myself—Myth-Maker and Magician," in which he examined his own childhood belief in God to support the argument that the mythmaking of children could be compared to the fashioning of religion in primitive cultures. Obviously, he had to disclose that he was Jewish. This fact did not endear him to his advisor.[15]

But Lowenthal was never one to hide in the face of adversity. If anything, his year at Harvard strengthened his Jewish identity. Very early on he visited Louis Brandeis who asked him "to organize, select and in a measure train [together with Jacob de Haas] some public speakers from the Harvard Zionist Society who are to be sent about Boston and Vicinity (as far as Worcester) to lecture on Zionism. . . . I agreed to give 2 or 3 nights a week to the work, and consented to talk myself, if necessary, a couple times a week." Now Lowenthal was hooked. His chores, which he discharged loyally and in good spirits, ranged from an engagement "to talk to some German Jewesses on Zionism and try to allay their suspicions that we were trying to prevent them from mingling with the upper Gentile strata" to "telling the Jews of Manchester that their only hope in life was to become Zionists."[16]

His visit to Manchester, New Hampshire, was particularly valuable for him because it counterpoised the protected world of Har-

vard, its high-minded talk and genteel manners, with an impression
of reality that deeply affected the philosophy student. He wrote to
his parents: "I thought Manchester was a town—it is a city of
85,000 inhabitants. 20,000 work in one cotton mill—of which 25%
are children from 12 to 15 yrs of age. . . . I'm sometimes ashamed
that I'm a human being, of the same specie [!] as these child-
devouring monsters." Lowenthal was scheduled to speak before a
group of two hundred Jews. The first address of the evening was in
Yiddish. "Manchester has no Reform Jews (I sometimes feel it
should be spelled Reformed Jews, for they are often people who
though unfortunately born Jews, have realized their crime, and
have since reformed), so I didn't have to *prove* to my audience that
the Jews are a race, and that they really are suffering damnably in
Europe." The collection at the end was meagre; no surprise, because
"there are practically no rich Jews in Manchester, and what few
there were, are of course not interested." [17]

It was Lowenthal's strong commitment to the reconstitution of
the Jews as a people, that is as a national entity complete with
language, culture, and territory, that prevented him from feeling
excluded, as other Jewish students did, from certain niches of Harvard society, from the Old Boston crowd that kept even a Brandeis
off their guest list for social occasions. [18] Lowenthal divided his work
time evenly between his academic training in philosophy and his
Zionist activities, and his leisure hours between visiting the Kallen
family in Roxbury and touring New England with his Harvard
roommate and best friend, Eugene Taylor, a fellow-"Strangler" from
the University of Wisconsin.

As Commencement approached, Lowenthal had already left Harvard in spirit and started on a new life. Hence he felt the "expense
of a gown useless." At the last minute a close friend of Kallen's,
Harry Wolfson, lent him his so that Lowenthal could take his degree
with the other students in the Stadium. The exercises held no fascination for him. "I was bored with the continual harping on Preparedness— (when the only Preparedness they intend is military—
not economic or social). Good Heavens, if all these people are so
intent on fighting . . . why don't they go to Europe!" Lowenthal
had other fights to think of. When Brandeis and de Haas asked him
to head the Zionist Bureau of the Pacific Coast, which they were

about to open, he jumped at the offer. "Every man I enlist," he wrote home, "every dollar I get, is a bit toward rebuilding the nation of our fathers; and a bit toward adding to the value and self-respect of the Jew in America, and in all the world."[19]

Lowenthal began his work in San Francisco at a salary of $2,000 a year in September 1916; his campaigning in Boston had trained him, so that he now proved to be quite successful. In the summer of 1919 the Zionist headquarters called him back to New York. Lowenthal was ambivalent; he loved San Francisco and his work there; he had recently married, and his wife, Sylvia, had a good job in the municipal government. On the other hand Lowenthal had resumed writing and was producing reviews and essays for magazines like the *Dial*, the *New Republic*, and the *Menorah Journal*. He thought that his presence in New York could further his career. But more important were two other considerations. Moving back to the East Coast would make it easier to visit his recently widowed mother in Pennsylvania. And his mentor, too, would be within visiting distance. In the spring of 1918 Kallen had resigned from his teaching job at the University of Wisconsin because of a deep falling out with the faculty and the president over matters of academic freedom.[20] He was on the lecture circuit for a year and in 1919 was invited to join the founding faculty of the New School for Social Research in New York City.

Eventually, the Lowenthals moved back east where Marvin continued to work for the Zionist Organization of America but with less enthusiasm. He wanted to be a writer. The letters to Eugene Taylor, who to Lowenthal's great chagrin though with his help had bought a farm in Huron, South Dakota, are filled with writing plans and reports on his latest readings. On 29 August 1920 he cried out: "I am going to take the bull by the horns and plunge into deep water—in[to] the Rubicon. I'm leaving the Zionist Organization, and will try to storm the literary world. There is only one way to become a writer, I guess, and that is to write. I sold $100 worth of stuff to the Menorah Journal this month and I count on about that much monthly from them. This will be a start." Seven weeks later, on 6 October 1920, his thirtieth birthday, he surprised Taylor with the news that he had "just concluded arrangements for editing on the Menorah Journal—two days a week—for $2000 a year, plus two cents a word for all I write and an understanding [that] I write *at least* $500 worth a year. This will come in handy as a regular income on the side." [21]

Beginning with the February issue of 1921 Lowenthal signed as associate editor of the *Menorah Journal*. Fittingly, the issue opened with his fourth lengthy article for the magazine, an essay on "Jewish Realities in America." His comment to Taylor: "Speared $75 for that." From now on he would contribute reviews and articles regularly and write a four- to five-page column, "The Adversary's Notebook," for each issue under the pseudonym H. Ben-Shahar. But he was still restless. He had not yet found his subject, the theme that would turn him from a two-cents-a-word journalist into a writer.

In August 1921 the Lowenthals planned to pack up and go to Europe. "We figure that in low-exchange countries (Italy, Germany, France) we can live on an average of $25 a week for both. Now I can earn that amount, easily, writing over there." Dream became deed in February 1922. For a year the Lowenthals lived in Florence ("100% celestial"), London, and Berlin. It is difficult to say precisely how living in Europe affected Lowenthal, because the letters to his mother discontinue in 1922 and with his other major correspondent, Taylor, he shared intense literary and philosophical, but no Jewish interests. It is clear, however, that just as Paris for Lewisohn in 1924, Berlin in 1922 was a major turning point for Lowenthal. The four-part series on "The Jews in the European Scene" he was writing for the *Menorah Journal* in the spring of 1922 was quite alarming. [22]

He began his exposition with an account of the trial of the thirteen accomplices in the assassination of Germany's Jewish foreign minister Walter Rathenau which revealed "in the heart of Germany's population a nest of semi-secret, semi-military organizations motivated, in great part, by anti-Semitism." What he found particularly shocking about the Rathenau case was not "that it was a Dreyfus affair but that it was not a Dreyfus affair; no man dared be a Zola." In the rest of the series Lowenthal showed how widespread and virulent anti-Semitism was in Germany and its eastern neighbors. With astonishing foresight he warned against Hitler. He quoted two resolutions adopted by Hitler's party in Munich in

February 1923 "urging that all Jews in Germany be interned" and that "if the Allied forces did not leave the Rhineland in the near future all German Jews should be treated as hostages and shot." Lowenthal made it abundantly clear that the European Jew "better prepare for his immediate future," which would bring terror, but he had very little practical advice to offer.

It speaks for Lowenthal that he did not advocate Zionism as a simple solution. The Jews, he wrote toward the end of the last installment, "must fight, of course, as they do with particular *élan* in Poland; but like Rabbi Ben Zakkai, they must prepare anew for an exile, and look about for a new Jabneh. This new exile will not be enacted in terms of immigration so much as seclusion; it promises a new return to an inner life, to a severely Jewish culture. The Zionists have, it is true, the perfect but the impossible solution— impossible, that is, of saving European Jewry. Their tragedy is that as fast as Europe renders the existence of the Jew insupportable, the Jew loses the economic means to escape—to Palestine or elsewhere."

For American Jews who watched the onset of the destruction of the European Jews in safety but behind closed doors—the Johnson Act of 1924 had restricted immigration drastically—Lowenthal saw little and yet very much to do. "If we want to help European Jewry hold through, we must strengthen them with our protest—not back-door whisperings in diplomatic chancelleries, but vigorous, widespread, public protest—of which the world has heard so far very little, especially from America. And we must help them strengthen their inner moral resources by giving them the means to develop and intensify their faith, culture, and common life. Not relief money, but munitions for a siege."[23]

Alas, no outcry rocked the foundations of the earth. But Lowenthal was shaken. To his gentile friend Taylor he divulged very little of his terrifying discoveries, of an "atmosphere so thick with hatred against the Jews" that his report may have seemed paranoid to his Dakota friend.[24] Occasionally he gave him a glimpse of his new direction, his turn toward the study of Jewish history and culture. On 9 October 1922 he wrote from Berlin: "Due to a stiff leg, I am at home reading Glückel von Hameln's memoirs of Jewish life in Germany in the 17th century, and enjoying every word the simple and strong lady has to say. (I can read German now like a fish, providing it is written by simple old ladies or kindergarten children)." Glückel, born in 1646, was neither that old nor that simple when she began to write her zikhroynes (memoirs) in 1690. She was remarkably well educated and seasoned by the experiences of war, expulsion, the plague, the hysteria triggered by Sabbtai Zevi, and last but not least, by the tough life of a woman who bore fourteen children and had to run a seventeenth-century business. Lowenthal played down how much he was affected by Glückel and her story. He was about to find his subject as a writer. He would be the one to record Jewish life in Europe and thus preserve at least its memory should the destruction he foresaw become a reality.

It would take Lowenthal another ten years to ripen into that chronicler. When he was finally ready to proceed from the production of articles to the writing of books he launched his major phase in 1932 with a translation of the *Memoirs of Glückel of Hameln*. It was followed a year later, when Hitler had risen to power in Berlin, by Lowenthal's most important book for post-Shoah Jewry, *A World Passed By: Scenes and Memories of Jewish Civilization in Europe and North Africa* (1933).[25] It describes the major Jewish communities in France, Spain, Italy, Germany, Austria-Hungary, Poland, the Balkan countries, and North Africa, which ceased to exist a decade after the publication of the book. In 1935 Lowenthal took a vacation from his subject to create his favorite book, *The Autobiography of Michel de Montaigne*, from the Frenchman's essays and to translate it into English. Then he reembarked on his most painful work, *The Jews of Germany: A Story of Sixteen Centuries*.

Published a year after the Nuremberg Laws, in 1936, when the world celebrated the Berlin Olympics, *The Jews of Germany* was designed to shock Americans, or at least American Jews, out of their complacency by showing that German anti-Semitism was not a recent, passing phenomenon, that it was not the invention of a crackpot politician strategically used to win a campaign, but, rather, deeply ingrained in the German people as part of their history, and that the Jews of Germany and perhaps the peoples of Europe were doomed if the world did not wake up to the reality of the impending nightmare. "The world and Germany," Lowenthal foretold, "has but a few years to decide whether it will choose liberty, or—in a battlefield too horrible to contemplate—it must choose death."[26] Well spoken and not heard.

Lowenthal's publications of the thirties are the fruit of ten years of intense study and observation in Europe; a decade lived in an atmosphere thick with hatred had sharpened his perception and taught him that the high culture of Europe had a barbaric underside which was beginning to show where the cloak of refinement was worn threadbare by the economic depression. The Lowenthals left Europe, in February 1923, with a certain relief; but Marvin longed to return, particularly to London. The pull of his subject was strong. When the *Menorah Journal* appointed him European editor, he was delighted. The Lowenthals were back in Paris in the fall of 1924, just in time for the grand funeral of Anatole France (18 October), whose writings Marvin very much admired. Ludwig Lewisohn and his companion Thelma Spear arrived in Paris the same year. Both couples would stay for a decade, but there is no evidence that they ever met.

Both writers traveled to Palestine in 1925, Lewisohn for the *Nation*, Lowenthal for the *Menorah Journal*, and were enchanted by what they saw. "It is only too easy to envision the proximity of God," Lowenthal wrote to Taylor. Earlier he had tried to explain his fascination with Palestine: "You once said you couldn't understand my Zionist passion—you couldn't feel excited about Jutland or Friesland where the Anglo-Saxons hailed from. Dear fish, you see the difference! Who the hell could get excited about Friesland. . . . The difference is that . . . Jews have mixed the rocks of Erez Israel with dreams—and even a cold relativist like myself gets all heated up at the thought of sleeping in the hills of Judea. It is the power of the word. Of the hope of a happy, united mankind. . . . Hold the skirt of a Jew and say, we have heard that God is with you, let us worship him together on the Mount of Zion, for out of Zion shall go forth the Law, and the word of the Lord from Jerusalem, and nation shall not lift up sword against nation, nor shall they learn war any more. They never talked that way in Jutland." Nevertheless, Lowenthal had to admit after his visit to Palestine, "I can't say that in any sense it is 'my' world—as I feel Italy to be—but it is endlessly more fascinating, more beckoning."[27]

England, whose literature had been a staple in Lowenthal's intellectual life and which he therefore expected to be intensely familiar to him, disappointed in a similar way. Lowenthal informed Taylor on 6 October 1926: "If you are in England long enough, you begin to realize that the culture of England which is yours, which is most profoundly and altogether you does not mean that England is yours, that the life and human character which bred and created this culture is yours. . . . [Understanding England] is not a mystic question of blood, of *nationality*—but a palpable question of geography and social environment. I've read lately Emerson's 'English Traits' and I'm pleased to discover that he too finds himself a foreigner in England. I'm amazed and puzzled at Henry James."

Like many American expatriates, Lowenthal made Paris his home. Not the least of its attractions was the ready availability of rare and not so rare books which Sylvia had made her business. Taylor in South Dakota was one of her good customers. In the winter of 1926 she traveled to New York where she arranged en passant her husband's literary affairs so that upon her return Marvin found himself in the enviable position of having a publisher and no manuscript. "My publisher," he boasted to Taylor, "is eager to have my Jewish history (not written), my [Adversary's] Notebook, then a book in defense of the skeptical life." But Lowenthal did not yet have the *sitzfleisch* necessary for such productions; he needed to see more of Europe and to participate somehow in its political life. He wanted to cut himself loose for a while from the journalistic routine. "I've given up my Menorah work, and make my living out of representing the American Jewish Congress at Geneva [Congress of Minorities] and writing amusing letters to Rabbi Wise." [28]

Between 1927 and 1931 Lowenthal served as the representative of the Jewish minority interests at the League of Nations, toured Europe and North Africa extensively, continued to contribute to the *Menorah Journal* and other magazines, and finally landed a job as secretary to the World Conference for International Peace through Religion, and, more lucrative, as editor for Harper and Brothers. Here, he came to rest for a while (1931–34). The company produced his first two books, *The Memoirs of Glückel of Hameln* and *A World Passed By*.[29] The increasing political gloom in Germany turned him toward Montaigne whose skepticism he shared. A reporter overheard Lowenthal talking at a party about his plans for a Montaigne book as appropriate for this time of crisis and filed a rather curious write-up:

> Montaigne lived in worse times than these, if they could be worse; continuous disorder and violence. . . . He went through it all very calmly, implying occasionally that it would all come out in the wash. . . . This looks like the ideal method, from a distance; but Marvin Lowenthal's wife was at the party, and said that her husband was a perfect Montaignist and declined to worry about anything whatever which nearly drove her frantic.[30]

In fact, Lowenthal worried a great deal. He relocated to America in 1934; and as soon as the Montaigne book was done and placed with a publisher (Houghton Mifflin), he resumed work on his history of the German Jews. Shortly after the boycott of Jewish stores in Germany on 1 April 1933, Lowenthal was questioned about the situation in Germany by an American audience. In his answer he made a distinction between the Germans who would soon emerge from the hysteria of Hitlerism and the Nazi thugs who were bent on eliminating all Jewish life from Germany. By 1935, Lowenthal's distinction was worthless. Hitler and his party had complete control over all political and social institutions. The Nuremberg Laws of 15 September 1935 deprived German Jews of their citizenship. Thirteen further decrees added over the next few years would outlaw them completely. These additions were hardly needed. The fate of the German Jews was sealed in 1935.[31]

The British Commissioner for Migration and Statistics in Palestine, Eric Mills, came to Germany in the fall of 1935 to discuss the financial aspects of the emigration of German Jews to Palestine. He wrote after his meetings with German officials in a private letter: "While before I went to Germany I knew that the Jewish situation was bad, I had not realized as I now do that the fate of German Jews is a tragedy, for which cold, intelligent planning by those in authority takes rank with that of those who are out of sympathy with the Bolshevik regime, in Russia; or the elimination of Armenians from the Turkish Empire." Mills added: "The Jew is to be eliminated and the state has no regard for the manner of this elimination."[32] Lowenthal did not have Mills's political contacts, but his study of the Jews in Germany which inevitably became a history of anti-Semitism in Germany led him to the same conclusion. Observing the triumph of Nazism, he writes, "Nothing in the material circumstances of Germany can be reckoned upon to divert or soften the effort toward [the] extermination [of the Jews]."[33]

Lowenthal's jeremiad, *The Jews of Germany*, left him exhausted. His journal of the time is filled with literary fragments, essay sketches, and writing plans, but nothing larger materialized. The war came and disaster overtook the remaining Jews of Germany and those in the Nazi-occupied territories. Lowenthal abandoned projects like "Edward de Vere, 17th Earl of Oxford—is he Shakespeare?" and "Reality in Art and Life." They added nothing to the time but their own uselessness. The high culture of Europe had taught mankind exactly nothing. Thousands of times the Germans had listened admiringly to the words of Shakespeare: "Hath not a Jew eyes? Hath not a Jew hands, organs, dimensions, senses, affections, passions?—fed with the same food, hurt with the same weapons, subject to the same diseases, healed by the same means, warmed and cooled by the same winter and summer as a Christian is? If you prick us, do we not bleed? If you tickle us, do we not laugh? If you poison us, do we not die?" Common sense and compassion, which Shylock appeals to, sometimes deep faith, or sheer moral decency induced a few individuals and nations to render the Jews whatever assistance was possible. But it was clear that survival after the catastrophe depended not on external help, but on the realization of Herzl's impossible dream.

In 1941, Lowenthal returned to the only spark of hope in a darkened world—to the women and men committed to Zionism. He wrote and edited the *Life and Letters of Henrietta Szold* (1942) whom he had not found very appealing thirty years earlier. Though deeply rooted in American life, she had become a Zionist even before Herzl. She founded the Zionist women's organization Hadassah, which gave her a certain stature. But she became truly famous when, shocked by Hitler's rise to power in 1933, she practically took over the so-called Youth Aliyah, the emigration of Jewish children from Nazi-occupied territories to Palestine. She was then seventy-three years old. She continued to work twelve hours a day until long beyond her eightieth birthday. Her letters pulse with life and inspire one to join her effort.

The *Life and Letters of Henrietta Szold* aroused Lowenthal from his gloom. There was work to be done. After collaborating with Frank Monaghan on a rather curious book, *This Was New York: The Nation's Capital in 1789* (1943) which was clearly designed to instill Americans with a sense of pride during wartime, Lowenthal became again active in Zionist affairs. From 1946 to 1949 he served on the Zionist Advisory Commission and from 1952 to 1954 edited the *American Zionist*. He then began his last major work, a one-volume edition and translation of *The Diaries of Theodor Herzl* (1956). The first (incomplete) German edition appeared in Berlin in 1922–23. Lowenthal's German had not been good enough then to read the three volumes comfortably. A few years later he was able to write a character study of Herzl based on these diaries for the *Menorah Journal*.[34]

But it needed more than a thorough knowledge of German to comprehend the vision Herzl unfolded in his diaries. After the Second World War, the Shoah, and the founding of the State of Israel, Lowenthal looked back with new appreciation to the diaries of this peculiar man, not devoid of vanity, who in a flash had imagined a new life for Europe's Jews and then dedicated his remaining years (1894–1904) to the political realization of his "immortal romance." For that one needed a touch of megalomania. "I believe," Herzl noted in 1895," that for me life has ended and world history begun." Lowenthal, discreet as ever, did not comment on Herzl's love of the grand gesture. His editorial comments show reverence for the man whose ideas (mediated by Kallen) persuaded him to put his talents at the service of the Jewish people.

It is good to remember that Lowenthal was above all an American. He did not see the struggle of the Jews for first class status in America and among the nations as an isolated, parochial concern. As long as a single Jew was threatened, the civil rights of all were threatened and vice versa. "We must learn that when a Negro burns, it is a Jew burning: when a labor picket is shot, it is a Jew who falls; when a Ku Klux rides down a Catholic, it is riding down a Jew. . . . We must realize that Jewish rights are bound up and are one with everyone else's rights; . . . and, that, in sum, Jewish liberty can never rise higher than its source, which is the liberty of all men."[35] Marvin Lowenthal was a classic Jewish liberal. He died

in 1969 when the genteel anti-Semitism of the Old Boston crowd
had finally died out and a new, radical anti-Semitism was just
beginning to arise.

Notes

1. Shmuel Ettinger, "The Modern Period," in Haim Hillel Ben-Sasson, ed.,
   A History of the Jewish People (Cambridge: Harvard University Press,
   1976), 939; Walter Laqueur, *A History of Zionism* (New York: Holt,
   Rinehart and Winston, 1972), 187–205; David Vital, *Zionism: The Cru-
   cial Phase* (Oxford: Clarendon Press, 1987).
2. This pocket diary is in box 1 of the Lowenthal papers (P-140) in the
   Archives of the American Jewish Historical Society (Waltham, Mass.).
   The note reads: "Fregt di welt an alte kashe: tra-la-tra-di-ri-de-rom /
   Entfert men: tra-di-ri-di-rei-lom / oi, oi, tra di ri de-rom / Un as men wil
   ken men doch sagen trai dem / Blaibt doch weiter di alte kashe tra-la-
   tra-di-ri-de-rom." (The world asks an old question: Tra-la . . . ? /
   Comes the reply: Tra-di . . . ! / And if you wish you may say: Trai
   dem! / But still the old question remains: Tra-la . . . ?.) I would like
   to thank Helen Goodman and Rabbi Jerome Fishman for assisting me in
   researching and understanding this song.
3. Lowenthal, letters to his parents 27 December 1904; 1 January 1905;
   Christmas 1912; 2 October 1913 (postmark), and others. Lowenthal
   papers, box 3. All letters quoted in this essay are unpublished and held
   by the Archives of the American Jewish Historical Society in Waltham,
   Mass. Lowenthal's papers were arranged for the Archives by Jonathan
   Sarna. I would like to thank the Archives for permission to quote. I
   have edited the letters slightly, amending obvious errors and idiosyncratic spelling.
4. "I reported to the Registrar's office at 9:30 this A.M. and after telling me
   that one member of the Committee was dead against admitting me under the submitted credentials—poor requirements which I showed, the
   Registrar ended up by saying that it was finally decreed that I should be
   admitted as a Special Adult Student. . . . The whole thing, in view of
   the liberal wording of the Wis[consin] Catalogue, struck me as red-tape
   and bush-wak—but I suppose they must be careful and allow themselves the privilege of refusing entrance to undesirable persons, regardless of entrance requirements." Lowenthal, letter to his parents, 5 February 1912. In those days "undesirable persons" was a code word for Jews.
5. Susanne Klingenstein, *Jews in the American Academy, 1900–1940: The
   Dynamics of Intellectual Assimilation* (New Haven: Yale University
   Press, 1991), 49.
6. Sarah Schmidt, "Horace Kallen and the Americanization of Zionism"

(Ph.D. diss., University of Maryland, 1973); cf. also her article bearing the same title in *American Jewish Archives* 28 (April 1976): 59–73. Ben Halpern, *A Clash of Heroes: Brandeis, Weizmann, and American Zionism* (New York: Oxford University Press, 1987), 101–4.

7. Lowenthal, letters to his parents, 16 May 1912; 20 September 1912; 8 October 1912; 9 October 1912. In 1913 Lowenthal would take on secretarial and press work for the theater, increasing his workload to twenty-four hours a week. In 1914 Kallen liberated him from the Orpheum by hiring him as his secretary.

8. Mark Krupnick, "The 'Menorah Journal' Group and the Origins of Modern Jewish-American Radicalism," *Studies in American Jewish Literature* 5 (Winter 1979): 58; cf. also Robert Alter, "Epitaph for a Jewish Magazine: Notes on the 'Menorah Journal,' " *Commentary* 38 (May 1965): 51–55. R. E. Neil Dodge, "The Menorah Prize of Wisconsin," *Menorah Journal* 4 (April 1918): 123–24.

9. Lowenthal, letter to his parents, 1 November 1912; preceding quotes are from his letters of 6 October 1912, and 13 November 1913, and from his letter to Eugene Taylor of 6 October 1926.

10. Klingenstein, *Jews in the American Academy*, 35; Lowenthal, *The Jews of Germany: A Story of Sixteen Centuries* (Philadelphia: Jewish Publication Society of America, 1936), 306.

11. Lowenthal, letters to his parents: 24 November 1914, Sunday A.M. 1915; Madison, Christmas 1912; 16 November 1912; Chicaco, Ill, Tuesday [New Year's 1913]; Friday, P.M. [envelope postmarked 8 November 1913].

12. References in this paragraph are to Lowenthal's letters to his parents of 2 February 1914; 18 April 1914. The quotes are from Horace M. Kallen's essay "Judaism, Hebraism, and Zionism," *Judaism at Bay: Essays toward the Adjustment of Judaism to Modernity* (New York: Bloch, 1932), 38–39; Schmidt, "Horace Kallen" (diss.), 40; cf. also Klingenstein, *Jews in the American Academy*, 41, 46.

13. Halpern, *A Clash of Heroes*, 110–13.

14. Lowenthal's letters to his parents of late 1914 and early 1915 have no exact dates. The quotes in this passage are from a four-page typed letter with the dateline "Wednesday" and the penciled addition "1914–5" not in Lowenthal's hand.

15. In an undated letter to his parents Lowenthal asks them not to be upset about some of Hocking's comments on his paper: "Don't you know you mustn't take a religious criticism too literally. When Hock[ing] said I was rash, he merely meant I was no Christian; and I agree with him. You don't know (of course) that he spent a year trying to prove the existence of God, Heaven, Hell, Original Sin, Conscience, Salvation— and that, I'm sure is sufficient to make anyone rash." Lowenthal's master's thesis is kept in box 1 of his papers.

16. The quoted letters to Lowenthal's parents have no exact dates: Thurs-

day (postmarked 8 October 1915); Sunday (no envelope, date 31 October 1915 inferred); letter postmarked 16 March 1916.

17. Lowenthal to his parents: postmark 16 March 1916; Tuesday—Rainy afternoon (postmarked 5 October 1915).

18. Halpern, *A Clash of Heroes*, 80.

19. Lowenthal, undated letters to his parents, probably from mid-June 1916.

20. Kallen to Lowenthal, 15 February 1918; Lowenthal papers, box 6.

21. Lowenthal to Taylor on 29 August 1920; 6 October 1920; Lowenthal papers, box 6.

22. Lowenthal to Taylor, 14 August 1921; 30 May 1922; 3 May 1923.

23. Lowenthal, "The Jew in the European Scene, I," *Menorah Journal* 9 (June 1923): 77, 78, 79, 71; "The Jew in the European Scene, IV," *Menorah Journal* 10 (February 1924): 65, 66.

24. Lowenthal, Erich Gutkind, Morris R. Cohen, *Proposed Roads for American Jewry: A Symposium* (New York: National Council of Jewish Women, n.d.), 14. In his speech Lowenthal said about his impression of Berlin in 1922: "I was amazed at the strength and spread of German antisemitism; and yet I had a fairly high standard to judge by. For I came from our America of 1921 when Henry Ford . . . was trying to sell the American people not only cars but the *Protocols of Zion [sic]* and *The International Jew*. Still . . . it seemed amazing to me . . . to live and move in an atmosphere so thick with hatred against the Jews." I was reminded of this passage recently by a Jewish friend from Scarsdale, New York, who after coming across Paul Lawrence Rose's stunning book *Revolutionary Antisemitism in Germany from Kant to Wagner* (Princeton: Princeton University Press, 1990) told me, "Growing up in America you would just never think that all of that was real. There is nothing in this country that prepares you for that, not even slavery."

25. This book was reprinted by Joseph Simon under the title *A World Passed By: Great Cities in Jewish Diaspora History* (n. p.: Pangloss Press, 1990).

26. Lowenthal, *The Jews of Germany*, 421.

27. Lowenthal to Taylor, 25 May 1925; 8 March 1925; 25 May 1925.

28. Ibid., 19 December 1926.

29. Lowenthal wrote to his uncle Simon from Paris on 31 August 1931: "I am concluding arrangements with Harper and Brothers to edit for them a series of books on Jewish subjects. Harpers are only going into this tentatively and the fate of the plan will depend on the reception of the first few books." Lowenthal papers, box 3, Personal Letters to Relatives.

30. "Turns with a Bookworm," *New York Herald Tribune*, 2 April 1933. Lowenthal papers, box 1. To Taylor, Lowenthal wrote on 10 April 1927: "I lack the concentration and application to achieve positive views

myself. . . . I suspect that life forever escapes formulae, that it can never be pinned down with a thumping fist, but at best can only be indicated with a transient gesture, the pointed finger that moves as it points. I would have been more at home in Montaigne's tower."

31. "Says Nazi Oppression Was Planned in 1922 on Definite Schedule," *New York World Telegram* 5 April 1933, Lowenthal papers, box 1. William L. Shirer, *The Rise and Fall of the Third Reich: A History of Nazi Germany* (New York: Simon and Schuster, 1960), 233.
32. Quoted in Martin Gilbert, *The Holocaust: A History of the Jews of Europe during the Second World War* (New York: Henry Holt, 1985), 48–49.
33. Lowenthal, *The Jews of Germany*, 417.
34. Lowenthal, "Herzl's Diaries: A Character Study of Theodor Herzl," *Menorah Journal* 10–11 (1924–25).
35. Lowenthal et al., *Proposed Roads for American Jewry*, 40. The term "first class status" is Alan Dershowitz's coinage in *Chutzpah* (Boston: Little, Brown, 1991). On the new anti-Semtism, see his chapter 3 "At Harvard: Quotas, Conflicts, and Honors;" and Henry Louis Gates, Jr., "Black Demagogues and Pseudo-Scholars," *New York Times*, 20 July 1994, A15.

CHAPTER 10

The Education of Maurice Samuel

Emanuel S. Goldsmith

Maurice Samuel occupies a singular position among the ranks of American Jewish intellectuals. He played a major role in the emergence of the American Jew's sense of Jewish identity and in the evolution of the American Jew's definition of Jewishness. He was the leading spokesman of Jewish rejuvenation and creative survival in America for half a century, beginning his work in the 1920s when first-generation American Jews scrambled to divorce themselves from their immigrant forbears. Yet in large measure because of his own contributions, he lived to witness the dawn of an American Jewish intellectual and cultural renaissance, both academic and popular, of magnitude and significance. In addition to his work as an expositor of Jewish spiritual and cultural values and as a translator from Yiddish and other languages, Samuel was a lecturer, debater, and polemicist of note. His devastating denunciations (both oral and written) of anti-Semitism, anti-Zionism, and Jewish self-deprecation were matched by his lucid expositions of the differentia of Judaism, Zionism, the birth and early history of modern Israel, the Yiddish language, the biblical heritage, and Judaic themes and characters in modern literature. Finally, Samuel was a creative intellectual and a man of letters who brought his own literary personality and refined taste and judgment to the discussion of the Jewish experience.

Samuel's family migrated from Rumania (where Maurice was born on February 8, 1895) to Paris and then to Manchester, England, when he was five years old. He was educated in Manchester's elementary schools and spent three years at the University of Manchester which he left without taking a degree. In 1914 he migrated to the United States, where three years later he was drafted into the army and sent with the American Expeditionary Force to France. There he did intelligence work and, after the war, served as interpreter for the American Pogrom Investigating Committee in Poland headed by Henry Morgenthau, Sr., and for the inter-Allied Reparations Commission in Paris, Berlin, and Vienna. During his stay in Poland, Samuel discovered deep sources of affection and joy in his identification and integration with East European Jewry. Returning to the United States in 1921, he worked for the Zionist Organization of America until he resigned in 1928 to pursue the career of a lecturer, translator, and freelance writer. From 1924, when his book *You Gentiles* was published, until his death on May 4, 1972, Samuel published over twenty original works on Jewish themes, the last being *In Praise of Yiddish* (1971), as well as numerous articles and essays on Jewish literature and life. Through his writings and lectures he became the voice of self-affirming American Jewry and a pre-eminent shaper of Jewish values among English-speaking Jews the world over.

In one of his books Samuel states that by the time he was a young man, he had to all intents and purposes forgotten whatever Yiddish and Hebrew he picked up as a child and had to sit down to learn them again. Moreover, for years he was indifferent to the destiny of the Jews, ignorant of Jewish culture, and an uncentered cosmopolitan outside of the inner circles of Jewish life.[1] In fact, before he became a Zionist he flirted with rationalism, Marxism, atheism, mechanism, positivism, and nihilism. It was only after he came to America and met the Zionist orator Shmarya Levin and later the poet Chaim Nachman Bialik that Samuel drifted back into Jewish life and became a Zionist.[2] (He later translated Levin's autobiography and many of Bialik's poems into English.) Eventually Samuel decided to put his erstwhile estrangement to good use and place his reborn interest and affection at the service of other outsiders. He felt, interestingly enough, that his knowledge of what it meant to be ignorant of Jewish things would be an advantage in his role as a mediator of Jewish values. The returned outsider would be able to combine the appreciations of a stranger with the love of a kinsman and serve as an interpreter between two worlds.[3]

Samuel's Jewish writings, whatever their ostensible theme, record his personal confrontations with, and education in, things Jewish. To Samuel interpretation was everything and he believed that consciously or unconsciously every writer who reveals his beliefs also reveals his personality. It was indeed the interweave between personality and formal beliefs that constituted for him a writer's real, three-dimensional thesis.[4] Samuel's books are all simultaneously primers and fundamental expositions of their subjects, as well as commentaries and personal interpretations of the matters discussed. Sprinkled with personal reminiscences, they are tourists' guides through what for many readers are the uncharted regions of Jewish life.

As a writer, Maurice Samuel was concerned with both the content and the form of his message. He saw himself as protagonist, propagandist, and teacher; as one of the *maggidim*, the wandering preachers of East European Jewry; as a one-man Anti-Self-Defamation League; and as an unofficial Minister for Jewish Self-Improvement. He viewed himself as an employee of the Jewish people with a lifelong contract on which only one signature appears.[5] His objective was to help Jews acquire an interest in Jewish knowledge with the hope that they would transmit it to their children.[6] At the same time, however, he had what he called "the craftsman's compulsions":

> I want to see how accurate and evocative I can make a description, how concisely, gracefully, and tellingly express an idea; most troublesome of all, because here I am weakest, how natural, organic, and unnoticed I can make the progress of a paragraph, a chapter, a book; and as a protagonist, which I am more than artist *pur sang*, how proleptic I can make my argument, anticipating in it the maximum of possible objections.[7]

The richness and variety of Samuel's contribution is apparent from the characterizations of his critics and admirers. Ludwig Lewisohn credited him with developing "a complete interpretation of the meaning of the history of Western civilization" and making "a massive and permanent contribution to man's thinking about himself and his destiny."[8] Harold U. Ribalow wrote that he could not think of a single English-language writer who had enriched Jewish literature as Samuel had done.[9] Cynthia Ozick spoke of him as the best polemicist of our time for whom "the Jewish view is never yielded up through simple declaration or exposition; it is wrested out of the engagement with, and finally a disengagement from, an alternative world view."[10] Milton Hindus noted "a sharp edge of amusement in Samuel's exposition of his favorite subjects" and saw as the complement of this quality "an unaffected eloquence which aspires, not vainly, to the plane of the sublime."[11] John Murray Cuddihy described him as "the great historian of the *shtetl* and of Eastern European Jewry."[12]

Five of Samuel's books were about Zionism and Israel (*What Happened in Palestine*, 1929; *On the Rim of the Wilderness*, 1931; *Harvest in the Desert*, 1943; *Level Sunlight*, 1953; and *Light on Israel*, 1968) with substantial sections of several others devoted to this theme. During the years he worked for the Zionist Organization of America, he got to know Chaim Weizmann whom he had first met in 1911 during his student days in Manchester. During Weizmann's trips to America on behalf of the Zionist cause, Samuel was sometimes assigned to him as secretary for months at a time. He also accompanied Weizmann on fund-raising trips on behalf of the movement. An intimate friendship developed between the two men which became a constant source of inspiration for Samuel. In Weizmann, he saw the personification of what he held to be essential in Zionism. Weizmann showed Samuel Jewish history working in the Jewry he knew. He converted the words "the Jewish people" from an idea into Samuel's own family and childhood memories.[13] In later years, Samuel was to verbalize the impression Weizmann made on him: "He speaks as my people would speak if it were articulate; he acts as it would act if it were awakened; he is what I want my people to become!"[14] Weizmann strengthened Samuel's espousal of the Ahad Ha-Amian or essentially cultural approach to Zionism and prevented him from identifying with chauvinistic or jingoistic trends within the movement. Samuel dedicated his second book, *I, the Jew*, to Weizmann and, towards the end of the latter's life, collaborated with him on his autobiography, *Trial and Error*.

Samuel's characterization of the Zionist achievement was undoubtedly influenced by his having lived for ten years in Palestine.
He viewed as altogether remarkable that the ancient organism
called the Jewish people should have been able to put forth the
necessary effort for its own remaking, produce a pioneering class,
pull itself together, and reassert itself on the very brink of its dissolution in the oceans of modern life.[15] Comparing Jewish ties to the
land with those of the Arabs, he wrote:

> The love of the Jewish people for its ancient homeland is of a different
> kind from that of the Arab. Its potency was hitherto known only to
> Jews—and not to all of them. Only a great and potent love could
> have created Israel. Homelessness, oppression, humiliation cannot
> explain it. Though the majority of Jews have come to Israel because
> they had nowhere else to go, the foundations were laid by Jews who
> were drawn to it by an overwhelming passion. . . . Israel has made
> its brilliant record because the decisive motivation was the love for
> the land transmitted without diminution across sixty generations.[16]

Samuel saw Zionism as a manifestation of an impulse for the
renewal of Jewish life among East European Jews in the last decade
of the nineteenth century. The secular Zionist leadership came
primarily from the intellectual stratum of Yiddish-speaking Jewry
that had broken only with part of the ritualistic side of Judaism.
They were as completely of the historic Jewish tradition as the
formally religious leaders and were the representatives of a Jewish
renaissance that illumined the Jewish people for nearly fifty years.[17]
The Palestinian pioneers between 1881 and 1939 too were loyal to
the moral and prophetic aspects of Judaism. The creation of the
Jewish homeland was connected in their minds with the renaissance of Judaism as an evolving way of life and a special vision of
humanity and the world. The strength of Zionism in the early
formative and decisive days came out of its historical and religious
passion; statism and refugee relief were incidentals which only
later were made into dominants by unforseen circumstances.[18] The
creation of the Jewish homeland was thus bound up with a continuing world Jewry, and with the millennial universal Jewish outlook.
    Even during his years of professional work on behalf of the Zion-
ist Organization of America, Samuel was at odds with the organiza-

tion on several points. He felt that it concentrated on the promotion of immigration into Palestine, but paid little attention to the spiritual needs of the Jewish people; it neglected working with and for the Jewish communities of the world; it gave inadequate attention to the younger generation and failed to enlist talented young writers in its cause; its intellectual level was low. Its preoccupation with practical results made it oblivious to the need for a Jewish spiritual and cultural renaissance. Moreover, there crept into it "a repellant Jewish jingoism" which only increased with the establishment of Israel. Although many leading Zionists also disapproved, the organization could not make such disapproval its concern.[19]

Perhaps even more serious was the fact that, in an astonishing contradiction, the Zionist movement distorted the interpretation of the Exile (*Galut* or *Goles* in Hebrew and Yiddish). Thus the youth of Israel became poisoned against Judaism outside of Israel. Samuel saw the contempt of the young Sabras for Jews who did not come to Israel, and their rejection of a possible Judaism anywhere but inside the ancient homeland, as a major failure of the Zionist movement. He explained it as follows:

> On the one hand, we said that the creation of a Jewish homeland would add dignity and content to Jewish life everywhere. On the other hand, when we spoke of the Chalutzim, and of all those that went to build Palestine, we would by contrast depict the life of Jews outside of Palestine as being, in its nature, irremediably debased. We did not quite mean it. We had in fact the picture of a realizable ideal of American Jewish life, a dignified and creative life. We spoke that way out of admiration of the Chalutzim, out of propagandist exaggeration, out of traditions carried over from past humiliations, out of a present frustration (non-existence as yet, of a Jewish homeland), out of a feeling of guilt that we had chosen the easier way, and out of irritation with our opponents, whose timidity about Jewish and Zionistic values was a debasement of both Judaism and Americanism. We carried over into our extramural utterances our intramural Yiddish self-criticisms, which have always been hyperbolic.[20]

Commenting on his own concern with the preservation of Jewish life outside of Israel, Samuel wrote that he had always looked upon the building of the Jewish homeland as an enterprise intended to serve Jews who remained outside of it no less than those who went to it and became a part of it. Channels of communication would always be needed between Israel and the Jewries scattered throughout the world. That the homeland in the making needed such intermediaries was obvious. That the need would continue when the task was completed occurred to few. Little attention was paid to the ultimate implications of Zionism; no one paused to consider Zionism in the total setting of Jewish history, to analyze it as a dynamic process within which the creation of the Jewish homeland was but a phase.[21]

According to Sol Liptzin, "although Samuel is best known as a popularizer of Zionism, his most original contributions were not primarily in the formulation of Zionist philosophy but rather in the clarification of anti-Semitism as an occidental phenomenon."[22] Six of Samuel's books explore various aspects of anti-Semitism: *You Gentiles* (1924), *I, the Jew* (1927), *Jews on Approval* (1932), *The Great Hatred* (1940), *The Gentleman and the Jew* (1950), and *Blood Accusation* (1966).

When as a young man Samuel decided to return to his people and tradition, he discovered that the rejected values of his childhood and boyhood environment were at work within him. "I had been touched with the Jewish tradition, the non-combative, non-competitive ideal; this tradition, which I had not acquired from books, but from unbookish people, from parents and relatives and neighbors— this tradition is separated by a tremendous gulf from the tradition of the western world."[23] Samuel gradually felt estranged from his fellow Englishmen because of what he saw as the combative impulse and the competitive philosophy that were so deeply imbedded in the English people and, by extension, in all of Western civilization.

> The non-Jewish civilization has set up an immense structure of moral substitutions which may best be described as the sporting formulation of life. Life is conceived as a game, and good behavior consists in scrupulously following the rules of the game. Therefore by definition a good man is one who always "plays the game." To find moral guidance, to achieve the right attitude toward his fellow men, to perfect his discipline, a man must go in constantly for games. The purpose of games is only in very small part physical exercise, which

is merely athletics. Their essential function is to express and keep alive the combative spirit. They are a moral cult. They are, in fact, the moral cult.[24]

On re-reading the Bible and Jewish history, Samuel came to realize that Judaism had always lacked a sports-fixation, that it was in fact characterized by a rejection of sports and the combative ethic. The rejection of sports was in fact the result of a moral fixation rooted in the writings of the Hebrew prophets. Nowhere in the Bible can one find evidence of a Jewish bent toward the sporting expression of life. Moreover, the frustrations of poverty and the displacements of exile had not obliterated the moral idiosyncrasy of Jewry. "The pacifist fixation of my boyhood world, expressing itself in abhorrence of violence, and in contempt for the mimicry of violence, was not a stratagem of slaves. It was an ancient tradition that had been born in freedom."[25] Through all of its known history, the Jewish people had been haunted by the need to formulate and affirm a morality in which the ritual of sports is rejected, and the prophets' concept of the nation as a moral instrument affirmed.[26] The prophetic vision was not of a prosperous nation but of a nation permeated with a moral spirit. For them a nation that was not a moral instrument had no reason or "right" to exist.[27]

Once, as a boy, Samuel had sneaked his way into a local church on a Sunday morning and heard the minister's sermon. Although terrified by the frequent invocation of the name of Jesus, he was amazed to discover that the ethics of Christianity were not unlike those of Judaism and that both faiths were at odds with the sporting ethic taught in English schools.

The sermon . . . had nothing whatsoever to do, in spirit or in sub-stance, with that gay, magnanimous, adventurous and gamesome world which I had come to hear glorified. It did no proclaim, in new and unimaginable attractive phrases, the cosmic rightness of the life of Greyfriars, *The Revenge*, *The Charge of the Light Brigade*, and the cricket team. In a most unbelievabe way it rehearsed what I had been learning in *cheder!* It appeared that among the Christians, too, the meek and the humble were blessed. It appeared that when someone hit you, you did not answer laughingly with a straight left, and you did not invite your friends to stand around in a circle while you

236 EMANUEL S. GOLDSMITH

carried on with the Marquis of Queensbury rules. Not a bit of it! You turned the other cheek! And what was my stupefaction on hearing that anyone who called anyone else a fool was in danger of hell-fire— a straight lift from *The Ethics of the Fathers!* It appeared that the peacemakers, not the soldiers, not the manly, laughing killers, were the blessed. This was not Tom Merry's world at all. It was my *Rebbi's.*[28]

Samuel was later to discover in the Christian world, alongside the biblical ethic, a rival world, a rival literature, and a rival pantheon. It was pagan, playful, and destructive. Yet it had universal and coeval status, and was widely accepted within Christendom. In that world the gentleman as a killer was respected.[29] "The two worlds are so intermingled that the escape does not even call for a formal defection. One could attend church on Sunday morning, hear the sermon I first heard in a church; and in the evening one could burst with pride hearing *Gunga Din* recited by the pastor."[30] In the Jewish world, by contrast, the summation of life as a game, with the concomitant implication of life as a hideous tragedy, was completely unknown. "Fighting was not a lark; armies were not masquerades; and sporting contests, the charades of war, with their wild practice excitations, were an abomination to the Hasideans who fought Antiochus the Fourth, and a foolishness to the Jews among whom I grew up. If competitive brutality existed among them in the ordinary daily struggle—and it did—there was no philosophy to make it seem the proper order of the universe."[31]

Anti-Semitism, as Samuel saw it, had to be viewed in terms of this pagan identity of Christendom denying the Semitic identity of its Christianity.[32] It was an expression of the concealed hatred of Christ and Christianity, rising to new and catastrophic levels in the Western world.[33] It sought to put an end to the Christian episode in human history and had to be clearly distinguished from anti-Jewishness which was simply group prejudice, the dislike of Jews as persons.[34] Anti-Semitism, on the other hand, was a special disease of the Western mind. It was the concealed rejection of the Jewish moral concept through the open rejection of the Jew.[35] Though directed against the Jewish people, anti-Semitism had nothing to do with reality since it was obsessed with the fantasy of a far-flung conspiracy against the Western world.[36]

In the Nazi onslaught on the Jews during the Holocaust, Samuel saw more than an act of genocide, since it was as much an attempt to destroy an idea as to wipe out a people. "There glowered in the Nazi mind a maniacal loathing of something spiritual, something with which the Jews and Judaism are historically associated. . . . They were seeking universal admiration as the first unashamed and consistent protagonists of a Jew-free world."[37] The Nazis set out to destroy everything in Western civilization that smacked of Jewish influence and the destruction of the Jews themselves was but a first step toward that end. It was a call to arms against the restraints of morality; it was an offer to lead western man out of the labyrinth of ethics and back into the lost paradise of the primitive, pre-Christian world.[38] The Nazis, in effect, concentrated their insane hatred on the Jews in order to conceal their attack on Christianity. They vented it on the people that had produced Christ.[39]

During the Second World War, the Arabs too viewed Hitler as a promise, not as a menace. They saw in the war against the Jews an action parallel to the Nazis' war against human progress. "That it did not come off was a bitter disappointment to the Germans and the Arabs. The Germans have come to terms with it. Not so the Arabs."[40] In their struggle with Israel today, are the Arabs anti-Semitic or merely anti-Zionist? asked Samuel. Most Jews today are Zionists as far as the Arabs are concerned, insofar as they are proud of Israel and ready to help her. Besides, the distinction between Jews and Zionists is made only rarely by Arab spokesmen. The Arabs have also reissued *The Protocols of the Elders of Zion* and sought to revive interest in it all over the world. Their effort, however, is self-defeating. If they succeed, the Arabs will bring Jews to Israel sooner and in larger numbers than will Zionism.[41]

> The creation of a Jewish homeland is infinitely more than an answer to anti-semitism; and the paradox of it is that if there were no anti-semitism there would be no opposition to the creation of a Jewish homeland, at least ideologically. More than that, the nonexistence of a Jewish homeland is itself a cause of anti-semitism, for it is an abnormality, reflecting on the status of the Jewish people and therefore on the status of the individual Jew who elects to remain Jewish. It is further a confirmation of the ancient superstition that the Jewish people forfeited the right to a homeland by an act of deicide.[42]

According to Samuel, Nazi anti-Semitism, followed by the miracle of Israel reborn, set up a tremendous ferment in American Jewry. Rejection of the Jewish heritage, on the one hand, and nostalgia for it, on the other, were replaced by thoughtfulness and a process of re-Judaization. The rebirth of the Jewish state was more than a political event for American Jews. Its impact was psychological, moral, and proto-religious. "The Jewish people which in the decline of the democracies had fallen to the nadir of human status, rose after the victory of the democracies to an eminence of accomplishment which could not be matched in history." [43] The question "*Why* should I be a Jew?" came to be replaced by "*How* can I be a Jew?" A re-Judaizing generation arose in American Jewry which, although a minority, came to be the dynamic catalyst in Jewish life. A historic change unforeseeable before the birth of Israel, was taking place. The dawning perception of something remarkable in the Jewish heritage was finding confirmation. [44]

Samuel believed that it was idle to dream of an American or any other Diaspora Jewry deeply versed in Jewish tradition. Nevertheless, American Jewry needed to acquire enough of its tradition to realize that its predominantly progressive and intellectual character had been largely bequeathed to it. The line of transmission went back to a choice made by a remote ancestry in the territory now called Israel. [45] Jews had to realize that their ethics and their intellectualism were infused into the Jewish people thousands of years ago and perpetuated through the generations. The perpetuation was conscious, systematic, disciplined. The tradition had to be renewed from father to son by arduous effort. If the effort is relaxed, the character will die. Indeed, relaxation is the portent of death. [46]

Those who wished to associate themselves with Judaism and its contribution to humanity and human survival could not do so simply by accepting its moral principles. Judaism was a method and a destiny as well as a revelation. "Judaism calls for education in the history of the Jewish enterprise and self-identification with it not simply by approval on general grounds, but by participation in it, and by the absorption and transmission of its tradition. [47] Jewish values could not be explained; they had to be acquired by conscious effort since they are associated with a body of knowledge. This body of knowledge is in turn associated with the Jewish idea that without knowledge there is no Jewishness. This is the Jewish tradition of intellectuality, the dissipation of which is a loss to every country with a Jewish community.[48] What was needed was a serious lifting of Jewish cultural standards among Jews.

> It must begin in the home, with parents participating, both for themselves and for their children; it must permeate the religious centers; it calls for secular institutions, like the community centers; it calls for an extension of the Jewish day-school system and of the Jewish-oriented summer camps. We cannot speak of the revival of Hebrew as the spoken language of the Jewish home—it was never that in the Diaspora or even in the post-Babylonian Jewish commonwealth—but it has been the additional language of the cultivated Jew, the language of his prayers and meditations and of his literary activity. But the chief mainstay of the Jewish tradition has always been and must always be its organic attachment to the land of its birth and finest flower, and a renascence of the Jewish tradition in America will be authentic only when it leads to the gradual migration of some hundreds of thousands of American Jews to Israel.[49]

"I have been drawn to, I have experimented with, other forms and materials," wrote Samuel, "but my dominant interest for thirty years has been the essay on a Jewish subject. . . . I have found moral satisfaction in spreading information on Jewish history, Jewish literature, Jewish folkways and ways of thought; in presenting as attractively and readably as I could the elements of Jewish problems; in pondering the nature of the relationship between the Jewish and the non-Jewish worlds."[50] Samuel's manifold contributions to the re-Judaizing of American Jewry include his interpretation of the nature of the Jewish people, of the specific role of America and American Jewry in Jewish history, of the significance of the Yiddish language and culture in the Jewish heritage, and of the significance of the Bible in both Jewish and general life.

The Jewish people, according to Samuel, is first of all a world people and a world observer. Whatever happens anywhere in the world happens to some part of the Jewish people and is communicated to the rest of it. "If humanity is trying to create One World, Jewry is the pilot plant. At the same time, in the tenacity with which it has held on to its identity for some three and a half millennia, it proclaims the vital principle that One World does not mean One Face."[51] The Jewish people is also an ethical people. A Jew who identifies with his people is aware that this identification implies an ethical obligation even if he considers himself an atheist. For Samuel there are no Jewish atheists, and what we call secular Jewish nationalism is actually deeply involved in the Jewish religion.[52]

A particularly Jewish idea, one that harks back to the prophets, is the motif of the redemption of the idea of the nation. "To derive a social-moral impulse from a national need and tradition, to devote the impulse, in turn, to the nation as a whole, to make morality and nationhood a unity, is Jewish as theme and experience; the highest Christian fellowships have denied nationhood instead of redeeming it; they have therefore denied the organizing needs of mankind, and placed them first in a vast and unmanageable abstraction."[53] Samuel believed that when Israel became politically and economically secure, it would have to continue the specific Jewish contribution to the world, together with world Jewry. The contribution can be described as the purification of nationalism, and the clarification by example of its creative and universal function.[54]

Samuel pointed out that if America had not welcomed European Jewry between 1880 and 1921, there would be practically no Jewish people today. Moreover, if Jewry had not been rescued by the United States, there would be no Israel. The creation of a great American Jewry was, in fact, a prerequisite to the creation of the Jewish state. Before 1920, America's open doors made it possible for Palestine to draw to itself only those Zionists who were psychologically prepared to build a Jewish state. America's defeat of Nazi Germany in World War II should be viewed as saving the Jewish name from infamy, even as it rescued the Jewish people from extinction. Is it any wonder that America's Jews have always laid claim to a special love of America? They have so often known the meaning of tyranny, oppression, and discrimination that they therefore appreciate freedom with a vitality that non-Jewish immigrants and non-Jewish native-born Americans have never experienced.[55]

American Jews think of America with love and gratitude, not only because of what they escaped from. In America, Jewish life thrived as nowhere else in the history of the Diaspora. America's destiny, her struggles with herself, her successes, failures, and perplexities, have engaged the Jew with a special intimacy.[56] American Jewry, together with Diaspora Jewry as a whole, can play an important role in bringing general Western values to Israel.

> When American Jewry will come into its own—and this will perhaps coincide with Israel's coming of age—it will produce an outlook and a literature as different from Israel's as, let us say, the Mishnaic was from the prophetic. We will not feel Israel's temptation to suppress the middle past. We will cultivate the memory of the founding of American Jewry, and of its roots in Europe. Our tradition will cherish the manifold experience of our people and faith in the heart of the Western world; and this will be our contribution to the widening of Israel's horizon, and to the mitigation of her egocentricity.[57]

Ronald Sanders has described Maurice Samuel's exuberant love for languages as one of the central features of his personality. He was "the only writer who ever turned the mental processes and enthusiasms of the translator into the stuff of literature in its own right."[58] Samuel devoted three of his books to the Yiddish language and literature: *The World of Sholom Aleichem* (1944), *Prince of the Ghetto* (1948), and *In Praise of Yiddish* (1971), in addition to translating Sholem Asch, I. J. Singer, Isaac Bashevis Singer, and other Yiddish writers into English. In a chapter entitled "The Fossil Creates a Language" in *The Professor and the Fossil* (1956), he wrote: "I wish to describe a Jewish cultural phenomenon of first-rate importance; and I wish to place in evidence part of the continuous spiritual creativity of the Jewish people."[59] The power of Yiddish, Samuel believed, derived from its dual character as a language strongly polarized by practicality and mercantilism, on the one hand, and by other-worldliness or Messianism, on the other. Its beginnings lay in simple economic necessity. Jewish traders in the Rhine Valley eight or nine hundred years ago had to learn the local dialects, and turned them into a language which ultimately absorbed the non-economic element of their lives, their Jewishness.[60]

The Yiddish language, like the Bible, must be viewed from its meta-literary aspect. It is redolent with spiritual meaning. "You cannot read Yiddish intelligently as a whole without feeling God, the Sabbath, the High Holidays, the Exile, the Return at the center, all created by the Bible. If you are a *veltlecher*—a secularist—you get at least an echo of them."[61] A cultivated Jew in Israel or the Diaspora cannot do without Yiddish since it mirrors Jewish life in its totality. To Yiddish poets like Chaim Nachman Bialik (who wrote in Yiddish as well as Hebrew), Aaron Zeitlin, Jacob Glatstein, and Chaim Grade, Samuel applied the phrase that each of them has "struck one clear chord to reach the ears of God."[62]

Although Maurice Samuel devoted only one of his books to the Bible—*Certain People of the Book* (1977)—there are important chapters interpreting biblical ideas in *The Gentleman and the Jew*, *The Professor and the Fossil*, and several of his other works. In addition, two volumes of his radio conversations on the Bible with Mark Van Doren were published posthumously under the editorship of Edith Samuel—*In the Beginning, Love* (1973) and *The Book of Praise* (1975). He considered what we think of the Bible today to be of vital significance. "I cannot permit myself to be frightened off by the complexes that have accumulated round the subject. My picture of man, of Christendom, of Jewry, and of myself has the Biblical experience at its center."[63]

Samuel believed that the Bible could not have become the determinant of Jewish history if it consisted only of what he termed "explanatory myths." Such myths it contains, but its essence is something else: the folk transmission of a factual experience.[64] Of the belief in miracles in the Bible and its theory of retribution, he wrote that they are "the stylization of the age." The essence of the biblical utterance, on the other hand, is timeless.[65] "The man who does not see in the prophets, in the Moses narrative, in the Ruth story, in Job, in the Song of Songs, the highest type of individual genius, should apply his literary faculties exclusively to the study of crossword puzzles."[66]

Of the prophets, Samuel wrote that they move us to a condition in which not to do good seems to be an inexplicable stupidity, a privation, a confinement or an unnatural restriction.[67] The prophets give meaning to life and thereby illuminate the whole universe.[68] They release us from the mechanistic or purely materialistic view of the world. He paraphrases the prophetic message to the individual as follows: "The prophet makes us see goodness as self-subsistent; he makes us see that life has meaning, that the meaning expresses itself in goodness, and that life is impossible without goodness. Not impossible in the sense that it cannot continue without goodness—though this may also be the case—but rather as we say that so-and-so is an impossible person.[69]

The following passage from *The Gentleman and the Jew* encapsulates Maurice Samuel's credo, *Weltanschauung*, and legacy:

> I, Maurice Samuel, an American citizen, and a lover of this country, feel that the best I can offer it springs from my identification with the development of Judaism. In the deep moral struggles of America (as of the rest of the Western world) the issue lies between the cooperative and the competitive interpretations of life, between essential Christianity and its matrix and ally, Judaism, on the one hand, and paganism, open or concealed, on the other. If I identify myself with Judaism that is such in name only, hence with an Israel that is a purely nationalistic state, I serve neither Judaism nor America, whatever approvals I can obtain for the deception. If, under the slogan of an exclusive Americanism, I disassociate myself from creative Judaism and a creative Israel, I am practicing another deception: I am depriving America of my best potentialities, and calling it good Americanism. For this deception it is particularly easy to obtain approval; but though there is a popular—and singularly immoral—advertising cliche: "Such popularity must be deserved," I must look for guidance to more serious considerations.[70]

Milton Hindus has described Samuel as an essayist who refused to lower himself to the demands of the fickle audience of the marketplace. Throughout his career he remained concerned with literary style and his writings contain flashes of both poetry and humor.[71] Samuel's influence on the generation of thinking Jews (both committed and estranged) for whom he wrote cannot be overestimated. His stance was that of the Jew with deep roots in the lore and life of his people, painstakingly analyzing its vicissitudes and their inner meaning. Here was an urbane, modern intellectual uniquely capable of infecting others with his fascination for things Jewish despite the prevailing fashion of defection and decline. The depth of understanding, breadth of perspective, commitment, and devotion with which he approached his literary subjects were refreshing and invigorating. Many a university position in Jewish studies, rabbinic pulpit, and leadership post in the English-speaking world today is filled by a devoted reader of Samuel's books. One could do worse than recommend them to those still in need of Jewish knowledge, pride, and inspiration.

Notes

1. Maurice Samuel, *Prince of the Ghetto* (Philadelphia: Jewish Publication Society, 1948), 3–4.
2. Maurice Samuel, *Level Sunlight* (New York: Knopf, 1953), 8.
3. *Prince of the Ghetto*, 3–4.
4. *Level Sunlight*, "Advice to the Reader," and Maurice Samuel, *The Gentleman and the Jew* (New York: Knopf, 1963), 276.
5. Maurice Samuel, *Little Did I Know* (New York: Knopf, 1963), 276.
6. Ibid., 286–87.
7. Ibid., 267.
8. Ludwig Lewisohn, "A Jewish Philosophy," *Congress Weekly*, October 9, 1950, p. 13.
9. Harold U. Ribalow, "Modern Day Maggid: Maurice Samuel," *Jewish Heritage*, Winter 1962–63.
10. Cynthia Ozick, "Foreword," *The Worlds of Maurice Samuel: Selected Writings*, ed. Milton Hindus (Philadelphia: Jewish Publication Society, 1977), xix.
11. Milton Hindus, "Introduction," *The Worlds of Maurice Samuel*, xxv.
12. John Murray Cuddihy, *The Ordeal of Civility* (New York: Basic Books, 1974), 141.
13. *Level Sunlight*, 9.
14. Ibid., 10.
15. Ibid., 50.
16. Maurice Samuel, *Light on Israel* (New York: Knopf, 1968), 105–6.
17. *Level Sunlight*, 21.
18. Ibid., 22.
19. *Little Did I Know*, 281.
20. *Level Sunlight*, 223–24.
21. Ibid., 43.
22. Sol Liptzin, *Generation of Decision: Jewish Rejuvenation in America* (New York: Bloch Publishing, 1958), 250.
23. *The Gentleman and the Jew*, 96.
24. Ibid., 97–98.
25. Ibid., 108–9.

26. Ibid., 190–91.
27. Ibid., 132.
28. Ibid., 34–35.
29. Ibid., 49.
30. Ibid., 205.
31. Ibid., 206.
32. Ibid., 257.
33. Maurice Samuel, *The Great Hatred* (New York: Knopf, 1940), 36.
34. Ibid., 39.
35. *Level Sunlight*, 253.
36. Ibid., 256.
37. *The Gentleman and the Jew*, 276–77.
38. Ibid., 278.
39. Ibid., 244.
40. *Light on Israel*, 88.
41. Ibid., 182.
42. Ibid., 38.
43. *Level Sunlight*, 236.
44. Ibid., 237.
45. *Light on Israel*, 189.
46. Ibid.
47. *The Gentleman and the Jew*, 315.
48. *Little Did I Know*, 306.
49. *Light on Israel*, 197.
50. *Level Sunlight*, 43.
51. *Light on Israel*, 198.
52. Ibid., 199.
53. *The Gentleman and the Jew*, 273.
54. *Light on Israel*, 207.
55. *Level Sunlight*, 242.
56. *Light on Israel*, 134.
57. *Level Sunlight*, 267.
58. Ronald Sanders, "Maurice Samuel: An Appreciation," *Midstream*, Vol. 19, No. 2 (February 1973): 57–58. This essay also discusses Samuel's six published novels.
59. Maurice Samuel, *The Professor and the Fossil* (New York: Knopf, 1956), 40.
60. *Little Did I Know*, 283.
61. Maurice Samuel, "My Three Mother-Tongues," in *The Worlds of Maurice Samuel*, 381.
62. Ibid., 379.
63. *The Gentleman and the Jew*, 110.
64. Ibid., 178.
65. Ibid., 117.

66. Ibid., 168.
67. Ibid., 122.
68. Ibid., 125.
69. Ibid., 126.
70. Ibid., 300–301.
71. Milton Hindus, "Introduction," *The Worlds of Maurice Samuel*, xxv.

CHAPTER 11

Charles Reznikoff

Milton Hindus

When it comes to literary recognition, it might be said that the first hundred years are always the hardest. I mean, of course, true and lasting recognition, not an ephemeral simulacrum of it, which may be produced by mere publicity or even occasionally by the enthusiasm of a whole generation. We continually witness the sort of newspaper fame which goes up like a rocket and comes down like a stick. And if we live long enough, we see fashions that are more lasting but also fade and perish. Then there is the kind of recognition that may be very slow and modest in its growth, and which may be compared to the process of sifting and re-examination that leads to the canonization of a saint by the church. A Jewish equivalent of this may be the legend of the *lamed-vav:* the thirty-six righteous, often obscure individuals, whose merits alone persuade the Lord to let a sinful world continue on its destructive course.

The arts, too, have their saints, some of whom, like the Dutch painter Vermeer, have literally taken centuries to come into their own, and of this number, I dare to suggest, Reznikoff may have been one. Since he lived into his ninth decade (he was in his eighty-second year when he died in 1976), he fortunately witnessed the initial glimmerings of the enduring reputation that was to be his. Now that we are approaching his centenary (he was born in Brooklyn, New York, on August 31, 1894), we ought to take stock once again of the value of the work he has left us. To help us do so, The Black Sparrow Press in 1989 published a one-volume text of his

Complete Poems, which had begun to appear thirteen years earlier in two volumes.

My own recognition of Reznikoff preceded that of the world in general (insofar as it can be said to exist now), yet in a way mine paralleled it as well, for it was produced by development rather than by a bolt from the blue, the proverbial "shock of recognition." There was, indeed, a great deal working against such recognition. We belonged to different generations. He was twenty-two and a newly admitted member of the Bar of the State of New York when I was born in 1916. Between the generations, as I noted very early, there is a great wall of separation, thick and soundproof enough to make one side virtually inaudible to the other. Still, there were important things we had in common. We were born New York children of immigrant Russian Jews, who somehow escaped deep alienation from our parents and grandparents, while necessarily finding for ourselves original forms of unorthodox affirmation. We were both also precocious schoolboys, if graduating from high school and entering college before we were sixteen made us so. At that point, however, our paths diverged somewhat, for Charles was evidently more enterprising than I was, if equally naive. Knowing early that his destiny was to be a writer, he struck out bravely from New York for the unknown Middle West, a feat which proved beyond me before I was thirty. At fifteen, he was attracted by the adventure and promise of a new academic enterprise: a School of Journalism established at the University of Missouri.

It took him a year to realize his mistake and return home, not in failure or disgrace (for he published a good deal of competent if not creditable verse) but with the disillusioning realization that journalists were interested primarily in news rather than in the way it was written, and that they defined news in a way that emphasized the sensational and melodramatic rather than the ordinary happenings of everyday life, which were precisely the things that interested him most profoundly. Born journalists preferred man-bites-dog stories which to him seemed trivial and cheap. If he had formulated his idea in the manner of Ezra Pound, whom he had read early, he might have said that his own preference was for "the news that stays news."

His contributions to the *University Missourian* during the year

1910 are of marginal interest to the student of his work. They are, for the most part, imitations and/or parodies of various poetic styles, usually romantic. Occasionally, there is a mere hint of the possibility of something better for the reader of his later work, as in this set of lines, which he postscripts "after Dean Swift":

> Lives there a man who with malice embittered
> Wounding doth keep you at your distance,
> Why weep? Rather rejoice, thou Fool, that he keepeth
>   His at the same time.

Faced with the problem of earning a living, Reznikoff was willing to enter his family's millinery business, as he did later on when he became a salesman. But the economic instability of all business argues in all immigrant households for the wisdom of entering a recognized profession. Charles's younger brother, Paul, became a physician. Charles himself apparently considered taking a doctorate in history and entering the academic profession. He decided upon the study of law, he tells us, encouraged by the notable example of the poet Heine. Motivated by a desire to avoid a repetition of his experience with journalism, Reznikoff became for years a conscientious student of American law, finding its history, philosophical principles, and socially beneficial possibilities more intriguing than its drier technical or corporate problems, but devoting himself sufficiently to the literature dealing with the whole body of the science to graduate second in his class at the New York University School of Law and subsequently to become one of the youngest to pass the Bar examination.

He was no more suited, however, for the rough-and-tumble of the courtroom or its histrionics than he had been for news gathering as defined by journalism, and so, after losing a painful case on behalf of a relative, he decided he needed additional preparation and enrolled in a postgraduate course at the Law School of Columbia University. With the Declaration of War against Imperial Germany in 1917, he joined the Reserve Officers Training Corps, but the war was over before he could be sent overseas. He did not suffer the sense of disappointment at this, which F. Scott Fitzgerald describes having experienced. On the contrary. How he felt about the tragedy of the war, as it related to the truncated lives and promise of young artists and poets like himself, is memorably indicated by some lines published in 1918, dedicated to the memory of Gaudier-Brzeska, a brilliant young Polish-French sculptor befriended and touted by Ezra Pound (whose head Gaudier-Brzeska immortalized in stone) in a little book published in 1916 after he was killed in battle the year before.

In the first gathering he made of his own verses, Reznikoff included

On One Whom the Germans Shot

How shall we mourn you who are spilled and wasted,
Gaudier-Brzeska,
sure that you would not die with your work unended,
as if the iron scythe in the grass stops for a flower?

I think that I have detected in this last line, much admired and commented on by the poet May Swenson, when it was reprinted nearly half a century later by New Directions, a wry and ironic allusion to a famous early poem by Robert Frost, "The Tuft of Flowers," in which isolated men mowing a field at different hours are presumed to be united by a single bond, their love of natural beauty, manifested by a silent decision to spare the same clump of wildflowers.

Surviving the anxieties of the war, Reznikoff still faced the relentless struggle for personal and economic survival. Journalism had been ruled out as a calling and the practice of law had proved distasteful. There was still his parents' business which he worked for until it, too, went down in a crisis in which enterprises of much greater magnitude foundered. He found refuge for a while in a scholarly adjunct to legal studies when he went to work for a publication called *Corpus Juris*, described as an "encyclopaedia of law for lawyers." He held down a demanding job there until his work proved too meticulous for his supervisor, whose interest was in productivity more than in quality and who complained of Charles's excessive care for detail in his reports of cases, saying: "I thought I was hiring a carpenter and you turn out to be a cabinet-maker!"

All the while that painful choices of regular remunerative jobs were being made, he was also trying his hand at a variety of literary forms—not only verse, which he enjoyed most and at which he was most successful in his own estimation, but experimental "haiku" dramas (as they have been described), autobiography, fiction, translations from German, and commissioned histories of American Jewish communities. He did some professional editing jobs as well, notably that of the two volumes of legal papers of Louis Marshall, the prominent lawyer and Jewish communal leader, who had been considered for appointment to a seat on the Supreme Court of the United States before Louis Brandeis. It was a hard struggle for economic survival and personal fulfillment, as is indicated by these lines from *Five Groups of Verse* (1927), no. 19:

> After I had worked all day at what I earn my living,
> I was tired. Now my own work has lost another day,
> I thought, but began slowly,
> and slowly my strength came back to me.
> Surely, the tide comes in twice a day.

The reference here may be to the laborious legal research he was doing on cases tried in the courts of different sections of the United States during the last decades of the nineteenth and the first decades of the twentieth centuries. It was this employment that provided grist for the mill that eventually produced the volumes of his own epical *Testimony*, the collection of concentrated narratives in a form which he described as "recitative" of life in the United States between 1885 and 1915, as reflected in its law reports. The methods he worked out in *Testimony* proved useful to him during his last years in the composition of his own version of *Holocaust*, based on the records of the Nuremberg Trials in Germany and the Eichmann Trial in Jerusalem.

Although Reznikoff was hardly twenty when some of his poems were accepted for publication by the legendary editor Harriet Monroe, whose *POETRY: A Magazine of Verse* in Chicago was the most prestigious periodical in the country entirely devoted to new creations in the most exacting of verbal arts, he at once asserted his courageous independence and self-confidence by refusing to heed the suggestions and textual emendations made by the great editor. So unwilling was he to leave aesthetic decisions to anyone's judgment other than his own that he withdrew from consideration poems already accepted for publication. When one reflects on the vanity of young poets and what it must have taken to turn down the opportunity to exhibit one's work in so notable a place, it is clear that what we have here is a young man of unusual maturity and integrity. To these qualities must be added enterprise as well, for he was willing to undertake the considerable expense and labor of printing his own work on a press of his own which produced solidly bound little editions that, it is pleasing to report, he lived long enough to see valued highly by rare-book dealers and collectors.

It was this enterprise and recalcitrant individualism, reminiscent of Walt Whitman's setting type himself for the initial printing of *Leaves of Grass*, which caught the favorable attention of Ezra Pound when it was reported to him in a letter from Louis Zukofsky. The story can be read in the Pound–Zukofsky correspondence published by New Directions in 1987. It was Zukofsky who was the friend and protégé of Pound, not Reznikoff, who never met him and only contributed the (edited) entries on Pound and Zukofsky to *The Encyclopaedia Judaica*. It was also Zukofsky, of course, who was an early and influential impresario of the poetry of Reznikoff, upon whom he placed the weighty role of example for the so-called Objectivist school or movement. This was launched in the pages of the issue of *Poetry* that Harriet Monroe, at the instigation of Pound, invited him to edit. He succeeded in eliciting Pound's endorsement of Reznikoff's writing as "very good," an accolade the master did not bestow lightly or upon more than a handful of his contemporaries. Reznikoff could not have failed to be moved by this approval from a man he had regarded with profound respect both as poet and critic. This may explain the restrained gentle irony of his conclusion in his earliest entry on Pound: "Although Pound's influence as a poet and teacher of poetry has been, and still is, great, the influence of his contributions to anti-Semitism has been slight, because in his time there have been far more vigorous and voluble anti-Semites and because his own contributions are in the least regarded of his prose and in his dullest verse." He completely revised this, however, in the 1971 edition.

Reznikoff was no more capable of denying the centrality of aestheticism in his vision of the world than Proust would have been. Who but a profound Platonic aesthete—for whom the beautiful merges imperceptibly together with the good—could have written such lines as the following (from *Separate Way* [1936], 3, I) in the very year, 1933, which witnessed Hitler's accession to power in Germany:

> I will write songs against you,
> enemies of my people; I will pelt you
> with the winged seeds of the dandelion.
> I will marshal against you
> the fireflies of the dusk.

Such restrained irony is based on the recognition that the poet's kingdom is not that of the world of brutal power.

I first encountered Reznikoff's work without notable enthusiasm in the fall of 1944 when, at the request of Clement Greenberg, who was editing the magazine *Contemporary Jewish Record* (a predecessor of the magazine *Commentary*, which he later helped edit), I reviewed a group of three novels with Jewish themes, one of which was Reznikoff's *Lionhearted*, which dealt with the massacre and expulsion of the Jews of York in England in the twelfth century. The irony of the title appealed to me, but little else did. The title had been expropriated from the famous Crusader King Richard and bestowed upon the fugitive small people of strangers in his realm, who were hunted down and killed by an inflamed, envious populace, welcoming the opportunity of improving their own lot by taking the lead against the helpless from the hands of the lords of church and state. The review I published in October 1944 indicates that, though I sympathized heartily with the subject of the book and what the writer was attempting to do with it, I did not think he had succeeded in his aim: "Reznikoff's book is in the worst tradition of historical fiction in the sense that the characters are pasteboard creations serving merely as vehicles for the author's ideas. I liked Reznikoff's frankly partisan tone, but I failed to see his purpose in spinning a story so thin that he himself gives it up before the end of the book and turns to straight historical narrative. Had he done so from the beginning, his book would have been much stronger."

I did not know at the time of Reznikoff's initial attraction to the field of history, and he may have taken my advice sufficiently to heart to publish six years later in collaboration with Uriah Engelmann, a history of the Jews of Charleston, South Carolina, which I am certain would have pleased me more than *The Lionhearted*. There was an aspect of the novel to which I had a more positive response. It was what I perceived as his "insistence on the importance of racial purity in a time of crisis. . . . Throughout the book the romantic love which binds individuals together is shown to be far less important than a tie of each individual with his ethnic group."

I knew nothing of Reznikoff personally at the time. I had no notion of his marriage to Marie Syrkin, and her name would have meant nothing to me, for I was not a reader of the *Jewish Frontier*. I had no awareness of what it was revealing in those years of the horrors that were being visited on the Jews of Eastern Europe. Years later, I reread the book with a much more sympathetic eye, though my critical reaction to it did not undergo any great change.

I understood better, however, the way my words may have registered on the sensibilities of the hardworking author, and it is distressing to reflect that it could have been a review such as mine that triggered an epigram (*Inscriptions: 1933–1945*, 3) by Reznikoff addressed perhaps to a confident young critic (I was twenty-eight at the time, Reznikoff had just turned fifty):

You are young and contemptuous.
If you were the sentry,
you would not fall asleep—
of course.
Wounded
you would not weep.

Truly, the generations often seem almost incomprehensible to each other, and it is late indeed that one learns the true meaning and importance of charity, tolerance, forbearance, generosity, which the least of us as well as the greatest and supposedly most invulnerable are always so much in need of. Whatever the personal references may have been, and there is no way of recovering it now, that is the lesson which the past has to teach us.

Years after reviewing *The Lionhearted*, in the early 1950s I came across Reznikoff's work again. It was in the form of a group of verses (later to be included in the collection entitled *Inscriptions: 1944–1956*) printed in the pages of the magazine *Commentary*. This time I was not asked to comment on them in print, but remember being greatly impressed by them, far beyond anything in the book of prose fiction I had reviewed. I was impressed to the point that I began to discuss his work with others, and if they had read him before and discounted him to urge them to reconsider on the strength of this latest publication. One oddly shaped set of verses, in particular, connected with my own sensibility, and I read them over and over. The Latin title was striking—*Te Deum*—but the victory that was being celebrated was not of a public but of a private kind. It was a celebration of the simple life, the ordinary man, and the virtue of a philosophical, perhaps religious, resignation to one's lot, however obscure, in the scheme of things. The theme reminded me of Emily Dickinson's "I'm Nobody! Who are you?" or possibly Whitman's psalm for the republic of the uncommon common man. The phrasing recalled to my mind that of a short poem by Dylan Thomas. Yet Reznikoff's hymn of thanksgiving was somehow absolutely his own, uniquely original in the totality of its effect:

Te Deum

Not because of victories,
I sing,
having none,
but for the common sunshine,
the breeze,
the largess of the spring.

Not for victory but for the day's work done
as well as I was able;
not for a seat upon the dais
but at the common table.

It was hard to say which was the more satisfying to my sense, the substance of what was being said or its form. It repaid attention to examine carefully the concatenation of unexpected rhymes, unemphatic meter, and concealed echoes in words of such different signification as "day's" and "dais." I found it hard to understand how I could have read the work of so "able" a writer (to say no more of him) without the care and respect he so obviously deserved and called for.

It was not until 1961 that I was able to address my attention to Reznikoff again in print, seventeen years after I had first done so. By 1961 I had long been teaching at Brandeis University, where one of my colleagues was Marie Syrkin, who, I was told, was married to Charles Reznikoff, though I never met him at that time and never, to my best recollection, had any conversation about him with her. I did not, however, make any secret of my admiration for Reznikoff's verse to anyone who would listen. I remember, in particular, reciting some verse of Reznikoff to the head of our English department who was a poet. It was probably Marie, therefore, who presented me, in 1959, with a copy, uninscribed, of Reznikoff's latest little book, printed by himself in that year: *Inscriptions: 1944–1956.* Reading his verses again with even more feelings of respect than before, I made up my mind that I would write an unsolicited review of it for a magazine in New York, the *New Leader,* for which I had reviewed many books over the years. Despite this, I anticipated that the editors might be less than enthusiastic about reviewing a book by an author they had never heard of and for which no recognized publisher was taking responsibility. The proposal might strike them as too personal for their pages. Though the magazine lacked a mass-circulation, it had a discerning and intellectually prestigious readership. (T. S. Eliot had once described it as the best magazine being published in America.) I, therefore, worked hard to make my review persuasive to the few initiated readers of poetry, who might by chance come across it, as well as the many uninitiated, before presenting it to the editor, who may have been a member of either group but whose position compelled him to keep watch over the interests of the second. I submitted my short review some time in 1960, but the new managing editor did not get around to printing it before the beginning of 1961. Of the hundreds of reviews I have published in a multitude of periodicals both here and abroad, there is not one I can think of now that seems more important to me, more judicious, or more productive of the good I sought, immediate and long-range. Reznikoff, whom I had not yet met, later told me that, as soon as the review appeared, he had heard from friends who had been out of touch with him for years. By 1962, a paperback selection of his lifetime accumulation of verse had been published jointly by New Directions and the *San Francisco Review*, which was greeted with ecstatic praise in the pages of the *Nation* by Hayden Carruth. He was being invited to give poetry readings on various college campuses. We must not exaggerate. It was hardly the triumph of a Lord Byron when he woke one morning to find himself famous. But it seemed a decisive turn-around in the fortunes of a forgotten author, and he was humble enough to attribute to me excessive credit for it instead of to the quality of his own work. He seemed really to suffer when being praised. He once stopped what he took to be the effusiveness of his friend George Oppen with the crushing commonplace: "We all do the best we can." But he did not just say it; he truly believed it.

The opening of my essay was from T. S. Eliot's early essay *Tradition and the Individual Talent:* "Honest criticism and sensitive appreciation are directed not upon the poet but upon the poetry. If we attend to the confused cries of the newspaper critics and the *susurrus* of popular repetition that follows, we shall hear the names of poets in great number; if we seek not Blue-book knowledge, but the enjoyment of poetry, and ask for a poem, we shall seldom find it." I went on to point out that the literary fate of Reznikoff seemed to be the reverse of Eliot's hypothetical case, since he had produced some real poems, but had almost entirely escaped the rumor-mongers. There was no mention of him in any of the standard references works, and I had searched without much success for readers to share my enthusiasm for the distinction of his epigrammatic verse. Yet he could hardly be denied a place in the literary history of the movements of Imagism and Objectivism in the earlier part of the twentieth century. I cited some readers—like Lionel Trilling, Kenneth Burke, and Louis Zukofsky—who had praised his work thirty years before, and I noted the difference between my pleasurable reaction to his verse and my feelings at my first encounter with his prose. The rest of the review was given over to concrete illustrations of his work—beginning with *Te Deum*, which, in my estimation, belonged in the anthologies among the choicest specimens of verse in his time, but had been inexplicably overlooked. But I also pointed out some wonderfully bitter lines, worthy of the pencil of a Roman satirist, in which, without mentioning names, he had pinned "wriggling against the wall" persons he had known intimately over the years and treated gently, even lovingly, elsewhere. Passing resentments against friends may be frozen and, in a literary sense, immortalized in some vigorous lines. In the following ("By the waters of Manhattan," *Inscriptions: 1944–1956*, 39) for example, which I quoted, I thought I recognized much later, as I learned more of him and his story, his wife, Marie Syrkin, his early admirer and literary friend, Maurice Samuel, and Marie's father, Nachman Syrkin, the founder of Labor Zionism, who had died in New York in the 1920s. I have never said this before, and knowing such facts, even if my surmise were correct, adds or detracts nothing from the force of the poem, though other readers like Ben Halpern apparently came to the conclusion I did about the reference.

I remember very well when I asked you—
as if you were a friend—whether or not
I should go somewhere or other,
you answered: "It does not matter
you are not at all important."
That was true. But I wonder
Whom you thought important.
He who has been in his grave
these ten years or more?
He is not important now.
Or is he who is wearing out a path
in the carpet of his room
as he paces it
like a shabby coyote in a cage,
an old man hopelessly mad.
Yourself no doubt
looking like one
who has been a great beauty.

Here are eighteen lines inspired by such powerful feelings that even they were insufficient to discharge them completely, for there are another eleven lines elsewhere in Reznikoff ("Autobiography: New York," XI) evidently originating in the same situation:

> "Shall I go there?" "As you like—
> it will not matter; you are not at all important."
> The words stuck to me
> like burrs. The path was hidden
> under the fallen leaves, and here and there
> the stream was choked. Where it forced a way
> the ripples flashed a second.
> She spoke unkindly but it was the truth:
> I shared the sunshine like a leaf, a ripple;
>
> thinking of this, sunned myself
> and, for the moment, was content.

There is undoubtedly grist for the mill of a biographer here, particularly if one succumbs to the temptation to explain such lines by connecting them with what is revealed about the Reznikoff–Syrkin marriage and relationship in the very interesting pages of Reznikoff's posthumously published fiction *The Manner Music*. But this was not available to me when I wrote my review, and as I never had any biographical ambitions in this area, even if it had been available, I am not optimistic about fathoming the depth of the connection between poetry, fiction, and the experienced reality which underlies both. No one has ever refuted, or is likely to refute, the validity of Proust's generalization in *Contre Sainte-Beuve* that "a book is the product of a different *self* from the self we manifest in our habits, in our social life, in our vices." No biographer is likely to cast any light on the inventiveness which enables Reznikoff (in *Inscriptions: 1944–1956*, 3) to refresh the theme of mutability, which we should have guessed had been outworn long ago:

> One of my sentinels, a tree,
> Sent spinning after me
> this brief
> secret on a leaf:
> the summer is over—
> forever.

Consider the inventiveness it took to treat a sentimental theme
without succumbing to its sentimentality, to resist the temptation
of the lachrymose with just a dash of the bitters of self-mockery (in
Inscriptions: 1944–1956, 43):

> These days when I dare not spend freely
> and the friends I meet are uneasy
> that I might ask for a loan, I dreamt of you:
> my friend at school.
> I was going to ask you a question
> and afraid you might find it foolish
> (you were somewhat older and sensible).
> The faces around you were shadowed
> but yours was smiling, fresh and pink.
> And I must be in my dotage
> for I find myself weeping that you are dead—
> who have been dead for a long time.

The space for my review had been limited, or else I might have
hazarded a comparison between the pathos in this expression of a
poet, old and poor, and the deeply moving latter half of his Medita-
tion on the winter festival of Hannukah, which celebrates the victory of the Maccabees more than a century before the Christian era,
recounted in the Apocrypha. The speaker's identification, here as
everywhere, is with the poor, especially among his own people, but
not limited to them and extending not only to the poor of other
nations but, at times, the animal kingdom as well, destined for
slaughter. His comfort is the great and famous verse of the prophet
Zacharia, which is twice repeated, the second time with an almost
imperceptible variation that infuses it with an affective power I
still find quite thrilling after scores of readings (*Inscriptions: 1944–
1956*, "Meditations on the Fall and Winter Holidays," IV):

> Penniless, penniless, I have come with less and still less
> to this place of my need and the lack of this hour.
> That was a comforting word the prophet spoke:
> Not by might nor by power, but my My spirit
>   said the Lord;
> Comforting indeed for those who have neither might
>   nor power—
> for a blade of grass, for a reed.

The miracle, of course, was not that the oil for the
            sacred light—
in a little cruse—lasted as long as they say;
but that the courage of the Maccabees lasted to this
            day;
let that nourish my flickering spirit.

Go swiftly in your chariot, my fellow Jew,
you who are blessed with horses;
and I will follow as best I can afoot,
bringing with me perhaps a word or two.
Speak your learned and witty discourses
and I will utter my word or two—
not by might nor by power
but by Your spirit, Lord.

Although he was continually attempting compositions of varying
length, he took to heart the observation that brevity is the soul of
wit in such pleasurable exercises as the one (in *Inscriptions 1944–
1956*, 37) condensing a familiar fable and copybook maxim into two
rhyming lines consisting of a dozen words and a mere fifteen syl-
lables:

The nail is lost. Perhaps the shoe;
horse and rider, kingdom too.

Stated thus, who can believe the moral, except the children whom
it was meant to caution? On the other hand, who can doubt it, on
the basis of the most extensive experience? Or consider the ironic
force and social comment implicit in such a fragmentary ejacula-
tion as this (*Inscriptions 1944–1956*, 24):

Scrap of paper
Blown about the street
you would like to be cherished, I suppose,
like a bank-note.

I don't know if this was written after reading a pamphlet by Pound
on Money or his 45th Canto on Usury. Probably not, but it could
have been a contributing factor. More likely, it was a response to
his own experience of standing in line with a thousand others
during a "run" on a bank in the Depression of 1930 where he had

deposited the first sizable advance of $1,000 he had received from the New York publisher, Boni, for the rights to his novel *By the Waters of Manhattan*, a beautiful title which served him again later for his volume of selected verse. I had the pleasure of introducing this novel in a new edition, more than half a century after it was first published.

That Reznikoff realized the nature of his own strength is clear from one of his daring *midrashim* (*Going To and Fro, and Walking Up and Down* [1941], no. X) in which he cuts down to size the conventionally recognized great, while building our respect up for the ingenuity and capacity of those thought to be of smaller stature, for example, the "other" New York Jewish Intellectuals.

> I do not believe that David killed Goliath.
> It must have been—
> you will find the name in the list of David's captains.
> But, whoever it was, he was no fool
> when he took off the helmet
> and put down the sword and the spear and the shield
> and said, "these weapons you have given me are good,
> but they are not mine"
> I will fight in my own way
> with a couple of pebbles and a sling.

Against the Goliath of the worldly, Reznikoff also is in need of no more than a concentrated couplet, a "haiku," a suggestive quatrain, a rephrasing of a familiar fable or prayer, a new angle or light upon hackneyed words in the Bible or in Aesop.

Reznikoff was emphatically not a member of the intelligentsia, either in the honorific East European sense or in the American one, which is described by the dictionary as "often derisive" and which makes titles like doctor or professor sound to many American ears (except perhaps in the case of physicians) faintly ironic. If any analogies are in order, he was more like an inventor, which is apparently the way the poet William Carlos Williams thought of himself. West of the waters of Manhattan, intellectuality is rarely identified with real intelligence, which gives rise to dark suspicions among parochial inhabitants of the island.

The last fifteen years of Reznikoff's life were happily his most secure. In my initial review, I had said that at age sixty-seven, he was still laboring without recognition of his merits by the world. It came to him afterwards, if not in such abundance that "the giving famishes the craving," at least sufficiently to satisfy his quite meager expectations. "A writer of verse," he once said, "must learn to fast and drink water by measure." He made friends feel that the honors, invitations, and anthology-inclusions, which came in the years after 1961, had amply compensated for whatever neglect he had suffered previously. I myself was asked to write half a dozen reviews of new books and reprints of old ones as they appeared, and I was able to include a chapter from his first novel, *By the Waters of Manhattan*, in a book I edited while he was still alive to see it. After 1976, I added to these two new books. One was a synoptic essay, the other a collection of memories of him, tributes and assessments of his work by writers mainly from the United States, Britain, and Canada. It was almost as if I had been magnetized like one of the rings in Plato's parable in his dialog *Ion*, which stretches from the reader through the writer all the way back to the inspiring Muse who stands behind all real poets by vocation.

For Reznikoff, writing poetry was not so much a life-enhancing activity as a life-sustaining one. He was not among the comfortable who can take it or leave it. He was not among those at ease or at home "in Zion" or anywhere else. He once turned down an invitation to visit Israel apparently with the excuse that he had not yet done with exploring Central Park. Writing for him was not a choice but a compelling need. This is one way in which he describes it (in *Inscriptions 1944–1956*, 2):

> The Indian of Peru, I think,
> chewing
> the leaf of a shrub
> could run all day.
> I, too,
> with a few lines of verse, only two or three
> may be able
> to see the day through.

I am reminded by this of a passage of about the same number of lines, though each line is generally longer, in Whitman's *Lilacs:*

> In the swamp in secluded recesses,
> A shy and hidden bird is warbling a song.
>
> Solitary the thrush,
> The hermit withdrawn to himself, avoiding the settlements,
> Sings by himself a song.
>
> Song of the bleeding throat,
> Death's outlet song of life (for well, dear brother, I know,
> If thou wast not granted to sing thou wouldst surely die).

Reznikoff's imagery is sparer, but essentially the import of both passages is similar. Whether the poet is suggesting a comparison between the Indian, seeking narcosis, and himself, or between himself and the hermit bird, each is saying that verse-making has a value for the poet by providing indispensable relief from pain and strain, and not because it produces a commodity for the marketplace.

Reznikoff's humor, which does not appeal to everyone I have found, is one of his charms for me. It is a scholar's humor, depending often on his learning in secular texts as well as sacred ones. In the following lines from "Sightseeing Tour: New York" (*Inscriptions 1944–1956*, 45), it is exercised against a seemingly harmless but single-minded enthusiasm, which has the effect of turning its object into a grotesque:

> Fraser, I think, tells of a Roman
> who loved a tree in his garden so much
> he would kiss and embrace it.
>
> This is going pretty far
> even for a lover of nature
> and I do not think it would be allowed
> in Central Park.

The taste for both classicism and neo-classicism (of the eighteenth century) goes back far in Reznikoff. He was hardly more than a schoolboy when, in addition to composing his quota of romantic verse (even Alexander Pope at fifteen wrote romantically and not with acerbic tongue in cheek), he was attracted to Swift among the moderns. Later he was drawn to Swift's sources among the ancients. The epigraph of the initial selection from his lifetime accumulation of verse is from Martial.

He consciously aims at communication with a maximum of transparency, clarity, and concentration. When he achieves it, as he does often, he is memorable indeed, as George Oppen has testi-fied, and as I can confirm from experience. Macaulay reminds us of an anecdote in Plutarch about Lysias, the celebrated advocate and speech-writer (satirized by Plato in the *Phaedrus*). One of Lysias's clients, for whom he had written a speech to be delivered in court, complained that, in reading it over and over trying to memorize it, he had become increasingly aware of its weaknesses. "You forget," Lysias told him, "that the jury will hear it only once." Perhaps we may seek in such cynicism some clue to the reason for Reznikoff's reaction against the practice of law in the courtroom. He was too scrupulous and respectful of words to waste them or use them idly. "Silence is legal tender everywhere," he tells us in one verse. "Of the first twenty sins we confess," he notes in *Day of Atonement*, "five are by speech alone." The result of such care is that the more carefully we read over his seemingly simple lines, the more we are likely to become aware of internal form and subtle connections in them, until at last they begin to seem inevitable and unforgettable. We memorize them almost without intention. He has somehow succeeded in carving his words in our memory like initials in newly laid cement. Poetry, for Reznikoff, was concentrated and memora-ble speech.

Faced with the necessity of a coda for a composition that is but another link of my involvement with the work of Reznikoff over the past thirty years, I am tempted to emulate the inconclusive conclusion of the last essay by William James, the ms. of which was found on his desk at the time of his death in 1910 and subsequently published in the *Hibbert Journal*. The title of the essay is "A Plural-istic Mystic" and the words are attributed to the subject of the essay, James's longtime friend and correspondent, the philosopher and poet Benjamin Paul Blood: "There is no conclusion. What has concluded that we should conclude with regard to it? There are no fortunes to be told, and there is no advice to be given. Farewell!" These words have left a marked impression indeed upon a number of those who have heard or read them and know nothing more about their author, not even that there is an essay by James about him. They continue to stand by themselves, on their own, in the bareness of their enigmatic challenge.

I am not going to try to interpret their meaning, which may be different for every reader. In my own mind they connect with two brief compositions of Reznikoff. One (*Jerusalem the Golden* [1934], no. 66) consists of a mere half-dozen lines, which Marie Syrkin asked me to read on her behalf at his funeral in New York in 1976. I repeated them at her own, thirteen years later in Santa Monica, California:

> If there is a scheme,
> perhaps this too is in the scheme,
> as when a subway car turns on a switch,
> the wheels screeching against the rails,
> and the lights go out—
> but are on again in a moment.

The other is the "Epilogue" he composed for his late collection of poems *By the Well of Living and Seeing*:

> Blessed
> in the light of the sun and at the sight of the world
> daily,
> and in all the delights of the senses and the mind:
> in my eyesight blurred as it is
> and my knowledge slight though it is
> and my life brief though it was.

Doubt that there is any patterning, "scheme," or meaning in the universe is probably what is most tormenting in intense grief or crisis, personal or social, when we feel as if we were suddenly plunged back into the primeval state of chaos and disorder that preceded the creation. What tides us over at such times is the "antiseptic" of faith which we may not even know we possessed, the conviction that all will be well again, that the lights which have gone out for us will come on again "in a moment," though it seem an eternity. It is then that the realization floods through us that there is no ending which is not also a new beginning, and that all reasoning, indispensably useful and pleasing as it may be, is also artificial and incomplete, because it is based on segmentations which are arbitrary.

I am tempted finally to quote the apologia with which James introduces his essay on the obscure but provocative thinker Benjamin Paul Blood: "I have always held the opinion that one of the first duties of a good reader is to summon other readers to the enjoyment of any unknown author of rare quality whom he may discover in his explorations." This could well serve, if I may say so, as a description of what has been my own continuing critical effort.

CHAPTER 12

A. M. Klein: The Intellectual As a True *Ohev Israel*

Rachel Feldhay Brenner

A Jew I am, the whole world knows it . . . I am the possessor, because of the education my bearded father gave me, of a rich legacy.
—A. M. Klein[1]

Irving Howe found that statements beginning "I am a Jew and . . ." were very difficult for his fellow New York Intellectuals to utter.
—Alexander Bloom[2]

An examination of A. M. Klein's stature as a Canadian and Zionist intellectual against the coterie of the New York Jewish Intellectuals reveals the irony of inverse symmetry. Despite their two-decades-long conscious endeavours to discard their Jewishness, the New York Intellectuals of the 1930s and the 1940s owe their name and distinctness, as a group, to their Jewish origins. Years later, in the sixties, Irving Howe, an eminent member of the New York group, reached the conclusion that "the main literary contribution of the New York milieu has been to legitimate a subject and tone we must *uneasily* call American Jewish writing."[3]

The Canadian Klein sensed the Intellectuals' uneasiness regarding their Jewish origins when he mocked them as "Americans by Jewish dissuasion [who] think that by travelling incognito, they will be mistaken for royal, or at least New England, personages."[4]

Declaring proudly: "I travel on my own passport," Klein claims against the assimilationists that he has "a contribution to make as a Jew, a contribution to the culture of the [Jewish] group." He meets other cultures "as an equal, not as an interloper."[5] Ironically, however, the absence of critical acknowledgment from the influential New York milieu precluded recognition of Klein's work beyond the confines of his native Montreal, and only recently have the diversity and the quality of his literary achievements been given due attention.[6]

A. M. Klein was born in 1909 in Ratno, Ukraine. In 1910 his family emigrated to Canada and settled in Montreal. In the years 1926–30 Klein attended McGill University, majoring in classics, political science, and economics. From 1930 to 1933 Klein studied law at the Université de Montréal and in 1934 he established a law firm. Klein married Bessie Kozlov in 1935 and they had three children.

Klein's literary work was informed by his deep attachment to Jewish heritage and a sensitive approach to the multicultural aspects of his environment. His first volume of poetry, *Hath Not a Jew* (Behrman's, New York, 1940) reveals emotional closeness to Jewish tradition in an array of folk stories, biblical motifs, and religious symbols. His second book of poetry (Jewish Publication Society, Philadelphia, 1944), deals almost exclusively with Jewish subject matters. Stylistically, both collections demonstrate a dominant influence of the English romantics, imagists, and the Elizabethan poets. In 1944 he also published *The Hitleriad* (New Directions, New York), a long satiric attack on Nazism. *The Rocking Chair and Other Poems* (Ryerson, Toronto, 1948) focuses on the French Canadian tradition and the social reality of Quebec. The volume won the Governor-General's Award. In 1949 Klein traveled to Israel, Europe, and North Africa. His only novel, *The Second Scroll* (Knopf, New York, 1952), is based on this journey. In 1954 he suffered a mental breakdown. Very little is known about his illness. Unfortunately, he ceased writing, withdrew from public life, and became a complete recluse. A. M. Klein died in 1972.

Klein was a lifelong dedicated Zionist. From 1928 to 1932 he served as educational director of Canadian Young Judea and edited its monthly magazine, the *Judean*; in 1936 he was on speaking tours for the Zionist Organization of Canada and edited its monthly, the *Canadian Zionist*; from 1938 to 1955 Klein served as an editor of the *Canadian Jewish Chronicle*; in 1949 he was sponsored by the Canadian Jewish Congress to travel to Israel and upon his return he lectured extensively on Zionism and the State of Israel in Canada and the United States.

Though little recognized by the United States Jewish community, Klein is still remembered in his native Montreal with awe and affection. Many of the Canadian Jewish poets and writers have acknowledged Klein's influence in their life and work. Suffice it to mention Irving Layton who, in his poetry, remembers Klein's "imperishable name with grateful tears and affection"; Leonard Cohen, who sees Klein as father and teacher and wishes to stay with him at times of despair and grief; Miriam Waddington, who tries to figure out Klein as a tragically split figure of an innovative poet.[7]

Both Klein and the New York Intellectuals saw the Jew as a universal symbol. The New York Intellectuals made intense efforts to replace their "minimal"[8] position of deliberate refusal to acknowledge affinity with Jewish history with the "American *idea*" of the universalist, better society "built in the shell of the old,"[9] which would make Jewish suffering and alienation the symbol of *la condition humaine*. This "minimal position" is quite a different matter from Klein's "maximal position" vis-à-vis Jewish history. Klein's concept of Jewish universality by no means bespeaks the individual's anxiety of exclusion; on the contrary, it expresses faith in human solidarity. Whereas the New York writers draw upon the exilic history of the Jew to depict social alienation, Klein celebrates the return of the Jew to the newly established Jewish State as the actualization of the prophetic vision of human brotherhood. In that sense, he interprets the unfolding present by contextualizing it with the past. On the eve of the Declaration of the State, Klein wrote in his editorial for the *Canadian Jewish Chronicle*:

> Who will gainsay, that there is in the New Jewish State the possibility for the creation of a way of life which will be the amalgam of the

best of the Orient and the best in the Occident—the efficiency of
Europe joined to the spirituality of Asia? Time was when there came
out of Zion a light whereby the whole world was illumined . . . what
was may be again.[10]

This global vision of redemption is not prompted by the desire to
escape Jewish particularism, neither does it generate from a naive,
uncritical subscription to Isaiah's eschatological vision. It is true
that the State, reborn soon after the cataclysm of the Holocaust,
must have signified to some a mystical or divine actualization of
biblical prophecy. Klein's notion of the centrality of Israel among
the nations, however, is rooted in the concreteness of his Zionist
humanistic creed. Global redemption seems possible thanks to the
return of the victimized people of Israel to its land and to the
restitution of its voice as a free nation. Klein's expectation of universal moral regeneration emerges from the unfolding actuality of
an unparalleled national revival.

Unparalleled, indeed, yet not unanticipated or unprepared for.
As Klein shows in the same editorial, the "miracle" of Jewish national revival issues from a continuous, centuries-long process of
revitalization of Judaism through constant Zionist reinterpretation
of its exilic history: Jewish Diasporic existence has always been
infused with the notion of return to Zion. Clearly, Klein establishes
the intellectual lineage of those whose longing and labor brought
the idea of Zionism to its fruition: he remembers "Rabbi Zadoc who
for the sake of Jerusalem fasted himself to a shadow," and recalls
Rabbi Yehuda Halevi who "blissfully perished on sacred soil"; he
commemorates "the untold *paytanim* on whose lips the hope of
Zion was never silent," he relates to "the Chovevei Zion, cherished
in their name and in their being," and he glorifies "the incomparable prince, Benyamin-Zev Herzl, who died fifty years too soon."[11]

Klein does not seem to differentiate between those Zionists who
for centuries projected the hope to return to Zion in their constant
re-reading of the old text and the political Zionists who actualized
the old text and implemented its promise. Thus he lists together the
rabbis, scholars, and *paytanim* (liturgical poets) who longed for
and dreamed about Zion and the Zionists, represented by Herzl,

whose objective was the *praxis* of Jewish sovereignty. He also mentions Chovevei Zion (Hibbat Zion), a pre-Herzl Zionist movement, which strove to converge and to implement the traditional and the political notions of Zionism.

Klein's reference to Chovevei Zion is particularly important in terms of his adherence to the ideology of cultural Zionism as propounded by Achad Ha-Am. Hibbat Zion was highly praised by Achad Ha-Am for its ideal of the Jewish State grounded in the renaissance of Jewish culture which will develop "through the expression of universal human values in the terms of its own distinctive spirit." [12] "Hibbat Zion," claimed Achad Ha-Am, "begins with national culture, because only *through* national culture and *for its sake* can a Jewish State be established in such a way as to correspond with the will and the needs of the Jewish people." According to Achad Ha-Am, the political ideal must be attained, but it must be anchored in the "living inner spiritual force of Judaism" which "unites us with the past and . . . [with] our historical foundation." The resumption of the position of "an ancient people which was once a beacon to the world" will not take place unless the spiritual unity of the Jewish people is restored. [13]

Klein's invocation of the long line of Zionists—ancient and modern, political and spiritual—demonstrates awareness of national cultural tradition in the spirit of Achad Ha-Am's reading of Jewish history. The new State unites not only the existing dispersions of the Jewish people, but brings into focus the past and its relevance to the State. In that sense, Klein adopts Achad Ha-Am's concept of national redemption through revival and maintenance of cultural continuity. Indeed, Klein was a lifelong follower of Achad Ha-Am's Zionist outlook. As early as 1928, he subscribed to Achad Ha-Am's thought, the vision which would guide him on his future intellectual and literary quests:

> It is to arouse the just recognition of the Jew to his own abilities, and to prompt him to use it *[sic]* for the creation of his own culture, that this Zionism exerts all its efforts. A culture not of one language (for in the Diaspora that is an impossibility), but of one thought, a literature not of one style, but of one spirit, a product singularly Jewish and yet remarkably cosmpolitan—that was the dream of Achad Ha'am, that was the goal of cultural Zionism. [14]

In view of Klein's subscription to the ideal of cultural Zionism, it is not difficult to understand his elation at the establishment of the State. Evidently, the reborn State in the wake of the Holocaust signified a climactic moment in the long years of Klein's Zionist endeavours, proving that *his* reading of history, as opposed to that of the assimilated American Jewish intellectuals, was correct. In fact, Klein never doubted the validity of his Zionist convictions. In a 1945 essay, poignantly entitled "Those Who Should Have Been Ours," the Canadian poet attributed the post-war sense of "troubled conscience" and "feeling of alienation" of the American intellectuals to their refusal to acknowledge "the atypicalness of their Jewish origin" and urged the American writers to reconsider their national-cultural position in light of recent history: "Will the plight of their race, recovering now from an ordeal which has cruelly lopped it to two-thirds its size, evoke in Jews, in artists whose trade is sensitivity, a feeling of oneness with the persecuted, tragedy shared with kith and kin? Will the inspiration of Palestine banish their sense of inferiority? Will the supercilious glaze fall from their eyes, as in the light of current history they survey again the treasures of their heritage?"[15] As for Klein himself, he had no difficulty grasping the far-reaching implications of the unfolding Jewish revival. A political entity at last, the Jewish people, according to the poet, has been redeemed from its a-historicity: the "ghost among the nations . . . has regained its voice,"[16] and with the establishment of the State, the cultural centre of Jewish life will effectively come into being.

The cultural significance of the State had become central to Klein's Zionist thought long before 1948. In 1932, for instance, he maintained that "the importance of Eretz-Israel lies in the spiritual influence it will have and already has on the Diaspora, as a cultural centre, as a vortex of Jewish life." The Jew in exile, he wrote poetically, will turn to Eretz-Israel as a heliotrope turns to the sun.[17] Israel, as Klein saw it, will provide the focus and frame, as well as the *raison d'être* and the inspiration for the continuation of Jewish cultural existence in the Diaspora.

Indeed, in his poetry, Klein very often amalgamated the cultural strata of Israel and the Diaspora in Jewish existence; he would turn, for instance, to the ancient land of the Bible for theme, while using linguistic and formal structures acquired in the exile. When the

Yiddish critic, Shmuel Niger, reproached him for being too Jewish for the Gentiles and too Gentile for the Jews, Klein reminded him that the Talmud is "a compilation in Aramaic," that Yiddish literature is "Slavic dressed up in Hebrew script," and that Yehuda Halevi wrote "Hebrew poetry in Arabic metres."[18] The viability of Jewish culture and, to an extent, its meaningfulness, submitted Klein, are predicated upon its openness and its adaptation to the cultural patterns of the host countries. In fact, Klein's 1941 ballad, "Yehuda Halevi, His Pilgrimage," represents an attempt to produce a universal work grounded in a Jewish theme, a text "singularly Jewish and yet remarkably cosmopolitan." The Jewish theme of longing for Jerusalem is presented in the guise of a Spenserian stanza and the chivalric plot of the imprisoned princess:

> Liveth the tale, nor ever shall it die!
> The princess in her tower grows not old.
> For that she heard his charmed minstrelsy,
> She is forever young. Her crown of gold,
> Bartered and customed, auctioned, hawked
> and sold,
> Is still for no head but her lovely head.
> ....
> Halevi sang her song, and she is comforted![19]

The motif of longing for Zion, set against a non-Jewish literary intertext, emerges in "Autobiographical" (1942), one of Klein's best-known poems which registers reminiscences of his childhood. The poet remembers how the paved streets of Montreal used to invoke fantasies of "pleasant Bible-land." This memory, however, plays a different role in the poet's mature age than the memory of the Romantic poet, such as Wordsworth, who seeks to spark his creative imagination through "recollection in tranquility"—the quiet reminiscence of a youthful experience of personal encounter with nature. The Jewish poet's creativity generates from the collective myth of his people which extends beyond time and space:

> .... in memory I seek
> The strength and vividness of nonage days,
> Not tranquil recollection of event.

It is a fabled city that I seek;
It stands in Space's vapours and Time's
haze . . .[20]

In a very early poem, "Greeting on This Day" (1929),[21] which celebrates the Jewish settlers in Palestine, Klein, though far away in "northern snows," declares his affinity, as both a Jew and a poet, with the holy city of Safed:

Your memory anoints my brain a shrine,
Your white roofs poetize my prose,
Your halidom is mine.

The recurring theme of national-historical origins in Klein's poetry underscores his ideological orientation of the cultural Zionist. The poet reiterates Achad Ha-Am's prescription that the consciousness of a common Jewish heritage, which ties the Diaspora to Eretz-Israel, is central to the concept of Jewish cultural renaissance. At the same time, as Klein demonstrates extensively in his poetry, Jewish culture need not be parochial; the Jewish intellectual should feel entitled to draw upon all sources of inspiration and, if possible, make a contribution to the cultural life of his host country. Nowhere, it seems, is Klein's deep sense of Jewish heritage more emphatically demonstrated than in the poet's comment regarding his "Quebec Poems," a volume of poetry thematically focused on the history, tradition, and life style of the Province of Québec which was later published under the title *The Rocking Chair* (1948) and won him the Governor-General's Medal. "For an interval," writes Klein, "I have abdicated from the Hebrew theme which is my prime mover to look upon the French Canadian in this province: we have many things in common: a minority position; ancient memories; and a desire for group survival. Moreover the French Canadian enjoys much—a continuing and distinctive culture, solidarity, *land*—which I would wish for my own people."[22]

It is Klein's proud self-acceptance as a Jew that enables him to identify with the "other." Unlike the universalist attitude of the New York Intellectuals which aimed to efface their Jewish identity, Klein's universalism emanates from a strong sense of Jewish self. Klein's relatedness to the "other," that is, his ability to discern the particularity and, at the same time, the similarity of his neighbor's situation derives from the consciousness of his own "otherness" rather than from the detached universalist stance which generalizes, and thus abstracts, the predicament of marginalized and oppressed minorities.

Despite his "ethnic" Jewish outlook, so different from the cosmopolitan world picture of the New York élite, Klein's dedication to Jewish heritage gained him a measure of recognition in American Jewish intellectual circles. Some American intellectuals of Zionist orientation admired Klein's undaunted cultural-ethnic *Weltanschauung* and applauded his poetic talent. The periodicals *Opinion* and the *Menorah Journal* frequently published Klein's poems, and the prominent men of letters Ludwig Lewisohn and Maurice Samuel became Klein's friends. In fact, Lewisohn, who praised Klein as "the first contributor of authentic Jewish poetry to the English language," implicitly, yet astutely, pointed out the distinction between Klein and his New York contemporaries. In his appreciation of Klein's poetry, Lewisohn claimed that true poetry cannot take root in self-denial: "We need not blindly accept our heritage; we may legitimately rebel against it. But he who frankly 'represses' it, denies it, flees from it cannot evidently be a poet."[23]

Lewisohn not only called attention to the avant-garde nature of Klein's work, which opens the vistas of Jewish poetry for the English reader; he placed Klein in the Jewish prophetic tradition of "legitimate rebels." In that sense, Lewisohn's view of Klein corroborates the notion of an intellectual as an innovator or an imaginative re-reader of his tradition. Indeed, Klein's own perception of the poet as a social reformer, often at odds with his own community, corroborates Lewisohn's complex view of the poet inherently steeped in his tradition, a tradition which is also the object of his rebellion. In an important essay, "The Bible's Archetypical Poet," written almost at the end of his poetic career, Klein outlines the dual relationship of proximity and distance that the poet establishes with his community. The poet is indelibly entrenched in his heritage: he "lives and labours within a tradition." However, as an intellectual, he is also the avant-garde thinker who, while remaining "rooted in the common soil . . . turns his eyes to new directions." The poet moves between "the ideas of convention and revolt, of tradition and innovation":[24] he is a revolutionary, yet not a destroyer. It is not the betrayal of the tradition but, rather, the desire to infuse the old with the new, that is, to posit the unconventional in order to revitalize the outlived premises that places the poet in conflict with his community.

Interestingly, Klein's understanding of the poet's role in society as both preserver of tradition and its cultural reformer illustrates Max Weber's view of the "culture mission" that the intellectual performs regarding his national group. Weber argues that intellectuals are individuals "who by virtue of their peculiarity have special access to certain achievements considered to be 'culture values,' and who therefore usurp the leadership of a 'culture community.' "[25] The intellectual thus emerges as both reformer and educator of his national group, a cultivator and a developer of its distinctive cultural features. The intellectual is also the individual, according to Weber, who, acting out of "intellectual integrity," confronts the "demands of the day." Those who procrastinate, waiting for the opportune moment to fulfill those demands, said Weber in 1918, should remember "[t]he [Jewish] people . . . who has enquired and tarried for more than two millennia, and we are shaken when we realize its fate."[26]

Klein, however, was not prepared to "tarry." Aligning himself with the Zionist ideology of Achad Ha-Am, he strove for Jewish unity through the rediscovery and revitalization of his nation's culture. His extensive translations from Hebrew and Yiddish poetry represent his efforts to create a cultural network for all Jewish people. In particular, Klein translated Bialik, the Hebrew national poet, who became his revered model of a Zionist poet *engagé*. His 1942 essay, poignantly entitled "Bialik Thou Shouldst Be Living at This Hour," establishes an intertextual connection with Wordsworth's "London, 1802,"[27] which opens with "Milton! thou should'st be living this hour" (220). Like Wordsworth who awaits Milton's voice to wake England from its spiritual apathy, Klein sees Bialik's poetry as a revolutionary force of national rebirth and invokes Bialik's "thundering voice" of the "Hebrew national renascence." The reference to Milton claims a share for Jewish poetry in Western tradition; at the same time, the inferred correspondence between Bialik and Milton proudly asserts Jewish cultural heritage. The

Jewish poet, says Klein drawing upon Bialik's example, is a fighting poet, a "part of the fighting forces, as much so, indeed, as is the trumpeter, marching into the fray."[28] Like the trumpeter, the poet does not abandon his people, but leads it toward new victories and achievements.

As a Zionist intellectual, who follows in the footsteps of Achad Ha-Am and Bialik, Klein's militant position of the poet *engagé* by no means implies the ideology of militant, expansionist nationalism. The Yishuv, as Klein saw it, was comparable to the Maccabees, who fought only when Jewish faith and freedom were at stake.[29] Pacifist at heart, Klein struggled for the recognition of Israel's equal status with other nations so that it may actualize its spiritual and cultural promise and thus contribute to the welfare of humanity at large.[30]

The Holocaust, however, deeply affected Klein's redemptive vision of the State as a symbol of global spiritual rebirth: the horror and the extent of Jewish destruction threatened the physical survival of the Jewish people. Unlike the New York Intellectuals who remained largely unresponsive to the increasingly precarious position of Jews in Europe, Klein followed the steadily worsening situation with growing premonition. Most of the New York Intellectuals misinterpreted the Nazi threat to both the Jewish people and the world at large.[31] In his examination of the New York Intellectuals' attitudes regarding the war, Alexander Bloom comments that "[t]he outbreak of war did not witness a significant increase in the discussion or the analysis of Jewish themes . . . the lack of discussion on the topic of Jews and their persecutions stands out starkly." Opposing the American participation in the war, the Jewish Intellectuals acknowledged the danger for "all culture, all real democracy, all social progress," but claimed that "[t]he American masses can best help [the German people] by fighting *at home* to keep their own liberties."[32]

Klein demonstrated a diametrically opposed attitude to the New York Intellectuals regarding the political developments in Europe. In an editorial occasioned by the victory of the Nazis in the 1932 elections to the German Reichstag, he observed starkly that "[t]he Jew stands condemned in Germany as the eternal alien; the deluded mobs who voted for the Brown Shirts now know where to find a scapegoat. . . . It is a scapegoat with a beard; it is a Jewish scapegoat."[33] Furthermore, in an editorial he wrote in response to *Kristallnacht*, Klein not only protested the atrocities committed against Jews, but claimed that it foreboded oppression for all people of conscience: "To-day it is the Jews who have been reduced to serfdom, decreed into helotry, made lower than the worm. But to-morrow? . . . To-morrow it will be Catholics, the Protestants, all Christians whose doctrine of love is anathema to the savages who have sprung up upon the seats of the mighty in Germany." At the same time, he admonished his community "happily situated in a free country on this side of the Atlantic" against indifference regarding the suffering of Jews in Europe. "[I]t is our duty," he postulated, "in this hour of sorrow, to manifest to the world at large, by organized meetings of Jew and Gentile and by responsible utterances, that our brethren in Germany are not utterly forsaken. . . . Let Canadian Jewry remember those who in this day and age, died *al kdushas hashem*."[34]

Indeed, Klein's poetry reveals the extent of his identification with his European brethren. In "Childe Harold's Pilgrimage," written in 1938, the Canadian poet dismisses the geographical distance that separates him from Europe and asserts his affinity with the persecuted Jew, trapped in Germany, barred from entrance into the free world:

> Always and ever,
> Whether in caftan robed, or in tuxedo
> > slicked,
> Whether of bearded chin, or of the jowls
> > shaved blue,
> Always and ever have I been the Jew
> Bewildered, and a man who has been tricked,
> Examining
> A passport of a polyglot decision—
> To Esperanto from the earliest rune— [35]

In the post-Holocaust poem, "Meditations upon Survival" (1946), the poet compulsively relives the death of the Holocaust victims; the guilt of survival evokes the impossible wish to have died with his brethren:

At times, sensing that the golgotha'd dead
run plasma through my veins, and that I must
                                                live
their unexpired six million circuits, giving
to each of their nightmares my body for a
                                bed—
inspirited, dispirited—
those times that I feel their death-wish
                        bubbling the
channels of my blood—
I grow bitter at my false felicity—
the spared one—and would almost add
                        my wish
for the centigrade furnace and the
                        cyanide
                            flood.[36]

Realizing the precariousness of Jewish physical survival in the
aftermath of the Holocaust tragedy, Klein intensified his Zionist
endeavours. The solution to the Jewish problem in the wake of the
Holocaust, maintained Klein, is certainly not the dissolution of the
Jewish people through the actualization of socialist ideology, as
Sartre would have it. In his review of Sartre's *Antisemite and Jew*,
Klein reiterates his position of Jewish authenticity through Jewish
self-assertion, that is, "an acceptance by the Jew of his lot and not
a flight from it, and a consequent self-development within the given
situation."[37] In his editorials, he continued to encourage Jews, in
both Palestine and the Diaspora, to adopt and implement the "principle of self-help" in building the future State; he also renews his
appeals to the free world to act decisively and swiftly with regard
to the official inclusion of the Jewish nation among the other members of the international community.[38]

However, the promotion of political Zionism as the safeguard of
the physical existence of the Jewish people never superseded the
significance that Klein attached to the nation's cultural survival.
Indeed, he stressed the importance of the development of Jewish
culture at this particular historical juncture. In his 1948 letter to
the American Jewish poet, Karl Shapiro, Klein said:

> Now the continuation of our own culture stands before the Jewish writer
> as *the challenge*. The hiatus of the Diaspora has been closed—closed

even for those who still remain therein. We do not write any longer *in vacuo;* we write in the aftermath of a great death, European Jewry's, and in the presence of great resurrection.[39]

The interdependence of Jewish physical survival and of Jewish cultural revival is of unprecedented significance in the wake of the conflating events of the Holocaust and the establishment of the State. Now the rediscovery of unifying links is all the more urgent in view of the destruction of the European tradition and the establishment of the natural center of Jewish culture. North American Jewry—the community of accidental survivors of the catastrophe—emerges as the only link which may ensure the continuity of Jewish cultural heritage. "[I]t is, it would seem," maintains the Canadian poet, "only the English-speaking Jewries who today, in our traumatic muteness, might perhaps supply our people utterance that is direct and authentic."[40]

Klein himself rises to the occasion magnificently in *The Second Scroll* (1951), his only fictional work and his final major piece of writing. The fiction is semi-autobiographical, based on Klein's own journey to Israel in 1949. The novel's protagonist is Melech Davidson, a former Talmudic scholar, a disenchanted communist and a Holocaust survivor—the proverbial Wandering Jew who pursues the Messianic mission of the Ingathering of Exiles in the newly established State of Israel. Significantly, Melech's odyssey is told by his Canadian nephew, who follows his uncle from Montreal to Europe, to North Africa, and finally to Israel. Thus the North American witness-outsider who did not experience the tragedy of the European Diaspora symbolically claims his share in the spiritual legacy of his people. Indeed, the connection is re-established by the survivor himself: in a letter to his Canadian nephew, Uncle Melech points out their common fate, claiming that "we were all in that burning world, even you who were separated from it by the Atlantic—that futile bucket."[41] The conclusion of the novel foregrounds reunification through the reaffirmation of the common history and ritual of the dispersed people. Israel's tragic past and its hopeful future are reconfirmed by the ritual of the *Kaddish* that the Canadian-born nephew recites at the grave of his European-born uncle in the reborn Jewish State.

Both the title and the structure of the novel reinforce the theme of national redemption through re-unification. Formally, the novel reiterates the first scroll of the Torah: its five chapters are named after the Five Books of Moses. As the analogy implies, to perceive the return to Zion as the reenactment of the story of Exodus is meaningful only in the context of Diaspora history. Just as Israel's coming into possession of the land of Canaan constituted a sequel to the Egyptian bondage, so the re-possession of the land in the post-Holocaust era is ineluctably tied to the history of Jewish exile. The reconfirmation of the covenant in the *second* scroll, as the title of the novel indicates, reaffirms the bond which both acknowledges and transcends the culturally and geographically diverse past of the people. In contrast with the New York Jewish Intellectuals who chose to identify the Jew as the symbol of the alienated, disaffected modern man, Klein identified the rebirth of the Jewish nation as a historical event of reaffirmation of life and humanism, the ramification of which may affect humanity at large.

Unfortunately, Klein did not see his ideal materialize. Instead of the anticipated convergence of the biblical and the Diaspora heritage in Israel, Klein witnessed the State's deliberate and determined estrangement from the heritage. In his 1949 editorial, entitled "The Dangers of Success," Klein vehemently repudiates the Zionist ideological notion of *shelilat ha-galut* (the negation of the Diaspora). He warns against the xenophobic attitude of the State which threatens to establish two categories of Jews: "the Israeli and the non-Israeli; and the non-Israeli is equated with non-Jew." Such an attitude, according to Klein, seeks "the nullification of Diaspora Jewry." The discord that it initiates not only harms the Diaspora Jewry by excluding it from *Klal Yisroel*; it deprives the Jewish State of two thousand years of Jewish heritage and tradition, a situation which threatens to reduce it to an insular and uncultured community of peasants. Klein asserts that the *"primum mobile"* of Jewish viability "is neither land nor language; it is people . . . the substance is *Amcho*—thy people." "What the time demands," admonishes Klein, "is not a negation of a Diaspora, but the affirmation of a total Jewry."[42]

It seems bitterly ironic that at the time of the fulfillment of the poet's most cherished hopes for his nation's sovereignty, he is impelled to embark on yet another campaign, this time against the State's ideological position which undermines his own Jewish identity. In fact, Klein's predicament is not new. Already in 1909, in an essay entitled "The Negation of the Diaspora," Achad Ha-Am argued against those who wished to eliminate the Diaspora altogether. Investigating the premises of contention between the Yiddishist autonomists, who claimed that Jewish national life can be fulfilled in the Diaspora, and the Zionists, who claimed that Jewish life can be fulfilled only in the Jewish State, Achad Ha-Am postulated that the Diaspora cannot disappear because it represents a principle which supersedes all other principles, namely that "[t]he Jews as a people feel that they have the will and the strength to survive whatever may happen, without any ifs or ands." And while "the dispersion must remain permanent," it will be strengthened by the State which will provide "a single permanent center, which can exert a 'pull' on all of [the dispersions], and so transform the scattered atoms into a single entity with a definite and self-subsistent character of its own."[43]

Interestingly, in his denunciation of Israel's policy vis-à-vis the Diaspora, Klein reiterates Achad Ha-Am's argument. As Klein observes in his editorial, Israel's position of *shelilat ha-golah* was an error as "grave" and "fatal" as that of the Bundists, "though reversed": while the Yiddishist autonomists dismissed the possibility of the State, the Zionist State dismissed the existence of the *galuth* [Diaspora]. To Klein's dismay, the national reunification of the Jewish people, as celebrated in *The Second Scroll*, has proven an illusion with Israel's rejection of the history of the Jewish Diaspora. It became clear that Achad Ha-Am's solution of the State as a consolidating cultural-national center was discarded by the Zionist political leadership. Let us recall Weber's perception of the intellectual as the transmitter of national cultural values, the bearer of the "culture mission" of his national group. By denying the Diaspora, the Jewish State has denied the Diaspora intellectuals their *raison d'être* by invalidating their cultural values, rendering their mission meaningless.

As if in a nightmare, the death of the fictional Melech Davidson, the Wandering Jew whose life has become the emblem of the history of Jewish Diaspora existence, assumed realistic dimensions. Indeed,

Klein's powerful last essay, "In Praise of the Diaspora," is both a eulogy and an elegy of the Diaspora. In this commemorative lamentation over the history of Jewish dispersions, the metaphorical Uncle Melech becomes Uncle Galuth, symbolically buried by "eight sabras" [Israeli-born Jews]. His burial procession consists of "a host of personages" which represents the endless variety and the enormous wealth of Jewish culture accumulated during the long years of *galuth*.[44] Yet, though buried, the cultural heritage of the Diaspora cannot disappear altogether. In the final lines of the eulogy, Klein addresses the descendants of Uncle Galuth and reconfirms his faith in the continuity of Israel's history:

> We shall remember him. In the hour of prosperity his memory shall be to us as a warning; and in the hour of adversity that same memory shall be strength impregnable. Our kinsman . . . is with us still. . . . His body we have lowered into the grave, but his spirit . . . now summoned to tasks easier than any of those he has already vanquished, now for constructiveness and not simply for survival 'bound in the bond of the living'—his spirit shall prevail![45]

Devoted to the ideal of Jewish sovereignty and cultural unity, Klein, the true *ohev Israel* (lover of Israel) to the very end, continues his "culture mission" of an intellectual as both reader and interpreter of the historical text. His vision of the Jewish State's future redesigns the function of the Diaspora. The two-thousand-year history of Jewish physical and cultural survival will henceforth become the frame of reference for the young and inexperienced Jewish State. Now the exilic past of the Jewish people will assume the constructive task of guiding the new State through triumphs and defeats. The consciousness of *netzach Israel* (the eternity of Israel) is the most precious legacy that the Diaspora can offer the State. The legacy of survival "without any ifs or ands," to recall Achad Ha-Am, constitutes a model of undaunted spirit of resilience, endurance, and persistence. It is a lesson that demonstrates to the fledgling State the art of prevailing under the most adverse circumstances.

To a remarkable extent, Klein's reading of the Jewish cultural future in the spirit of Achad Ha-Am's cultural Zionism has proven correct. In Israel, we have been witnessing the relatively recent need to reevaluate Israeli attitudes to the Diaspora, as it emerges in today's Hebrew literature. Israeli writers and playwrights, such as Shulamith Hareven, David Grossman, Aharon Megged, David Lerner, Yehoshua Sobol, and many others, have been examining, often quite critically, the implications of the ideology of *sheliat ha-golah* upon the Israeli *Weltanschauung*. The monumental Museum of the Diaspora in Tel Aviv attests to the survival of the Diaspora spirit in the Israeli consciousness. In Canada, as mentioned before, practically all of the younger generation of Jewish writers—Henry Kreisel, Irving Layton, Miriam Waddington, and many others—have acknowledged Klein as their teacher and spiritual father, a moralist and a guardian of Jewish culture and heritage. In the United States, the State of Israel has become a center of interest and concern to some of the staunch New York Intellectuals, such as Irving Howe and Norman Podhoretz,[46] and the problematic of the Jewish State has pervaded the fiction of leading American Jewish writers, such as Saul Bellow and Philip Roth.

Klein's unflinching faith in cultural Zionism thus enabled him to read history correctly and urged him not to "tarry" in his response to the "demands of the day." As an intellectual, Klein combined outstanding oratorical talents, erudition, and poetic inspiration with the emotional dedication of a true *ohev Israel*. Today, in retrospect, we appreciate the clarity and the accuracy of his vision, so deeply rooted in his intellectual integrity as a proud Jew.

Notes

1. Klein quoted in Miriam Waddington, *A. M. Klein* (Vancouver: Copp Publishing, 1970), 118.
2. Alexander Bloom, *Prodigal Sons: The New York Intellectuals and Their World* (New York: Oxford University Press, 1986), 24.
3. Irving Howe, "The New York Intellectuals: A Chronicle and a Critique," *Commentary* (October 1968): 42 (my emphasis).
4. A. M. Klein, "Those Who Should Have Been Ours," *Literary Essays and Reviews*, ed. Usher Caplan and M. W. Steinberg (Toronto: University of Toronto Press, 1987), 247.
5. A. M. Klein quoted in Waddington, *A. M. Klein*, 119–20.
6. Posthumously, Klein's work has been increasingly recognized. The proceedings of the 1975 A. M. Klein's Symposium, edited by Seymour

Mayne, were published by the University of Ottawa Press in the Re-appraisals: Canadian Writers series; in 1982 Usher Caplan published Klein's literary biography, *Like One That Dreamed;* in 1984 the *Journal of Canadian Studies* published an issue entitled *A. M. Klein's Montreal* (Vol. 19, No. 2); in 1982, 1983, and 1987 the University of Toronto Press published respectively Klein's *Editorials, Short Stories,* and *Essays and Reviews* edited by M. W. Steinberg and Usher Caplan; two volumes of Klein's poetry edited by Zailig Pollock have been recently (1990) published by the University of Toronto Press. Full-length studies of Klein are by Miriam Waddington, *A. M. Klein* (Vancouver, 1970), G. K. Fischer, *In Search of Jerusalem: Religion and Ethics in the Writings of A. M. Klein* (Montreal, 1975) and Rachel Feldhay Brenner, *A. M. Klein, The Father of Canadian Jewish Literature: Essays in the Poetics of Humanistic Politics* (Lewiston, 1990). Michael Greenstein discusses the significance of Klein's contribution to Canadian Jewish literature in *Third Solitudes: Tradition and Discontinuity in Jewish-Canadian Literature* (Kingston, 1989).

7. For a detailed discussion of writers who have paid tribute to Klein, see my *A. M. Klein, The Father of Canadian Jewish Literature.*
8. Trilling quoted in Bloom, *Prodigal Sons,* 22.
9. Alfred Kazin quoted in Bloom, *Prodigal Sons,* 136.
10. A. M. Klein, *Beyond Sambation: Selected Essays and Editorials 1928–1955,* ed. M. W. Steinberg and Usher Caplan (Toronto: University of Toronto Press, 1982), 320.
11. Ibid., 320.
12. Achad Ha-Am, "The Law of the Heart," *The Zionist Idea: A Historical Analysis and Reader,* ed. Arthur Hertzberg (New York: Atheneum, 1986), 255.
13. Achad Ha-Am, "The Jewish State and the Jewish Problem," *The Zionist Idea,* 268–69.
14. *Beyond Sambation,* 5.
15. *Literary Essays and Reviews,* 247, 250–51.
16. *Beyond Sambation,* 319–20.
17. Ibid., 25.
18. A. M. Klein quoted in Introduction, *Literary Essays and Reviews,* xiii.
19. A. M. Klein, *Complete Poems, Part 2: Original Poems, 1937–1955 and Poetry Translations,* ed. Zailig Pollock (Toronto: University of Toronto Press, 1990), 556.
20. Ibid., 566.
21. *Complete Poems, Part 1,* 142–43.
22. Klein quoted in Usher Caplan, *Like One That Dreamed: A Portrait of A. M. Klein* (Toronto: McGraw-Hill Ryerson, 1982), 149.
23. Lewisohn quoted in Caplan, *Like One That Dreamed,* 71.
24. *Literary Essays and Reviews,* 148.

25. Max Weber, *From Max Weber: Essays in Sociology*, ed. H. H. Gerth and C. Wright Mills (New York: Galaxy, 1958), 176.
26. Ibid., 156.
27. William Wordsworth, "London, 1802," *Norton Anthology of English Literature*, Fifth Edition (1986), 220.
28. *Literary Essays and Reviews*, 33.
29. See, for instance, "The Modern Maccabee," *Beyond Sambation*, 9–11.
30. See, for instance, "Zionism—Our National Will-to-Live," *Beyond Sambation*, 25–26.
31. See Bloom, *Prodigal Sons*, 125–33. For instance, *Partisan Review*, the New York Intellectuals' important magazine, assigned the American intellectuals, even after the war had begun, the task of demonstrating their integrity and to "signalize their opposition not only to war in the abstract but specifically to American entry into this war."
32. Bloom, *Prodigal Sons*, 139–40.
33. *Beyond Sambation*, 30.
34. Ibid., 36–37.
35. *Complete Poems, Part 2*, 475.
36. Ibid., 663.
37. *Literary Essays and Reviews*, 267. It is interesting to note the implied criticism of the New York Jewish Intellectuals in Klein's subsequent ironic comment: "The espousal of such a solution [assertion of Jewish authenticity], of course, would bring Sartre into the camp of Rabbi Mordecai Kaplan, and would make out of the *Partisan Review* but a supplement of the *Reconstructionist*."
38. See, for instance, the following editorials in *Beyond Sambation*: "The Patria" (31 August 1945), 247–48; "The United Palestine Appeal" (22 March 1946), 255–57; "The World's Conscience" (24 January 1947), 296–99.
39. A. M. Klein quoted in Caplan, *Like One That Dreamed*, 164.
40. *Literary Essays and Reviews*, 246.
41. A. M. Klein, *The Second Scroll* (Toronto: McClelland and Stewart, 1969), 30.
42. *Beyond Sambation*, 333–34.
43. *The Zionist Idea*, 271, 276.
44. *Beyond Sambation*, 468–69.
45. Ibid., 477.
46. See, for instance, Alan M. Wald, *The New York Intellectuals: The Rise and Decline of the Anti-Stalinist Left from the 1930s to the 1980s* (Chapel Hill and London: University of North Carolina Press, 1987), 329, 355.

PART THREE

Spiritual Leaders

CHAPTER 13

Mordecai M. Kaplan

Jack J. Cohen

In a life that spanned over a century (1881–1983), Mordecai M. Kaplan frequently anticipated the decades to come. His mind was always on the future, but he never lost sight of the fact that the future is hewn out of the past and present. Consequently, his thought paid careful attention to the demands of history and to the possibilities and dangers that inhere in the decisions of today.

Kaplan's perspective on time enabled him to avoid much of the surrender to intellectual faddism that characterizes less careful thinkers. He was, of course, no less a product of his time than anyone else, but his involvement in the affairs of his Jewish and general environments distanced him from trying to impose an abstract intellectual system on a reality with which it had little or no connection. The Kaplan of the thirties and forties acted out an approach that had been formulated during the experience of the first half-century of his life.

Kaplan was a major force in the Jewish community long before 1930, even though he often regarded himself as a failure. Most particularly, he berated himself for not yet having published a major volume on any of the issues that occupied his mind. In 1930, Kaplan was forty-nine years old, a late age for a person who aspired to produce a corpus of significant works.

Mordecai Kaplan was born in a small town in Latvia.[1] His father, Rabbi Israel Kaplan, was a strictly Orthodox Jew, whom Kaplan loved and respected for his probity and willingness to expose his son to heterodox views. Despite the elder Kaplan's adherence to traditional Jewish thought, he believed in openness to the world about him, trusting that Mordecai's loyalty to Rabbinic Judaism would be strengthened, rather than weakened, by such exposure. The story of Mordecai Kaplan's subsequent wrestling with tradition has been well documented and need not be repeated here. But it is pertinent to observe that Kaplan learned from his own experience that following the path of freedom does not necessarily lead to the results desired. Nonetheless, even if the future does not turn out as we might like it to be, we should continue to adhere to freedom rather than try to force our offspring into our own patterns of thought and behavior. Kaplan knew of no other way than that of intellectual persuasion to convince others of the correctness of his message. Almost always, he was sure that his views were sound, so that when they were rejected by his audiences or his readers, he would occasionally attribute his failure to a weakness in his formulation or delivery or style, rather than to the quality of the ideas themselves. Nonetheless, his diaries demonstrate that Kaplan did not permit his vanity to interfere with his intellectual integrity and judgment. Those same diaries abound in constant re-thinking of his premises, analyses, and recommendations. Frequently, the self-criticism takes the form of self-flagellation for his outbursts of temper or his lack of adequate scholarship. At one point, he says about himself, "Mine is the hell of being a mediocrity and knowing it."[2]

From his mother, whom he depicted as something of a tyrant, Kaplan acquired stubbornness, single-mindedness, and determination, but he tempered these traits with the capacity to correct mistakes and to see when his assumptions or objectives were misguided. He was able to achieve this level of character, because he learned the lesson of his mother's life. She was an unhappy woman, and Kaplan attributed her unhappiness to her blind, unalterable piety. She was simply unable to adjust to a changing world or to conceive that her son had to be free to live his own life. Kaplan's mother was so determined that he should become the Chief Rabbi of England that she looked upon his departure from traditional Judaism as her own personal tragedy. Kaplan retained his mother's strength of will, but he directed it toward the attainment of truth rather than the domination of the will of others.

These observations on Kaplan's character can help us to understand how he was able emotionally to cope with the critical problems that faced the Jewish people during the two decades between 1930 and 1950. They do not, however, describe the unusual features of Kaplan's way of thinking that enabled him both to grasp the essence of the Jewish experience of those days and to contribute notably to the molding of the decades ahead. That two-fold ability was a result of broad reading and his insistence that experience is the key to wisdom. He made this point vividly when he wrote, "I am always fascinated by life rather than by books, even the finest. After all, I am by nature an activist, and theorizing is with me a means to an end and not an end in itself."[3]

Kaplan read assiduously in history, anthropology, sociology, psychology, philosophy, literature, comparative religion, and the arts. He followed the advances in the physical sciences. He never lost sight of the limits of his knowledge in each of these fields, but he was confident in concluding from what he knew that reason and experience held the keys to wisdom and prevented imagination from running wild. Tradition had to be adjusted to what had been discovered by the best minds among humankind. If tradition opposes the truths and values common to the world's accepted authorities, it had to give way. But Kaplan's predilection for modernity did not blind him to the need to give a fair hearing to the heritage of the past. He argued that life is far more than intellect alone, and he therefore never abandoned the exploration of the classic sources of Judaism for their untapped resources, even in the regions of mysticism in which he would tread with great trepidation. His love of Judaism and his dedication to effectuating the creative continuity of the Jewish people were founded both on his emotional ties to his forebears and on his belief in the ability of his fellow Jews to utilize the Jewish heritage for universally valid and worthwhile purposes.

These affirmations drew Kaplan to the cause of the Jewish people and its civilization rather than to the application of his talents to an academic career in anthropology, sociology, or education which was offered to him at various times. Kaplan was an intellectual who believed that the human mind must not be blocked in its journey through time by the restraints of group loyalty, but he set out to prove that the intellect could be every bit of a tool for universality when it is applied to the problems of a single society as it is held to be when it embraces the human condition as a whole. Let us remember that this assertion was far from evident in some leading intellectual circles, including Jewish ones, in the thirties. The assumption was widespread, for example, that the problem of anti-Semitism would be resolved when the plight of those who suffered from colonialism and economic oppression was alleviated. According to this cosmopolitanism, Jews sustained their culture, because they had no other outlet. However, as soon as they were free to choose their means to salvation, they would join the human mainstream. According to this view, the Jewish people would simply disappear. This was the conception of the communists and their many fellow travelers and of some leading anthropologists.

Kaplan perceived that the cosmopolitanism of the thirties was a spurious one. The universal salvation, preached by both fascists and communists, was actually a form of nationalistic imperialism. In retrospect, this phenomenon should have been apparent to every intelligent observer; but Kaplan himself flirted with communism for a few years, until he understood fully that its universalism was an illusion. Intellectually and morally, fascism presented no problem for Jewish intellectuals inasmuch as its avowal of rule by brute force was sufficient to drive it outside the pale of respectability. Communism, however, was a different story. Marxism, after all, rested on a universal ethic of social responsibility—"from each according to his ability, to each according to his need"—which could easily be accommodated to the ethical foundations of Judaism. It was this feature of communism which appealed to Kaplan for a while. That principle, however, was too circumscribed for his taste, and he soon turned his back on Marxist and communist doctrine. His opposition may be summed up in a remark he made during a discussion he had in 1936 with students of the School for Jewish Social Work. Kaplan maintained that, "official Communism or Marxism, in demanding the acceptance of the Marxist outlook, precluded its being accepted by those of us who believe that the spiritual aspect of life, though determined in its form and content by the economic factor, can and does achieve an independence which enables it to determine the development and utilization of the economic factor."[4] Subsequently, Kaplan developed a much broader theory of the causes of social conflict and change, but it is apparent from his reasoning about communism and fascism that the nationalism of the Jewish people, in his view, would have to accord with a moral and spiritual system immune to any misuse of power.

The interplay of cosmopolitanism and nationalism occupied Kaplan's mind when he thought about the Jewish people. On the one hand, he believed that the Jews had always been and would continue to be universalist in their national aspirations and could therefore be depended upon to treat their nationalism as a responsible and creative spiritual force. At the same time, the Jewish people was in a shambles. Kaplan was fully aware of the dangers to Jewish survival that lurked in the free world. Deculturation, intermarriage, and the lack of visibility of Jewish community and culture all led to assimilation. Furthermore, Jewish survivalists seemed to have no inkling as to what had to be done in order to plan for the future. By 1930, Kaplan had already completed the blueprint of his theory of Jewish civilization, which he called Reconstructionism.

In defining Judaism as an evolving religious civilization, Kaplan based his thought on several assumptions, from which he never departed:

1. Judaism is not an entity unto itself; it is the product of the living Jewish people.
2. Since the Jewish people inevitably has to change as it adjusts itself to the vicissitudes of life, so must its culture undergo evolution from one form of expression to another.
3. A civilization contains every variety of spiritual, ethical, social, economic, political, linguistic, and aesthetic creation that the genius of its adherents can conceive.
4. The genius of the Jewish people has been most clearly evident in its understanding of and creativity in the field of religion. Any plan for the future of Judaism has to take into account all the elements of the Jewish heritage, with special emphasis on religion.

At the foundation, then, of Jewish civilization, there must be a clear conception of Jewish nationhood or peoplehood. Basic to Kaplan's position is the intuition that the Jewish people has to recast its self-identity in radical ways. In the first place, it has to accept the fact that it is a natural group. The doctrine of divine election had to be abandoned in favor of the adoption of a national vocation responsive to the ethical challenges of the moment.[5] This revolution in self-identity necessarily entailed a new theology and philosophy of nationhood, to which Kaplan had already addressed himself early in his career. He concluded that the Jews must see themselves as a transterritorial people whose center in Eretz Yisrael would be surrounded by a periphery of a viable Diaspora—that is to say, of all those Jewish communities free to work out their own destinies.

Kaplan came to grips with the full impact of freedom on Jewish polity. If Eretz Yisrael is to occupy the central role in Jewish creative survival, it has to be so chosen by the Jews as indispensable to the creation and retention of a high national culture. Kaplan was alert to the fact that countless Jews would need Eretz Yisrael as a refuge and that the bulk of its potential settlers would come as refugees. But such a rationale could not suffice to satisfy the spiritual purposes for which a nation requires a land; nor could it serve as a basis for building the land as a living space for the Arabs and others who already dwelt on the soil. So Kaplan wrestled with all these questions.

While the return to Eretz Yisrael in traditional Judaism always laid a heavy burden of responsibility on the Jews to behave in such a way as to merit the restoration of the Land to them, it was God who would effectuate it. Under freedom and voluntarism, however, it was the people alone who would decide. Therefore, reasoned Kaplan, it would be unrealistic to expect that the Ingathering of the Exiles could ever be actualized in its entirety. As long as Jews can find freedom in the Diaspora, a large percentage of them will remain there. Furthermore, no country in the world, and especially a small one, can be expected to provide for the needs of persons of all sorts of skills, temperaments, family responsibilities, and aspirations. Mankind is in movement. State borders are increasingly being crossed. National exclusivism, buttressed by laws to keep strangers out and natives in, are becoming an anachronism. The Jewish nation is destined to be in the vanguard of this process and should define itself henceforth as a spiritual people, centered in Eretz Yisrael.[6] Its Diaspora communities, tied to the core in Eretz Yisrael by bonds of religion, culture, and ethical aspiration, would each have to create a distinctive but nonetheless Jewish culture befitting the unique circumstances of its environment.[7]

Kaplan argued that American Jewry and Jewries in other open societies in the Diaspora should organize themselves into one form or another of voluntary organic communities. He posited that without such a structure, it would be impossible to cope with the centrifugal forces set in motion by freedom. The Jewish people in dispersion needed a new polity which could simultaneously guarantee freedom of expression for all who wished to identify themselves as Jews and provide a visible framework for that identity. Although Kaplan insisted that these organic communities would operate according to the rules of democratic polity, he was opposed by those organizations and movements that feared to lose some of their autonomy and power. Others, principally the American Jewish Committee, deplored any move that might cause Jews to be viewed as a separatist group within the larger body politic of the state. Although Kaplan's view has never been adopted in its entirety, it remains as a challenge to this day. At least in the United States, whose future most engaged Kaplan's interest, there is considerable communal organization—the Federation of Jewish Welfare Funds, the National Community Relations Advisory Council, the United Jewish Appeal, the various unions of synagogues, to say nothing of the many local efforts at coordination. However, all these structures have avoided dealing with the purposes of Jewish creative continuity. Until they do, there will be little or no ability on the part of American Jewry to combat the powerful forces of assimilation that are decimating its ranks.

Kaplan is often portrayed as a naive optimist about Jewish survival in the United States, but this is most certainly a misreading of both the mood and content of his analysis of American Jewry and his hopes for its future.[8] He feared that all that would remain of Judaism in America would be a sterile Orthodoxy. He respected the survival power of Orthodoxy but deemed it hardly worthwhile to survive on that level of vitality. It is now clear that Kaplan erred in his evaluation of the ability of at least some segments of Orthodoxy to adapt to a modern, pluralistic society, but he was correct to be concerned about the kind of Judaism that could emerge out of the tottering structure of the Jewish community of this era.

Kaplan's vision of Jewish peoplehood was Zionist to the core. The rebuilding of Jewish life in Eretz Yisrael was a *sine qua non* of creative Jewish survival. Nonetheless, Kaplan's conception of Zionism was always critical of crucial elements in the theory and practice of the Zionist movement and of the way in which it operated in Eretz Yisrael. He sought to devise a strategy for survival in the Diaspora, despite his fear that the venture might be in vain. Moreover, he looked upon Jewish life outside of Eretz Yisrael as capable of bringing salvation to the individual Jew and of insuring the creative continuity of the Jewish people. He knew, of course, that Jews would now have to choose between two styles of life, that of a responsible, autonomous majority and that of a free minority. Since that choice would and should be made by each Jew in accordance with his temperament and life circumstances, Kaplan posited that the Jewish people would have to engage for the foreseeable future in a two-fold process of establishing a humane and culturally creative society in the Jewish homeland and a free, minority existence wherever possible in the lands of dispersion. Therefore, he opposed those who negated the possibility or desirability of a Diaspora Judaism and those who believed that there could be a Jewish future under freedom without a creative Jewry in Eretz Yisrael.[9]

Kaplan aligned himself with Aʿhad Ha-Am, A. D. Gordon, and others who empathized with the national feelings of the Arabs. Periodically, he criticized the Zionist leaders for their shortsightedness in not involving the Arabs in the building of a shared economy and in ignoring their national feelings and needs. Unfortunately, Kaplan expressed his criticisms only sporadically and lightly in his published writings. Here is a typical passage:

> The White Paper of 1939 is the penalty Jews are paying for having mishandled the problem of their relations with the Arabs—Jews should have realized that they have to live with the Arabs, and should not have attempted to build a Jewish economy by discourag-

ing employment of Arabs. They should have tried to develop a single high-level economy in which exploitation of both Arab and Jewish labor would have been precluded.[10]

For the most part, however, he concentrated is his public essays on supporting the historical claim of the Jewish people to its home-land. This, he felt, was what the hour demanded of Jewish leaders.

Privately, in his diaries, Kaplan was most frank. He notes that as a result of the failure of the Arabs to develop the land, Jews tended to despise them.[11] In 1929, he comments, "Instead of deploying some of the abler and more fiery spirits among the Arabs by giving them positions in some of the financial and industrial undertakings, the Zionist Administration fostered a spirit of Jewish chauvinism and a Western air of superiority which is bound to antagonize the na-tives."[12] In this same reflection, which was aroused by a conversa-tion he had had with Joseph M. Levy, the noted correspondent of the *New York Times,* he went on to observe that the mentality which served the Zionists in their dealings with Diaspora Jewry and foreign governments could not be serviceable in relating to the Arabs. Kaplan's empathy for the Arabs was deep. In a diary entry of 1929, he wrote that the Zionist movement had made a serious mis-take in not first negotiating with the Arabs before turning to the European nations to support the Zionist endeavor.[13] In subsequent years, Kaplan added further reservations about Jewish behavior toward the Arabs, but he never developed a clear and practical plan of action for the integration of the two peoples in a setting of Jewish sovereignty.

The disparity between Kaplan's departures from popular Zionist rhetoric, as expressed throughout the diaries, and his published declarations can be partly explained by his reluctance to take a public position, except in general terms, on a matter in which he was only peripherally involved. Moreover, he hesitated to add to the difficulties of the Jewish people at a time when its very exis-tence and the possibility of implementing the drive for autonomy were threatened. Nonetheless, the stand taken in the diaries was fully consonant with Kaplan's vision for reconstructing the Jewish people and its tradition. Concerning the latter, he was far less reticent about voicing his ideology. He insisted that any Jewish

society or state that would be established in Eretz Yisrael must be
in accord with the ethical standards of enlightened democracy.
During the two years that he taught at the Hebrew University
(1937–39), he saw the threat that halakhic extremists posed for
the yishuv; and he was equally concerned by the extreme secular
abandonment of all connection with the rich tradition of classical
Judaism. He asserted strongly that a religionless Judaism, whether
in Eretz Yisrael or in the Diaspora, was a distortion of Judaism and
would eventually deprive Jews of their morale and of their reason
for perpetuating the Jewish people.

Kaplan did not rest at this point. Indeed, from his earliest days in
the rabbinate, he attempted to evolve a general philosophy of religion and a new orientation to Jewish religion that would meet the
requirements—intellectual, spiritual, and moral—of that philosophy. His basic premise was what he called his Copernican revolution—turning religion on its head and using as the point of departure not revelation of God's will for man but rather man's search for
salvation or self-fulfilment. In the course of this search, he affirmed,
man will experience the reality of God by virtue of his (man's)
discovering resources in himself and beyond himself that will enable him to satisfy his needs, at least to a reasonable extent.

A full exposition of Kaplan's theology and religious ideology
would take notice both of the complex of issues with which Kaplan
knew he had to come to grips, and their solution, which he sought
but did not find. He envisioned a group of thinkers from various
disciplines who would pool their intellectual skills toward the development of what he termed the science of soterics, the purpose of
which would be the search for a unifying principle or principles
regarding the dimensions of human salvation. He never abandoned
this effort to gather an effective group, whether in the Rabbinical
Assembly, the Reconstructionist movement, or in Israel after his
aliyah late in life. He even attempted, together with the liberal
Protestant theologian, Henry N. Wieman, to establish an interreli-
gious association of thinkers who were prepared to respond to the
challenges of secularization and the advance of scientific method.
For some reason which I have not yet discovered, the plan did not
materialize, but the idea is indicative of Kaplan's conviction that

Judaism could only benefit from close cooperation with other religions in the search for truth and for the furtherance of human salvation on earth.[14]

Having determined that religion should be located in those elements in the life of every people that derive from the drive to satisfy the human need for self-fulfillment, Kaplan concluded that a rational philosophy of religion ought to begin with an attempt to locate those basic requirements of the human person. Here would be the meeting point of science, philosophy, and theology. Both philosophy and theology would have to remain attached to experience and the scientific method, if religion is to keep pace with the expanding horizons of the human intellect. This premise in no way put Kaplan into the camp of scientism and radical empiricism. He was careful to acknowledge the limitations of science, in the light both of frequent mistakes and of the enormous domain of the unknown, as well as of its inability to handle the dimensions of value and aesthetics. Man's imagination is capable of extending into the far reaches of the realm of transcendence. All Kaplan sought to do was to prevent the misuse of imagination by religionists who permitted it to ignore the authority of reason and warranted assertability.

Kaplan never ceased studying the nature of man. More accurately, he persisted in learning about the physical and psychic make-up of the human being, because he was convinced that in order to approximate the cosmic role that humans ought to play, a theologian must first acquire a well-grounded knowledge of the human body and mind. Kaplan never fell prey to the fallacy of any type of reductionism that might have led to equating the "is" and the "ought" or deriving the spiritual from the physical, but he insisted that all ethical judgments must avoid distorting what is natural to the functioning of body and mind. Thus, for example, many of the roles that women have been forced to play in society have derived from misconceptions on the part of males as to the nature of the physiology and psychology of the female sex. Nonetheless, science should not be so construed as to eliminate the reality of a realm of transcendence without which man cannot aspire to fulfillment. Kaplan returns to this theme many times, but I cite here one of his late statements, that illustrates his sense of balance: "Although man transcends mechanistic and scientific law, some would reduce life and mental events to pure mechanism and scientific formulae. Transcendence does not imply overstepping the limits of natural law. It merely implies taking into account a dimension within human nature which some scientists ignore. That is the dimension of value which differentiates human nature from subhuman nature."[15]

Theology, it is sometimes forgotten, deals not only with God but with the cosmos and man, as well. That is to say, any concept of God entails views about the physical universe and about man that befit, or should befit, the way in which the particular theologian perceives the Deity. Similarly, every concept of man or the universe requires a parallel idea of the other dimensions of reality that is consanguine with that vision. Inevitably, theology, like all other disciplines, has to undergo constant metamorphosis.

Kaplan has yet to be accorded his due as a major theologian. The reasons for this lack of recognition are several, but detailing them would take us far beyond the confines of this brief account.[16] It is pertinent, however, to declare that Kaplan realized how tenuous and conditional theological statements must be, how necessary it is to consider seriously both the rational and mystical approaches to reality and how aware one must be of the limits of and need for both systems of mind. He should be credited with being one of the few Jewish scholars of the twentieth century who tried to make sense in theological terms of the impact on Judaism of the discoveries of the physical sciences and the insights of the human sciences. Many theologians, it is true, recognized that a new world was aborning, but for the most part they argued either that Judaism had already anticipated it or that it need have no effect on the essentials of Jewish theory and practice. Kaplan underestimated the holding power of supernatural habits of thinking, but his challenges to these habits remain unanswered: How shall religious Jews respond to the scientific study of the classical Jewish texts, especially of the Bible? Do not the findings of that study undermine the foundations of halakhic Judaism? And if so, what must religious-minded people do about prayer, many of the mitzvot, the authority of the rabbinate, the status of women, and many other issues that are connected with the assumptions of supernatural revelation?

The unwarranted attacks on Kaplan and the equally unfortunate ignoring of his theology have characterized, as well, those who regard the whole theological enterprise as outmoded. For much of the thirties, for instance, little credence was given by Jewish intellectuals to religious thinkers of any stripe. Both the Marxists and their opponents were at one in their derogation of religion. In the forties came neo-Orthodoxy and existentialism and their assault on the power of reason. Kaplan's efforts to refine rational methods of solving spiritual problems were declared to be shallow and secular.

The semantics of all normative disciplines constitute a never-ending problem. Value words, in particular, possess so many overtones that communication between educated persons often founders on mutual misunderstanding of the intent in their use of identical terms. Kaplan was troubled by having to resort to language that had become associated in the popular mind with supernatural connotations. Therefore, he either had to invent a new vocabulary, or to elicit from the old vocabulary meanings that inhere in it in the light of today's universe of discourse. He chose the latter method, although he also had to have recourse to neologisms or the borrowing of terms from other disciplines in order to get his points across. I shall touch sketchily on just two terms—God and mysticism.

I have already referred to Kaplan's insistence on the importance of transcendence in his system. Nonetheless, his critics continue to assert that Kaplan's theology lacks any sense of the mystery of existence and of any reality beyond the mere immanent. The passage I quoted above concerning man's transcending nature illustrates Kaplan's problem. For him, the transcendent and the supernatural are not necessarily related. Traditionalists speak of God as supernatural, that is, as completely separate from the natural order and as capable at any time of overthrowing it. On the other hand, Kaplan sees the transcendent as a facet of the natural, in the sense of "the whole is greater than its parts." Transcendence is an essential category of the thinking process, Tomorrow transcends today, natural law transcends natural phenomena, the human person is always far more than he appears to be to himself or to others at any given moment. These and many other examples show how a word can be transposed from the key of the supernatural to that of the natural. It should not require too much imagination in order to apprehend why certain theologians should be dissatisfied with Kaplan's transposition and be unwilling to credit him with a theologically respectable application of the term "transcendence."

All the more is Kaplan criticized for his unorthodox usage of "God." In this respect, he suffered the same fate as John Dewey, who was taken to task for applying the term to man's ideal ends. A God, it was held, who resided only in human imagination is no God. Dewey, they argued, simply muddied the waters. Whatever be the validity of that criticism or of Dewey's subsequent rejoinder, Kaplan's terminological dispute with his critics is far more significant. As could be expected, he is still called an atheist in certain circles, the argument being that a God who lacks absolute power and freedom cannot be the true God. But the critics from all sides have paid no attention to the crucial distinction that Kaplan made between "God" and God. Of the latter man can know nothing with certainty. Indeed, all he can do is to attempt more or less educated guesses about God, based on his experience. And since that experience is always limited, so must man's knowledge about God ever be severely circumscribed. As for experiencing God, that too is an aspect of man's experience with what he identifies as the true, the good, and the beautiful. It is a matter of our attaching these designations to what in the universe indicates that there is a force operating in it that helps us to become truly human. In other words, Kaplan has taken theology out of the realm of certainty and conferred upon it the dignity of all other efforts of man to define his place in the cosmos. That dignity stems from man's determination to posit purposes for himself and to achieve them in the face of an imperfect and an unfinished creation. For Kaplan, belief in God is the assertion that the search for salvation, within the realistic bounds set by man's mortality, is supported by the thrust of the cosmos for improving the quality of existence. There can be no proof for such a faith, but it is supported every time a good deed is done, every time the cause of a disease is discovered, and every time a work of art is created or appreciated.

Nor did Kaplan dodge the problem of evil that arises in every theological system and that became especially poignant for sensitive men and women during the decades under discussion. Kaplan's treatment of the existence of evil is summed up in his published works in a chapter on the subject, published in 1948.[17] He distinguishes between natural and moral evil, with the former constituting the real theological difficulty. How can a good, omnipotent God create or permit floods, disease, and other natural disasters that destroy innocent lives? Kaplan's response is unequivocal. "The question why evil exists is one to which the human mind should never expect to find an answer. It seems to be a necessary condition of life which we expect as part of existence. For, as human beings, we can never know why anything exists. But if the existence of evil is part of the mystery of the world that baffles human understanding, the existence of the good is no less a part of that mystery."[18] Thus Kaplan saw the Holocaust as a problem of the moral condition of the human race. The reasons for the inhuman behavior of the Nazis and the culpability of the nations that permitted them to take their toll were, in Kaplan's eyes, available to examination by scientists and other students of men's ways. On the other hand, the unprovoked suffering that most persons undergo at some point in their lives and the unfair distribution of pain, not caused by man's inhumanity to man, found Kaplan as agonized and perplexed as any other theologian. In the privacy of his diaries he went beyond the mere acceptance of evil as a fact of life. He did, in the last analysis, concern himself with the mystery to which he knew man could not supply an answer. But he was humble enough to keep these reflections to himself.

For instance, inasmuch as the existence of evil cannot be denied, Kaplan inquired as to its status in relation to good. In one of his reflections during the thirties he remarks that, "Good by no means presupposes evil, as evil does good. The absence of good is not necessarily evil. whereas the absence of evil is necessarily good, for existence is per se good."[19] Starting as he does with the normative Jewish view that the Creation is good, Kaplan is hard put, as is everyone else, to explain the presence of evil. All he can do is to accept the polar character of reality and search for ways to minimize what is harmful to man's salvation. One of his major steps in this regard is to eschew granting to evil the power of an independent force. It exists, because there is a basic tension in all of reality which God and man alike seek to overcome. In the course of that endeavor, the universe makes its slow progress of improvement. This is not a theology for those who want certainty, but it offers an honest and plausible evaluation of what can be asserted at this stage of civilization about the problem of natural evil.[20]

When it comes to the term "mysticism," Kaplan is again misread. He had enormous respect for what the Jewish mystics had tried to do. He wrote that "Jewish mysticism caught the true spirit of the kind of religion man needs. The keynote of its thinking is the truth that man shares with God the power to create."[21] No honest thinker can ignore the fact that while man has reached into the vast regions of space, he is still surrounded by an even more enormous unknown. Kaplan always sought to learn more about reality. He joined those free spirits who believed that much of the inexhaustible cosmic mystery can be appropriated for the fulfillment of human destiny. Nevertheless, he avowed that mere knowledge of nature and the pantheism that one is tempted to advance in its wake leave us cold. Man needs a feeling that there is a direction to existence that confers meaning on his striving for self-improvement. There is plenty of room in this image of reality for mystical assertions, depending, of course, on what is meant by "mystic." As Kaplan remarked:

> It is not at all necessary to resort to the befuddling terminology of mysticism in the effort to give expression to experiences which do not fall within the ordinary concepts of reason. And it is dangerous to disparage the function of reason in checking the wild extravagances of uncontrolled imagination. All that is necessary is to enlarge the scope of reason to limits beyond the traditional categories.[22]

Given such a position, it seems to me that an objective reading of Kaplan must conclude that he paid careful and favorable attention to the essential role of mystical thought in Judaism and in all well-rounded intellectual systems. He was, in fact, as vociferous in attacking the excesses of rationalism as in attacking those of mysticism.

Kaplan's naturalistic theology was applied by him to all other aspects of Jewish life. It is hard to determine in the dynamics of his system, whether he derived his theology from his anthropology or vice versa. But while that is a subject that might be of some interest to ontologists, psychologists, and others who are absorbed in the development of ideas, it is sufficient here to draw attention to Kaplan's effort to relate phenomena in some organic way. Thus, a God located in the transcendent realm of the natural order cannot be said to have "chosen" the Jewish people for a special cosmic assignment. Kaplan was virtually alone among Jewish thinkers of the twentieth century who deemed it necessary to eliminate the doctrine of divine election from the Jewish mind. The logic of his theology left no room for a supernatural chooser. Nor did his ethical vision permit arrogating to any people a monopoly on moral responsibility for the welfare of mankind. That obligation rested equally on all peoples, depending on the circumstances surrounding each of them at any one time. The Chosen People doctrine, Kaplan understood, is woven of many threads, each of which introduces into the fabric of Judaism a source of spiritual deficiency. Altogether, they cast the Jewish people into the comparative mood, whereby the worth of Judaism is determined by whether or not its uniqueness also bears the signs of superiority. The implications of this mood for Jewish education and for intergroup relations reach far beyond the Jewish people. Strains of the doctrine are to be found in almost every tradition and cause untold damage to the perceptions that each has of the other.

In place of election, Kaplan urged the Jews to accept the burden of their historical situation and, by endeavoring to respond to its challenge with ethical rectitude, contribute their share to the humanization of mankind. In other words, once election is removed from the theological framework, its message of responsibility for each person and each nation can be unambiguously held up for examination. It is this moral purpose of national life that informed Kaplan's philosophy of education. In this connection, too, Kaplan's intertwining of theory and practice stands out. His life work includes: sixty years of association with the Jewish Theological Seminary, during which he helped establish and lectured at the School for Jewish Social Work; two years spent teaching the philosophy of education at the Hebrew University; his lecturing throughout the length and breadth of the United States; his role in conceiving and establishing the University of Judaism in Los Angeles; his participation in endless seminars and educational committees; and his contribution to the scope of educational philosophy at Teachers College of Columbia University. Kaplan's entire professional career is an intellectual saga awaiting a master narrator.

Kaplan had many faults as a pedagogue. Yet he had few peers in transmitting to his students an awareness of his dedication to intellectual honesty. No teacher, he taught, may violate the freedom of mind of his students or lead them to believe that freedom justifies their holding any idea without being willing or able to expose it to the collective judgment of the best minds of their generation. Kaplan loved the Jewish heritage, but he also recognized its weaknesses. He appealed for profound study of classic texts, but that erudition must stimulate new and creative ideas and forms of expression, unknown to our ancestors.

Education was the key to the advance of all civilizations, and Kaplan was particularly eager to strengthen it by binding it ever more closely to the democratic way of life. Here again, we see his passion for organic thinking. Democracy's whole success depends upon the ability of the masses to bring to their decisions a fund of knowledge, a power of analysis and a wisdom born of tolerance of difference. He always wanted to know the educational implications of any of his ideas, and he was equally eager to understand why some of those ideas, in which he placed great stock, were not acceptable to his audiences or his students. Kaplan's life might be described as one of unending educational tension.

Since education is the key to salvation, progress in that direction is inevitably slow and uncertain. Human beings, Kaplan maintained in his tough-mindedness, must cultivate a morale based on a realistic acknowledgment of the mortal condition. In this respect, there is much similarity between his reading of reality and that of Bertrand Russell, who preached a gospel of human dignity and defiance in the face of a cosmos bent on destroying itself and all that reside in it.[23] Kaplan, instead, depicted a universe of inexhaustible creative power, striving to bring order out of chaos and capable of injecting into existence new and improved forms of matter and mind. In the morbid atmosphere of the thirties and forties, during the unspeakable period of nazism and the Cold War between East and West that ensued at its conclusion, Kaplan's voice spoke of man's need to strive toward perfection, even though the best he could hope to achieve was a limited alleviation of his pain and sorrow. In contrast to the spreading existentialism of the period, Kaplan urged his fellow human beings to take advantage of the enormous freedom that is available to them and to create a more beautiful world.

One of the repeated criticisms leveled at Kaplan is that he lacked a poetic sense and was devoid of the emotions that are associated with the aesthetic and spiritual dimensions of life. Nothing could be further from the truth. His published works and his activities in fashioning a modern curriculum for the Jewish school are distinguished, among other ways, by their emphasis on the need to heighten the artistic and emotional elements in Jewish life. Kaplan was largely responsible for the introduction of musical and artistic self-expression as a major objective in the education of Jewish children. Moreover, in his efforts to restore the creative spirit to public worship, one of his main aims was to infuse beauty and emotional power into what has become a moribund repetition of a formula that is largely irrelevant to the concerns of the worshipers.

A study of Mordecai Kaplan's intellectual career should be revealing to anyone interested in the dynamics of cultural history. In the first place, what drove a man with such obviously catholic and universal interests to devote almost a whole century of intellectual endeavor to the central question of creative Jewish survival? The answers to this question—for clearly there is no single explanation—would entail an examination of such issues as particularism and universalism and their bearing on chauvinism, the role of parental and other environmental factors in the framing of mind, and the impact of individual temperament on life decisions.

Secondly, it will be noticed that, in many instances, Kaplan concerned himself with matters that exercised the Jewish public only a generation or more later. This is manifest in his urging Jewish women to struggle for the equalization of their status,[24] in his efforts to democratize the institutions of the Jewish community and to bring them into organic coordination, in his constant call for a new covenant which would bind world Jewry into a single people around an agreed platform, in his appeal to the non-Orthodox religious denominations to join the World Zionist Organization and in his incessant efforts to induce rabbis, educators, and laymen to study the Bible and other Jewish classics in the light of the new intellectual reality. Some of his recommendations were adopted in the course of time, frequently without mention of his role in their promulgation. But others still remain to be considered. What, then, determines when the time is ripe for the implementation of an idea?

Cultural history is replete with accident. Kaplan's critics declare that his philosophy and his program are passé. But that judgment might very well tell us more about the lack of vision of this generation of thinkers than it does about what Kaplan actually said. Of one thing I am convinced. Mordecai Kaplan's writings cannot be dismissed or ignored in the cavalier fashion that has become common since his death. I accept the evaluation of a student of philosophy, Dr. George E. Vernon, who stated that

> Whatever his inadequacies, Kaplan's achievement finally looms larger than his detractors could imagine and that his partisans would dare suspect. Standing at a momentous crossroads in the history of thought, he glimpsed new paths that he himself could not recognize. The stature of the man and the scope of his vision may no longer brook denial. To accord him, a rightful place in the Judaic and Western traditions simply pays an homage long past due.[25]

Vernon referred to Kaplan, the theologian. His words, it seems to me, apply equally to Kaplan the sociologist, the educator, the moral activist, the Zionist, and the dreamer.

Notes

1. For a more detailed description of Kaplan's life, see the essay by Mel Scult, in Emanuel S. Goldsmith and Mel Scult (eds.), *Dynamic Judaism* (New York: Schocken/Reconstructionist Press, 1985), 3–13; Kaplan's autobiographical reflections, "The Way I Have Come," in Ira Eisenstein and Eugene Kohn (eds.), *Mordecai M. Kaplan: An Evaluation* (New York: Jewish Reconstructionist Foundation, 1952), 283–321; also Richard Libowitz, *Mordecai M. Kaplan and the Development of Reconstructionism* (New York and Toronto: Edwin Mellen Press, 1983).

2. Kaplan's *Diaries*, March 22, 1936. Kaplan was an inveterate diarist. More accurately, he kept a journal that was packed with reflections about himself, his family, and a panoply of the people he met from all walks of life. He recorded important events in Jewish history; he used the journal to work out his sermons, his disparate ideas, and those that were eventually published in ordered form. The journal contains hundreds of pages of his efforts to systematize the science of soterics mentioned later on in this essay. It contains many passages in Hebrew and quotations in a number of languages that Kaplan thought were especially striking. The entries began in 1913 and ceased, I believe, in 1979, when Kaplan was no longer able to concentrate. Most of the excerpts that I quote in this chapter are taken from the two decades of special interest for this book.

3. *Diaries*, December 19, 1947.

4. *Diaries*, February 13, 1936. For an excellent account of Kaplan's encounter with communism, see Rebecca T. Alpert, "The Quest for Economic Justice: Kaplan's Response to the Challenge of Communism, 1929–1940," in Emanuel S. Goldsmith, Mel Scult, and Robert M. Seltzer (eds.), *The American Judaism of Mordecai Kaplan* (New York: New York University Press, 1990), 385–400.

5. References to the Chosen People doctrine are scattered throughout Kaplan's works and need not be detailed here.

6. *Judaism as a Civilization* (New York: Schocken, 1967), chaps. 17–19. (The first edition of this magnum opus was published by Macmillan in 1934)

7. Kaplan readily acknowledged the influence that Aʿhad Ha-Am had upon his conception of Jewish polity. Nonetheless, he refined Aʿhad Ha-Am's conception of Eretz Yisrael as the spiritual center of the Jewish people in a crucial way. Whereas the great essayist left the impression that Jewish creativity in Eretz Yisrael would provide cultural enrichment for the Diaspora communities, Kaplan looked to the vitality of the yishuv as a catalyst that would galvanize those Jewries to create their own authentic forms of Judaism.

8. Kaplan stated clearly the problem that underlay all his endeavors: "To me . . . the burning question is, can Jews and Judaism survive in the Diaspora? All other questions seem to me to be of an academic nature" (*Diaries*, May 26, 1949). Nor did Kaplan have any illusions about the future of the Jews in Europe were Hitler to have his way. He wrote that, "the Jewish people is confronted with the menace of gradual extermination accompanied by mental and physical torture" (*Diaries*, August 12, 1936). The danger to Jewish survival came from the exposure of body and soul to forces that would require unified resistance. Kaplan was not naive.

9. Perhaps the most penetrating summation of Kaplan's perennial hopes

and doubts about the Jewish future in homeland and Diaspora is his quip, penned in Hebrew during his sojourn at the Hebrew University: "Regarding the contrast between Judaism in the golah and here, it can be said that from chaos it is possible to create a world, but from nothing it is impossible to create chaos" (*Diaries*, December 8, 1937).

10. *Future of the American Jew* (New York: Macmillan, 1948), 136.
11. *Diaries*, July 18, 1935.
12. Ibid., June 3, 1929.
13. Ibid., September 27, 1929.
14. Ibid., May 1, 1947.
15. *The Religion of Ethical Nationhood* (London: Collier-Macmillan, 1970), 89.
16. A blatant example of the inability of certain thinkers to read Kaplan carefully is the chapter which David Hartman devotes to him in his *Conflicting Visions* (New York: Schocken, 1990). I attribute this genre of criticism to the incapacity of many modernists to step into the post-modern era. They recognize the problems, but they hesitate to attempt solutions that would necessarily set aside hallowed traditions and habits of mind.
17. *Future of the American Jew*, 231–43.
18. Ibid., 235. In a significant entry in his *Diaries*, Kaplan suggests that salvation should be conceived as escape from evil, rather than the attainment of good. But he points out (July 12, 1940) that the determination by man of what is evil is often misplaced. I might add that Kaplan's suggestion is similar to the idea that Judaism teaches us to eschew and combat idolatry more than to make positive claims about God.
19. *Diaries*, December 24, 1939.
20. Ibid., July 10, 1940.
21. *The Meaning of God in Modern Jewish Religion*. (New York: Reconstructionist Press, 1962), 78. (First published in 1937.)
22. *Diaries*, July 24, 1940.
23. Bertrand Russell, "A Free Man's Worship," in *Why I Am Not a Christian* (New York: Simon and Schuster, 1957), 104–16.
24. "The Status of the Jewish Woman," in *The Reconstructionist*, February 21, 1936.
25. George E. Vernon, *Supernatural and Transnatural—An Encounter of Religious Perspectives: The Theological Problematic in the Modern Judaic Worldview of Mordecai M. Kaplan* (Ph.D. dissertation, Santa Barbara, University of California, 1979), 407–8.

CHAPTER 14

Milton Steinberg

Simon Noveck

Among the rabbis who preached in American synagogues and were active in Jewish organizational life during the 1930s and 1940s, none was more gifted intellectually than Milton Steinberg. His brilliant sermons were based not only on Bible and Midrash but on philosophical and literary sources. The lucidity of his thinking and his skill in putting his thoughts into systematic discourse, his historical novel *As a Driven Leaf*, which made such a profound impact on numerous readers, his series of popular books on Jewish survival, on contemporary Jewish problems, and on basic Judaism, his polemical articles on Zionism, Conservative Judaism, and on Reconstructionism, and his penetrating theological essays written with the same lucidity and persuasiveness which characterized all his writings—all these reflected a creative mind and a personality who not only influenced his generation, but also those who have read his books in the ensuing years. More than any other rabbi of his time (or of our time) his life and career dramatically illustrate the fact that intellectualism, standards of excellence, and literary style are not incompatible with success in the rabbinate.

Early Background and Influences

How did it happen that such a gifted young man, whose family background and early upbringing were somewhat different from those of other American rabbis of the time, made such a career choice? In those years most rabbis came from religiously observant parents, often the sons of rabbis, cantors, or other religious functionaries and usually had years of training in a yeshiva before entering the Seminary. Young Steinberg had none of these advantages.[1] His father had studied Talmud in his youth in Lithuania and knew his way in rabbinic literature, but he had lost his piety and given up his religious interest even before settling in Rochester, New York, where Milton was born. In search of new moorings and for people who would be receptive to his "free ideas," Samuel Steinberg began to gravitate toward the local branch of the *Arbeiter Ring* (Workman's Circle) and to attend forums at the Labor Lyceum, a few blocks from his home where he heard Morris Hilquit and other socialist speakers talk about the new society they wanted to build in America. In the "Progressive Library" nearby, Samuel began to read articles by Eugene Debs, Abraham Cahan, and Victor Berger of the Socialist movement and he often took his precocious son along. In later years Milton would refer to these early influences, to the love of ideas, the passion for justice, and for intellectual debate that he gained from his father and from the socialist lecturers.

Young Steinberg learned to read before he entered public school and at an early age was already a frequent visitor at the little neighborhood library on Joseph Avenue near his grandparents' home.[2] The librarian was amazed to find this nine-year-old little boy reading Dostoyevsky's *The Brothers Karamazov* and other Russian novels. In junior high school young Steinberg excelled in his studies and at East High School he led his class in all subjects except physics and geometry. He was particularly fascinated by the study of Latin. Milton Steinberg, as his teachers and friends have testified, was a natural student to whom acquiring knowledge came easily and gracefully.

While his father was not religious, living as the family did with his mother's parents Milton also absorbed an emotional attachment to Judaism. His grandmother was a completely pious woman and Milton never forgot the Friday afternoons in her home when "one could almost feel the *Shabbos* coming in. As twilight fell, out came the spotless white table cloth, gleaming candlesticks and the silver *kiddush* cup; and the smell of my grandmother's Sabbath fish first roused appetites long before sundown."

His grandfather, a nervous, hot-tempered man, a peddler like Milton's father, was also an observant Jew with a profound reverence for Jewish tradition. One of Milton's earliest and dearest childhood memories was "carrying my grandfather's *tallis* and *mahzor* to the synagogue. I was very young, so young that I had to break into a run from time to time to keep up with him, but I can still recall across the years, the feel and appearance of his *mahzor*—its smooth, shiny, leather binding, mottled brown in color, the yellowing edge of its pages and their musty smell when they were opened after being untouched for a full year."

In spite of the early religious influences, however, it never occurred to any of his relatives or friends at the time that "Michele" Steinberg would become a rabbi. He received only a few years of formal Jewish education, just enough to prepare him for his bar mitzvah which took place in the Leopold Street Synagogue in November 1916. In view of his logical mind and his ability to express himself, his contemporaries were all convinced that this lean, gaunt adolescent with the probing brown eyes would study law. That he turned to rabbinical studies instead can be explained only by the move of the family in the winter of 1919 to New York City, where he acquired new friends and teachers and a philosophically oriented rabbi took a personal interest in him.

Choosing a Career: From Philosophy to Religion

Milton Steinberg was fifteen and a half when the family resettled on West 119th Street at the corner of Lenox Avenue in Jewish Harlem. In contrast to Rochester's thirteen thousand Jews, Harlem had a population of approximately one hundred thousand. It was a vibrant, intimate neighborhood, densely populated and bustling with Jewish activity. In the area from 100th Street to 125th Street and between Madison and Seventh Avenues, an enclave of Jewish institutions of all kinds had been established, including the uptown Talmud Torah, the Yeshiva of Harlem, Oheb Zedek, the Institutional Synagogue, the reform Temple Israel, and Anshe Chesed—a liberal Conservative congregation with organ, choir, mixed seating, and late Friday evening services—whose rabbi was Dr. Jacob Kohn.[3]

The Jewish atmosphere in Harlem was especially noticeable on Sabbath and holidays. While a few years later the trend of the more affluent Jews was to move to West End Avenue and Riverside Drive, in 1919 Jewish Harlem was at its peak, a staunchly middle-class community populated by the more successful Jews whose children would make their mark in American life.

Milton attended DeWitt Clinton High School where he displayed the same drive to excel as in Rochester. In January 1920, on his first report card, he received 105 in English, 100 in Physics, 95 in Economics and American History, and 97 in Latin. On the same block where Steinberg lived in an apartment house just across the way also lived Myron Eisenstein, the same age as himself, and his "kid brother" Ira. Their grandfather, J. D. Eisenstein, was a well-known Jewish scholar who had published a series of books and encyclopedic works in Hebrew on Jewish law and Jewish thought. Myron and Milton became friends and participated in many activities together—movies, walks, occasional rides on rented bicycles in Central Park, and from time to time shared their reactions to books they had read. However, when the Eisenstein brothers took Hebrew lessons with a private tutor three times a week, Milton did not participate. But together with Myron, he did join the Sohi Club at the Anshe Chesed Synagogue, the meaning of which its seventeen members were pledged to keep secret. Milton also agreed to take a course at the synagogue in biblical Hebrew, but he made it clear to Rabbi Schwefel, the teacher, that his interest was in the language for its own sake and not for religious reasons.[4]

Unlike the Eisenstein brothers, Milton rarely attended services at the synagogue. Even before entering college he had read Herbert Spencer's *First Principles*, in which the famous philosopher rejected traditional ideas of God and insisted that no one possessed sufficient knowledge about the universe to base religion on such a view. He had also read the three essays on religion by John Stuart Mill, who denied that the Intelligence probably responsible for the order of the universe was concerned with the good of human beings. These thinkers confirmed for him the negative attitude to religion he had gained from his father. On one or two occasions, however, he yielded to his friends' entreaties and went along with them to Anshe Chesed. Soon he discovered that he enjoyed "going to shul." The service always included a few English readings and seemed to be a happy blend of modernism with traditional Judaism. He was also fascinated by the thoughtful, philosophically oriented sermons of Rabbi Kohn, whose rational logical approach to Judaism appealed to him.[5]

Kohn was a friendly man of thirty-nine, who had come to the ministry through philosophy. On his graduation from high school in Newark, New Jersey, he had received a scholarship to New York University, where he studied theistic philosophy and avidly read books by Bowne, Royce, and James, all of whom helped to confirm him in his religious point of view. When Solomon Schechter arrived from England to head the reorganized Jewish Theological Seminary, Kohn decided to study for the rabbinate. After serving in a pulpit in Syracuse, he accepted the call to Ansche Chesed. The New York congregation was truly "Conservative" in that it introduced family pews, organ, and choir. The nucleus of the group consisted of German Jews of Alsatian background, many of whom were devoted to tradition. Among those who attended services regularly on Saturday mornings were Henrietta Szold, at that time in charge of Zionist educational work, Alice Seligsberg, a co-worker with Miss Szold on Zionist projects, and Jesse Sampter, American poet and Zionist writer. The congregation also attracted a smattering of rabbinical students who came to compare Kohn's style of preaching with that of Dr. Kaplan, their homiletics professor.

For a time, Milton found it difficult to accept many of Kohn's doctrines because of his earlier socialistic upbringing and agnostic views. But as he heard more of the Rabbi's sermons, he found himself reexamining what he had read and his youthful presuppositions. The fact that one cannot know much about the Reality called God, Kohn pointed out, was no reason to assume that one cannot know anything about that Reality. The Spencerian view, if applied to other objects of thought, would make all knowledge impossible.

When Kohn discovered how interested Milton was in his theological expositions, he invited him to his home and took him for long walks in the park, where he tried to stimulate his imagination

about the problem of God and other aspects of the philosophy of
theism. Kohn communicated to Milton his conviction, partly derived from Royce and Bowne, of the complete compatibility of
philosophy and religion. He showed Milton how medieval Jewish
thinkers like Saadia and Maimonides had employed philosophy to
clarify their faith. Kohn also tried to implant in him a taste for
what he called "metaphysical philosophy." He pointed to the indispensable role which faith must play not only in religion but also in
science and other areas of life. Scientists, he pointed out, do not
begin with facts, but rather with hypotheses about the orderliness
and rationality of nature and the intelligibility of the universe,
presuppositions which cannot be proved. All these themes would in
later years appear in Steinberg's writings as foundation stones of
his own world view. These philosophical discussions with Kohn
convinced Milton that the "first principles" from which he should
begin were not those of Spencer or Mill, but those of a God on
which all other religious affirmations are based. If a philosophical
approach to religion became the basis of Steinberg's orientation to
Judaism, and metaphysical speculation an indispensable passion
influencing even his pulpit addresses and sermons, this stemmed in
large part from Rabbi Kohn's influence. In a letter to Kohn many
years later, Milton reminded him of those "talks about Judaism and
the Jewish people, the universe and its problems," and what they
had meant to him.[6] They led him slowly, shyly, and almost secretly
to practice the traditional rituals of Judaism. He began to put on
tefillin [phylacteries] regularly, and with the new understanding of
religion he had acquired, came affection and love for the ancient
usages of Judaism.

In February 1921 Milton entered City College, a half-hour from
his home. He threw himself into his secular studies with his usual
energy and determination. He was undoubtedly thinking of his own
college days when later he urged a young undergraduate to study
"out of the joy and zest of exploration."

> For these are the years of intellectual adventuring in your life, of
> roaming far afield, of flight of the spirit, yes, and of the laying in of
> your basic mental capital. Travel far, boy, and among all sorts of and
> conditions of ideas. And acquire generously of those treasures of

which, as the ancient Rabbis put it, a man eats the yield in this world and the principal remaineth unto eternity.[7]

For Milton Steinberg, those were truly years of intellectual adventuring. During his first semester, he registered not only for the usual classes in English literature, algebra, and public speaking, but also for courses on Homer in Greek and on Cicero, Livy, and Horace in Latin. The following year he studied the history of philosophy, Plato in Greek, Roman lyric poetry, and Greek drama, as well as the standard courses in economics, American government, and medieval and modern history. We can only guess what attracted him to the Greek dramatists and philosophers and to the Roman poets, but undoubtedly he must have responded to their rational outlook and spirit as well as to their literary merit.

Milton would have done well in any college. But City College in the 1920s was particularly suited to his type of intellectualism. The school had acquired a first-rate faculty, attracted to it by its location, academic standing, and comparatively high salaries. Perhaps its best-known member was Morris Raphael Cohen, who after several years in the mathematics department had received an appointment to teach philosophy. Cohen had already become a veritable folk hero about whose mental prowess tales were recounted with loving exaggeration.

The nature of the student body, too, helped to create a milieu in which one with Milton's inclinations could feel at home. The typical City College student at that time has been described as an argumentative, sometimes brilliant, loquacious, and rather truculent young man who was partial to radical politics, disrespectful of authority, and often knew more on a given subject than his teachers. Careless in dress and gauche in worldly matters, he concentrated on classroom accomplishments with a fierce competitiveness. Even in this highly competitive milieu, Milton made his mark. By the end of his second year, he had earned A in at least fifty credits and won a medal for the highest average attained by any student for that year. He was also awarded a prize for excellence in Greek, a certificate of merit in logic and shared the prize in philosophy with Paul Weiss who later became an eminent philosopher and metaphysician.

While Milton majored in the classics, the courses that provided him with the greatest stimulation were those given by Morris Raphael Cohen. Cohen's unusual erudition, his Socratic method of teaching, the encyclopedic range of his knowledge, and his logical analysis of every issue made his classes exhilarating. For Milton these courses achieved special importance because of his hope that through philosophy he would find the grounding he needed for his new religious orientation. In Cohen's classes Milton learned to overcome his occasional tendency to what his teacher called "sloppy thinking," and to discipline himself always to be orderly and logical in his presentations. In later years the analytical, logical nature of Steinberg's sermons and addresses was to be a hallmark of his preaching and teaching. Part of his appeal would be not only a powerful intellect but the clear way in which he presented the material, breaking down his exposition of ideas with phrases like "In the first place . . . in the second place." This logical approach stemmed at least in part from the example set for him by Morris Cohen. "Much of what is straight and wholesome in my thinking," he wrote years later to Cohen's son Felix, "is due to the instruction in straightness and wholesomeness of thought which your father imparted."

Unlike many of his classmates, Milton did not mind that Professor Cohen often acted the devil's advocate and occasionally subjected students to his wit and ruthless logic. Once when one of Milton's friends angrily walked out of class in protest, Milton went after him and brought him back. Milton himself was so full of reverence for Cohen's keen mind that he was able to forgive unpleasant aspects of his personality.

> In those days, the person I admired most in all the world was a professor, a man of staggering erudition, vast profundity, dazzling brilliance. To know what he knew, to think thoughts as deep and creative as his, to be capable of his felicity of expression—this was my highest aspiration.
>
> It did not seem important to me then that he was cruel in debate, not only with his colleagues who were presumably his equals, but also with his students. What was it to me that it was his pleasure to demolish students with crushing remarks, or that he was not above

baiting some slow witted youngster into tearful confusion. He was learned, brilliant, and that was all that mattered.[8]

But when Cohen applied this approach to Judaism, going out of his way to shock the students, many of whom came from religious homes, Steinberg became annoyed. Like Nietzsche, Freud, and other contemporary critics, Cohen was without any underlying sympathy for religion and always stressed its "dark side," the wars and persecutions perpetrated in its name. He insisted that religion instilled mental attitudes antithetical to those gained from scientific training. Cohen could see no logical force in the theistic argument that "the entire universe must have a person as its cause, designer or director." For him, all forms of theism were anthropomorphic, and it was "blind arrogance," he said, to put one's confidence in such a personalistic explanation.[9]

Later, under the impact of the Nazi threat, Cohen was to modify his views. But in 1923 he seemed to Milton more critical of religion than was necessary. The "rationalists" in the class, like Sidney Hook and Ernest Nagel, welcomed these views, but most of the students violently disagreed. Steinberg alone had the courage to do so openly. The professor, he declared, was overstating the case by giving the "dark side of religion" without mentioning its many contributions. A rational approach, Milton argued, was desirable, but reason, valuable as it was, had its limits. Milton felt somehow that the very future of Judaism was at stake and resolved to meet the professor on his own intellectual ground. To his parents' dismay, he began to stay up later and later at night, preparing for Cohen's class. Paul Weiss recalled that he heard much talk around the college of the "many long battles the professor and Steinberg had in class, with Milton quoting the Bible and passages from Graetz's history" as well as arguments from Royce, who had become for him, as for so many other earnest but intellectually troubled people at the time, a kind of prophet.

Though he had the encouragement of his classmates, it was an unequal debate between the Socratic master and the inexperienced youth. Recognizing that he needed more knowledge in the philosophy of religion, Milton turned to Rabbi Kohn, who organized a study group to help him and his friends meet Cohen's criticisms. "They were to tell me all the destructive bombs which Cohen had dropped on the structure of their religious lives," Kohn later wrote, "and it would be my duty to analyze what the professor had said to see if there was not another side to the matter under discussion. It became an exercise of Kohn contra Cohen."[10]

As a result of these sessions, Steinberg emerged from his classes with Cohen with his theistic faith intact. In a way, Morris Cohen completed the work of Rabbi Jacob Kohn, by helping Milton to argue his way philosophically to a religious view.

During this period, Milton gave a good deal of thought to what career he would choose after graduation. In spite of his interest in philosophy, it did not appear to him to provide the complete vision of life to which he could dedicate himself. It has been suggested that Steinberg might have made philosophy his career were it not for the difficulty in obtaining university appointments experienced by Jews in the 1920s. To be sure, an academic career was not easy for a Jew to achieve at that time. However, there is no reason to believe that Milton Steinberg would not have attained the same success as his classmates Sidney Hook and Ernest Nagel. That he did not choose academic philosophy as a career was at least partly because he was not satisfied with teaching and research as a way of life. He preferred a profession which would lead to a more direct involvement with life. Jacob Kohn suggested that he consider entering the Jewish Theological Seminary where he would be able to further his interest both in Judaism and in philosophy. Milton was attracted by the idea and after a great deal of thought, in September 1923, at the beginning of his last semester at college and just before his twentieth birthday, he applied for admission to the Seminary. At the entrance examinations he had no difficulty with questions on the Bible and managed to write a Hebrew composition, though not without several grammatical errors. But when he was examined in Talmud by Professor Louis Ginzberg, the eminent talmudist, it became obvious that he was not very knowledgeable. Nevertheless, Steinberg's general background was so impressive that the admission committee accepted him with the proviso that he take extra private instruction in Talmud and Hebrew grammar.

A few months later, in February 1924, Milton Steinberg graduated from City College *summa cum laude*, an honor achieved by only four of the three hundred members of his class. Prior to graduation he received an appointment to teach Latin and Greek at Townsend Harris, the preparatory division of City College. Having a semester to wait before he could enter the Seminary, he accepted the assignment with alacrity. He enjoyed the experience and "remained ever after," as he put it, "an ardent Hellenist." Nevertheless, when the dean of City College offered him a position to teach Latin and Greek at the college itself, he turned it down. Milton had his heart set on his rabbinic studies and had no intention of changing his mind.

That summer, while waiting for Seminary classes to begin, he registered for two courses in philosophy at Columbia University. The first given by Professor William P. Montague, was a survey of the leading ideas of speculative thought from the Greeks to Bergson. The second, by Herbert Schneider, dealt with recent philosophical thought in the United States.

Rabbinical Student

Steinberg enjoyed most of his courses at the Seminary, particularly the one on modern Hebrew literature where he read for the first time the poignant stories of Mordecai Zev Feierberg, the poetry of Hayyim Nachman Bialik, and the essays of Aᶜhad Ha-Am. He was fascinated by the spiritual biographies of these men, the inner conflicts they had suffered in an attempt to reconcile Jewish loyalties with the world at large. His teachers sensed that he was not only a serious student who prepared carefully for each class, but was also "a thinker." They respected him, as did most of his fellow students, for his intellectual superiority and his ability to articulate his thoughts so beautifully. At the end of his first year he won a scholarship of three hundred dollars for attaining the highest average in the school on the final examinations.

However, while he found the Seminary a satisfactory experience scholastically, Milton was disappointed in his hope that his studies would help him to find answers to some of his lingering theological doubts. He was not the only one among the students with intellectual misgivings about some aspects of tradition and about their ability to adjust to their future spiritual role. A few years later, in a revealing letter to a young Seminary student who complained that he was not altogether happy at the institution, Steinberg confessed that during his own first year, he too had been "filled with ups and downs" and was "alternatively elated and depressed." Time and again he and his friends asked themselves if they were fitted for the rabbinate "and we were constantly haunted by the question as to our adjustment to it."[11]

In later years Steinberg averred that these doubts were nothing of which to be ashamed. Quite the contrary, he affirmed, "every man of soul in the Seminary must traverse this particular bit of wilderness. The only men I knew who didn't have this experience were rabbinical oxen. While mental disturbances are no guarantee of effectiveness in the rabbinate, I certainly think that the absence of them is a serious reflection in any student."[12]

That Milton did not leave the Seminary and register at law school was primarily because of Mordecai Kaplan, one of the most influential personalities on the faculty at the time. In contrast to Jacob Kohn's philosophical emphasis, Kaplan was influenced by the sociological approach to religion he had acquired at Columbia where he had studied under Franklin Giddings, one of the founders of the new Science of Society. He had also read the works of Charles Cooley and Emil Durkheim who helped him to understand the reality of social life and its impact on the individual.[13] Kaplan was also very much influenced by A'had Ha-Am, with his emphasis on group consciousness and the will to live of the Jewish people.

Kaplan was not in favor of abstract theology; what was important for him was the experience of the group. Judaism, in his view, did not contain a fixed set of doctrines incumbent on all Jews, since such doctrines were always changing and evolving. Religion was a manifestation of group life rather than a revelation of absolute and eternal truths. Thus, Kaplan insisted, Jews were more than a religious fellowship or Philosophical Society, as Reform Judaism thought. Jews must seek to create in the United States the elements of a real community, because were they to have nothing in common other than their religion, their life as a people would be in danger.[14] Thus, while he and Kohn were both progressive in their attitude to

Jewish law, their outlooks were based on different philosophic grounds.

Milton studied with Kaplan for two hours every Wednesday morning, for him the two most exciting hours of the week. He approved of the way Kaplan tried to jolt the students out of their lethargy. Though more deliberate in his thought processes than Morris Cohen, Kaplan seemed to Milton to be equally exciting as a teacher. To be sure he could roar with prophetic wrath when a student misused a Midrash or made what he considered a particularly stupid remark. But unlike the City College professor, Kaplan felt it his duty to reconstruct Judaism.

Steinberg, fresh from his debates with Morris Cohen and from his reading of Royce, regretted that Kaplan had little to say about the nature of God, the problem of evil, or of faith and its relation to reason. But he recognized the cogency of Kaplan's sociology and of his broad definition of Judaism. He gained from him an understanding of the serious crises confronting the modern Jew and the economic and intellectual challenges to be overcome. Kaplan helped him to realize the inadequacy of existing programs for Jewish survival. He also furnished Steinberg and the other students with a view of religious observance as folkway, and with a vision of a new type of communal structure. If later, as a rabbi, Steinberg saw Judaism in broad comprehensive terms as a complete civilization, if he had clear-cut views on all aspects of Jewish peoplehood—culture, Zionism, and the Jewish community—these were based for the most part on the integrated outlook given him by Mordecai Kaplan. Milton readily acknowledged his debt to this bold, stimulating teacher for furnishing him with a creative program for Jewish living, and a rationale which enabled him to continue his rabbinical studies.[15]

Midwest Pulpit

When Milton was about to graduate from the Seminary in June 1928, Dr. Kaplan invited him to become his assistant at the Society for the Advancement of Judaism in New York. Milton turned the offer down because, as he put it, he didn't want to become a shadow in the light of a great man. He preferred to start out on his own, even in a less prestigious congregation, and accepted a pulpit in Indianapolis, on the way to becoming a prosperous industrial center.

Everything seemed to go smoothly at the beginning of his Indianapolis career. "The Rosh Hashanah services in this outpost of Jewish civilization," he boasted in a letter to his friend Ira Eisenstein who was still at the Seminary, "were a triumphant success and the stock of Conservative Judaism has gone up 100%. For the first time in the history of Indianapolis, members of a Reform congregation visiting a second-day service failed to get the smug feeling of an experience in intellectual slumming. The future is particularly roseate at the immediate present."

From the first, Steinberg put his emphasis on his sermons. His initial two talks on Rosh Hashanah entitled "Reality of the Moral Law" and "The Kingdom of God," were a foretaste of the theological emphasis that was to characterize his preaching. When he launched the late Friday evening services early in October, he devoted the first few sermons to the philosophy of Conservative Judaism. "Jewish civilization," he pointed out, "is not static, and it is imperative to change and modify it according to the times." Orthodoxy was no longer relevant to modern Jewish life, and Reform Judaism had gone to extremes. The Conservative program, he insisted, was best suited for the people of Indianapolis and for modern American Jews everywhere.

In addition to theological themes, Steinberg took up a variety of other topics. On several Friday evenings he dramatized the lives of Jewish personalities like "Sabbatai Zevi, the last of the great false Messiahs." During the Christmas season he spoke on "Judaism and the Teaching of Jesus." In a sermon entitled "Whither America?" he reviewed *Middletown*, the then recently published sociological study by Robert and Helen Lynd about Muncie, Indiana.

Initially there was an enthusiastic response to these sermons. But after a few weeks, Steinberg discovered that there were difficulties in preaching regularly to the same congregation. For some of his congregants his sermons were too abstract and intellectual, and even his vocabulary was too difficult. Many were too fatigued from the day's work to be receptive to a thoughtful message. There were

also physical difficulties. The acoustics in some parts of the synagogue were not good, and the temperature not always conducive to
listening to a profound sermon.

Steinberg tried to be sympathetic. But soon he realized with
dismay that the congregants were unwilling to have their minds
taxed by discussions about God and morality; they wanted to hear
"interesting sermons" on recent novels or current events, rather
than serious religious discussion. Though disappointed by these reactions, he refused to cater to the taste of the congregation. The
purpose of the sermon, he explained, was not to entertain or amuse,
but to educate, stimulate, and clarify. He urged them to make the
intellectual effort to think through with him some of the problems
of Jewish life.[16]

Gradually however, the congregation became accustomed to his
intellectual approach. They recognized his great talents and grew
deeply fond of him. There was a sweetness about this young rabbi
and a dedication that they liked. While he was not much of a
fund-raiser or an administrator, his great ability as a speaker, the
intellectual stimulation he provided for the younger people in the
congregation, the enthusiasm and zeal which characterized everything he did, and the warm personal relationships he developed,
won for him almost universal admiration.

He, in turn, found the rabbinate a constant challenge and derived satisfaction especially from the study circles he organized
primarily for the young married couples. Little by little the doubts
he had entertained about the ministry were dispelled. In a letter to
the son of one of his congregants, who was a student at the Seminary and like Steinberg in his time had begun to develop doubts,
he wrote:

> Once you are in the rabbinate your problem will solve itself. You
> must learn that the Jewish people needs the best and finest type of
> conscientious leadership. You may suffer from a sense of defeat and
> frustration, you may find yourself unable to effect your ends, but you
> will never feel that what you are doing is not worthwhile. The Jewish
> cause may be doomed in this country, but even that gives no support
> for abandoning it. The fact that a cause is lost is no reflection on
> its goodness.
>   I feel so thoroughly the value of the rabbinate that I want to

repeat my old advice. Stick to your guns and learn all you can. Prepare yourself to the full and allow your intellectual hesitancies to resolve themselves in the course of time.[17]

Steinberg served as a rabbi in Indianapolis for five years when he received a call from Dr. Louis Finkelstein, registrar of the Seminary, inquiring whether he would be interested in becoming the rabbi of the Park Avenue Synagogue in New York. It was a small semi-Reform congregation with an impressive building on the Upper East Side whose dwindling membership had been searching for a dynamic young rabbi who would revitalize the congregation. Though it meant a one-third decrease in salary, Steinberg saw great potentialities in this new congregation and, anxious to be back in New York City in the heart of Jewish life, he welcomed this new opportunity. Once again a move to New York meant a turning point in his life.

Park Avenue Synagogue

Steinberg began his career at the Park Avenue Synagogue in September 1933 with some trepidation. The fall of 1933 was hardly the most auspicious time to begin building a run-down congregation into an effective religious institution. The country had not yet recovered from the Depression. The economic situation was still desperate. The congregation itself was beset by problems—lack of membership, financial difficulties, absence of any planned programs, no Hebrew school to speak of, and from Steinberg's point of view, the untraditional character of its service. But Steinberg was determined to take this inert and almost bankrupt congregation and make a go of it.

As we have seen, Steinberg was hardly Orthodox, but he was committed to traditional ritual practices. In his view they ministered to "man's thirst for beauty, pageantry and mystery in life" and were a way of preserving the Jewish people and its way of life.[18]

Early in his tenure he made it clear to the officers that he could not in good conscience officiate in a synagogue so much at variance with the Conservative movement in Judaism. They had agreed in advance to discontinue the collection of money on the Sabbath and to require all worshipers to cover their heads. After a great deal of discussion, wearing the *tallis* at Sabbath and holiday services also became the accepted practice. Later, as families of East European background joined the congregation, more Hebrew was gradually introduced. Steinberg was also unhappy about the non-Jews in the choir, since in his judgment they could not participate in the worship service in any genuine fashion. However, he did not insist on their being replaced immediately, preferring to wait until they resigned. Within two or three years the prayer book was replaced by a more traditional text, smoking on the synagogue premises was prohibited on the Sabbath, and in place of the miniature *Sukkah* [booth] on the pulpit, a real *Sukkah* was built at the rear of the synagogue.[19]

When Steinberg began his ministry at the Park Avenue Synagogue, it had only 120 dues-paying families, not enough to solve its financial problems or to carry out the programs he had in mind. But he was convinced that at least some of the unaffiliated Jews in Yorkville—physicians associated with Mount Sinai Hospital, attorneys, accountants, teachers, and wealthy businessmen—could be won over to Jewish life. Many, of course, were so involved in the activities of the city—the Broadway theater, concerts at Carnegie Hall, the Metropolitan Opera, the art galleries up and down Madison Avenue—that they felt no need for religion. But there were others, Steinberg was convinced, who with the rise of nazism in Europe and the emergence of anti-Semitism in the United States, might be more receptive to Jewish identification.

At a membership meeting early in January 1934, he outlined his plan for increasing the membership. It consisted in the formation of small, intimate study circles to meet in the homes of some of the more devoted congregants to which non-affiliated friends could be invited. Social groups were soon organized and night after night the new rabbi made his way up and down Park and Fifth Avenues and over to the West Side, leading discussions on current Jewish problems and aspects of Jewish history and religion.

Steinberg was very effective at these sessions. He was helped by his encyclopedic knowledge, his liking for people, and his collection of humorous stories. His enthusiasm was contagious and he enjoyed teaching. "More than the calf wants to suck," he would say, quoting the ancient rabbis, "the cow wishes to be sucked." Though originally many came to these study circles invited by a friend, the pleasantness of the experience often led to regular attendance.

Gradually all kinds of people began to affiliate with the synagogue. To the original German "mainline families" were now added many congregants of East European extraction. Many of these were to make names for themselves in the general and Jewish communities. After the membership had increased and the financial situation had improved, some of Steinberg's friends felt guilty that their "brilliant young rabbi" had been obliged to go hat in hand to various homes asking people to join. But Steinberg did not seem to mind. By 1938, after five years of his leadership, the congregation had expanded from the original group of 120 to 350 families. Each year thereafter saw new additions. The proportion of prominent citizens and professional persons was especially high. But besides presidents of movie companies and of department stores, Steinberg was pleased that the new members also included small shopkeepers, machinists, and mechanics. By 1942 the membership had reached the "saturation point" of 425 families and the financial situation completely stabilized itself. In 1949 when I arrived to serve as Steinberg's associate, the congregation numbered more than 750 families.

Philosophical Preacher

One of the main attractions that drew people to the Park Avenue Synagogue was Steinberg's eloquent and stimulating preaching. Unlike many of his colleagues, he spoke in a simple and direct manner without affectation. He did not rely on anecdotes, sensational themes, or gimmicks, but held his audience through the content and poetic quality of his sermons. They dealt with many different themes, one of the most frequent being the problems of Jewish survival. This type of sermon, usually given at the late Friday evening service, was based on Steinberg's conviction that Jews were more than a religious communion but constituted an ethnic or social grouping, a people with cultural interests, a sense of community and a dedication to Palestine as a national homeland. His sermons therefore dealt with such topics as "What's Wrong with Jewish Leadership?"; "What's Wrong with Jewish Education?"; "The

Future of Zionism in America"; "The Crisis in Zionist Leadership"; "The Partition of Palestine"; "The Issue of Dual Loyalties"; "Jewry and Its Lost Jewish Intellectuals."

From time to time he took up a historical theme or discussed a historical personality in an effort to give his congregants insight into the Jewish past. Examples are such topics as "The Prophet Elijah: Man, Legend and Symbol"; and "Maccabees and Puritans: Must Religious Zeal Always Become Religious Intolerance?" On successive weeks he summed up the life and contributions of Rashi, Moses Maimonides, and Moses Mendelssohn, after which he dealt with such themes as "A Jewish View of Jesus" and the question "Who Crucified Jesus?"

Occasionally he took a Jewish book as his point of departure. Among those he reviewed on a Friday night were *The Jews of Rome* by Leon Feuchtwanger, Franz Werfel's *Hearken Unto the Voice*, Ludwig Lewisohn's *Renegade*, Irving Fineman's *Hear Ye Sons*, Sholem Asch's *East River*, I. J. Singer's *The Brothers Ashkenazi*, Maurice Samuel's *World of Sholom Aleichem* and Mordecai Kaplan's *The Future of the American Jew*.

His eloquence and analytical powers were particularly manifest on the subject of faith and its uses. As he had done when he first came to Indianapolis, he devoted the first few Friday evenings at the Park Avenue Synagogue to the question of ideology, discussing such topics as "What Should Be Our Philosophy of Jewish Life?"; "Can We Be Orthodox? Shall We Be Reform?" His purpose in these talks was to win his listeners to a point of view. He made it clear that despite his traditionalism and his strong emotional sympathy with Orthodox Judaism, Orthodoxy was not his program. Nor did he find Reform an adequate or logically consistent philosophy. It reduced Judaism to a pallid kind of religiosity by stripping from the tradition the rich poetry of Jewish observance, allowing Hebrew to become a dead tongue, and in its classic version insisted that the Jew forget his dream of a homeland. As much as he respected colleagues and friends in the Reform rabbinate like Levi Olan, Philip S. Bernstein, Joshua Liebman, and Charles Shulman, he could not agree with some of the practices in their synagogues. In his opinion, a more traditional approach was necessary, and he felt his congregants were entitled at the very outset to know his basic religious convictions. Thus on one occasion he took as his theme "A Modern Confession of Faith: What Can a Man Believe?" His answer was very explicit.

> I believe in God because the universe as the manifestation of a creative mind is the only plausible basis for the order of the spheres. I believe in immortality because I cannot believe that consciousness is not more than the reaction of material brain cells. I believe that when the body dies, consciousness does not die with it; there is nothing in science than can positively contradict this.
>
> I believe that there is a real moral law as surely as there is a law of Nature. I believe in the Bible; not in its miracles or in its science, nor that it is literally inspired nor even that it is the final morality. But I do believe that the Bible is the great moral teacher of law, justice, mercy, the Kingdom of God.
>
> In addition, there are certain things I believe in as a Jew. I believe in the value of Judaism as a rich culture, as a way of life, as a contribution to the civilization of the world. I believe in Zionism and the future of the Jews in Palestine despite Arab riots. I believe we shall succeed in building in Palestine a rich new Jewish culture that will be an inspiration to us, a crowning glory to the Jewish past. . . .
> And first and last I believe in man and in the essential goodness of human nature, in spite of war and bestiality, injustice, poverty, corruption of ideals and hypocrisy. . . . I believe that man will mount up from the slopes of Hell to the ideal society that the prophets call the Kingdom of God.[20]

In the following months he elaborated on his outlook by discussing such themes as "Athens and Jerusalem: The Eternal Struggle of the Greek and Jewish Spirit"; "Can an Irreligious Man Be a Good Jew?"; "Does Morality Require Religion?"; "Is Religion Inborn or Can It Be Acquired?"; "What Value Has Prayer?"; "Floods, Earthquakes, and the Goodness of God." From time to time he gave a series of sermons on the same topic so he could develop, in three or four successive weeks, various aspects of such philosophic subjects as "The Utopian Dreams of Man," "The Search for Happiness," and "Science and Religion."

The philosophy behind this kind of preaching was a conviction that if the people understood the role and purpose of religion, they would develop a greater concern for it. What Steinberg wanted to get across was the view that religion is an indispensable element in life, that faith as well as intellect is necessary for the good life. He was a religious rationalist who appealed to human intelligence and common sense. In his interpretation, Judaism does not expect its followers to accept anything that is unreasonable, that runs counter to modern science and its laws. But intellect, he insisted, is not sufficient by itself to grasp the truth about the universe. Democritus, Socrates, Plato, and Aristotle had thought so, but then Greek reason ran into a stone wall, and unable to prove its own validity, gave way to the mysticism of Plotinus. The same process was being repeated in modern times. Descartes had been convinced that man could solve all his problems by the power of reason, but Locke, Hume, and Kant had demonstrated that men could not achieve ultimate truth, a fact that was confirmed by non-Euclidian geometry. Faith, too, is necessary to work out a *Weltanschauung*.

The pulpit, Steinberg believed, also had a responsibility to apply Jewish teachings to the American scene. He therefore rejected the view that a rabbi should avoid controversial issues.

> Those who protest against pulpit discussion of economic problems, seem to forget that Judaism teaches the divinity of man; that it has always insisted upon the social use of wealth and upon human cooperation as the ideal principle for the ordering of society. They seem to forget that Moses legislated against exploitation, that Amos, Isaiah and the rabbis of the Talmudic age were intensely concerned about the social problems of their day.[21]

Steinberg's concern with social problems, while not new, was intensified by his appointment to be chairman of the Rabbinical Assembly's Committee on Social Justice. In this capacity he issued a statement together with Rabbi Elias Margolis, the president of the assembly, protesting against lynchings in Maryland, California, and Missouri, and calling for legal protection for the victims. At its annual convention in June 1934 at Tannersville, New York, the assembly, under his direction, adopted for the first time a statement expressing its official attitude to social problems:

> We affirm that the discussion of problems of social and economic justice . . . is not only legitimate but even necessary subject matter for treatment from the pulpit by ministers of religion.

> Teachers of religion must, if they are to be true to their calling,
> give voice in unequivocal terms to those ethical values which are
> relevant to man's organized living.[22]

Several members of the synagogue board, conservative in their political and social outlook, objected to this use of the pulpit to express what were to them radical ideas. A number of manufacturers in the congregation were especially annoyed by his defense of trade unionism. But Jacob Friedman, president of Park Avenue Synagogue, understood that a rabbi must follow the dictates of his conscience, and at no time did he try to discourage Steinberg from stating his own convictions. At a testimonial dinner in Friedman's honor, Steinberg paid tribute to the synagogue president for his restraint in "withdrawing from any gesture which might in the least impede the free movement of my personality."

Ideologue of Conservative Judaism

As a graduate of the Jewish Theological Seminary, Steinberg was, of course, proud of his alma mater and always encouraged his congregants to support its program and activities. But with the passage of the years he began to find fault with the direction the Seminary was taking and developed misgivings about what he called its "theological evasiveness." By this he meant its failure to articulate where the Conservative movement stood on many religious issues. As he saw it, the Seminary was drifting toward a neo-Orthodoxy which he did not think was consonant with the purpose of the movement. In his opinion, the crystallization of an ideology was indispensable to avoid intellectual confusion, to clarify the relationship of Jewish to American loyalties, and to make the movement more efficient and purposeful. Also there were problems in his own rabbinate on which he needed guidance. Until Conservative Judaism formulated a point of view, this guidance, he insisted, would not be forthcoming.

Except for Mordecai Kaplan, the Seminary faculty rarely mentioned the term "Conservative Judaism," conceiving their task to be the development of a Judaism without qualifying adjectives. They

While most of his colleagues respected Steinberg both as a rabbi and as a thinker, they resented the attitude reflected in his letters. They too recognized the importance of making the prayer book relevant to the needs of the new generation, but they were also concerned that it maintain a continuity with the tradition. To be sure, the idea of the Chosen People had been vulgarized in many circles, but the remedy, they thought, did not lie in its elimination. The doctrine, they insisted, was historically sound and psychologically necessary—an indispensable factor for Jewish survival. Moreover, recent biblical scholarship indicated that the concept was associated in Jewish thought not with belief in an inherent personal or group superiority, but rather with the highest responsibilities which come to Jews as the custodians of the Jewish way of life. Also, to Steinberg's disappointment, the commission retained the traditional structure of the *Musaph* because of its stress on sacrifice as an ideal, and for the hope it expressed in the restoration of Palestine.[26]

Steinberg was deeply troubled by this illiberal spirit in which he felt the commission was working. He could not accept what he thought was a "fear of making the least modification of the traditional text, the readiness to engage in complicated argument all for the purpose of proving that the words which stand written are the only proper and acceptable words."

> That is what haunts me—this paralysis of our hands, hearts and imaginations, this readiness to sacrifice the truth as we see it out of the excess of the virtue of reverence for the past, this mood of "if our ancestors were angels, we are mortals; if they were mortals, we are asses."
>
> I, too, love the Jewish tradition—but not with such total subservience of spirit nor with such neglect of the needs of contemporary Judaism.[27]

In Steinberg's view, the prayer book contemplated by the commission would be, at best, a better standard prayer book, more gracious in style, with supplementary readings arranged so that congregations might more conveniently select appropriate passages for special occasions. However, it would still include "things which none of us believe and wanting from it things we all believe without any token of the fact that the world and Jewish life have changed so mightily in the past five hundred years."

> I say that we have made nonsense of half of what little ideology we possess, that we suffer from all of the powerlessness of our Orthodox brethren without either the sanctions or the comforts of an Orthodox theology; that we are throwing away our great chance which I am convinced is Judaism's last chance in America. For this I weep—for a Conservative Judaism once so rich in promise—a promise which, thanks to the caution and pusillanimity of its leaders, is being constantly frittered away.[28]

Early Theological Essays

In enumerating Milton Steinberg's activities, I have left for last his theological essays, for they represent, I believe, his most important contribution. In the early 1940s in the midst of the war, Steinberg decided to write a book on what he called a "reasonable faith." The mood of intellectual uncertainty resulting from the war, from recent scientific developments, and from sociological challenges of the time persuaded him of the need for a volume devoted to the theoretical beliefs of Judaism. Developments in philosophy, he felt, confirmed this need. Theism as a philosophic doctrine had been losing ground since the mid-seventeenth century and for many philosophers had become an unacceptable view. Christian thinkers were also coming to the conclusion that religious metaphysics was necessary to an understanding of Christianity. In the Jewish community, too, there were at least a few voices urging the need for theological reflection.

Because the time seemed ripe and because of his interest in the field and his hope of being invited to teach at the Seminary, writing such a book appealed to him. He planned to call it *An Anatomy of Faith* and hoped it would provide the same analysis for religious faith that his *Making of the Modern Jew* had done for Jewish survival. He had three types of readers in mind: religionists who were troubled in mind, ex-religionists who would like to make their way back, and anti-religionists who had developed misgivings about their position. His aim was to present for all three groups a rationale for the religious life, an acceptable theory as to the nature of religion and a demonstration that religion is possible without the least sacrifice of intellectual integrity.

However, after beginning the project he soon realized that he needed to do more reading than he had had time for up till now and a period of sustained reflective thinking. He recognized that what he had been able to do in the case of the *Making of the Modern Jew*, to write the book in three months during one summer, would be impossible with this book on theology. He therefore decided to publish a series of articles on theological themes and let the book emerge out of these more limited studies, chapter by chapter.

His first essay appeared in the *Reconstructionist* of March 7, 1941, and was basically a reply to an earlier article by Eugene Kohn on the "Attributes of God Reinterpreted."[29] Kohn had presented Dr. Kaplan's view that God was not a divine person, as in traditional Jewish thought, or an absolute Being, but rather a process at work in the universe. Kohn also agreed with Kaplan's repudiation of religious metaphysics, insisting that a concept of God is important not for what it says about the nature of the Deity, but for how it functions in the life of the Jewish people. In the Kaplanian view, the whole of existence is so constituted as to help the individual find "salvation," or self-fulfillment. "God is manifest in all creativity and in all forms of sovereignty which make for love and for the enhancement of human life."

Steinberg respected the motives behind this conviction of the futility of metaphysical speculation, and the desire to retrieve from the historical God idea its most meaningful elements. However, for him the riddle of the universe was not so readily dismissed. Faith was not only a psychological and ethical venture but also an affirmation concerning the ultimate nature of things.

It was convictions of this kind which were the basis of the disagreement with Kaplan and Kohn which emerged at this time. In Steinberg's opinion, Kohn's view represented "an inadequate theism." For a God who is merely an aspect of reality, the sum total of life-enhancing forces, is not enough of a God. Not only traditional religionists, Steinberg said, but sophisticated philosophers like Royce and Bergson, looked upon God, among other things, as a "principle of explanation through which an obscure universe takes on lucidity." Also, the God of Jewish history is the Creator not of one aspect of reality but the whole of it. To Steinberg, therefore, the theology of a God who is a "process at work in the universe" might well lead to the bizarre necessity of positing a second Godhead.

The Kaplan-Kohn concept seemed to Steinberg to be merely a name without any objective reality to correspond with it. As he confided to Jacob Kohn, he did not derive his theology from Kaplan.

> It is one of Kaplan's limitations that he has almost no metaphysi-cal interest, perhaps no metaphysical sensitivity. To him God is a concept, at least so he always speaks of God, rather than an existen-tial reality, the reality of all realities, the *vrai vérité*. Or, to put it otherwise, to Kaplan God represents the psychological and sociologi-cal consequences of the God-idea rather than the cosmic *Ding-an-sich*. It is for its sociology of Jewish life that I am a Reconstructionist, not for the clarity or the utility of Kaplan's theology. I have often challenged Kaplan on that point. His response is that metaphysics is "personal" religion as opposed to the tradition-sanctioned group expression. I have never been able to see the value or the validity of the distinction he makes.[30]

Steinberg was convinced that it is possible for modern men to have a God who is more than an idea—the reality of all realities, the source, sanction, and guarantee of man's moral aspiration. Such a God, he insisted, is inescapable both on intellectual and moral grounds. This was his first public assertion of theological difference with his teacher. But it by no means indicated any alienation of theological difference from the Reconstructionist cause or any dimunition of his personal affection for Dr. Kaplan.

> With all my reservations as to Kaplan's theology, with all my awareness of emotional bias in him, I am at home only in the Recon-structionist group. Conservative Judaism is, for want of a philosophy, jelly-fish in character. Reconstructionism for all its inadequacies is to me an adequate sociology, the only one in contemporary Jewish life which takes cognizance of all aspects of the Jewish tradition.[31]

For his next essay, Steinberg chose as his topic "Toward the Rehabilitation of the Word Faith." In writing his novel *As a Driven*

Leaf, he had done a good deal of thinking on the nature of the act of faith and its relation to the rational life and he felt that he would have a "larger, fresher and more generous contribution to make with this subject then with any other." Here he was concerned with those who were unable to find their way back to religion because faith was a requirement. They understand faith to mean a readiness to believe that which cannot be completely proven, he pointed out. Since they are unable to accept religion's supposed rejection of scientific research and free inquiry, they remain alienated. Steinberg put forth the view that both science and philosophy are also based on beliefs or hypotheses which cannot be logically established. Unless men were prepared to make such assumptions, empirical science would be impossible. If one may believe the unproved in one realm, why not in another? In science, to be sure, hypotheses and postulates are used only under fixed and rigid restraints. But this is also possible in theological belief, Steinberg insisted. The religionist should use the same standards as the scientist for his hypotheses—congruity, practicality, and simplicity.[32]

In general, Steinberg's thinking in these early essays focused not on the traditional Jewish concepts of God, Torah, and Israel, or on theories of the nature of Jewishness, but on his general philosophy of religion. His interest was, as he put it on one occasion to Dr. Finkelstein, "in systems of religious metaphysics," in the "cosmological and ontological aspects of the Jewish religion, that is, in man's thinking concerning God and the ground for faith in Him and concerning his manifestations in life."[33]

In Steinberg's cosmology, the entire universe is the "outward manifestation of Mind—Energy, of Spirit, or to use the older and better word, of God." God is the essential "being of all beings," whose reason expresses itself in the rationality of the universe and makes the world a cosmos rather than a chaos. God is endowed with mind and consciousness, a truth which Steinberg felt had been played down by Kaplan in his zeal to make the implications of God's existence plain.

Why is there so much evil in the world? At this stage, this was for him the crux of the religious outlook. He recognized that one cannot entirely account for evil, particularly for natural disasters like floods and earthquakes, but he was convinced the effort must

be made. His own interpretation, at this time, was that evil represented the survival into the human condition of lower stages of
reality—mineral, vegetable, and animal—out of which man has
emerged. Traces of these earlier stages will be eliminated in the
course of time as God's purpose unfolds. Some day man will become
completely and purely human.

Steinberg knew that these essays represented only a beginning
and that much work lay ahead. But he decided to publish these
early theological thoughts. Written in a vivid and colorful style,
these articles reiterated his optimistic outlook on man and the
world's evil. Men are "participants even if in the smallest degree in
God's travail as he gives birth to a new order not only of things but
of being." . . . To those who hold onto it, the God-faith "furnishes
a confident hope, an assurance of a final victory over evil."[34]

Later Theological Essays

At the end of December 1943, while on a trip to army camps in the
Southwest on behalf of the Jewish Welfare Board, Steinberg suffered
a severe heart attack in Dallas, Texas. After several months of
convalescence he decided to limit himself only to essentials in his
rabbinate and to devote most of his time to his writing. In the next
two years (1945 and 1946) he managed to complete two new
books—*A Partisan Guide to the Jewish Problem* and *Basic Judaism*,
both still in print after more than forty-five years. Then once again
he turned to his program of reading in theology. This was not only
a continuation of what he had started during the war, but also
proceeded from what he still considered a desperate need in the
Jewish community. During the immediate post-war period a new
climate was developing, at least among intellectuals, a disenchantment with liberal culture and a reevaluation of such established beliefs as rationalism, humanism, faith in progress, science,
the use of intelligence in human affairs, and the perfectibility of
human nature. In technical philosophy, America seemed to be at
the beginning as well as at the end of a cultural epoch. Ideas
were being imported from abroad—the existentialism of Sartre and
Heidegger, the new sophisticated version of Catholic Scholasticism

of Jacques Maritain in Paris, and logical positivism from Vienna—all of which were leading to a radical revision of pre-war philosophical ideas.

What was happening in the world of philosophy was also true of Christian theology. The "theological revolution" which for many theologians had its beginnings in 1919 with Karl Barth's *Epistle to the Romans*, now began to have a perceptible impact on American Christian thought. The works of Kierkegaard, Barth, and Brunner were now widely read, as were those of other existentialist writers, such as Buber and Berdyayev. While these men exerted only limited influence in academic philosophical circles in the United States, they had a decided impact on Protestant theology. Milton Steinberg sensed that they also had implications for Judaism.

With the help of two friends, Will Herberg and Professor Albert Salomon, with whom he often discussed his readings, Steinberg now familiarized himself with the works of several German thinkers—Max Scheler, Wilhelm Dilthey, and Max Weber. He then read long selections from Karl Barth, re-read many of the essays of Charles Pierce, the founder of Pragmatism, and went through several of the major works of Kierkegaard whose emphasis on the subjective life of passion, anxiety and dread represented for Steinberg a completely different type of religious thinking. In quick order he tackled *Either-Or, Fear and Trembling* with its famous doctrine of the "theological suspension of the ethical," *Philosophical Fragments and Concluding Unscientific Postscript*. Though Kierkegaard's ideas ran counter to the basic presuppositions of normative Judaism as he understood them, Steinberg found him a "highly original and richly endowed spirit." However, he could not accept Kierkegaard's repudiation of intellect or his total reliance on faith. To him, the Danish philosopher represented an example of the wrong use of faith. Out of these readings came several new essays and papers, beginning with a lengthy article on Kierkegaard in the *Menorah Journal* in which he tried to explain why a Jew could not accept this type of theology. In this article Steinberg describes Kierkegaard's viewpoint as marginal, idiosyncratic, and somewhat extreme, but which he considered as representative of Christianity in an intense and distinctive way. Kierkegaard's basic premises, as Steinberg interpreted them, emphasized the desperate plight of modern man, beset by sin and bewilderment, and were based on a conviction that reality cannot be grasped through reason. Faith to Kierkegaard was not supplementary to intellect but its natural enemy. Goodness could not save the individual. When God asks it, moral principles have to be put aside, as Abraham had done in his readiness to sacrifice his only son, Isaac. Our concern must be for the individual soul rather than for the community and for the one true event in history—the self-revelation of the Eternal.[35]

As a religious rationalist, Steinberg was unable to accept any of these conclusions. In Judaism, he wrote, the ethical is never suspended, not for anyone or under any circumstances. Kierkegaard's interpretation of the *Akedah* [sacrifice of Isaac] and his delineation of the relation of the individual to society were therefore alien to the Jewish position. Nor can Judaism embrace the notion that man can do nothing to alleviate his own spiritual plight. It has confidence in man's powers of self-renewal and in the regeneration of society. Though he felt existentialism had made a contribution by its emphasis on inwardness, its mystical sensibility, and its feeling for the dilemmas and torments of human existence, Steinberg regarded its abandonment of reason as a grave failing. "I would sooner stand on objective critical thought whether on God or anything else," Steinberg wrote, "than on the total subjectivism and relativism of the existentialists. For in the former case there is a universal universe of discourse; in the latter only private worlds."[36] To another correspondent he reiterated that while existentialism and the crisis theology "deepened the religious consciousness in our time," they are in the long run "adverse to clear thinking and wholesome feeling on religious matters and hostile to the entire enterprise of perfecting the world under the kingdom of the Almighty." His own convictions, he said, remained "in great measure the consequence of a rationalist-pragmatic metaphysics."[37]

Whatever the merits of Steinberg's attitude, his essay was unquestionably a brilliant analysis, based on a careful reading of Kierkegaard, particularly the philosophical treatises. It was characteristic of Steinberg that he was able in so short a time to become acquainted with Kierkegaard's vocabulary, to absorb his ideas, and to write a critique from the point of view of Judaism. It also revealed his fair-mindedness and his tolerance for an outlook incompatible with his own.

Just before the Kierkegaard paper went to press, Steinberg received an invitation to deliver a paper on recent trends in Jewish theology at the June 1949 convention of the Rabbinical Assembly. The invitation was prompted by the renewed interest in theology sparked by Martin Buber, Will Herberg, Emil Fackenheim, and Jacob Taubes, whose articles were appearing in various journals. Members of the assembly, it was suggested, would welcome a survey of their ideas and also of recent trends in Protestant thought both here and in Europe. It was a complex, scholarly assignment, involving a program of readings few rabbis were qualified to undertake. Today, in the 1990s, Buber and Rosenzweig are well known in the Jewish community, and works of Barth, Brunner, Heidegger, the two Niebuhrs, and Tillich are all available in paperback. But in 1949 most rabbis were just becoming aware of these names. It was no mean feat for Steinberg to synthesize the various theological currents into a coherent paper and present his own evaluation.

The paper began with an evaluation of the tendency of contemporary theology, characteristic especially of neo-Reformationist continental thinkers, to reject the intellect as a tool and to rely exclusively on faith. Once again, Steinberg admitted that there was some value to the existentialist protests against rationalism's transformation of the living God into an abstract idea. He also found something valuable in the existentialist criticism of the modernists for pretending to look to Scripture for the truth when in fact they were not. He stated again his earlier view that religious certainty would not be achieved by logic. But he cautioned that although the recent anti-intellectual trend in philosophy was sound as a protest, it was "gravely perilous" as a program. Contrasting Judaism with Protestantism, he pointed out that anti-rationalism is not essential to Judaism as it might be to some forms of Protestantism. Moreover, Steinberg saw an "intellectual disingenuousness" in the existentialists' use of reason to justify their rejection of it. Reason, he pointed out, is also indispensable to them, if only so that each person might, according to existentialist doctrine, establish his own interpretation of Scripture.

Turning to recent thinking about the concept of God, Steinberg agreed with Kierkegaard that the modern immanentist notion of God as within the world is not wholly consonant with biblical tradition. Revelation to many modernists, he pointed out, is perhaps little more than man's own discovery of the truth, couched in pietist language. But he warned that the new transcendentalism, in some of its extremist versions, like that of Barth, had "inflated a half-truth to a whole and so perverted even the half." In Steinberg's view, God must be conceived as present within and animating men and affairs, and at the same time as an Absolute Being above and apart.

This brought him to another theological novelty—the proposal of a non-absolute God advocated by thinkers like James, Pierce, Whitehead, and Hartshorne. Subject to several reservations, Steinberg felt this notion had considerable merit, and he acknowledged the influence on his own thinking particularly of Pierce and Hartshorne.

Religion, Steinberg emphasized in this paper, as he had done so many times before, has a cognitive function to help us comprehend the universe. Turning to Kaplan's work, Steinberg again suggested that his teacher's refusal to engage in philosophical speculation concerning God was a deficiency in his theology. Since Kaplan, in his recent book, *The Future of the American Jew*, had reiterated his conviction that metaphysics was unnecessary, Steinberg found it necessary to repeat some of his earlier criticisms of his teacher's theological views.

In the last part of the paper Steinberg devoted himself to such theological problems as the "rediscovery of sin," the "depreciation of man's moral powers," and the "retreat from meliorism as found in the writings of Barth, Tillich and Niebuhr." He expressed his gratitude to these men for supplying him with a frame of reference for comprehending the social horrors of the 1940s. But he repeated his view that even Niebuhr, who represented the sanest version of this school, had overemphasized man's sinfulness. Steinberg made clear that he preferred the more balanced Jewish view on this topic.[38]

Steinberg's Philosophy of Religion

Among the many projects that remained uncompleted at the time of his death in March 1949, Steinberg probably would have regarded the volume on theology, *An Anatomy of Faith*, as the most important. He was very much aware of the fact that he had not yet worked out a total "theology of Judaism." Nevertheless, his published essays did constitute, if not a Jewish theology, at least the beginnings of a philosophy of religion.

Steinberg's theological writings are marked by a complete openness and receptivity to truth whatever the source, and by a sense of fairness in stating points of view different from his own. Written with the lucidity, force, and persuasiveness which characterized all his writings, his theological essays are never shallow or superficial. His point of departure is always the Jewish tradition, for which he shows a constant sense of reverence. Steinberg described himself as a "traditionalist". "Jews," he said, "ought not to play fast and loose with their past lest they lose contact with it." But he also referred to himself as a "Hellenist." In his later years the Greek view played less of a role in his outlook than in earlier years, but the rational emphasis of Greek thought, its intellectual freedom and scientific spirit as well as its aesthetic values, remained permanent influences. He continued to believe that the ideal pattern for living would be a synthesis of Hellenistic philosophy, science, and art with Hebraic religion and morality.

Aside from Jewish tradition and classical philosophy, the intellectual framework out of which Steinberg's religious outlook grew was the entire range of modern philosophy from Descartes to Whitehead. However, for the most part it was from the insights of twentieth-century theistic thinkers that he drew the universe of discourse for his thinking about religion. He was not a detached thinker who engaged in "pure speculation for its own sake." His religious speculation was part of his quest for insight, meaning, and goodness in life. Science cannot provide such understanding, he said. It explores particular categories rather than "things as a whole." It deals with phenomena which can be weighed or measured, not with the true or the good or with ultimate reality. Its function is to explain how things come to be, not issues of value and purpose, which are the responsibility of a God faith. Given such a God faith, Steinberg tells us with a sort of suppressed excitement, "the whole universe bursts into lucidity. The rationality of nature, the emergence of life, the phenomena of conscience and consciousness become intelligible."[39]

Such a *Weltanschauung* can make a great deal of difference in a person's life, for "as a man thinks of ultimates, so he tends to deal with immediates." In Steinberg's view, the failure to achieve such an intelligible religious faith was responsible for some of the severest aberrations of his time—"the upsurge of anti-intellectualism, cultism and religious authoritarianism, the proliferation of neuroticisms and the latter day worship of the state, race or economic class,"[40] which he described as modern forms of idolatry.

Steinberg used several terms to define his theological approach. He frequently described himself as a "modernist," summing up his creed as follows: faith in intellect, confidence in the essential goodness of man and the remediability of evil, and a strong sense of the reality of progress as part of the scheme of things. In addition, he said, the modernist respected science and felt that Judaism should be adapted to modern ideas and circumstances.

Steinberg also referred to himself as a "religious rationalist" whose convictions were in great measure the consequence of a "rationalist-pragmatist metaphysics." However, to him rationalism did not mean the abstract, analytic, and deductive operations of the mind as found in geometry or the bold "quest for certainty" of a Spinoza, who designed his metaphysics and ethics mathematically. Nor did it mean the extreme of rationalism of Hermann Cohen, composed only of demonstrable propositions from which all undertones of mystery and mood have been eliminated. A religion confined only to the logically establishable and indifferent to the emotional hungers of men, he said, would "misinterpret the universe and feed its communicants stones for bread." Religion is also acquired through intuition and feeling, through tradition, revelation, and mystical experience, and through morality and group solidarity or a combination of these. Such nonrational approaches, however, at best furnish "tentative conclusions" which then require reason to confirm or upset them.

But even the rational process can provide only "plausible interpretations with a high measure of probability." Descartes and Locke, Steinberg asserted, had taught that the senses cannot be completely trusted as sources of information concerning reality. Lobachevski and the non-Euclideans had thrown a shadow over the certainty of the results obtained from Euclidean geometry. And Freud had shown that underneath logic there is the irrationality of the life drive. Thus step by step men gradually stopped looking to reason for the disclosure of complete truth. Steinberg saw evidence of this in the popularity of Bergson's intuitionism and in the ascendance of William James over Josiah Royce. Nevertheless, though the vision reason provides is "blurred, astigmatic, doubt-ridden, and always open to challenge," Steinberg insisted that it still remains the "most reliable of our powers, the only one which is universally shared and readily communicated."

Several critics have contended that in his last years Steinberg's theological orientation underwent a basic change. After his heart attack, they insist, he reached a "turning point" in his intellectual life, during which he came to "share with the Bible, Pascal, with Kierkegaard, with Buber and Rosenzweig, the conviction that the religious life begins not with judgment of rational assent but with an unconditional act of faith."[41] To be sure, several modifications in Steinberg's theology did take place during the last year and a half of his life. Out of his study of existentialist literature came a greater awareness of the nonrational factors in life. Also, he began to recognize the "depth of evil" of which human nature was capable, and that progress is not as inevitable as he had thought. The extravagant optimism which he had shared with many liberals of the prewar period gave way to a more sober attitude to human nature. But a comparison of Steinberg's later essays with his earlier ones does not reveal any radical change in his methodology. There is no evidence of any new direction in his philosophical orientation, as occurred with Whitehead after he came to the United States or with Hermann Cohen after he retired from Marburg University.

Perhaps, had Steinberg lived to give the course on Rosenzweig and Buber he was planning for his synagogue adult education program, and the seminar with the students of the Seminary, he might have shifted his outlook to a greater extent. Undoubtedly the appearance of *Judaism* magazine, *Tradition*, and other theological publications during the 1950s, and the general trend toward existentialism among Jewish thinkers, would have had an impact. But it is more likely that he would have developed a form of metaphysical theology along the lines of Hartshorne and Brightman and remain within the rationalist tradition. All of this, however, is pure conjecture. What actually happened by March 1950 was not a change in direction but a partial shift of emphasis, a widening of horizons and a deepening perspective.

Steinberg did not live long enough to fully expose his thought. He died in 1950 at the age of forty-seven. His essays, therefore, leave many questions unanswered, insights undeveloped and ambiguities unexplained. In spite of this, his theological writings are still very much worth reading and studying. They remind us of the overly practical bent of American Judaism and of the need for philosophical reflection in religion. As a sophisticated religious thinker, sensitive to philosophical issues, he raised many of the questions essential for the development of an acceptable theism.

In the present age, when so much play is given to enthusiasm and the nonrational element in religion, his plea that reason not be abandoned in the theological enterprise continues to be a source of encouragement and stimulation.

Notes

1. According to the transcript of his elementary school record, young Steinberg received A in literature, history, geography, science, mathematics, and Latin. However, in physical training, penmanship, drawing, and sheet metal, his mark was B.
2. As late as 1972, the little library was still there, and on a visit to Rochester I found the Russian novels still on the shelf in the corner where he used to sit and read.
3. For further details about Jewish Harlem at that time, see Jeffrey S. Gurock, *When Harlem was Jewish, 1870–1930* (New York: Columbia University Press, 1979).
4. Judah Schwefel to Simon Noveck, October 15, 1953. Mss. held at American Jewish Historical Society, Brandeis University. Rabbi Schwefel later moved to Israel where he changed his name to Shuval.
5. Outline of the series of sermons delivered by Dr. Kohn during 1919–20 on "Jewish Faith and Its Social Significance" and on the Jewish prayer

book will be found in *Problems of the Ministry* (New York Board of Ministers, 1927), 31–36. See also ibid., 36–39, for two additional series delivered during the 1923–24 and 1925–26 seasons.

6. Milton Steinberg to Jacob Kohn, December 31, 1942.

7. Milton Steinberg to Arthur A. Cohen, January 17, 1946.

8. Milton Steinberg, *A Believing Jew: The Selected Writings of Milton Steinberg* (New York: Harcourt Brace, 1951), 235.

9. *Campus*, April 26, 1921.

10. Jacob Kohn unpublished memoir, 11. The manuscript is in the hands of his daughter, Mrs. Eleazar Lipsky, in New York City.

11. Milton Steinberg to Mordecai Brill, December 21, 1932.

12. Ibid.

13. Simon Noveck, "Kaplan and Milton Steinberg: A Disciple's Agreements and Disagreements," in *The American Judaism of Mordecai Kaplan*, edited by Emanuel S. Goldsmith, Mel Scult, and Robert M. Seltzer (New York: New York University Press, 1990), 148–49.

14. Ibid.

15. How strongly Steinberg felt about Professor Kaplan can be seen from the letter which he wrote on behalf of himself and his fellow students to Cyrus Adler in 1927. "There is preeminently one man among our teachers who is responsible for what faith and courage and vision we may lay claim to. It is from him that we have acquired the hardihood to go on in a difficult and discouraging cause for it was he who has given the Judaism we are expected to teach the content and vitality we have elsewhere sought in vain. . . . We have seen in him that clear and simple passion for spiritual honesty which we believe is the first desideratum in American Jewish life."

16. Milton Steinberg, *Only Human* (New York: Bloch Publishing, 1963), 161–65 and 167.

17. Milton Steinberg to Mordecai Brill, December 21, 1932.

18. Address before the New Jersey branch of the National Women's League in Asbury Park, N.J., November 11, 1936. See also unpublished sermon on Uriel da Costa, 1940.

19. In introducing these various changes, which also included the observance of two days of each festival rather than the one-day observance followed by the congregation heretofore, as well as the custom of calling up individuals to the reading of the Torah, Steinberg acted slowly, gradually, and with patience, biding his time until the people were ready to accept these innovations. There were no demands of any kind, no firm insistence on what later came to be known as the "standards" of Conservative Judaism. Steinberg tried to achieve his goals by persuasion, without alienating or hurting anyone in the congregation. To him, the religious feeling of each individual seemed more important than the adherence to a norm.

20. Unpublished sermon delivered on Friday night, November 25, 1933.

21. *Reconstructionist*, April 25, 1935, p. 4.

22. *Proceedings of the Rabbinical Assembly* 5 (1933–38): 156.

23. The outlooks of the three groups were presented in a symposium at the 1948 convention of the Rabbinical Assembly entitled "Toward a Philosophy of Conservative Judaism." See *Proceedings of the Rabbinical Assembly* 10 (1948): 110–92.

24. Milton Steinberg to Jacob Kohn, January 25, 1943.

25. Milton Steinberg to Robert Gordis, May 7, 1944.

26. Robert Gordis, "A Jewish Prayer Book for the Modern Age," *Conservative Judaism* (October 1945): 12, 14–15.

27. Milton Steinberg to Robert Gordis, May 17, 1944.

28. Judah Goldin, who was a member of the commission, later came to the conclusion that Steinberg was not justified in many of his criticisms. He blamed his friend Milton's involvement with Reconstructionism for his attitude as well as Steinberg's naiveté. Interview with Judah Goldin.

29. *Reconstructionist*, November 29, 1940.

30. Milton Steinberg to Jacob Kohn, no date. Solomon Goldman too did not agree with Steinberg on this point. See *Reconstructionist*, June 26, 1942, pp. 24–25.

31. Milton Steinberg to Jacob Kohn, no date.

32. *Reconstructionist*, April 5, 1942.

33. Milton Steinberg to Louis Finkelstein, May 9, 1942.

34. *Reconstructionist*, April 30, 1943.

35. *Menorah Journal*, March 1949. The essay is reprinted in *An Anatomy of Faith: The Theological Essays of Milton Steinberg*, edited by Arthur Cohen (New York: Harcourt Brace, 1960).

36. Milton Steinberg to Arthur A. Cohen, November 2, 1947.

37. Milton Steinberg to Simon Rifkind, May 27, 1948.

38. "Theological Problems of the Hour," in *Proceedings of the Rabbinical Assembly of America* 13 (1949): 356–408. This paper is also reprinted in Cohen, *An Anatomy of Faith*.

39. Steinberg, *A Believing Jew*, 19–21.

40. "The Uses of Faith," unpublished article prepared for the *Nation*, May 1949.

41. David Silverman, unpublished address delivered at the Emanuel Synagogue, Hartford, Connecticut, in November 1962; Will Herberg, *Commentary*, March 1951, p. 501; Cohen, *Anatomy of Faith*, 57–58.

C H A P T E R   1 5

Will Herberg

David Dalin

When Will Herberg died in March of 1977, American Judaism lost one of its most provocative religious thinkers of the post–World War II generation. Like Herman Cohen and Franz Rosenzweig before him, Herberg came to Judaism from the outside. A Marxist and atheist through much of his young adulthood who had received no education or religious training in his youth, Herberg turned to the study of Judaism only after his romance with Marxism ended. A prolific and influential Jewish theologian and sociologist of religion, beginning in the late 1940s his spiritual journey from Marxism to Judaism was unique in the American Jewish intellectual history of this century. The only Jewish ex-Marxist to embrace Jewish theology and the study of religion as a full-time vocation, Will Herberg was the quintessential "Baal Teshuvah" of his generation.

Herberg was born in the Russian village of Liachovitzi in 1901. His father, Hyman Louis Herberg, who had been born in the same russian *shtetl*, moved his family to the United States in 1904. When his family arrived in America, his parents, whom he would later describe as "passionate atheists," were already committed to the faith that socialism would bring salvation to mankind and freedom from the restraints that had bound Western societies for centuries. His father died when Herberg was ten and his mother shared her husband's "contempt" for the American public school system.

Although he attended Public School No. 72 and Boys High School in Brooklyn, Herberg was largely self-taught, his real education taking place at the kitchen table of an apartment on Georgia Avenue in a lower-middle-class neighborhood of Brooklyn. A precocious and versatile student from his early youth, Herberg had learned Greek, Latin, French, German, and Russian by the time he was a teenager. Graduating from Boys High School in 1918, Herberg later attended CCNY and Columbia University, where he studied philosophy and history, without apparently ever completing the course work for an academic degree.

Herberg inherited his parents' "passionate atheism" and equally passionate commitment to the socialist faith. Entering the communist movement while still a teenager, Herberg brought to radical politics a theoretical erudition that helped elevate American Marxism as an intellectual proposition. While less prolific than Max Eastman, or the novelist John Dos Passos, Herberg, the editor and critic, was perhaps the most "catholic" of Marxist polemicists during the 1920s and early 1930s. A regular contributor to communist journals such as the *Working Monthly*, Herberg was also a familiar ideologue and polemicist in the *Modern Quarterly*, one of the chief theoretical journals of the Old Left generation.

Herberg wrote scores of articles and editorials on an amazingly diverse number of topics, critiquing Edmund Wilson's views on proletarian literature, arguing with Sidney Hook over the textual validity of Marx's ambivalent position on revolution, and explicating the relationship between Freudian psychoanalysis and communist thought. His attachment to communism was no mere affectation, but reflected intellectual conviction as well as moral ardor. So earnestly did he embrace Marxism that he even sought to reconcile it with Einstein's theory of relativity. Indeed, perhaps his boldest contribution to the radical thought of the period was his effort to reconcile Marxism to the new Einsteinian cosmology, the "second scientific revolution," that had been virtually unnoticed amongst radical writers in America. While most communists then still condemned Einstein for rejecting Marx's "scientific materialism," Herberg insisted that both Marxism and the theory of relativity were "scientifically true." As a radical Jew, moreover, Herberg hailed Freud, as he did Marx and Einstein, as a modern prophet. "The world of socialism—to which nothing human is alien and which cherishes every genuine manifestation of the human spirit," he would write during the 1930s, "lays a wreath of homage on the grave of Sigmund Freud."

Herberg's first disenchantment with orthodox Marxism came in 1920, when he, Bertram Wolfe, and other young intellectuals and labor organizers joined a group headed by Jay Lovestone, which split off from the main Communist party within the American Party leadership. Lovestone, an American supporter of the Soviet Marxist theoretician Nikolai Bukharin, had, like Bukharin, advocated more autonomy from Soviet control for national Communist parties. In 1929, Stalin struck back by demoting Bukharin in the Soviet Party and by ousting Lovestone and his followers from leadership of the American movement. After breaking with the official Party in 1929, Herberg became a staff member and then editor of the Lovestonite opposition communist paper, *Workers Age*, many of whose contributors would later become bitter anti-Stalinists.

As the 1930s progressed, Herberg became progressively disenchanted with his earlier Marxist faith. The grotesque Stalinist purges, the communist "betrayal" of the Popular Front on the battlefields of Spain during the Spanish Civil War, the Russian invasion of Finland and the Stalin-Hitler Nonaggression Pact of 1939 all contributed to his growing disillusionment. The Moscow trials, Herberg maintained, indicated the extreme barbaric measures to which Stalin would resort to suppress all resistance to his bureaucratic rule within Russia. For Herberg, as for so many ex-Marxists of his generation, the cynical, opportunistic Molotov-Ribbentrop agreement of 1939 dispelled any remaining belief, once held, that "only a socialist government can defeat totalitarianism." His final break with orthodox Marxism, which came in 1939, was no mere change in political loyalties, no mere repudiation of the political radicalism of his youth. For, as he would confess in recounting his journey from Marxism to Judaism on the pages of *Commentary* in January 1947, Marxism had been, to him and to others like him, "a religion, an ethic and a theology; a vast all-embracing doctrine of man and the universe, a passionate faith endowing life with meaning."[1]

Put to the test, however, this Marxist faith had failed. Reality, as Herberg would later express it, "could not be forever withstood," and by the late 1930s he had begun to recognize that the all-encompassing system of Marxist thought could not sustain the values that had first attracted him to revolutionary activity. "Not that I felt myself any the less firmly committed to the great ideals of freedom and social justice," he would reflect in 1947. Rather:

> My discovery was that I could no longer find basis and support for these ideals in the materialistic religion of Marxism. . . . This religion itself, it now became clear to me, was in part illusion, and in part idolatry; in part a delusive utopianism promising heaven on earth in our time, and in part a totalitarian worship of collective man; in part a naive faith in the finality of economics, material production; in part a sentimental optimism as to the goodness of human nature, and in part a hard-boiled amoral cult of power at any price. There could be no question to my mind that as religion, Marxism had proved itself bankrupt.[2]

Perceiving Marxism as a "god that failed," rather than as a "mere strategy of political action," Herberg was left with an inner spiritual void, "deprived of the commitment and understanding that alone made life livable."

As the god of Marxism was thus failing him in the late 1930s, Herberg chanced to read Reinhold Niebuhr's *Moral Man and Immoral Society*, a book that was to profoundly change the course of his life. "Humanly speaking," he would later write,

> it converted me, for in some manner I cannot describe, I felt my whole being, and not merely my thinking, shifted to a new center. . . . What impressed me most profoundly was the paradoxical combination of realism and radicalism that Niebuhr's "prophetic" faith made possible. . . . Here was a faith that warned against all premature securities, yet called to responsible action. Here, in short, was a "social idealism" without illusions, in comparison with which even the most "advanced" Marxism appeared confused, inconsistent, and hopelessly illusion-ridden.[3]

More than any other American thinker of the 1930s and 1940s, Niebuhr related theology to politics through a realistic assessment of human nature that seemed inescapably relevant in a time of the breakdown of the Marxist (and liberal) faith in progress and human enlightenment.

Some of Herberg's acquaintances would later liken his rejection of communism, and return to Judaism, to Paul's conversion on the road to Damascus. The comparison may have pleased him, for Herberg always felt that similarly, his return to Judaism was the product of events unanticipated and dramatic. His memorable road to teshuvah, inspired by his first encounter with Niebuhr, was unique in the annals of American Jewish intellectuals of the past generation. In an autobiographical passage in one of his essays, Herberg said that his encounter with Niebuhr's thought in 1939 was the "turning point," even before he met Niebuhr personally, who was then teaching at Manhattan's Union Theological Seminary.

Like Franz Rosenzweig before him, whose writings he began to read during the early 1940s, Herberg went through a wrenching inner struggle over whether to become a Christian. After several soul-searching meetings with Niebuhr, Herberg declared his intention to embrace Christianity. Niebuhr counseled him, instead, to first explore his Jewish religious tradition and directed him across the street to the Jewish Theological Seminary, where Herberg went to study. The professors and students at the Seminary undertook to instruct Herberg in Hebrew and Jewish thought.

Throughout much of the 1940s, while he was earning a living as the educational director and research analyst of the International Ladies Garment Workers Union, Herberg also devoted much of his time and energy to the study of Jewish sources. Not having received a traditional Jewish education in his youth, Herberg was introduced to the classical sources of Judaism through the writings of Solomon Schechter and George Foot Moore, and through the instruction of Judaic scholars who became his friends, such as Professors Gerson D. Cohen and Seymour Siegel, and Rabbi Milton Steinberg. As Seymour Siegel has reminisced, Herberg was "extraordinarily moved" by the realistic appraisal of human nature in the rabbinic literature, especially as expounded by Schechter.[4] He was impressed, also, by the theological writings of Martin Buber and Franz Rosenzweig who, together with Niebuhr, would shape his evolving views on religious existentialism and biblical faith.

Herberg was inspired and excited by what he learned. In Judaism he found, after years of searching, a faith that encouraged social action without falling into the trap of utopianism. Throughout the

1940s, he met regularly with rabbis and students at the Seminary, developing and explicating his emerging theology for journals such as *Commentary* and the *Jewish Frontier*, and he began lecturing on religious faith and the social philosophy of Judaism to synagogue groups and on college campuses. In much demand as a speaker, he traveled widely, and gained the reputation of being "the Reinhold Niebuhr of Judaism." He met regularly, moreover, at his home with rabbinical students and others to discuss his theological ideas. "In those early days," as one of these students has remembered, "when the naturalistic theology so brilliantly expounded by Professor Mordecai Kaplan was the main intellectual influence in Jewish religious circles, we were fascinated by Herberg's espousal of the orthodox ideas of a supernatural God, Messiah and Torah, expounded with fervor and yet interpreted in a new way."[5]

Out of these intellectual encounters, and out of several essays published in *Commentary* and elsewhere in the late 1940s, came Herberg's first major work, *Judaism and Modern Man*, which appeared in 1951. Widely acclaimed as a carefully reasoned and intensely written interpretation of Judaism in the light of the newest existentialist thinking, *Judaism and Modern Man* was highly praised by Jewish scholars, while Niebuhr, in a review of the book in the *New York Herald Tribune*, (December 16, 1951), himself stated that the book "may well become a milestone in the religious thought of America."

Herberg's central theological concern, as he describes it in *Judaism and Modern Man*, is the plight of modern secular man, his spiritual frustration and despair. One by one, Herberg examines the various "substitute faiths" in which modern man has placed his hopes and aspirations—Marxism, liberalism, rationalism, science, and psychoanalysis, among others—and finds that each is a way of evading ultimate theological issues. As a religion, as a basis of faith, each of these secular ideologies is found wanting: Modern man, claims Herberg, requires belief in an absolute God. "Man must worship something," Herberg often wrote. "If he does not worship God, he will worship an idol made of wood, or of gold, or of ideas."[6] Faith in God, asserts Herberg, is essential to one's being. Moreover, intellectual affirmation is not enough. A "leap of faith" is called for, a return to the living God of Abraham, Isaac, and Jacob and a total commitment to Him.[7]

In presenting his view of God and Judaism, Herberg criticized those theologians of the 1930s and 1940s who espoused a liberal, rational approach to God and, in so doing, reduced God to an idea.[8] For the religious existentialist, such as Herberg, who was deeply influenced by the dialogical I-Thou philosophy of Buber and Rosenzweig, the "idea of God" is meaningless: God is important only if there is a personal relationship to Him. Thus, for Herberg, Jewish faith and theology cannot be predicated upon an abstract idea of God such as, for example, the Reconstructionist notion of "a power that makes for salvation." Rather, the God of *Judaism and Modern Man* is a personal God to whom we can pray with an expectation of a response,[9] with whom we can enter into a genuine dialogue.

In many respects, as Seymour Siegel has noted, Herberg's theology was quite traditional. He believed in revelation, covenant, the resurrection of the dead, and the coming of the Messiah.[10] He also affirmed, unequivocally, the traditional theological doctrine of "chosenness": Jewish existence, argued Herberg, "is intrinsically religious and God oriented. Jews may be led to deny, repudiate, and reject their "chosenness" and its responsibilities, but their own Jewishness rises to confront them as refutation and condemnation."[11]

At the same time, however, Herberg was not a fundamentalist: That is, he did not view Scripture and the Tradition as literally God's word. Thus, for example, while believing in revelation, Herberg did not accept "the fundamentalist conception of revelation as the supernatural communication of information through a body of writings which are immune from error because they are quite literally the writings of God. . . . The Bible is obviously not simply a transcript from His dictation."[12] Rather, Herberg regarded revelation as "the self-disclosure of God in His dealings with the world,"[13] through His active intervention in history, and the Torah as a "humanly mediated record of revelation." In this, and in other respects, his theology, while traditional, was at variance with Orthodoxy.

Herberg argued, moreover, that a Jewish theology relevant to the postwar period would have to be predicated upon a less optimistic image of man, upon a sober recognition of human sinfulness and human limitations. The barbarities of Stalinism and, especially, the Nazi Holocaust, seemed to Herberg to have destroyed the very foundations of the prevailing liberal faith, shared by Reform and Reconstructionist Judaism alike, in the "natural goodness" of man. Liberal Jewish theology, he maintained, failed to answer the critical question of how evil regimes and institutions could possibly have arisen if man is essentially good. The answer, Herberg wrote, could be found in "Niebuhr's rediscovery of the classical doctrine of 'original sin,' which religious liberalism and secular idealism combined to deride and obscure." Sin, Herberg wrote, "is one of the great facts of human life. It lies at the root of man's existentialist plight." Without an "understanding of the nature of sin," he concluded, "there is no understanding of human life . . . or man's relation to God."[14]

Herberg's existentialist approach to Jewish theology struck a responsive chord in the hearts of many within the Jewish community and beyond, who were searching for religious roots and spiritual inspiration. The publication of *Judaism and Modern Man* was greeted with praise and enthusiasm by several respected Jewish reviewers, such as Milton Konvitz and Rabbi Milton Steinberg. Indeed, Steinberg, who was reader of the manuscript, penciled in the margins that Herberg "had written the book of the generation on the Jewish religion."

Herberg's theological writings, culminating in *Judaism and Modern Man*, had little impact within the secular Jewish intellectual world of which he had once been a part. Herberg had once looked to the New York Jewish intellectual community to inspire and guide America's religious revival. In so doing, he was sadly disappointed. Herberg's call for "a great theological reconstruction" and a renascent Jewish neo-Orthodoxy, first voiced in his *Commentary* article of 1947, met with an inhospitable reception amongst many of his fellow Jewish ex-Marxists who now contributed to *Partisan Review* and Dwight Macdonald's magazine *Politics*, and were playing such an influential role in shaping secular Jewish intellectual life and cultural tastes.[15] They were, for the most part, cultural modernists who had little interest in serious theological reflection or personal affirmations of religious belief. They found Herberg, quite simply, too religious; and his passionate involvement with Judaism, too extreme.

To these secular critics, such as Irving Howe, Herberg's nascent theological concerns and commitments bespoke a "new failure of nerve" which they were quick to dismiss. Herberg's call for a religious revival, they claimed, represented "an escape from the responsibilities of political life and uncertainties of worldly experience." Howe, in particular, unfairly castigated Herberg for turning political moralist, lamenting his conversion "from Lovestone to Jehova."[16] Herberg's theological convictions also troubled Sidney Hook and Daniel Bell, who could not accept his argument that democracy rests on "religio-philosophical" truths about man's fallibility and that theology may be a possible bulwark against totalitarianism.[17] These were sentiments shared by other New York Jewish intellectuals as well.[18] The "defeatist" retreat to religion that Herberg espoused thus found little support amongst most of the participants in *Partisan Review*'s 1950 symposium on "Religion and the Intellectuals" who, as John P. Diggins has pointed out, "regarded with aloof disdain the religious revival supposedly taking place in America, as though it were an ironic reenactment of the "false consciousness" that Marx promised would disappear with industrial progress."[19] Not surprisingly, the appearance of *Judaism and Modern Man* the following year went unnoticed in the *Partisan Review*, while other important New York intellectual journals also failed to review it.

Although *Judaism and Modern Man* served to make Herberg's reputation as a theologian, it did not immediately serve to secure for him the entrée into academia that he actively sought. Since 1948, his duties with the ILGWU had diminished to the point where his occupation was listed on his income tax return as "writer and lecturer." He offered courses on a part-time basis at the New School for Social Research in 1948 and 1949 and for a brief period, from May 1951 to June 1952, served as editor of the new quarterly journal *Judaism*. Much of his income between 1948 and 1954 came, however, on a freelance basis, from the writing of numerous articles and book reviews, and from his lecturing on college campuses, and to synagogue and church groups, far and wide. At least some of his time and energies, after 1950, were devoted to the research and writing of *Protestant-Catholic-Jew* which was published in 1955.

While there is much to question in Herberg's analysis,[20] *Protestant-Catholic-Jew* remains a work of enduring value to anyone hoping to understand the sociology of American religion. It has become a classic work in American religious sociology, one that Nathan Glazer, in his review in *New Republic*, November 14, 1955, called "the most satisfying explanation we have been given as to just what is happening to religion in America." The critical and public acclaim that greeted the publication of *Protestant-Catholic-Jew* brought Herberg instantaneous public recognition as one of the country's best-known sociologists of religion, a reputation which he would enjoy until the end of his life.

The critical acclaim that greeted the publication of *Protestant-Catholic-Jew* also brought Herberg the academic recognition, and position, he had long sought. In 1955, he obtained a full-time academic appointment as professor of Judaic Studies and Social Philosophy at Drew University, a Methodist institution in New Jersey, where he would teach until his retirement in 1976, the year before his death.

During the 1950s and 1960s, while teaching at Drew, Herberg also lectured at numerous universities, synagogues, and churches throughout the United States and Europe. He published scholarly anthologies on the works of Martin Buber, Karl Barth, Jacques Maritain, and other modern existentialist theologians, and a collection of some twenty of his articles on aspects of biblical theology, *Faith Enacted into History*, appeared in print in 1976.

During the 1950s and 1960s, moreover, Herberg became part of a remarkable group of ex-communists and ex-Trotskyists that included James Burnham, Willmore Kendell, Frank Meyer, Max Eastman and Whittaker Chambers, among others, who transformed the *National Review* into the preeminent intellectual journal of American conservatism. As religion editor of the *National Review*, Herberg emerged as one of the recognized leaders of the post–World War II conservative intellectual movement in America. His new conservatism found its most eloquent expression in his views on religion and state.

Herberg's views on religion and state were generally dismissed or

ignored within the secular world of the New York Jewish Intellectuals, of which he had once been a part. As Neil Jumonville has
recently noted, several of the best known of the group, such as
Sidney Hook, Irving Howe, and Philip Rahv, were alarmed about
the dangers inherent in "a religious orientation afoot"[21] within the
public square. Committed to the secular faith that religious values
and concerns had no legitimate role to play within American politics and public life, they shared the liberal Jewish separationist
assumption that religious freedom is most secure where church and
state are rigidly separated, and least secure where government and
religion are intertwined, which differed profoundly from the position that Herberg had begun, during the early 1950s, to fervently espouse.

Earlier than most other American Jewish intellectuals, Herberg
called for a reassessment of the prevailing liberal Jewish consensus
concerning church-state separation and the role that religion
should play in American life. "By and large," he wrote in 1952,
those who speak for the American Jewish community

> seem to share the basic secularist presupposition that religion is a
> "private matter." . . . The American Jew must have sufficient confi-
> dence in the capacity of democracy to preserve its pluralistic . . .
> character without any absolute wall of separation between religion
> and public life. . . . The fear felt by Jewish leaders of the possible
> consequence of a restoration of religion to a vital place in public life
> is what throws them into an alliance with the secularists and helps
> make their own thinking so thoroughly secular.[22]

And a decade or so later, frustrated by liberal Jewish support for
the 1963 Supreme Court decisions banning The Lord's Prayer and
Bible Reading in the public schools, he entered a plea for a restoration of religion to a place of honor in American public life:

> Within the meaning of our political tradition and political practice,
> the promotion [of religion] has been, and continues to be, a part of
> the very legitimate "secular" purpose of the state. Whatever the
> "neutrality" of the state in matters of religion may be, it cannot be a
> neutrality between religion and no-religion, any more than . . . it
> could be a neutrality between morality and no-morality, [both of
> which] are necessary to "good government" and "national pros-
> perity."[23]

"The traditional symbols of the divine presence in our public life,"
he warned, "ought not to be tampered with."[24]

Throughout the 1960s, Herberg's warning went generally un-
heeded within the American Jewish community. In more recent
years, however, Herberg's views on church-state relations have
gained more adherents. Today, more than a decade after his death,
his perceptive critique of a public life devoid of religious values
is now reflected in the thought of a growing number of Jewish
intellectuals who have come to share Herberg's belief that an American political culture uninformed by religious beliefs and institutions itself poses a danger to the position and security of America's
Jews.[25]

Notes

1. Will Herberg, "From Marxism to Judaism: Jewish Belief as a Dynamic
   of Social Action," *Commentary* (January 1947): 25.
2. Ibid., 27.
3. Will Herberg, "Reinhold Niebuhr: Christian Apologist to the Secular
   World," *Union Seminary Quarterly Review* (May 1956): 12.
4. Seymour Siegel, "Will Herberg (1902–1977): A Ba'al Teshuvah Who
   Became Theologian, Sociologist, Teacher," *American Jewish Year
   Book*, 1978, 532.
5. Ibid.
6. Janet M. Gnall, "Will Herberg, Jewish Theologian: A Bibliographical
   Existential Approach to Religion," (unpublished Ph.D. dissertation,
   Drew University, 1983), 51.
7. Will Herberg, *Judaism and Modern Man* (New York: Farrar, Straus and
   Young, 1951), 25–43.
8. Eugene Borowitz, "An Existentialist View of God," *Jewish Heritage*
   (Spring 1958).
9. Gnall, 54.
10. Siegel, 533.
11. Will Herberg, "The Chosenness of Israel and the Jew of Today," *Mid-
    stream* (Autumn 1955): 88.
12. Herberg, *Judaism and Modern Man*, 244–45.
13. Ibid., 246.
14. Will Herberg, "The Theological Problems of the Hour," *Proceedings of
    the Rabbinical Assembly of America* (June 1949): 420.
15. See, for example: Harold Rosenberg's "Open Letter to Will Herberg,"
    Commentary (February 1947); 145–51, which was written in response

to Herberg's *Commentary* article, "From Marxism to Judaism," the previous month.

16. John P. Diggins, *Up from Communism: Conservative Odysseys in American Intellectual History* (New York: Harper & Row, 1975), 279.
17. Ibid., 280.
18. For a thoughtful discussion of the attitudes of the New York intellectuals to religion generally, and to Judaism in particular, see: Edward S. Shapiro, "Jewishness and the New York Intellectuals," *Judaism* (Summer 1989): 282–92; and Edward S. Shapiro, "The Jewishness of the New York Intellectuals: Sidney Hook, A Case Study," in Seymour Martin Lipset (ed.), *American Pluralism and the Jewish Community* (New Brunswick, N.J.: Transaction Publishers, 1990), 153–71.
19. Ibid., 296.
20. See, for example: David G. Dallin, "Will Herberg in Retrospect," *Commentary* (July 1988): 42.
21. Neil Jumonville, *Critical Crossings: The New York Intellectuals in Postwar America* (Berkeley: University of California Press, 1991), 104.
22. Will Herberg, "The Sectarian Conflict over Church and State: A Divisive Threat to Our Democracy?" *Commentary* (November 1952): 459.
23. Will Herberg, "Religion and Public Life," *National Review*, August 13, 1963, p. 105.
24. Will Herberg, "Religious Symbols in Public Life," *National Review*, August 28, 1962, p. 162.
25. See for example: Jonathan D. Sarna, *American Jews and Church-State Relations: The Search for Equal Footing* (New York: American Jewish Committee, 1989), 29–31; Milton Himmelfarb, "Church and State: How High a Wall?" *Commentary* (July 1966); Seymour Siegel, "Church and State," *Conservative Judaism* 17 (1963): 1–12; Seymour Siegel, "Church and State: A Reassessment," *Sh'ma*, December 1, 1970; reprinted in Carolyn T. Oppenheim, *Listening to American Jews* (New York: Sh'ma, 1986), 130–34; Jakob J. Petuchowski, "Logic and Reality," *Jewish Spectator* (September 1962): 20; David G. Dalin, "Leo Pfeffer and the Separationist Faith," *This World* (Winter 1989): 136–40; and the contributions of David G. Dalin, Nathan Lewin, David Novak, Hadley Arkes, Milton Himmelfarb, Dennis Prager, Richard L. Rubenstein, Ruth R. Wisse, and Marc Gellman to the Symposium on "Judaism and American Public Life," in *First Things* (March 1991).

Contributors

RACHEL FELDHAY BRENNER was born in Poland, grew up in Israel, and emigrated to Canada where she taught at York University in Toronto. She is now a professor in the Department of Hebrew and Semitic Studies at the University of Wisconsin at Madison. Her publications include *A. M. Klein, The Father of Canadian Jewish Literature: Essays in the Poetics of Humanistic Passion* (1990) and *Assimilation and Assertion: The Response to the Holocaust in Mordecai Richler's Writing* (1989).

STANLEY F. CHYET is a professor of American Jewish history and director of the Edgar F. Magnin School of Graduate Studies at the Hebrew Union College-Jewish Institute of Religion in Los Angeles. He is a past associate director of the American Jewish Archives. His writings include *Israeli Poetry: A Contemporary Anthology*, translated and edited with Warren Bargad (1986), and numerous books and articles on various aspects of the American Jewish experience.

JACK J. COHEN, a retired director of the B'nai Brith Hillel Foundation in Israel, taught philosophy of religion at the Jewish Theological Seminary, the Hebrew University of Jerusalem, and the David Yellin College of Education in Jerusalem. He also served as rabbi of the Society for the Advancement of Judaism and as director of the Jewish Reconstructionist Foundation. Among his publications are *The Case for Religious Naturalism, Jewish Education in Democratic Society*, and *The Reunion of Isaac and Ishmael*.

DAVID DALIN, an ordained rabbi, is a professor of American Jewish history at the University of Hartford. He is a member of the Academic Advisory Council of the American Jewish Historical Society and a member of the editorial board of *Conservative Judaism*. He is the author of *From Marxism to Judaism: The Collected Essays of Will Herberg* (1989), and numerous articles and reviews that have appeared in a wide range of publications.

IRA EISENSTEIN is president emeritus of the Reconstructionist Rabbinical College, editor emeritus of *Reconstructionist* magazine, and a former national president of the Rabbinical Assembly of America. He co-edited the Reconstructionist *New Haggadah*, the *Sabbath Prayer Book*, and the *High Holiday Prayer Book*, and he is the author of a number of books including *Judaism under Freedom* (1956) and his personal memoirs, *Reconstructing Judaism* (1986).

EMANUEL S. GOLDSMITH is professor of Yiddish language and literature and Jewish studies at Queens College of the City University of New York, and rabbi of Mevakshe Derekh of Scarsdale, New York. He is the author of *Modern Yiddish Culture: The Story of the Yiddish Language Movement* and *Modern Trends in Jewish Religion*. He is a co-editor of *Dynamic Judaism: The Essential Writings of Mordecai M. Kaplan* and *The American Judaism of Mordecai M. Kaplan*.

ARTHUR A. GOREN is Russell Knapp Professor of American Jewish history at Columbia University and emeritus professor of American studies at Hebrew University. He is author of *New York Jews and the Quest for Community*, *Dissenter in Zion: From the Writings of Judah L. Magnes*, and *The American Jews*.

MILTON HINDUS, a founding member of the Brandeis University faculty, served as the Edytha Macy Gross Professor of Humanities until his retirement. Awarded the Walt Whitman Prize by the Poetry Society of America, he is the author or editor of fourteen books, including two on Charles Reznikoff, and he has contributed to leading periodicals here and abroad. His *Crippled Giant* was the first book on Louis-Ferdinand Céline in English, and his latest book is *Irving Babbitt: Literature and the Democratic Culture* (1993).

CAROLE S. KESSNER is a professor of comparative literature and Judaic studies at the State University of New York at Stony Brook. She is the recipient of the Marie Syrkin Fellowship for 1994. She served as book editor of *Reconstructionist* magazine for twelve years. Among many essays and articles, she is the author of "Milton's Hebraic Herculean Hero" (1974), "An Essay and Annotated Bibliography of Novels Documenting the Jewish-American Immigrant Experience" (1978), and "The Emma Lazarus-Henry James Connection: Eight Letters" (1991). She is currently working on a biography of Marie Syrkin.

SUSANNE KLINGENSTEIN is a professor in the program in writing and humanistic studies at MIT. She was born in Baden-Baden (Germany) and received her Ph.D. from Heidelberg University. She has lived in the United States since 1987 and taught as instructor and lecturer in American literature at Harvard University. She is the author of *Jews in the American Academy, 1900–1940: The Dynamics of Intellectual Assimilation* (1991), and she has contributed essays to many books and journals.

MILTON R. KONVITZ was professor of industrial and labor relations at Cornell University and emeritus professor of law at Cornell University. He was a visiting professor at Hebrew University, associate director of the Truman Center for Peace Research, a fellow of the American Academy of Arts and Sciences, the Jewish Academy of Arts and Sciences, chairman of the editorial board of *Midstream* magazine, and the author of *Judaism and Human Rights* (1972) and *Judaism and the American Idea* (1978), among many other books, essays, and articles.

DEBORAH DASH MOORE is professor of religion at Vassar College and director of its American culture program. In 1988–89 she served as research director of the YIVO Institute for Jewish Research. An historian of American Jews, she has written two books, *At Home in*

America: Second Generation New York Jews and *B'nai B'rith and the Challenge of Ethnic Leadership,* and edited *East European Jews in Two Worlds* and co-edited *Jewish Settlement and Community in the Modern Western World.* She currently serves as editor of the *YIVO Annual.* Her next book is *To the Golden Cities: Pursuing the American Jewish Dream in Miami and L.A.*

SIMON NOVECK is the author of *Milton Steinberg: Portrait of a Rabbi* and the editor of the B'nai Brith series of volumes on great Jewish personalities and thinkers. He has taught Jewish history and philosophy at Brooklyn College and the Hartford Seminary Foundation, and political and social philosophy at the City College of New York.

ROBERT M. SELTZER is a professor of history at Hunter College and the Graduate School of the City University of New York, the chairman of the Hunter Jewish Social Studies Program, director of the Joseph and Ceil Mazer Institute for Research and Advanced Study in Judaica at the CUNY Graduate School, and editor of the *Encyclopedia of Religion,* the author of *Jewish People, Jewish Thought,* a co-editor of *The American Judaism of Mordecai M. Kaplan,* and of studies on Eastern European Jewry.

Index

Rahv, Philip, 66, 362
Ratner, Joseph, 133
Reconstructionism: Milton Steinberg and, 340; Mordecai Kaplan and, 295, 299–300; Trude Weiss-Rosmarin and, 115; Will Herberg and, 359, 360
Reconstructionist, 339
Reflex (publication), 57
Reform Judaism, 153, 211, 331
Religion. *See* Judaism; Secularism; Theology
"Renegade Jew," 160
Revelation, 359
Reznikoff, Charles, 247–67; "Autobiography: New York," 259; *By the Waters of Manhattan* (novel), 262, 263; "By the waters of Manhattan" (poem), 258; *By the Well of Living and Seeing*, 266; classicism and, 264–65; *Complete Poems*, 247–48; contributions to *University Missourian*, 247–48; *Day of Atonement*, 265; "Epilogue," 266; *Five Groups of Verse*, 251; *Holocaust*, 251; humor of, 264; *Inscriptions: 1933-1945*, 254, 255; *Inscriptions: 1944-1956*, 255–61; *Jerusalem the Golden*, 266; journalism and, 248–49; *Lionhearted*, 253–54; *The Manner Music*, 259; Marie Syrkin and, 58, 67–68, 254, 256, 258–59, 266; "Meditations on the Fall and Winter Holidays," 260–61; "On One Whom the Germans Shot," 250; practice of law and, 249, 265; *Separate Way*, 253; "Sightseeing Tour: New York," 264; *Te Deum*, 255–56, 258; *Testimony*, 251; value of verse-making for, 263–64, 265
Ribalow, Harold U., 231
Rice, Elmer, 183
Rivlin, Yosef Yoel, 103
Robinson, James Harvey, 147
Rochdale Institute, 147
Rosenfeld, Isaac, 92
Rosenwald, Julius, 209, 210
Rosenwald, Lessing, 36
Rosenzweig, Franz, 104, 345, 349, 353, 357
Roth, Philip, 66, 285

Royce, Josiah, 132, 146, 210, 213, 321, 325, 339, 349
Rubenstein, Charles A., 185
Rubin, Reuven, 297
Ruppin, Arthur, 76–77
Russell, Bertrand, 308

Sachar, Abram L., 63, 65
Sachs, Nellie, 66
Salomon, Albert, 343
Sampter, Jesse, 317
Samuel, Maurice, 228–46; A. M. Klein and, 276; Charles Reznikoff and, 258; combative ethic and, 234–36; contribution as writer, 230–31; credo of, 243; early life of, 228–29; *The Gentleman and the Jew*, 242, 243; on Hayim Greenberg, 37, 46–47; *I, the Jew*, 231, 234; Marie Syrkin and, 55–56; Palestine and, 232; *In Praise of Yiddish*, 229, 241; *The Professor and the Fossil*, 241, 242; *The World of Sholom Aleichem*, 241, 331; writings on anti-Semitism, 234; writings on biblical ideas, 242–43; writings on Yiddish, 241; writings on Zionism and Israel, 231; *You Gentiles*, 229, 234
Sanders, Ronald, 241
Santayana, George, 136, 145, 146, 147, 192, 210
Sapir, Edward, 140
Sartre, Jean-Paul, *Anti-Semite and Jew*, 280
Satyagraha ("soul-force"), 34
Schechter, Solomon, 117, 147, 317, 357
Scheler, Max, 343
Schen, Israel, 115–16
Schiller, F. C. S., 146, 147
Schneider, Herbert, 133, 323
Schneidman, Jonah, 106
School for Jewish Social Work, 307
School of the Jewish Woman, The, 105–7, 109–10
Schwefel, Rabbi, 316
Science, 301–2, 318, 321, 341, 347–48
Secularism: Ben Halpern and, 89, 91; Hayim Greenberg and, 42–45; Maurice Samuel and, 240; Mordecai